The Subordinate Sex

Vern L. Bullough

with the assistance of Bonnie Bullough

The Subordinate Sex

A History of Attitudes toward Women

University of Illinois Press

Urbana Chicago London

To my parents,
    D. Vernon and Augusta Ruckert Bullough

To those who raised Bonnie,
    Ruth Uckerman and Clyde Uckerman

Contents

Preface   vii

one
The Background   3

two
Formation of Western Attitudes   19

three
The Pedestal with a Base of Clay   50

four
The "Rise" of Women and the Fall of Rome   77

five
Christianity, Sex, and Women   97

six
Byzantium: Actuality Versus the Ideal   121

seven
Sex Is Not Enough: Women in Islam   134

eight
On the Pedestal: The Beginning
    of the Feminine Mystique   153

nine
The More Things Change, the More
    They Remain the Same   195

ten
China and India: Inferiority
    Is Not Only Western   230

eleven
Role Change and Urbanization   263

twelve
The American Experience   295

thirteen
Some Questions about the Past and the Future
   by Bonnie Bullough   335

Guide to Further Reading   355

Index   367

Preface

Any attempt to study women throughout history probably takes a kind of foolhardiness which is usually condemned in scholarly circles. In my defense, since I am not normally a rash person, it might be said that if this book dealt with the history of males instead of females it would probably be regarded simply as a textbook and treated as such. Unfortunately, the way in which men have looked at women is a little-explored field, and it will be a long time before standard texts appear. In the meantime studies such as this might serve as guidelines for monographic studies.

In this day of woman's liberation there might well be criticism for a man writing a book on women. Again in my defense, since most of the historical sources have been compiled by men, all I am doing is really indicating that what men said about women only rarely reflected what women themselves thought or felt. Originally I had hoped to have my wife as coauthor, as she has been on numerous other books, but other commitments prevented her from assuming that role, particularly a grant to work on improving the health-care delivery system. As an articulate and opinionated woman, however, she continued to criticize what I wrote and also found time to write the final summary chapter. Though giving her the last word does not really compensate for the loss of her collaboration, her criticism and our arguments about the other chapters hopefully kept to a minimum some of the excesses that have plagued much of the recent writing for and about women.

The book does not espouse any particular theory about the development of civilization nor do I have any simple theory for the past subjugation of women with which the book is mostly concerned. Even more lacking is a satisfactory explanation of why women have been willing to be subjugated, a problem which is only now beginning to receive attention. In a sense the book grew out of various projects which I have been engaged in. Several years ago I wrote a study of prostitution, and my wife and I have done several studies of nursing, both "women's" occupations, and although there is a world of difference between them, there are also striking similarities. I also did a textbook on Western civilization, which gave me a broad overlook. For the past three years I have been doing research on attitudes toward sex under the sponsorship of the Erickson Educational Foundation. These activities inevitably led to the present volume, which I hope will enable the reader to understand some of the historical forces that formed our society and still influence our attitudes. To me, as a historian, the problem seems to be the need to understand these forces and to eliminate the myths that stand in the way of sexual equality, or at least to take more positive steps in this direction.

I would like to acknowledge some of the friends and colleagues who have helped me in the study. Most obvious is my wife, who is listed on the title page for her contribution of the final chapter. I should like to thank Reed Erickson and the Erickson Educational Foundation for the encouragement and support they have given me over the years. My colleagues Allen Dirrim and Rena Vassar proved particularly helpful in helping me track down obscure references in various languages and periods. The students in my course on the history of women also deserve thanks for serving as guinea pigs for some of the ideas expressed here. I am also, like all historians, indebted to librarians and I wish to thank those at California State University, Northridge, University of California, Los Angeles, the Huntington Library, San Marino, Newberry Library and the library of the University of Chicago both in Chicago, the British Museum in London, the National Library in Edinburgh, and the Bibliotheque Nationale in Paris. Special thanks should also be given to Martha Barcus, Margaret Ball, Selma Rosen, Nancy Meadows, Mary Alvarez, and particularly to Joy Thornbury for their help in getting the manuscript into presentable form. I also am indebted to Kerry Hoover, who conceived of the project while he was at the University of Illinois Press, to Bruce A. McDaniel (Ms.), and to Richard L. Wentworth, who carried it through.

The Subordinate Sex

chapter one

The Background

Women have existed as long as men. Along with their menfolk, they have suffered through plague, war, depression, famine, tragedy, and have had the added burdens of childbirth. Yet compared to men, only a handful of women have managed to break into the pages of history. Men have been generals, kings, writers, composers, thinkers, and doers; women have been wives, mistresses, companions, friends, and helpmates. The very word woman, in fact, emphasizes this passive anonymous position. It derives from the Anglo-Saxon *wifman*, literally "wife-man," and the implication seems to be that there is no such thing as a woman separate from wifehood. As individuals, with few exceptions, women did not count. They were mothers, wives, daughters, sisters, proper and forgotten.

Unfortunately we do not know how most women in the past regarded either themselves or their role since almost all we know about them comes from the writing of males. Until comparatively recent times few women have left real records of themselves as individuals. We can surmise that women accepted their subordinate role but even if they did not there was little society permitted them to do about it. One of the few ways women could make a living on their own was by selling themselves, and it is worthy of comment that until almost the nineteenth century, history records more famous prostitutes and mistresses than it does women writers, composers, or artists. In fact, about the only way a woman managed to appear as an individual in the historical record was when she scandalized her contemporaries. Even if a woman held a powerful position she is much more likely to be remembered if her actions, particularly her sexual actions, shocked her contemporaries. Simply being a queen was not enough. It was the scandalous conduct in her position as queen which counted for more. Theodora, the Byzantine empress, is remembered because of her irregular sex life before she became empress rather than for her accomplishments as empress. Eleanor of Aquitaine, Hatshepsut, the Egyptian Pharaoh, Cleopatra, the Ptolemaic queen, Catherine the Great of Russia, and Lucrezia Borgia are others who scandalized their contemporaries, and the list could go on and on. Even the great Queen Elizabeth is no exception. In Elizabeth's case it was her insistence in not marrying and her unconsummated love affairs which have been the focus of attention. Some nineteenth-century historians believed they could explain everything by claiming that Elizabeth was really a male in drag. In a sense this was a credit to her abilities because such writers could not understand how a woman could be an outstanding ruler. The obvious answer to them was that she was a man. This one incident helps explain the difficulty of any study of women in the past.

Since both the actions which went into the making of history and the records kept by a society have in general been determined from a male point of view, any history of women must of necessity be primarily a history of man's attitudes toward women. This not infrequently is a depressing kind of history since men have usually tended to see women from two extremes, as the perfect mother symbolized by Mary or as temptress symbolized by Eve. Only rarely is she pictured as a real living human being with ideas and emotions like those of other (male) human beings. Inevitably, also, history has been written to emphasize that the proper role of woman is to be subordinate to man. As a leading American historian of the early twentieth century explained, everything in women's "existence is subordinate to their indispensable functions of continuing and rearing the human race and during the best years of their life, this work, fully discharged, leaves little room for any other."[1] But why such self-assured consignment of women to a subordinate role? Oscar Wilde, who always tried to say clever things, had one of his better moments when he pointed out that "All women become like their mothers. That is their tragedy. No man does. That is his."[2]

Men accept the fact that they are the superior sex but is it not pos-

1. Francis Parkman, *Some of the Reasons against Woman Suffrage*, pamphlet written for the Massachusetts Association Opposed to the Further Extension of Suffrage to Women (Boston, 1910).

2. The quotation can be found in W. H. Auden and Louis Kronenberger, *The Viking Book of Aphorisms* (New York: Viking Press, 1962), p. 175.

sible that they both fear and envy women? Biologically of course woman is different from man, and as the French say, *Viva la differ-ence*. Usually this statement has been taken as a paeon of praise to the pleasures of sex, but can it not just as easily be taken as a man's way of asserting his relief that he is not a woman? If woman's biological differences set her apart from the male of the species, these differences in the past have tended to hamper her rather than help her in any struggle with the male. During the prime of their lives, women were usually pregnant, probably at least every other year until the menopause. The long periods of gestation cut them off from the freedom to roam and help account for the male monopoly on hunting and fishing. Even though there was a high proportion of miscarriages and a high infant mortality in the past, still the continued pregnancies and the slow development of the child from infancy to puberty curtailed the scope of feminine activities. Men on the other hand were free to leave the home, to roam at will in the forest, to hunt, to fight, even to contemplate. In spite of the current male tendency to make fun of female fashions, originally it was men who had the time to put feathers in their hair, rattles on their wrists and ankles, to paint their faces, and to more fully develop their personalities. This does not mean that women were not productive in advancing civilization. They were. Anthropologists in general believe that women were the key innovators in basketry, weaving, pottery, in domesticating grain and improving its seed-bearing ability. Their contributions to agriculture are held by some to have created one of the major revolutions in human history. Still women were subordinate and their very subordination is demonstrated by the fact that once agriculture developed and specialization occurred, most of the tasks previously done by women were taken over by men, although they were often assisted by their wives or daughters. It is also possible that women simply lacked physical energy to assert themselves. Biologically women are prone to anemia and the lack of protein in their diet probably made them more willing to accept male domination.

John Stuart Mill, the nineteenth-century advocate of rights for women and a major figure in modern thought, held that the reason for women's submission was the superior strength of the male.[3]

3. John Stuart Mill, *The Subjection of Women* (reprinted, Cambridge: MIT Press, 1970), p. 9.

Perhaps strength is its own law, at least until organized society was well advanced, but is it the whole cause for the supremacy of the male throughout so much of history? This problem has intrigued investigators from a variety of disciplines. Some of the answers they have formulated are important in placing this study in context, although few of their theories would be acceptable to scholars today. Much of the hypothesizing is connected with the question of the origin of society, something about which we know little and about which we often speculate. Great concern over the question was expressed in the middle of the nineteenth century as the intellectual community began to accept the fact that the biblical account of creation left unaccounted for millions, even billions, of years. As scholars, with the discoveries of Charles Darwin and others, began to challenge the Judeo-Christian account of the beginnings of man, biblical justifications for the subordination of women no longer seemed valid, and inevitably there was an attempt to find other reasons. Two early theoreticians who wrote about the nature of society and women's place were Sir Henry Maine and J. J. Bachofen, both of whose works appeared in 1861. Maine held that the patriarchal system of authority was the original and universal system of social organization. The family was the original unit, and the eldest male parent held supreme authority in the household. From the family such authority had been extended into clans, from clans into tribes, and so on. Almost always men had been the rulers, although occasionally when for some reason or another women had outnumbered men, matriarchy temporarily existed but only as an unstable and degrading form of organization.[4]

Bachofen agreed that patriarchy was a superior kind of organization to matriarchy, but he did not feel it was the original or universal system of social organization. Instead it represented advancement on the evolutionary scale. Originally society had existed in a state of sexual promiscuity with no stable family life, and in such a state women, "defenseless against abuses by men" and exhausted by male "lusts," felt the need for regulated conditions and purer ethics. Since mothers were the only parents the younger generation knew with certainty, they could use their position to lay the foundation of a rule of women (*gynaecocracy*). Men accepted these new female constraints unwillingly, but in return for giving up the right of a man to any woman he wanted, women surrendered herself for a limited

4. Sir Henry Maine, *Ancient Law* (London: Murray, 1861), p. 122.

period to one man. In this evolution of society women were aided by religious beliefs since mankind at this stage in his development was wholly dominated by faith. It was women, according to Bachofen, with their profound sense of the divine presence through their ability to bear children, who capitalized on man's reverence for nature, and though physically weaker, they were able to assert their strength over the male as the repository of the first revelation. Eventually, however, men had usurped power, subjugated their women, and their society was able to advance further on the evolutionary scale. This was because women ruled only when society remained close to nature, but when intelligence was essential, men were needed to rule.[5]

Both Maine and Bachofen shared the assumption that societies passed through a series of differing stages. Several scholars set to work studying primitive societies to find out whether matriarchy or patriarchy was the earliest form of organization. The American ethnologist Lewis N. Morgan believed he had observed the transition from a system based on *jus maternum* (mother right) to *jus paternum* (father right) among the Iroquois Indians. From his observations he evolved a system of sex and family law for primitive peoples in which society progressed from the complete promiscuity of the primitive horde into the organized hunter tribes in which sex life was strictly regulated. At this stage the mother, since the father was unknown, remained the decisive factor in all questions of family relationship and inheritance. It was only when production developed enough for two human beings, man and woman, to maintain themselves economically by stock breeding and agriculture that the family split off and became a monogamous unit. In effect monogamy went hand in hand with the evolution of private property, and since economically the male was more active and physically the stronger, the woman fell under his domination, sexually and otherwise. The natural superiority of women, natural because she was more closely connected with offspring, was succeeded by the unnatural primacy of man.[6] Man held this primacy on the basis of his physical strength.

Probably the nineteenth-century arguments over whether society

5. J. J. Bachofen, "Mother Right," in *Myth, Religion, and Mother Right,* selected writing of Bachofen, trans. by Ralph Manheim, Bollingen ser., 84 (Princeton: Princeton University Press, 1967), *passim*; the quote is from p. 86.

6. See L. H. Morgan, *The League of the Iroquois* (Rochester, 1851) and *Ancient Society* (1871, reprinted, New York: World, 1963).

was matriarchal or patriarchal would have been forgotten, or relegated to debates among scholars,[7] if they had not become entangled with larger issues. Both the Marxists and the Freudians, for example, made use of such theories to buttress their own explanations about the original nature of society. The most influential Marxist theoretician was Frederick Engels, who, utilizing Bachofen and Morgan as his base, elaborated at some length on ideas earlier espoused by Marx. Engels held that the passage from matriarchy to patriarchy marked not only the great historical defeat of the feminine sex but also the development of private property. In the Stone Age when land belonged in common to all members of the clan, the rudimentary character of the primitive spade and the limited possibilities of agriculture meant that woman's strength was adequate for gardening. Though the two sexes in essence constituted separate classes, there was an equal division of tasks, with no one task more important than another. The men hunted and fished; the woman remained at home doing the essential domestic tasks. With the discovery of copper, tin, bronze, and eventually iron, and with the appearance of the plow, agriculture and other economic activity became so important that more intensive labor was required. To accomplish this man turned to the labor of other men whom he often reduced to slavery. Private property appeared, and as man became the master of slaves, he became the proprietor of women. Mother right was overthrown, simply by decreeing that the male offspring remain with their family while the female take up residence with her husband.[8] The male in effect took command in the home, the "woman was degraded and reduced to servitude," and the female "became the slave of his lust and a mere instrument for the production of children."[9] Man in his new-found sovereignty indulged himself in all kinds of sexual caprices simply because woman was subjugated and the only revenge the female had was through infidelity. Therefore, according to Engels, adultery was endemic in societies which emphasized private property.

As a good socialist Engels believed there could be no change in this subordinate nature of women until there was a change in the economic system allowing women to participate in the labor force on an

7. John McLennon, *The Patriarchal Theory* (London: Macmillan, 1885).
8. Frederick Engels, *The Origin of the Family, Private Property and the State* (4th ed., reprinted, New York: International Publishers, 1942), p. 49.
9. *Ibid.*, p. 50.

equal basis with men. As August Bebel, a disciple of Engels, emphasized, the problem of women could be reduced to their capacity to labor, and it was the resistance of the "capitalistic" paternalism which prevented the female from fully developing her personality. Bebel criticized the "bourgeois emancipationists" for failing to recognize that the "woman question," as he called it, could not be solved until the "social question," the economic reorganization, was solved.[10] In general the Marxists held that the repression of women by men had been an easy task, although there had been some areas where women rebelled. It was these rebels whose story was kept alive in the tales of the Amazons. To some Marxist theoreticians, in fact, the Amazons represented a last-ditch attempt by the matriarchy to assert itself.[11]

Tied in with controversy over the nature of the evolution of society is the debate over the original nature of marriage. Here also there were at least two camps: those who believed in original monogamy and those who upheld the hypothesis of promiscuity. The most important twentieth-century study emphasizing both promiscuity and mother right was Robert Briffault's, *The Mothers*, in which the side of mother right as a means of ending promiscuity was argued without compromise or reservation. Briffault went so far as to claim that mother right was the source of all social organization, that male influence was entirely irrelevant in the dawn of culture, and that kinship, political organization, the beginnings of law, economic life, magic, and religion were created and completely dominated by women until men had seized power.[12] Opposed to Briffault was Edward Westermarck, who held that monogamous marriage was a primeval institution, rooted in the individual family; that the matriarchate had not been a universal stage of human development; that group marriage never existed, much less promiscuity; and that the whole problem had to be approached using biology and psychology as well as a critical application of ethnological evidence.[13] Unfortunately neither Westermarck nor Briffault can be regarded as critical users of ethnological evidence.

10. August Bebel, *Woman under Socialism*, trans. from the 33rd German ed. by Daniel de Leon (New York: New York Labor News, 1904), p. 5.

11. Emanual Kanter, *The Amazons: A Marxian Study* (Chicago: Kerr, 1926).

12. Robert Briffault, *The Mothers: A Study of the Origins of Sentiments and Institutions* (3 vols., New York: Macmillan, 1927).

13. Edward Westermarck, *The History of Human Marriage* (5th ed., 3 vols., London: Macmillan, 1922).

Much more acceptable to the contemporary social scientists who investigate the problem was the answer of Ernest Crawley, who regarded sexual communism, mother right, and the total eclipse of the male sex as imaginary fantasies constructed against all evidence. Crawley, however, still felt that men were fearful of women. This fear he held was due to "physiological thought" rather than any primitive fear of matriarchy or its consequences.[14] By physiological thought he meant the concentration of the male upon physiological functions, particularly nutrition and sex. Theodore Besterman, who revised and enlarged Crawley's original work, held that the antagonism between the sexes was so great that man had continuously attempted to protect himself against women, and the result was a collective emotion of sexual solidarity in both men and women.[15] Following Crawley's path, he held that the fear of the female was due to the belief that human qualities could be or might be transmitted by contact with others. Since in savage psychology female inferiority was a firm assumption, Besterman held that men in such society would try to keep them in their place so the male would not catch the female weakness. It was when her femininity was most accentuated, at the time of her sexual crises such as menstruation or childbirth, that she was most rigidly secluded and avoided. This fear of the female was also present in sexual intercourse, and inevitably there were elaborate precautions taken in order to avoid its weakening effect and certain specific periods when sexual avoidance was required.[16]

Bronislaw Malinowski, one of the leading anthropologists of the twentieth century, believed that Crawley and Besterman were probably on the right track but felt that their view should be further explored before any final conclusions could be drawn.[17] As anthropologists have examined the problem, they have become increasingly reluctant to speak of matriarchy, and in fact most now would deny the existence of societies where women have been or are dominant

14. Ernest Crawley, *The Mystic Rose*, rev. and enlarged by Theodore Besterman (2 vols. in 1, reprinted, New York: Meridian Books, 1960), vol. 1, pp. 244–248.

15. Theodore Besterman, *Men against Women: A Study of Sexual Relations* (London: Methuen, 1934), p. 1.

16. *Ibid., passim*, esp. pp. 223–232.

17. Bronislaw Malinowski in an essay review of Briffault and Crawley which originally appeared in *Nature*, January 28, 1928, and which was reprinted in a collection of his essays and reviews entitled *Sex, Culture and Myth* (New York: Harcourt, Brace, and World, 1962), pp. 122–129.

regardless of whether promiscuity or monogamy turns out to be the original form of sexual union. As research into the question has progressed it appears that most of the so-called mother-right societies could better be called matrilineal societies in which descent is traced through the female, or matrilocal societies in which the husband lives with the wife's people. This kind of organization does not make them a matriarchy since authority is still vested in the male. He is the head of the household, the important position in most such societies.

Without delving further into the controversy, it is possible to conclude that the male has approached the female with mixed feelings, showing considerable fear, awe, and even reverence. As Joseph Campbell put it: "There can be no doubt that in the very earliest ages of human history the magical force and wonder of the female was no less a marvel than the universe itself and this gave to woman a prodigious power, which it has been one of the chief concerns of the masculine part of the population to break, control, and employ to its own ends. It is in fact more remarkable how many primitive hunting races have the legend of a still more primitive age than their own, in which the women were the sole possessors of the magical art." [18]

This early conception of woman as a magical force was due to her creative process. Some investigators feel that ancient man long thought, and some primitive societies apparently still hold, that the male played no part in conception. Somehow ancestral spirits in the form of living germs found their way into the maternal body. Sir Henry Maine, in fact, dated the origin of patriarchy from the discovery of paternity, but there is no consensus among historians about when and if such a momentous discovery took place in history. Certainly one of the most common representations which have survived from the paleolithic period are figurines with female characteristics such as hips and mammary glands considerably exaggerated. This might well indicate a worship of the generative power of the female, but it might also simply indicate that ancient men were the artists and took pleasure in portraying or observing the opposite sex, much as men do today. The *Playboy* centerfold, for example, is not necessarily indicative of the worship of the female but perhaps of a somewhat more mundane purpose.

It is not impossible that there was a downgrading of women when

18. Joseph Campbell, *The Masks of God: Primitive Mythology* (New York: Viking Press, 1959), p. 315.

men discovered that they too played a part in procreation. Since, moreover, the semen is visible while the ovum is not, it is easy to understand why throughout recorded history man has assumed that he was primarily responsible for procreation. This does not mean the female was entirely excluded, a difficult thing to do in terms of the biology of reproduction, but that she was often conceptualized as only carrying and nourishing the seed planted by the male. In the Greek period Aristotle gave women a slightly more important role than some of his predecessors in that he felt the fetus was formed from the union of sperm and menstrual blood, but it was the male who furnished the active principle while the women only supplied the passive element. For Aristotle the male principle represented form, motion, activity, while the feminine was equated with matter and potentiality. In the universe the earth represented the womanly and the maternal, hence mother earth, while the male represented the sun, the source of life. Those societies which followed such identification usually regarded the natural position for intercourse as that in which women were underneath the man, just as the earth was beneath the sun. Not all the Greeks agreed with Aristotle, and the compilers of the Hippocratic corpus, for example, recognized two kinds of seed, but the effect was the same since they regarded the female seed as weak and the male as strong. It was this male-oriented belief which dominated concepts of sexual reproduction in Western society until the time of William Harvey in the seventeenth century.

Even if we accept the theory that most societies have been paternalistic, with men holding the key positions of influence, we need to explain why seemingly in the past women have had periods of greater or lesser influence. Attempts to answer this have led to as many explanations as exist in the controversy over matriarchy or patriarchy. Many answers seem to rely on the concept of historical cycles developed by Oswald Spengler in his *The Decline of the West* (1917, 1921). Though most of the current generation of historians would regard Spengler's attempt to couple theories of social evolution and the organistic nature of society as historical poetry rather than social and institutional history, some of the concepts were adopted by Mathilde and Mathias Vaerting to explain the status of women.

The Vaertings believed that there had been various periods in history in which men were dominant while in others women had been. In those states where women ruled, woman was the wooer. The man contributed the dowry, and women extracted a pledge of fidelity from their husbands. Women had the sole right of disposal over the common possessions and she alone was entitled to divorce her partner should he no longer please her. In fact, much of what we regard as the proper roles of men and women were reversed with the women leaving home to attend to her occupation while the husband managed domestic affairs. The husband adopted the name and nationality of his wife, adorned himself in fancy clothes, and girl children were valued more highly than boys. The gods were for the most part feminine and males were regarded as somewhat less intelligent and somewhat more benevolent than the females. Most societies, they felt, had been a mixture of male dominant or female dominant with one sex having a slight edge over the other. Eventually they predicted there would be equality.[19]

Although the Vaertings classified ancient Egypt and several other societies as female-dominant ones, most historians would reject both their assumptions and their explanations out of hand. But then how do we explain why the influence of women seems to have waxed or waned at different periods? Instead of trying to define such modifications of position in terms of institution, where power and property are concentrated in the hands of one sex or the other, some recent investigators have turned to a study of attitudes. This implies that though institutions are persistent and last with little change into a period in which attitudes have altered considerably, it is possible for more feminine attitudes to be given currency in a patriarchal society. Recognizing this possibility G. Rattray Taylor, for example, proposed that past society be classified as patrist or matrist. He categorized the two as follows:

Patrist	*Matrist*
1. Restrictive attitude to sex	1. Permissive attitude to sex
2. Limitation of freedom for women	2. Freedom for women
3. Women seen as inferior, sinful	3. Women accorded high status
4. Chastity more valued than welfare	4. Welfare more valued than chastity

19. Mathilde and Mathias Vaerting, *The Dominant Sex: A Study in the Sociology of Sex Differentiation*, trans. from the German by Eden and Cedar Paul (New York: Doran, 1923), *passim*.

5. Politically authoritarian	5. Politically democratic
6. Conservative: against innovation	6. Progressive: revolutionary
7. Distrust of research, inquiry	7. No distrust of research
8. Inhibition; fear of spontaneity	8. Spontaneity; exhibition
9. Deep fear of homosexuality	9. Deep fear of incest
10. Sex differences maximized (dress)	10. Sex differences minimized
11. Asceticism, fear of pleasure	11. Hedonism, pleasure welcomed
12. Father-religion	12. Mother-religion

Taylor felt that these two patterns were extreme, and that as society changed there were intervening periods in which patterns would become confused, but owing to the nature of the Oedipal conflict there was a natural tendency to fall on one side of the fence or the other.[20] Taylor's listing was a modification of an earlier listing by J. C. Flugel,[21] but the whole catalog was value prone and not subject to any objective proof. Many of the characteristics he assigned to a female society could just as easily be assigned to a male society.

Both Taylor and Flugel based their key assumptions upon Freudian concepts. Freud, like Marx and Engels, posited an original state of nature which is no more subject to verification than theirs.

> We believe that civilization has been built up, under the pressure of the struggle for existence, by sacrifices in gratification of the primitive impulses, and that it is to a great extent forever being re-created, as each individual, successively joining the community, repeats the sacrifice of his instinctive pleasures for the common good. The sexual are amongst the most important of the instinctive forces thus utilized: they are in this way sublimated, that is to say, their energy is turned aside from its sexual goal and diverted towards other ends, no longer sexual and socially more valuable.[22]

Put in simple terms Freud seemed to be subscribing to a kind of organistic theory of history in which there was only a limited amount of vital energy in every culture and that the losses suffered through sex could not be replaced. In this he was following the historical beliefs advanced by such individuals as Henry Adams and Oswald

20. G. Rattray Taylor, *Sex in History* (New York: Vanguard Press, 1954), p. 83.

21. J. C. Flugel, *Man, Morals and Society* (London: Duckworth, 1945).

22. Sigmund Freud, *A General Introduction to Psychoanalysis*, trans. by Joan Riviere (New York: Garden City Publishing, 1943), pp. 23–24. See also Freud, *Civilization and Its Discontents* (London: Hogarth Press, 1930).

Spengler, but such analogies were unverifiable and misleading. The antiwomen implications Freud drew from his beliefs have been criticized by others, most recently by Kate Millet.[23] The criticism, however, is not new and several of his early disciples also disagreed. It was in part for his emphasis on "masculinity" that Jung parted company with him. Jung and his disciples have put considerable emphasis upon the concept of the "great mother,"[24] although in the popular culture it never gained the attention of the concept of "penis envy" held by Freud. Freud believed that the female held great feelings of inferiority over her lack of male genitalia, while the male, conscious of his possession, feared women wanted to castrate him. In brief, the narcissistic rejection of the female by male is liberally mingled with fear and disdain.[25]

It was some of the followers of Freud, however, who carried the arguments over female subjugation to an extreme. One of the early anthropologists, William Stephens, concluded that primitive tribes had greater sexual freedom than civilized communities,[26] thus emphasizing the need for sex control as a mark of civilization. Carrying the argument further was J. E. Unwin, who held that since the cultural conditions of any society were dependent upon the amount of its mental and social energy, and this in turn was dependent upon the extent of compulsory continence, creative societies could only exist when sexual outlets were highly restricted. He postulated that "No society can display productive social energy unless a new generation inherits a social system under which sexual opportunity is reduced to a minimum. If such a system be preserved, a richer and yet richer tradition will be created, refined by human entropy."[27] He

23. Kate Millet, *Sexual Politics* (Garden City, N.Y.: Doubleday, 1970), pp. 176–203.

24. For a discussion of this, and a thorough exposition of the concept, see Erich Neumann, *The Great Mother: An Analysis of the Archetype*, trans. by Ralph Manheim, Bollingen ser., 47 (New York: Pantheon Books, 1955). See also Ann Bedford Ulanov, *The Feminine in Jungian Psychology and on Christian Theology* (Evanston: Northwestern University Press, 1971).

25. Sigmund Freud, "The Taboo of Virginity," in *Collected Papers*, trans. by Joan Riviere (5 vols., reprinted, New York: Basic Books, 1959), vol. 4, p. 226, and "Some Psychical Consequences of the Anatomical Distinction between the Sexes," vol. 5, pp. 186–197.

26. William N. Stephens, *The Family in Cross Cultural Perspective* (New York: Holt, Rinehart, and Winston, 1953), p. 246.

27. J. D. Unwin, *Sexual Regulations and Human Behavior* (London: Williams and Norgate, 1933), pp. ix–x, 85.

then argued that historically the only way sexual opportunity had been kept at a minimum was under "absolute monogamy," where the husband had absolute power over his wife and children. Unfortunately, he wrote, no society ever tolerated this male domination for long since it made women and children legal nonentities, and as women made demands for changes the result was a reduction of marriage to a union made and broken by mutual consent, with a demand for relaxation of prenuptial continence. "As soon as a lack of compulsory continence became part of the inherited tradition of a complete new generation, the energy of each society decreased and faded away."[28] In effect women have to be kept in their place for civilization to progress. Unwin was not particularly happy with the subordination of women in absolute monogamy, but he believed that by historical accident this was the only way that regulations between the sexes had been accomplished in order to keep sexual opportunity to a minimum.[29]

More recently and with better scholarship H. R. Hays attempted to apply the findings of modern anthropology to attitudes toward women. He was influenced by Freud as well as Marx, but his conclusions can be better documented than those of Unwin. Hays held that male attitudes toward women and toward images of women were strongly influenced by deep anxieties that were almost universal. The anxieties, he felt, seemed almost basic to the kind of family relationships which mankind created, but they were further shaped by the pressures in the various cultures which were built as men compounded their fears by creating situations which rationalized and perpetuated them. Few human beings can easily face their own compulsions, and inevitably the male has tended to project his fears and antagonisms in terms of derogatory attitudes toward the female by insisting that women are evil, inferior, and valueless. Thus women should be made to obey, be kept in their place, or assigned to some unreal role which neutralizes them and removes them from the sphere of competition. Emerging from such attitudes are traditions and stereotypes which are used to justify male domination of the female.[30]

28. *Ibid.*, p. 87.

29. *Ibid.*, p. 108. Unwin further elaborated and clarified his views in *Sex and Culture* (London: Oxford University Press, 1934).

30. H. R. Hays, *The Dangerous Sex: The Myth of the Feminine Evil* (New York: Putnam's Sons, 1964), p. 281.

Hays found that in preliterate cultures there was almost a universal fear of women's sexual functions. This fear was institutionalized in sanctions and restrictions not unlike similar restrictions in more sophisticated societies. While economic factors might have influenced the treatment of women, Hays himself felt that psychological factors were the most important although it was often difficult to separate the psychological from other factors. He believed, for example, that the male's insistence on a monopoly of his wife's sexual services, but not vice versa, and the requirement that she be intact on marriage, but without restrictions for the male, was involved with feelings about private property. He also held that marriage in the past had been combined with the acquisition of property. Even as property, however, a woman's person was an extension of the male ego. Hays would emphasize that the continued existence of a double standard is largely dependent upon male anxiety. Such anxiety occured because the male was keenly aware that a woman's ability to perform sexually was limitless compared to his own; there was always the fear and suspicion that he had not fully satisfied her or that she would turn to more potent males. Inevitably a fanatical desire to control her sexual activity arose. This accounted for the fact that the faithless woman was made a stereotype and punished by male writers, while the faithless male (such as Don Juan) became a heroic figure regarded by males with considerable admiration.

The problem of the double standard is also tied up with the denial of the female's need for sexual fulfillment. Men have always assumed that they were the active element, women the passive. Mechanically of course, men are active, since they become aroused and carry out penetration. Though women can in theory still say yes or no, the determined male can usually force even the most recalcitrant woman to submit. On the other hand, a determined female still has the problem of arousing the male and then managing to submit.[31]

Though the status of women in society has varied in the past, sometimes higher, sometimes lower, there has been a practical universal unanimity of the male to ascribe a relative inferiority to the female. Associated with this is a feeling that an excess of female association might cause effeminacy, or at least weakness, in him. This attitude might be due to actual observation since the physiological process of detumescence following sexual intercourse usually leaves

31. *Ibid.*, p. 293.

a man feeling somewhat weakened. Inevitably man might ascribe this weakening to the influence of women. Many diverse tribes and cultures have enjoined continence on warriors and hunters, and our society usually demands abstinence of athletes—activities which demand strength and fortitude. There is also a fear of contamination from sexual intercourse. Usually this fear is greater in illicit intercourse, but it also exists in matrimonial intercourse. Again there is always the possibility of contracting venereal disease which might account for part of the fear, but this does not fully explain why illicit intercourse or intercourse without proper procedures or at the correct time might result in the blighting of crops, the ruination of hunting, or the appearance of sudden illness. Intercourse is also associated with the fertility of the earth and homeopathic or imitative magic seems inevitable, although some cultures believe sexual intercourse quickens the growth of trees while other societies hold to the opposite.[32] Inevitably woman is associated with all of these phenomenon in the male mind, and usually to her detriment. All of these factors should be kept in mind in this survey of the history of man's past, although rather than consciously adopting any of them, there has been an attempt to let the data speak for itself with a minimum of theorizing. It appears obvious, however, that if women have been subjugated, women as well as men have accepted and even encouraged this subjugation.

32. Geoffrey May, *Social Control of Sex Expression* (New York: Morrow, 1931), pp. 3–12. See also Edward Westermarck, "Subjection of Wives," in *The Origin and Development of the Moral Ideals* (3 vols., London: Macmillan, 1906), vol. 1.

chapter two

Formation of Western Attitudes

The cradle of civilization, or at least of Western civilization, was the river valleys of the Near East (sometimes called the Middle East), particularly in the area extending from modern Egypt to modern Iraq. Attitudes formed in these areas were incorporated into Jewish, Greek, and later Western Roman and Christian attitudes. Though the civilizations in these areas underwent considerable change, it is possible to generalize about attitudes toward women in them if only because the scarcity of source materials makes it difficult to reconstruct any one period in the detail possible in more contemporary periods.

It has been said that man's vision of the gods reflects his own vision of himself and his activities. If there is any merit to this statement it seems clear that the inhabitants of the Tigris-Euphrates Valley quite early held man to be superior to woman, and in fact relegated her to being a kind of property. There are hints that in the beginning of Sumerian society women had a much higher status than in the heyday of Sumerian culture, since in early Sumerian religious tradition goddesses occupy prominent roles in the Divine Assemblies. There is even the possibility that a kind of polyandry was practiced since the reforms or Urukagina in the middle of the third millenium B.C. referred to women who had taken more than one husband. Some have felt this might refer to the remarriage of a widow or divorcee, but the Sumerian text in itself does not support such a view. Nevertheless by the time the Babylonian theology was organized into the form in which it has come down to us the mother goddess was made clearly subordinate to male gods and monogamy had become the basic form of marriage.[1]

1. See Samuel Noah Kramer, *History Begins at Sumer* (Garden City, N.Y.: Dou-

The names and positions of the gods changed during different periods of Mesopotamian civilization as differing peoples achieved dominance. There were hundreds of deities but there were two major triads of gods: Anu, Enlil, and Ea; Sin, Shamash, and Ishtar. Over and above them was another god Marduk or Asshur. The only female in the group was Ishtar, or in Sumerian, Inanna, goddess of war and of love. Like humans, the gods had wives and families, court servants, soldiers, and other retainers. Ishtar, however, remained unmarried. Her lovers were legion but these unhappy men usually paid dearly for her sexual favors. She was identified with the planet Venus, the morning and evening star, and could arouse the amorous instinct in man, although she also had the power of causing brothers who were on good terms to quarrel among themselves and friends to forget friendship. If she perchance withdrew her influence "The bull refuses to cover the cow, the ass no longer approaches the she-ass, in the street the man no longer approaches the maidservant." Part of her difficulty was that she did not really know her place. In the poem translated as *Enki and World Order* the god Enki (whose powers are similar to Ea) assigned the gods various tasks. Ishtar, however, felt left out and complained to Enki. Her complaint applies to woman in general: "Me, the woman, why did you treat differently?/ Me, the holy Inanna, where are my powers?" [2] She was given various tasks as a result, but as an unmarried and erotic figure it was no wonder that sacred prostitution formed part of her cult. When she descended to earth she was accompanied by courtesans and prostitutes. The implication might well be, as we have indicated before, that woman was either to be wife and mother, or an unmarried professional, a prostitute.

The mere presence of Ishtar, or Inanna, in the heavenly triad is probably striking evidence of the great strength of the forces of nature which had been so deeply rooted in primitive society. She repre-

bleday, 1959), p. 99; Kramer, *Sumerian Mythology* (rev., New York: Harper, 1961); Joseph Campbell, *The Masks of God: Oriental Mythology* (New York: Viking Press, 1962), pp. 1–8ff.; and E. O. James, *The Ancient Gods* (New York: Capricorn Books, 1964), pp. 80–81. *Larouse Encyclopedia of Mythology*, ed. by Felix Guirand, trans. by Richard Aldington and Delano Ames (New York: Prometheus Press, 1960), pp. 57–58.

2. Kramer, *Sumerian Mythology*, recounts the myth in detail but these particular verses are taken from his *History Begins at Sumer* (Garden City, N.Y.: Doubleday, 1959), p. 98.

sented the blending of several different characters into one, most obviously the lady of love and the lady of battles, although these different aspects of her powers were worshiped at different places. If Ishtar chose to favor a mere mortal he could gain fame and riches, and she was much sought after. Sargon, the Akkadian conquerer, who lived toward the end of the third millenium B.C., felt himself to be under the protection of Ishtar and believed it was through her influence that he became king. As he himself said, his mother was a temple priestess who bore him in secret.

> She set me in a basket of rushes, with bitumen she sealed my lid.
> She cast me into the river which rose not [over] me.
> The river bore me up and carried me to Akki, the drawer of water.
> Akki, the drawer of water lifted me out as he dipped his e[w]er.
> Akki, the drawer of water, [took me] as his son [and] reared me.
> Akki, the drawer of water, appointed me as his gardener.
> While I was a gardener, Ishtar granted me [her] love. . . .

And then he became king.[3]

If the place of women in official mythology was somewhat circumscribed, it was even more so in actual life. Our chief source of information about actual conditions is the various law codes. Georges Contenau claimed that the early law codes granted to women rights, such as giving evidence in law courts and owning property, which in France have only been acquired in the twentieth century. This does not so much indicate how advanced women in Babylonia were but rather how subjugated French women have been.[4] Contenau himself admits that at least the Semitic-speaking portion of Mesopotamian society was unwilling to grant woman any true responsibility. Formal law codes are known from Ur-Nammu of the third dynasty of Ur (c. 2050 B.C.) and Lipit Ishtar of Isin (c. 1870). Neither of these codes is preserved completely and their great importance to us lies in the influence they had on later laws. In the Semitic dialects the first law code was that of the town of Eshnunna, dating from about 1800 B.C. The best known, however, was that of Hammurabi (c. 1700 B.C.), which contained about 250 laws. Later from the Assyrian

---

3. This brief autobiography is translated by E. A. Speiser under the title of "The Legend of Sargon," in *The Ancient Near East*, ed. by James B. Pritchard (Princeton: Princeton University Press, 1965), pp. 85–86.

4. Georges Contenau, *Everyday Life in Babylon and Assyria*, trans. by K. R. and A. R. Maxwell-Hyslop (London: Arnold, 1954), p. 250.

scribes there exists another legal corpus dating from 1100 B.C., which has a long section on women and marriage.

Women basically were property. They were neither to be seen nor heard. Monogamy was the normal way of life but monogamy in practice meant something different for the man than for the woman. A wife who slept with another man was an adulteress but a man could not only visit prostitutes but in practice also took secondary wives as concubines. Rich men and royalty often had more than one legal wife. Women were always under the control of a male. Until the time of her marriage a girl remained under the protection of her father, who was free to settle her in marriage exactly as he thought fit. Once married she was under the control of her husband. During the marriage ceremony a free woman assumed the veil which she wore from then on outside her home. In fact the veil was the mark of a free woman, and anyone who met a slave or courtesan wearing a veil had the duty of denouncing her. A concubine could only wear a veil on those occasions when she accompanied the legal wife out of doors. It was an offense for a woman to have any dealings in business or to speak to a man who was not a near relation.

Some scholars have argued that the earliest form of marriage required the bridegroom to purchase his bride, emphasizing even further the woman as property. In the earliest laws there were references to *terhatum* (bride money), which has been interpreted to be one of three things: the price paid for the bride, a gift made in order to ingratiate the bridegroom with the family, or simply a means of demonstrating that the union was a legal marriage. Regardless of its original meaning, by the time of the Hammurabic code it seems to have become earnest money in which the bridegroom assumed some pecuniary responsibility in case he did not live up to his undertaking. Often it was returned to him as part of the dowry.

The economic dependence of the woman upon the male was demonstrated by the various provisions allowing her to remarry. In cases where a woman's husband was taken captive and he had not left enough for her to eat, she could live with another man as his wife, although if her husband returned she was to go back to him. Any children by the temporary husband remained with him. If, however, the absence of her husband was malicious, motivated by a "hatred of king and country," he had no further claim upon his wife if she took a second husband. Women could also hold property. An unmarried daughter, for example, could be given either a dowry, a share of her father's property, or the usufruct, the right to the profits from the land. She was free to dispose of her dowry as she wished, but in other cases her property rights upon her death reverted to her brothers, except under special conditions.

The purpose of marriage was procreation, not companionship. The wife's first duty was to raise her children and a sterile marriage was grounds for divorce. The wife who gave birth to children, particularly to sons, was accorded special protection. The man who divorced the mother of his sons or took another wife was committing a culpable act. Her childbearing responsibilities were emphasized by penalties to anyone injuring a woman sufficiently to cause a miscarriage, and also in the statutes against abortion.

Adultery was not a sin against morality but a trespass against the husband's property. A husband had freedom to fornicate, while a wife could be put to death for doing the same thing. Free women were inviolable and guarded; a man who gave employment to a married woman not closely related to him was in difficulty. A man caught fornicating with an adulterous woman could be castrated or put to death, while the woman could be executed or have her nose cut off. Offenses with unmarried free women were treated differently from those of married women because there was no husband. If the offender had a wife, she was taken from him and given to her father for prostitution and the offender was compelled to marry the girl who was his victim. If he had no wife he had to pay a sum of money to the girl's father as well as marry her, although the father might accept money and refuse to give him his daughter. In any case the payment was for damaging property, lessening the value of the girl. If a man could prove by oath that an unmarried girl gave herself to him he was not compelled to surrender his own wife, although he still had to pay a sum of money for the damage he had caused. If a married woman was seized by a man in a street or public place and in spite of her efforts to defend herself was violated, she was regarded as innocent. If, however, she was acting as a prostitute either in a temple brothel or in the street the man could be convicted of engaging in an adulterous relationship only if he was shown to have had guilty knowledge.[5]

5. This description is taken from the various law codes. The standard collection in English is that edited by G .R. Driver and John C. Miles, *The Assyrian Laws* (Oxford:

These laws applied to freewomen. There were other women, particularly slaves. A slave had no human personality but instead was real property. If he was injured it was his master and not he who was entitled to compensation. A female slave was under obligation to give her purchaser not only her labor but also herself, without any counter obligation on his part. He could in fact turn her over to prostitution. Even when she became the purchaser's concubine and had children by him she still remained a slave liable to be sold. At her owner's death, however, she and her children received liberty. If a female slave was bought by a married woman either as her servant or as a concubine for her husband (as in the case of a childless woman), she remained the property of the wife. A male slave could, with his master's consent, marry a freewoman, and even if she lacked a dowry she and her children would still remain free. If she brought a dowry she could keep it, but any increase from investment was split with her husband's master. There were also temple slaves who were not confined to the temple but worked in the towns and hired out to private employers. Their legal status was harsher than that of ordinary slaves since they had no hope of adoption, while their children, even if their mother was a freewoman, automatically became the property of the gods. Children and wives of freemen were different from slaves, but the father still had almost total control. He could deposit his children with creditors, and apparently also his wife, although she could not be kept for more than four years. There was also a class of poor which existed at the beginning of the second millenium, who were above slaves but below freemen. Little is heard of them in later laws. Special exceptions must have been made for some women of this class since the Hammurabic code refers to "ale-wives," or women winesellers in taverns. Perhaps such women were regarded as prostitutes and not the freewomen with whom the laws were most concerned.

Other than tavernkeepers, the only other occupations for women mentioned in the law codes were as priestesses and prostitutes. There were various kinds of both. At the head of the priestesses was the

Clarendon Press, 1955). There are also translations of some of the codes by Albrecht Goetz and Theophile J. Meek, in *The Ancient Near East,* pp. 133–167. Reuven Yaron, *The Laws of Eshnunna* (Jerusalem: Hebrew University, 1969), has a comprehensive discussion of these particular laws. There are several other editions, particularly of the Code of Hammurabi.

Entu, the wife of the gods, or the "lady [who is] a deity." They were of very high standing and the kings could make their daughters Entu of a god. They were expected to remain virgins, although they might eventually take husbands, perhaps after menopause. A second class of priestesses was the Naditu, who were lower in rank but who were also not expected to have children. The Hammurabic code had several provisions attempting to ensure the rights of a priestess to dowry and other shares of her father's goods. Apparently their conduct was rigidly circumscribed since any priestess who went to a tavern to drink could be put to death. Prostitutes seem to have been quite common and there was a considerable variety of harlots and hierodules, each described by a different technical term. Some were attached to the temple and were known as *qadishtu* or *qadiltu*. It is possible that the term *kulmashitu* may have been used to refer to a similar class of women.[6]

With such a male-oriented society, few women emerged as real individuals in the history of the Mesopotamian civilizations. Two women seem to have exercised some influence as rulers, but they were comparatively late in the history of the area, and both seem to have merged to form the legendary figure of Semiramis. Herodotus, the Greek historian, reported the existence of two women rulers, Semiramis and Nitocris.[7] Later Diodorus Sicilus, the Greek historian who lived during the time of Roman Emperor Augustus, amplified the story considerably, combining both into the figure of Semiramis. It was in this legendary form that her name has survived. According to Diodorus, Semiramis was born of a goddess and married an Assyrian officer at the court of king Ninus. The king was so captivated by her beauty and valour that he took her as wife. Shortly Ninus died, leaving a son, Ninyas, by Semiramis, and in these circumstances Semiramis assumed power, reigning for many years, building Babylon, and turning to the conquest of distant lands.[8]

Modern historians believe that the legend of Semiramis was based upon a real person or persons who so impressed contemporaries that

6. See H. W. F. Saggs, *The Greatness that Was Babylon* (New York: New American Library), pp. 332–335. See also Vern L. Bullough, *History of Prostitution* (New Hyde Park, N.Y.: University Books, 1964).

7. Herodotus, *Persian Wars*, ed. and trans. by A. D. Godley (London: Heinemann, 1921), I, 184–185ff.

8. Diodorus Siculus, *Bibliotheca historica*, trans. by C. H. Oldfather *et al.* (London: Heinemann, 1933), ii, 1–20.

a legend developed which was passed on to the Greeks in garbled form. Semiramis herself is usually identified with Sammuramat, mother of the Assyrian king Adad-nirari III (810–782 B.C.). A memorial stele found at Ashur and an inscription at Kalakh (Nimrud) seem to indicate that she exercised considerable influence after the death of her husband, Shamshi-Ada V (824–810 B.C.), and in fact it was during her reign that the god Nabu (Nebo) was substituted for the former patron god at Kalakh.

The identification of Nitocris is somewhat more difficult. One authority has argued that she is simply a case of sex transformation, not uncommon in legend, in which Nebukadnezar somehow assumed a feminine form. Those who think she was a real historical figure believe they have found her in the person of Naqi'a, a wife of Sennacherib (704–681 B.C.) and the mother of his son, Esarhaddon (680–669 B.C.), whom he selected to succeed him. It was during the rule of Esarhaddon that the reconstruction of the neglected city of Babylon began. It is quite possible that Naqi'a took an active part in this as a sort of royal representative, since the king himself would by custom be unable to appear in the city until some of the official temples and buildings had been restored. Like Semiramis she managed to impress the populace enough to survive as legend, although over the passage of time her story became merged with her predecessor, perhaps on the ground that one outstanding queen could be understandable but two might challenge the male stereotypes too much.[9]

In both cases, however, women were only able to exercise authority as mothers, protecting the rights of their sons. It was only through their sons that women in the Mesopotamian civilizations seem to have had any influence at all. Even the wives of the king were not important enough to be regarded as queens since the use of the term was restricted to goddesses or to women who served in positions of power. The chief wife instead was usually called "she of the palace" and she lived along with the concubines and other wives in a harem guarded by eunuchs. Their way of life was carefully regulated by royal edicts, although in the last period of the Assyrian kingdom the

9. Hildegard Lewy, "Nitokris-Naqi'a," *Journal of Near Eastern Studies*, II (1952), 264–286. Daniel David Luckenbill, ed., *Ancient Records of Assyria and Babylonia* (Chicago: University of Chicago Press, 1926), I 260, no. 731, included the stele inscription of Semiramis.

influence of the king's wife and mother had somewhat greater power than before.[10]

Other than a few exceptional royal wives, only a handful of women managed to break through into the pages of history. There is an isolated reference to a woman physician at the palace in an Old Babylonian text, and we can assume that women attended other women in childbirth, but there is no further reference. The professional physician was usually a male. Women were also generally illiterate if only because in this period reading and writing were restricted to a professional class of scribes who underwent long training. Poetry, however, is a preliterate form of literature, and one of the most remarkable poets, in fact one of the few we know by name, was a woman, Enheduanna. She was the daughter of Sargon, whose administration marked the fusion of Semitic and Sumerian culture. As part of this fusion the Sumerian Inanna and the Akkadian Ishtar came together and in this process Enheduanna played an important role, at least if her identification is correct. She was a high priestess of the moon god, the first of a long line of royal holders of this office, and in this capacity she wrote a poem usually entitled "The Exaltation of Inanna." Her poetry served as a model for much subsequent hymnography and her influence was so great that she later seems to have been regarded as a god herself. Her poetic style was so unique, the stamp of her personality upon her poem so strong, that her editors believe it may well be possible to detect her authorship in other less preserved pieces.[11] Most of the cuneiform literature from the area is anonymous, or at best pseudonymous, so how many other women poets there were must remain unknown. The attitudes expressed about women in most of the poetry would tend to indicate that they had male authors.

In one of the great classics of Mesopotamian literature, the Gilgamesh epic, it seems obvious that woman's duty was to keep man calm and peaceful. In the beginning of the account Gilgamish was oppressing the city of Erech, taking the son from the father, the maiden from her lover. The people complained to the gods, who created a rival, Enkidu, from clay to deal with Gilgamish. Enkidu

10. A. Leo Oppenheim, *Ancient Mesopotamia* (Chicago: University of Chicago Press, 1964), p. 104.

11. William W. Hallo and J. J. A. Van Dijk, *The Exaltation of Inanna* (New Haven, Conn.: Yale University Press, 1968), pp. 1–12.

was a wild man whose whole body was covered with hair, who knew neither people nor country. When the existence of Enkidu was reported to Gilgamish he sent forth a temple harlot to ensnare the wild man: "Let her strip off her garment; let her lay open her comeliness;/ He will see her, he will draw nigh to her. . . ." Then with his innocence lost he could be more effectively handled by Gilgamish.

> The prostitute untied her loin-cloth and opened her
>   legs, and he took possession of her comeliness:
> She used no restraint but accepted his ardour,
> She put aside her robe and he lay upon her.
> She used on him, the savage, a woman's wiles,
> His passion responded to her.
> For six days and seven nights Enkidu approached and
>   coupled with the prostitute.
> After he was sated with her charms,
> He set his face toward his game.
> [But] when the gazelles saw him, Enkidu, they ran away;
> The game of the steppe fled from his presence.
> Enkidu tried to hasten [after them, but] his body was
>   [as if it were] bound.
> His knees failed him who tried to run after his game.
> Enkidu had become weak, his speed was not as before.
> But he had intelligence, wide was his understanding.

Eventually the woman persuaded him to set out for Erech, where he and Gilgamish engaged in combat and Enkidu was defeated. The two, however, became fast friends.[12] The legend suggests that woman was designed to ensnare man, to weaken him, to prevent him from realizing his full potentiality. In this forerunner of the stereotype of Eve, woman was both a source of pleasure and yet a delusion.

This ambiguous feeling toward the female is evident in a dialogue between a master and slave of comparatively late composition, entitled in translation, "The Dialogue of Pessimism."

> "Slave, listen to me." "Here I am, sir, here I am."
> "I am going to love a woman." "So love, sir, love.
> The man who loves a woman forgets sorrow and fear."

12. Alexander Heidel, *The Gilgamesh Epic and Old Testament Parallels* (2nd ed. Chicago: University of Chicago Press, 1949), tablet 1, col. iv, p. 22. Unfortunately Heidel, through some sense of false modesty, did not translate this portion into English but instead put it into Latin. In translating it from Latin I followed basically the form set by Saggs, *The Greatness that Was Babylon*, p. 372.

"No, slave, I will by no means love a woman."
["Do not] love, sir, do not love.
Woman is a pitfall—a pitfall, a hole, a ditch,
Woman is a sharp iron dagger that cuts a man's throat."[13]

Woman, nonetheless, was designed to be at the side of man, and as a proverb stated, "a house without an owner is like a woman without a husband."[14] The ideal wife was both passionate and able to bear sons: "May [the goddess] Inanna cause a hot-limbed wife to lie down for you;/ May she bestow upon you broad-armed sons;/ May she seek out for you a place of happiness."[15] Even a good wife was a burden and responsibility: "The man who does not support either a wife or a child,/ His nose has not borne a leash."[16] Or in a more hostile vein: "As the saying goes: 'Were not my wife in the cemetery, and were not also my mother in the river, I should die of hunger.' "[17] Women, as well as men, enjoyed sex. "Conceiving is nice," but "being pregnant is irksome."[18] It was also recognized that the "penis of the unfaithful husband" was no better "than the vulva of the unfaithful wife,"[19] but in most things a woman was discriminated against. "A rebellious male may be permitted a reconciliation;/ A rebellious female will be dragged in the mud."[20] Obviously women were regarded as a mixed blessing, and it was best that they be kept in their place.

Life in Mesopotamia was harsh and unpredictable. There were floods, famine, scorching heat, and cloudbursts, and always the danger of invasions. It might well be that in such a society the strong man was admired while the weak woman was regarded as a liability, but necessary because of her childbearing abilities. Inevitably the male would be forced to assert himself, to man the armies, to do the fighting, to keep his womenfolk in subordination. Is this an adequate explanation for male dominance? The difficulty with such a thesis is

13. W. G. Lambert, *Babylonian Wisdom Literature* (Oxford: Clarendon Press, 1960), p. 147.
14. *Ibid.*, p. 232.
15. Edmund I. Gordon, *Sumerian Proverbs* (Philadelphia: University Museum, University of Pennsylvania, 1959), p. 115, no. 1.147.
16. *Ibid.*, p. 120, no. 1.153.
17. *Ibid.*, p. 466, no. 1.142. This translation is by Thorkild Jacobsen rather than Gordon.
18. *Ibid.*, this is the translation by Saggs, *The Greatness that Was Babylon*, p. 407.
19. *Ibid.*, p. 496, no. 1.159. This is Jacobsen's translation.
20. *Ibid.*, p. 123, no. 1.156.

quite simply that these same attitudes are found in other cultures where environmental conditions are quite different. Nonetheless environment might have had some influence, since the place of women in Egyptian society seems to be quite different from that of Mesopotamian society.

At a superficial level, attitudes toward women in Egypt appeared to be so radically different from surrounding society that many of the early advocates of matriarchy felt that Egypt was the case that proved their thesis. From the time of Sir James Frazer and his late nineteenth-century compilation of the *Golden Bough* until today there have been a group of scholars who have clung to the belief that Egypt was a matriarchal society. Robert Briffault went so far as to argue that Egypt "never lost its essential matriarchal character" even though it had undergone a slow evolutionary process toward patriarchy.[21] Mathilde and Mathias Vaerting believed they had found their woman's state in ancient Egypt[22] and denounced all those who did not agree with them as being victims of patriarchal thinking. The evidence for a matriarchy, nonetheless, is highly debatable. Most recent studies would not regard Egypt as a matriarchal society but all would agree that the status of women was probably higher than in Mesopotamia and that women had the right to own and transmit property.

The controversy in part had its origins through the efforts of Sir W. H. Flinders Petrie, one of the founders of modern Egyptology, who held that in "question of descent the female line was principally regarded. The mother's name is always given, the father's may be omitted; the ancestors are always traced farther back in the female than in the male line."[23] He went on to state that Egypt was "based on a matriarchal system, the office-holder or farmer who married into a family was a secondary affair; the house and property went with the woman and daughters. This was a transition state from quasi-marriage to a patriarchal system eventually, where the man dealt with the property."[24]

21. Robert Briffault, *The Mothers* (3 vols., New York: Macmillan, 1927), vol. 1, pp. 378–379.
22. Mathilde and Mathias Vaerting, *The Dominant Sex* (New York: Doran, 1923), pp. 32ff.
23. W. M. Flinders Petrie, *Social Life in Ancient Egypt* (Boston: Houghton Mifflin, 1923), p. 119.
24. *Ibid.*, p. 109.

Giving support to Petrie was his contemporary and rival, the Frenchman Gaston Maspero, who served as director of the Egyptian Antiquities Service. He wrote: "The Egyptian woman of the lower and middle classes is more respected and more independent than any other woman in the world. As a daughter, she inherits from her parents an equal share with her brothers; as a wife, she is the real mistress of the house . . . her husband being, so to speak, merely her privileged guest. She goes and comes as she likes, talks to whom she pleases without any one being able to question her actions, goes amongst men with an uncovered face. . . ."[25] Though Petrie used matriarchy to describe what we now would call matrilineal or perhaps matrilocal society, and Maspero was considerably more cautious in his claims, inevitably Egyptian society in various encylopedic articles has been characterized for its "distinct preservation of matriarchy, the prominent position of women, and a comparative promiscuity in sexual relations."[26]

Most of the studies written about ancient Egypt which are more than thirty years old can no longer be regarded as accurate. In spite of this revolution in Egyptian studies one Egyptologist, Margaret A. Murray, recently wrote that the throne went strictly in the female line. "The Great Wife of the king was the heiress; by right of marriage with her the king came to the throne. The king's birth was not important, he might be of any rank, but if he married the queen he at once became king. To put the matter in a few words: the queen was queen by right of birth, the king was king by right of marriage."[27]

Few scholars would now agree with her. Most recent studies are ambiguous about the position of the queen. Typical is John A. Wilson, who argued that the legitimacy of the rule was conditioned "both by the royal descent of the mother and by that of the father. Pharaohs might have many wives, taken from many sources, but the purest line to carry on the seed of the sun-god Re would show a mother directly of the royal family. This was the reason for brother-sister marriages by some of the pharaohs, for the purpose of assuring the most divine strain and for the derivative purpose of cutting down

25. Gaston Maspero, *Life in Ancient Egypt and Assyria* (New York: Appleton, 1928), p. 11.

26. H. R. Hall, "Family (Egyptian)," in *Encyclopedia of Religion and Ethics*, ed. by James Hastings (New York: Scribner's, 1928), vol. 5, p. 733.

27. Margaret A. Murray, *The Splendor that Was Egypt* (rev., New York: Hawthorn Books, 1963), p. 102.

on the number of pretenders to the throne."[28] Some studies are out-right hostile to any such theory. Barbara Mertz has argued that the theory of inheritance through the female can only be supported by a series of exceptions and unreasonable explanations. Since this is the case, it is safest to hold that the inheritance of the throne was based on the simple notion of royal succession, that the king was succeeded by the oldest son of his chief wife. If the chief wife bore only daughters, the oldest one of them and the husband selected for her—preferably the king's son by a secondary wife or concubine—inherited the throne. Women could not rule in their own right and so an heiress princess needed a husband, but a properly legitimate crown prince could reign in his own right.[29]

Key to some of the theories of matriarchy was the marriage of brother and sister but scholars now doubt that it was very common. Professor Jaroslav Cerny after searching through hundreds of inscriptions concluded that the term sister had come to mean wife and lover rather than a sibling of the same mother and father. In his study of some 490 marriages in the twenty-second dynasty he found that only two can be taken as brother and sister, and even these have been debated, although marriage of half-brothers and sisters may have been more common. It was not until Greek times, in the time of the Ptolemies, that it became a rule for a pharaoh to marry his sister. This custom may have been imported from Greece rather than carried over from ancient Egypt. In sum, though we often encounter brother and sister couples in mythological stories such as Isis and Osiris, all we can say with certainty about ancient Egypt is that if marriages between siblings were legal, they were not very common.[30]

Part of the difficulty with reconstructing the real status of women in Egypt is that we lack the kind of comprehensive law codes present in ancient Mesopotamian society. We do, however, have numerous legal documents, particularly from the time of the Persians and the Greeks who occupied Egypt in the last half of the first millenium B.C. From these it would appear that women had the right to own property, to buy, sell, and testify in court. The Aramaic papyrus docu-

28. John A. Wilson, *The Culture of Ancient Egypt* (Chicago: University of Chicago Press, 1951), pp. 96–97.

29. Barbara Mertz, *Red Land, Black Land: The World of the Ancient Egyptians* (New York: Coward-McCann, 1966), pp. 76–80.

30. J. Cerny, "Consanguineous Marriage in Pharonic Egypt," *Journal of Egyptian Archaeology,* 40 (1954), 23ff.

ments dating from the fifth century B.C. found at Elephantine, although dealing primarily with a Jewish military colony, probably reflect Egyptian practices. From these it is apparent that women not only enjoyed full equality to own property but also could go about their transactions in the same manner as men. Moreover, they were allowed to regain the property they brought with them as dowry if their marriage broke up. If, however, the woman had committed adultery no such guarantee existed. Women were listed as taxpayers, and they could also sue.[31] Apparently a woman did not need a guardian to be able to execute legal acts, nor did it matter whether she was married or not. A daughter, at least in the Ptolemaic period, was entitled to equal succession in the estate of her father.[32] Women could acquire wealth or property through their parents, husbands, or purchase it. A wife was entitled to a third of her husband's possessions after his death, whereas the other two-thirds had to be divided among the children and sisters and brothers of the testator. If a husband desired his wife to receive more, he had the right to donate it to her before he died.

The comparative economic independence of women may have given them greater freedom than in Mesopotamia, and this would give support to Marxist theories about the reason for the subjugation of women. Such independence must have been limited to the upper levels of society. The ordinary peasant, whether male or female, lacked many possessions, and the slave was even lower on the scale. Nevertheless, women of all classes were recognized as important, evidenced by the numerous goddesses. Particularly important were the triads of gods composed of a man, woman, and child, almost always a son. This family portrait is evident in the Memphis triad of Ptah, his wife Skhmet, and their son Nefertum; in the Theban triad, Amon, his wife Mut, and son Khons; but most particularly in the triad of Osiris, Isis, and Horus. Isis became so popular that she supplanted all other goddesses. There were numerous other goddesses: Nephthys, sister of Isis and god of the dead; Hathor, the cow goddess

31. Reuven Yaron, *Introduction to the Law of the Aramaic Papyri* (Oxford: Clarendon Press, 1961), pp. 42–43. The best study of ancient Egyptian law is a series of articles in German by E. Seidl. See, for example, Seidl, "Eiführung in de Ägyptische Rechtsgeschichte bis zum Ende des Neuen Reiches," *Ägyptologische Forshungen*, vol. 10 (2nd ed., Glückstadt, 1951).

32. Raphael Taubenschlag, *The Law of Greco-Roman Egypt in the Light of the Papyri* (New York: Herald Square Press, 1944), p. 15.

and goddess of creation; and Hekhebet, goddess of childbirth. Mesh-khent, Taueret, and Renenet were also goddesses of childbirth or of suckling children. There were still others.[33]

Since goddesses were so important it would seem to follow that royal women would also be important if only because the pharaoh's first wife was the consort of a god. Inevitably, too, she became the "mother of the god" who would be the successor to her husband. At all periods in Egyptian society the queens were the first ladies of the land and originally the tombs of some were as big and as elaborate as those of the kings. During the pyramid period, however, the queens' pyramids were much smaller than those of the kings, emphasizing that while women were important, they were not as important as the men. There were exceptions. The Greeks preserved a legend of an early woman pharaoh, Rhodopis, the daughter of Cheops, the pharaoh who built the famous pyramid. All sorts of tales were told about her sexual ability that would tend to emphasize her mythical character.[34] There is, nonetheless, some corroborating evidence. The tomb of a fourth dynasty queen shows Khufu's daughter (Cheops to the Greeks), Hetep-hires II, as having blond hair instead of the conventional black hair. Since Rhodopis means "rosy cheeked" the resemblance is obvious. Her identity was probably merged with Queen Khent-kaus for whom the so-called fourth pyramid of Giza, actually a huge sarcophagus, was built.[35]

Legend and the reality of history are often different, and it was not until the eighteenth dynasty (c. 1570–1305) that the Egyptian queen achieved her highest prestige. The most influential of all was Hatshepsut (c. 1486–1468), who stole the throne from her young nephew and stepson, Thutmose III, and wielded the scepter for about twenty years. Hatshepsut, however, ruled as a king and not as a queen, an indication of the difficulties women had in ruling. The reigning monarch of Egypt had to be male: the titles, laudatory inscriptions, and ceremonies were all designed for men and were so deeply rooted in tradition and dogma that it was easier for a woman to adapt herself to fit the titles than to change the titles to fit her sex. Inevitably her reign is somewhat confusing since she is shown both

33. For a survey of the mythology, see *Egyptian Mythology* series of the *Mythologie Generale Larousse*, trans. by Delano Ames (London: Hamlyn, 1965).

34. Herodotus, *Persian Wars*, II, 135. See also Bullough, *History of Prostitution*, p. 24.

35. Wilson, *Culture of Ancient Egypt*, pp. 97–98.

in a man's kilt (and body) wearing the king's crown and artificial beard, and as a woman with feminine dress and queen's crown. She also has two tombs, one in her capacity as queen and one as king, the latter being larger. When she died or was driven from the throne by her nephew, Thutmose III, he destroyed almost anything Hatshepsut had ever touched, and even tried to obliterate all inscriptions which referred to her. Though Hatshepsut must have been a strong-willed woman, one of her great difficulties seems to have been her inability to lead an army. She recorded no military conquests or campaigns; her great pride was in the internal development of Egypt. Though there was nothing in her biological makeup that would prevent a woman from being a soldier or general, in fact, many of them disguised themselves as males to serve in the American Civil War, women almost without exception were not trained as soldiers. In the past when kings had to lead their armies this discrimination might have prevented more women from being rulers. Hatshepsut obviously was supported by the bureaucracy of the state, but civil powers can be diffused. In a military crisis, however, power must be centralized into the hands of one person, and though a woman might appoint a male to act as commander, there is little to stop him from turning against her, particularly if he has the loyalty of the troops. It might well be that Thutmose III used his military ability to regain the throne, since he either deliberately introduced military imperialism or was forced to expand in order to defend his countries' borders.[36]

Hatshepsut was not the only woman to sit on the throne. There were at least three others, although only as regents for their sons. The mother of Pepi II (2350–2200 B.C.) was mentioned in some of his inscriptions, but the other two queens in the twelfth and in the nineteenth dynasties were even more obscure. Tausert, who finished up the nineteenth dynasty, like Hatshepsut, took the title of king. Other than the fact that she was not the daughter of a king, we can say little more about her. More information is known about some of the other royal wives of the eighteenth dynasty, particularly queen Tiy, wife of Amenhotep III (1398–1361 B.C.) and her daughter-in-law, Nefertiti, wife of Akhenaton. Tiy is interesting if only because she is usually pictured as being ugly and a commoner. This raises

36. Barbara Mertz, *Temples, Tombs and Hieroglyphs* (New York: Coward-McCann, 1964), pp. 164–191.

questions of how she got to be queen. She must have been very bright, and we know she had considerable power both under her husband and under her son. Akhenaton also raised his own wife, Nefertiti, to a high position of power, but unlike Tiy, Nefertiti was and still is known for her beauty. Women continued to exercise considerable influence down to the time of Cleopatra, the seventh Macedonian princess of that name, and apparently the first Greek princess to be able to speak to the Egyptians in their own tongue. Though Cleopatra was Greek rather than Egyptian, her importance emphasizes the continuing influence of women in Egyptian affairs, whether foreign or native.

The relative importance of the queen mother was no indication that the king was restricted to one wife. Concubines and harems were common, but such women seldom appeared in public. The size of the harem probably varied and at times reached remarkable numbers. Ramses II (1290–1224 B.C.), for example, had at least seventy-nine sons and fifty-nine daughters. The members of the royal harem lived apart from the rest of the court. Employees of the harem were not eunuchs, as in Mesopotamia, but included normal men, many of them married, as well as numerous women. In general the harem women were chosen by the pharaoh either for political reasons or for their great beauty. It was through this last procedure that many non-royal women gained admission and some became queens. There were also a number of women of foreign birth. Inevitably there were conspiracies in the harem as various wives tried to maneuver their sons into key positions. When women were not in the harem for political reasons, their chief purpose was to amuse their lord. They were instructed in dancing and singing and other arts designed to arouse and delight the male. Some of the richer Egyptians also had harems and concubines but as a general rule Egyptians practiced monogamy if only because economic factors worked against polygamy. The husband could dismiss his wife if he wished to remarry or if his wife ceased to please him but he had to return her dowry and give other forms of settlement. Women had no such freedom.

Like most societies, Egypt practiced a double standard. Concubinage existed but not polyandry. Maidservants belonged to their owner and adultery for the male was not considered a sin. Prostitution was widespread. In the so-called "erotic papyrus" of Turin the adventures of an inexperienced man in a brothel were described in such great detail that the work has remained unpublished because scholars in the past regarded it as obscene. If a married woman committed adultery, however, she could be deprived of her property and be subject to punishment. We have two folktales from the Middle and New Kingdom of women committing adultery: in the first the woman was burned to death; in the second her husband killed her and threw her corpse to the hounds. In other folktales women appeared as very sexual creatures, willing to betray their husbands, use various kinds of tricks, and do other things in order to get the men who attracted them physically into bed. Gaston Maspero, the nineteenth-century editor of a collection of these stories, said that they indicated the Egyptian morals were lax,[37] and it is probably from such statements that the legend of the promiscuous Egyptian woman has arisen. Instead of female promiscuity, it seems possible that they might only indicate male wishful thinking. Before the late period of these tales the Egyptian woman was seldom pictured in any negative way in the literature. She was always the faithful caring wife, the princess with many suitors, or the mistress praised by songs and poems. Motherhood was her revered function. Not to have children was a terrible and lamentable situation, and mother and children were depicted at all times in Egyptian tombs and pictures.

Women seldom appeared in public life although some women did hold public offices. There are records of a woman director of a dining hall, a manageress of a wig workshop, the headmistress of singers, the supervisor of a house of weavers, and numerous mistresses of royal harems or superintendents of houses. In later Egyptian history wives of eminent persons or members of old noble families also were allowed to use honorary official titles. We know of at least one woman scribe who belonged to the household of the thirteenth-dynasty queen, and it is possible some queens and princesses knew how to write. Most women, even of the upper classes, could not. Women could also serve in the temples, and priestesses were recruited not only from the royal house, the civil service, or clergy, but also from the working class. Generally women served as musicians or dancers in the temple, although some might have become high priestesses.[38]

37. Gaston Maspero, *Popular Stories of Ancient Egypt*, trans. by A. S. Johns (reprinted, New Hyde Park, N.Y.: University Books, 1967), pp. xlvii, 14, 24, 136–140, 185ff.

38. Stephen Wenig, *The Woman in Egyptian Art* (New York: McGraw Hill, 1969), p. 25.

The extant literature seems to be from the hands of males, and it reflects the various attitudes of males toward women. Ptah Hotep, the semilegendary sage of the Old Kingdom who lived in the third millenium B.C., said: "If you are a man of note, found for yourself a household, and love your wife at home, as it beseems. Fill her belly, clothe her back; unguent is the remedy for her limbs. Gladden her heart, so long as she lives; she is a goodly field for her lord [that is, she will produce children if you cultivate her]. But hold her back from getting the mastery. [Remember that] her eye is her stormwind, and her vulva and mouth are her strength." [39] Though wives were good if kept in their place, care should be exercised in their choice. "If you take to wife one who is well nurtured, one who is cheerful, one whom the people of her city know, put her not away, but give her [food] to eat." [40] Women were also dangerous: "If you would prolong friendship in a house to which you have admittance, as master, or as brother, or as friend, into whatsoever place you enter, beware of approaching the women. It is not good in the place where this is done. Men are made fools by their gleaming limbs of carnelian. A trifle, a little, the likeness of a dream, and death comes as the end of knowing her." [41] In the New Kingdom, from the fifteenth to the twelfth centuries B.C., the same sort of advice was given. Motherhood was especially revered. "Double the bread that thou givest to thy mother, and carry her as she carried [thee]. When thou wast born after thy months, she carried thee yet again about her neck, and for three years her breast was in thy mouth. She was not disgusted at thy dung, she was not disgusted and said not: 'What do I?' She put thee to school, when thou hadst been taught to write, and daily she stood there [at the schoolhouse] . . . with bread and beer from her house." [42] When a man married he should keep the example of his mother in front of him. "When thou art a young man and takest to thee a wife and art settled in thine house, keep before thee how thy mother gave birth to thee, and how she brought thee up further in all manner of ways. May she not do thee harm nor lift up her hands to the Gods and may

39. Joseph Kaster, *Wings of the Falcon: Life and Thought of Ancient Egypt* (New York: Holt, Rinehart, and Winston, 1968), p. 170.

40. *Ibid.*, p. 171.

41. *Ibid.*, pp. 169–170.

42. Adolf Erman, *The Literature of the Ancient Egyptians*, trans. from the German by Aylward M. Blackman (London: Methuen, 1927), p. 239.

he not hear her cry."[43] A man had to be careful with his wife. "Act not the official over thy wife in her home, if thou knowest that she is excellent. Say not unto her: 'Where is it? Bring it to us,' if she hath put [it] in the right place. Let thine eye observe and be silent, that so thou mayest know her good deeds. [She is] happy when thine hand is with her. . . . Thereby the man ceaseth to stir up strife in his house. . . ."[44]

Women, in general, however, were a snare and a delusion. "Go not after a woman, in order that she may not steal thine heart away."[45] In particular beware "of a strange woman, one that is not known in her city. Wink not at her . . . have no carnal knowledge of her. She is a deep water whose twisting men know not. A woman that is far from her husband, 'I am fair,' she saith to thee every day, when she hath no witnesses."[46]

Yet a woman could also be a delight.

> When I embrace her and her arms enlace me,
>   it is as if I were in Punt,
>   drenched in her fragrance!
> When I kiss her with her lips opened,
>   ah, then I am drunk without beer!
> Hasten to prepare the bed, handmaiden!
> Place the finest linen for her limbs,
>   perfumed with precious unguents!
> O would that I were her Negro slave girl who bathes her,
>   then I would always see the color of all her limbs!
> O would that I were the one who washes her linen,
>   to rinse the perfumes which pervade her garments!
> O would that I were the ring upon her finger,
>   so that she would cherish me as something which
>   adds beauty to her life.
>
>   .   .   .
>
> Lovely are her eyes when she glances,
> Sweet are her lips when she speaks,
>   and her words are never too many!
> Her neck is long, and her nipple is radiant,
>   and her hair is deep sapphire.

43. *Ibid.*
44. *Ibid.*
45. *Ibid.*, p. 240.
46. *Ibid.*, p. 236.

Her arms surpass the brilliance of gold,
  and her fingers are like lotus blossoms.
Her buttocks curve down languidly from her trim belly,
  and her thighs are her beauties.
Her bearing is regal as she walks upon the earth—
  she causes every male neck to turn and look at her.
Yes, she has captivated my heart in her embrace!
In joy indeed is he who embraces all of her—
  he is the very prince of lusty youths!
See how she goes forth—like that one and only Goddess.[47]

In sum, the Egyptian woman had a relatively pleasant life and we do not need to resort to questionable generalizations like that of primitive matriarchy in order to explain it. Her somewhat higher status than the Mesopotamian woman still did not mean that she was considered equal to men. Women were clearly subordinate, and compared to men their lives were circumscribed. It might well be that the very passivity of living in Egypt due to the great fertility of the soil and to the regularity of life lent less emphasis to war and to the making of war. Women worked in the fields along with the men in ancient times, as they do now, although their assigned functions differed. Even the fact that women appeared as rulers does not mean that they had equality, since all apparently exercised their power in the name of their son or took a male name. It is also worthy of comment that most of the women rulers appeared at the end of a dynasty, apparently striving to keep the family in power either because their sons were young or their husbands enfeebled. Hatshepsut, of course, was an exception. Some Egyptian women worked outside of their homes, but the professions were not open to them nor were any of the crafts, except the traditionally feminine ones. They were not priests, nor were they carpenters, sculptors, or scribes. Woman's place was in the home, and it was as mothers that they had their greatest influence. If Egypt is the example of the power that women had under what some have called a matriarchy, their status in times past must never have been very high.

As far as attitudes toward women were concerned, ancient Judaism was more inclined to follow the attitudes of Mesopotamia than of Egypt. Judaism was a male-oriented religion with women clearly subordinate. Nevertheless there was considerable ambiguity expressed

47. Kaster, *Wings of the Falcon*, pp. 228–229.

toward women. The nature of this ambiguity is shown in the con-flicting versions of creation. In one version, God was said to have created the world in six days, including man (and woman), whom "God created in his own image, in the image of God created he them. And God blessed them, and God said unto them, Be fruitful and multiply, and replenish the earth, and subdue it: and have do-minion over the fish of the sea, and over the fowl of the air, and over every living thing that moveth the earth."[48] This account, however, is generally agreed to have been composed later, following the Baby-lonian exile, than the earlier and better known one of Adam and Eve. In this earlier version, the male was clearly superior to the female. God created man, Adam first, but then decided that it was "not good that the man should be alone; I will make him an helpmeet for him."[49] Then out of the rib of Adam, he made Eve. The very name woman according to the Bible meant that "she was taken out of man." The most striking evidence of this superiority of first creation is not found in Jewish but in Christian scriptures. The Apostle Paul emphasized: "For the man is not of the woman; but the woman of the man. Neither was the man created for the woman; but the woman for the man."[50]

Woman was created to assist man, to serve him, and to act as com-panion. Regardless of this intent, woman was troublesome. It was the women in Jewish literature who seemed to have the more con-stant, more aggressive sexual drive. It was Eve who led Adam astray, and so indirectly was responsible for all of his problems. For causing this disgrace God punished woman: "I will greatly multiply thy sor-row and thy conception; in sorrow thou shalt bring forth children; and thy desire shall be to thy husband, and he shall rule over thee."[51] Though ancient Palestine, like Mesopotamia, suffered from con-tinual invasion, thus demanding strong men, much of the ancient Jewish suspicion of women was due to the fact that they were so sexually enticing, and sex came to be more and more a problem in ancient Israel. In general there seems to have been very little preach-ing on sex in the pre-exilic period (before the sixth century B.C.). In fact there was little consciousness of sex as a special problem in the

48. *Genesis* 1:27–28, King James Version.
49. *Genesis* 2:18.
50. *I Corinthians* 11:8–9.
51. *Genesis* 3:16.

pattern of social conduct. After that, however, came a radical change which lasted through the Second Commonwealth and the entry of Rome upon the scene. In this period, when much of the scripture was put into written form, there was emphasis upon man as a weak, help-less creature, heir to inborn evil tendencies inherited from Adam, his original father. Man's greatest weakness was the lure of sexual plea-sures. The urge for sexual satisfaction made man almost a helpless victim in the hands of Satan. Inevitably a rigid code of sex morality developed in which even innocent social contact between the sexes came to be regarded with suspicion and condemned as immoral. If a man felt his soul was endangered by sex, women came to be feared and suspected since he was so conscious of the impact they had on him. Asceticism, particularly in sexual matters, became an ideal, and even legitimate sexual pleasures were condemned as sinful.

In a sense this explanation appears much too simple, since it ne-glects the fact that there were countercurrents within this period and large segments of the population were not in accord with such ascetic ideals. It was, nevertheless, these ascetic ideals which came to be in-corporated into the law and which exercised such great influence upon Christian thought. Why such hostility toward sex? One possi-ble explanation for this increasing rigidity of attitude, even overt hostility toward sex, is that it represented a reaction to the threat of assimilation. In order to preserve Judaism from what was regarded as the threat of disintegration from contact with outsiders, outsiders who were politically and militarily more influential, rigid codes were erected, separating Jew from non-Jew. Nowhere were these restric-tions more evident than in the increasing restrictions put upon social contacts between a man and a woman. Woman, after all, to the male mind is often equated with sex. She keeps reminding him of his sexual nature and therefore she must be evil. During the Talmudic period, coinciding with the first few centuries of the Christian era, when Judaism was temporarily more secure, there was again more permissiveness and a tendency to accept sex as good. The rabbis of this period even went so far as to ridicule the fear of the "dangerous" woman that had occupied the minds of the teachers of the earlier period. They denied that the flesh was evil, but emphasized instead that the legitimate pleasures of sex were essentially good. Even though sex was good, it was only within marital relationships that it could afford "legitimate" physical satisfaction and further God's purpose in perpetuating the human species. Moreover sex acts should always meet the standards of cleanliness and refinement set forth in the various codes. Still later in the Middle Ages sexual standards again became much more restrictive.[52]

The chief safeguard of sexual morality practiced throughout Jewish history was early marriage, as soon after puberty as possible. Even younger marriages were possible since the Jewish scholars regarded the boy as capable of the sexual act at nine and girls at three years of age.[53] In biblical times marriage took place around the age of fifteen, although girls were at least betrothed, if not married, at younger ages.[54] Young men who were still unmarried at eighteen might be called before the elders to account for their failure to take a wife. If the place of the bachelor was disapproved of, there simply was no place for a single woman. The aim of Hebrew society was to have every eligible person married. Tied in with this was the concept of levirate marriage, marriage of the widow to the brother-in-law. It is upon the husband's brother that the obligation was put to take the place of his deceased brother, both in providing a "name" for him and in caring for the widow, particularly if she were childless, since the childless person was cut off from the family tree and thus had to be artifically regrafted. The widow in return received care, sustenance, protection, and retained the social advantage of membership in her husband's family.[55]

Though levirate observance underwent definite and radical changes in the biblical period and probably disappeared altogether in the post-exilic period, there is still scholarly debate upon the subject.[56] Obviously the levirate marriage emphasized the nature of women as property. This also appeared in the *Decalogue*. "Thou shalt not covet thy neighbour's house, thou shalt not covet thy neighbour's wife, nor his maidservant, nor his ox, nor his ass, nor anything that is thy neighbour's."[57] This is in keeping with the fact that most of the biblical and talmudic references dealt with women

52. Louis Epstein, *Sex Laws and Customs in Judaism* (New York: Bloch Publishing, 1948), pp. 3–24.

53. *Abodah Zarah*, p. 179, trans. by A. Mishcon and A. Cohen in *The Babylonian Talmud*, ed. by Isidore Epstein (London: Soncino Press, 1953).

54. David Mace, *Hebrew Marriage* (London: Epworth Press, 1953), pp. 143–144.

55. Louis M. Epstein, *Marriage Laws in the Bible and Talmud* (Cambridge: Harvard University Press, 1942), pp. 79–80.

56. *Ibid.*, pp. 82ff.

57. *Exodus* 20:17.

from a male point of view. Inevitably also there was a double standard. Adultery existed in Jewish law but it applied only to the sex relations of a married woman with a man other than her husband. This could result in the death penalty,[58] but if a married man engaged in sex relations with other women there was no punishment. The subordinate status of women is also evident from the treatment of rape, most notably in the Talmud, where it is emphasized that there is always the possibility that the initial moral resentment on the part of the woman may gradually turn into an inward instinctual consent.[59] Though the sons of Jacob killed Shechem for raping their sister, Dinah, their father condemned them for it, although his condemnation might have been motivated by fear of what would happen to him and his family who were outnumbered by the unbelievers.[60] The case of Tamar, the daughter of David, and his son Amnon[61] was less one of rape than of incest, and incest was one of the crimes that Jews could not commit even under threat of death.[62] Rape under wartime conditions was not considered rape at all, and it was more or less standard practice for the Hebrew soldiers to ravish the women captured in war.[63] Some attempts were made to ameliorate such practices, but the custom was never fully abolished.[64]

Ancient Jews also practiced polygamy, and in the Bible it appears widespread, at least among the leaders. Gideon, the Israelite judge, had enough wives to bear him seventy sons.[65] Other polygamists included Jair, Ibzan, Abdon, David, Solomon, and Rehoboam, although sometimes it is difficult to separate wives from concubines since Abraham, Jacob, Gideon, Saul, David, and Solomon all had concubines. A concubine could be the slave girl of a man's wife, as was the case of Hagar and Sarah or Bilhah and Rachel, and several others, but a man could also buy a concubine for himself or take one captured in war. Woman's status in society depended to a large extent on her fruitfulness, and the inability to bear children was a cause

58. *Leviticus* 20:10.

59. *Kethuboth*, 51b, trans. by Israel W. Slotki in the *Babylonian Talmud*, ed. by I. Epstein (London: Soncino Press, 1936).

60. *Genesis* 34:30.

61. *II Samuel* 13:1–29.

62. *Leviticus* 20:11; Mace, *Hebrew Marriage*, pp. 159–164.

63. *Judges* 21:16–24.

64. *Deuteronomy* 22:10–14.

65. *Judges* 8:30.

of disgrace. The childless Sarah, for example, was despised by her handmaid Hagar, and poor Sarah was beside herself when Hagar gave Abraham a son.

Jewish law never prohibited sexual relations between unmarried persons but virginity in a bride was highly prized. There were, however, numerous Jewish ethical teachings extolling premarital chastity for both young men and young women, but no penalty was imposed for violation of this ideal. Children, whether born in or out of wedlock, were regarded as legitimate. The references to bastards refer only to offspring of unions that would have been impermissible in marriage, such as incestuous or adulterous relations or relations between a member of a priestly caste and a divorcée.[66]

The Bible also emphasizes the fact that women have special problems which further set them apart from men. A menstruating woman was held to be unclean: "And if a man shall lie with a woman having her sickness, and shall uncover her nakedness; he hath discovered her fountain, and she hath uncovered the fountain of her blood: and both of them shall be cut off from their people."[67] This seems to imply exile or death as punishment for sexual relations during menstruation, and we know that this was not normally the case. Traditionally, nonetheless, a woman was regarded as unclean for seven days and everything that she "lieth upon," "setteth upon," or "toucheth" also became unclean. "And if any man lie with her at all, and her flowers be upon him, he shall be unclean seven days: and all the bed whereon he lieth shall be unclean."[68] Since women were thought to be so obsessed with sex, they had to be protected from their own natural base instincts. Talmudic writers went so far as to prohibit a widow from keeping a pet dog for fear she might use it to commit a sexual indecency.[69] Widows were also enjoined from acquiring a slave for the same reason.[70]

The sexual nature of women is continually emphasized in the Bible. It was Potiphar's wife who tried to seduce Joseph,[71] and there

66. Mace, *Hebrew Marriage*, pp. 210–211.
67. *Leviticus* 20:18.
68. *Leviticus* 15:24.
69. *Abodah Zara*, 22b.
70. *Baba Mezia*, 71a trans. into English by Salis Daiches and H. Freeman in the *Babylonian Talmud*, ed. by I. Epstein (London: Soncino Press, 1935).
71. *Genesis* 39:7–18.

was quite frank sexual bargaining between Rachel and Leah for sex rights to their husband, Jacob.[72] Delilah was the cause of Samson's downfall.[73] Even when a woman was peacefully taking a sunbath, she caused trouble, as did Bath-sheba to David.[74] Since David was a man of God, the fact that he committed a mortal sin must have been due to Bath-sheba rather than to himself. Instead of the innocent victim she became the seducer and often is still so regarded. Frank S. Mead in his description of biblical characters, for example, describes her as a "dirty, apologetic gray."[75] The straying of Solomon, the "beloved of God," is also attributed to women. As the Bible says: "his wives turned away his heart after other gods: and his heart was not perfect with the Lord his God, as was the heart of David his father."[76] The term Jezebel, the name of the wife of Ahab, has even become a pejorative term in English because the biblical writers state that she led her husband to worship Baal.[77] In Proverbs, the most conspicuous and vividly developed theme is the importance of avoiding "strange women," or any women other than one's wife. Proverbs also characteristically presents the erring woman as more guilty than the man; while he is weak, she has deeply sinister designs upon him. A poor credulous man follows a woman just as an ox goes to the slaughter.[78] The author of Ecclesiastes through diligent search found one righteous man among a thousand, "but a woman among all those I have not found."[79]

There are, of course, other portraits of women in the Bible.[80] Intelligence, after all, was not a male prerogative, but the only woman who achieved a sort of political power by common consent was Deborah, the Prophetess, the Jewish Joan of Arc, who encouraged the doubters in the fight for Canaan and helped bring about victory over Sisera, leader of the Canaanite army.[81] Deborah helped Barak plan the strategy, organized the campaign, and accompanied Barak,

72. *Genesis* 30:1–24.
73. *Judges* 16:4–20.
74. *II Samuel* 11:2–27.
75. Frank S. Mead, *Who's Who in the Bible* (New York: Harper, 1934).
76. *I Kings* 11:4.
77. *I Kings* 16:31–33; 18:13, 19; 19:1, 2; 21:5–25; *II Kings* 9:7, 10, 22, 30, 36–37.
78. *Proverbs* 6:24–35; 7:10–27, *et al.*
79. *Ecclesiastes* 7:28.
80. For a survey see Edith Deen, *All of the Women of the Bible* (New York: Harper and Row, 1955).
81. *Judges* 4:1–24.

but once the Israelites had won, she gave all credit to God and took none for herself. In fact she only accompanied the troops at Barak's request.

Women were supposed to be loyal, particularly to their husband and their husband's family, and the story of Ruth and Naomi has often served as a moral lesson to impress all wives: "Intreat me not to leave thee, or to return from following after thee: for whither thou goest, I will go; and whither thou lodgest, I will lodge; thy people shall be my people, and thy God my God. Where thou diest, will I die, and there will I be buried: the Lord do so to me, and more also, if ought but death part thee and me."[82] The last chapter of Proverbs spells out what a good woman should do in great detail:

> Who can find a virtuous woman? for her price is far
>   above rubies.
> The heart of her husband doth safely trust in her, so
>   that he shall have no need of spoil.
> She will do him good and not evil all the day of her life.
> She seeketh wool, and flax, and worketh willingly with
>   her hands.
> She is like the merchants' ships; she bringeth her food
>   from afar.
> She riseth also while it is yet night, and giveth meat
>   to her household, and a portion to her maidens.
> She considereth a field, and buyeth it: with the fruit
>   of her hands she planteth a vineyard.
> She girdeth her loins with strength, and strengtheneth
>   her arms.
> She perceiveth that her merchandise is good: her candle
>   goeth not out by night.
> She layeth her hands to the spindle, and her hands hold
>   the distaff.
> She stretcheth out her hand to the poor; yea, she reacheth
>   forth her hands to the needy.
> She is not afraid of the snow for her houshold: for all
>   her household are clothed with scarlet.
> She maketh herself coverings of tapestry; her clothing is
>   silk and purple.
> Her husband is known in the gates, when he sitteth among
>   the elders of the land.

82. *Ruth* 1:16–17.

She maketh fine linen, and selleth it; and delivereth
   girdles unto the merchant.
Strength and honour are her clothing; and she shall rejoice
   in time to come.
She openeth her mouth with wisdom: and in her tongue is
   the law of kindness.
She looketh well to the ways of her household, and eateth
   not the bread of idleness.
Her children arise up, and call her blessed; her husband
   also, and he praises her.
My daughters have done virtuously but thou excellest them
   all.
Favour is deceitful, and beauty is vain: but a woman that
   feareth the Lord, she shall be praised.
Give her of the fruit of her hands; and let her own works
   praise her in the gates.[83]

It was perhaps from this description that someone coined the phrase
that while man works from sun to sun, woman's work is never done.
This is obviously again a male view of what a woman should do. Nowhere does it indicate that she should have any pleasures in life,
other than pleasure in a thing well done.

Women could also be an erotic figure.

Thy lips, O my spouse, drop as the honeycomb: honey
   and milk are under the tongue; and the smell of thy
   garments is like the smell of Lebanon.
A garden inclosed is my sister, my spouse; a spring shut
   up, a fountain sealed. . . .
My dove, my undefiled is but one; she is the only one of
   her mother, she is the choice one of that bare her. . . .
Thy navel is like a round goblet, which wanteth not liquor:
   thy belly is like an heap of wheat set about with lilies.
Thy two breasts are like two young roses that are twins.
Thy neck is as a tower of ivory; thine eyes like the fishpools
   in Hesbon, by the gate of Bath-rabbim: thy nose is as the
   tower of Lebanon which looketh toward Damascus.
Thine head upon thee is like Carmel, and the hair of thine
   head like purple; the king is held in the galleries. . . .
Set me as a seal upon thine heart, as a seal upon thine arm:
   for love is strong as death; jealousy is cruel as the

83. *Proverbs* 31:10–31.

grave: the coals thereof are coals of fire, which hath
a most vehement flame.
Many waters cannot quench love, neither can the floods drown
it: if a man would give all the substance of his house
for love, it would utterly be contemned. . . .[84]

Though the Song of Solomon owes its inclusion in scriptures to the idea that it portrays a close and loving relationship between God and Israel, and this allegorical interpretation was accepted by the early Christian church, most biblical scholars would hold that it should be interpreted much more literally. If combined with Proverbs it gives us two faces of woman: the dutiful housewife and loving mother on the one hand; the erotic lover, temptress of man, on the other. Nowhere was woman regarded as equal to man. In its positive aspects the ancient Jewish attitude led to a high regard for home and children and a high ideal of family life. Though woman's domestic and maternal virtues were esteemed, she was subordinate and naturally inferior to man, and she labored under various religious and social disabilities. Since the home remained the center of community life, the lot of the Jewish woman was not without either its compensation or its opportunities, but these were not to be compared, at least in the male mind, with those available to men. Women in the ancient Near East were everywhere subordinate, although their lot in Egypt was probably somewhat better than in Palestine or Mesopotamia. She had her greatest value as mother, but she was also important as a sex object. Though the Babylonians might have regarded her as property, it was the Jews who made her an object of evil. This facet of woman continues to appear through much of Western civilization.

84. *Song of Solomon, passim.*

chapter three

The Pedestal with a Base of Clay

Our nineteenth-century forebears put the Greeks on a pedestal. The classics played a great part in the education of the upper classes in Europe, as well as America, and the intrinsic greatness of much of Greek (and Roman) literature called forth unstinted admiration. The Greeks seemed to them to be the embodiment of wisdom and beauty and were regarded as setting standards by which epic, lyric, and dramatic poetry could be judged. The Greeks were called the fathers of history and geography, the founders of philosophy, regarded as having laid the theoretical basis for science, and creators of ideals which guided artists since their time. Though in recent decades we have tended to bring the Greeks down from their pedestal, to talk less in terms of the "glory that was Greece" and more in terms of historical reality, it is still troublesome to many historians, perhaps imbued with slightly more enlightened attitudes toward women than some of their ancestors, to find that the Greeks regarded women as such inferior creatures.

Though attitudes toward women differed over the long course of Greek history, during the period about which most is known, that of Athens in the fifth and fourth centuries B.C., the status of women seemed to have achieved some kind of nadir in Western history. Modern historians, who often are imprisoned in the attitudes of their own culture, recognizing that the Greeks were intelligent, rational, and sophisticated, just as they themselves are, find this attitude toward women contradictory and not a few have tried to explain it. H. D. F. Kitto, for example, in his popular (and scholarly) history of Greece, after pointing out the evidence for the depressed status of women, feels that the story is incomplete. In trying to develop a more accurate account, he compares himself to the detective in a mystery story who, though all the evidence seemingly leads to but one conclusion, does not fully accept it if only because there are still ten more chapters to go in the book before the real culprit is unmasked. Concerning Greek women, Kitto holds that what is wrong with the standard portrayal "is the picture it gives of the Athenian man. The Athenian had his faults, but pre-eminent among his better qualities were lively intelligence, sociability, humanity, and curiosity. To say that he habitually treated one half of his own race with indifference, even contempt, does not, to my mind, make sense. It is difficult to see the Athenian as a Roman paterfamilias, with a greater contempt for women that we attribute to the Roman."[1] The difficulty with such thinking is that the Greeks often treated a great many people with indifference, including other Greeks, and like most people before or since, were quite capable of brutality and callousness. The only way stereotypes about Greek attitudes can be challenged is by seeking new evidence and not by wishing things were different. Is there any evidence to the contrary? Arnold Gomme has argued that the negative view of women advanced by most scholars has been biased by the selection of sources from which it is drawn. A different view could be held since there is "no literature, no art of any country, in which women are more prominent, more important, more carefully studied and with more interest," than in the tragedy, sculpture, and painting of fifth-century Athens.[2] It is true that women do appear in the vase paintings, in the sculpture, and in the tragedies; particularly in the drama of Euripides women play an important role. The role, however, is highly restricted, namely that of housekeeper and mother. It is this very role which Greek males held in such low esteem. Or did they?

An American sociologist, Philip Slater, argues that the entire controversy over the role and status of women in Greece, and thus the attitudes expressed toward them in the extant literature, is based upon a "patriarchal delusion."[3] By patriarchal delusion he means the belief that power follows deference patterns, that because men were seemingly the most important they actually held real power. Slater also holds that a sizable power differential between the sexes was

1. H. D. F. Kitto, *The Greeks* (London: Penguin, 1951), p. 222.
2. Arnold W. Gomme, *Essays on Greek History and Literature* (Oxford: Basil Blackwell, 1937), p. 92.
3. Philip E. Slater, *The Glory of Hera: Greek Mythology and the Greek Family* (Boston: Beacon Press, 1968), p. 7.

never possible over any length of time, and that to believe the contrary was part of the patriarchal myth. According to Slater, once a scholar divests himself of such delusions, examines Greek society anew, the combination of derogation and of preoccupation with women ceases to be a paradox and becomes inevitable. This is because the rejection of the female by the Greeks was little more than the rejection and derogation of domesticity, of home and family life, and hence of the process of rearing young children. The fact that the Athenian adult male fled the home only meant that the Athenian male child grew up in a female-dominated environment. Later as an adult male he tried to convince himself, sometimes even successfully, that women were of no account, but deep down he knew that during the most important years of his psychological development the reverse was true. In his early formative years men were trivial to him, since the most important things at that period, at least as far as he could see, were decided by women. Using some twentieth-century studies as a basis for his theorizing, Slater argues that women, excluded from outside activities, inevitably assumed more decisions regarding household activities, emphasizing their role and influence over the young.

The difficulty with such an explanation is quite simply that ancient Greece was not twentieth-century America. The mother, in fact, was not the key figure she is in middle-class American society today, sacrificing herself and her independence to further her children's development, although this did sometimes happen in ancient Greece. Instead the most influential figure in reasonably well off Greek families, and it is this group with which Slater is most concerned, was the "nanny" who usually was also a slave.[4] Moreover girl children from the moment of their birth were regarded and treated as inferior to boys, a condition which young boys became conscious of if only because their slave nannies emphasized it in order to secure their own status. It seems doubtful, at least to us, that the combination of a doting "nanny" and the concept of superiority of the male so engrained in the young Greek male would lead to the kind of anxieties Slater feels existed.

It is undoubtedly true that the psychological influence of women should be separated from their social position, but Slater is highly

4. H. I. Marrou, *A History of Education in Antiquity*, trans. by George Lamb (New York: Sheed and Ward, 1956), p. 142.

selective of the psychoanalytic theory he chooses to buttress his position.

> The Greek male's contempt for women was not only compatible with, but also indissolubly bound to, an intense fear of them, and to an underlying suspicion of male inferiority. Why else would such extreme measures be necessary? Customs such as the rule that a woman should not be older than her husband, or of higher social status, or more educated, or paid the same as a male for the same work, or be in a position of authority—betray an assumption that males are incapable of competing with females on an equal basis; the cards must first be stacked, the female given a handicap. Otherwise, it is felt, the male would simply be swallowed up, evaporate, lose his identity altogether.[5]

It is precisely this mother-dominant, father-avoidant culture which Slater believes could explain the widespread existence in ancient Greece of male homosexuality and in which the mother would select the son as a kind of surrogate husband. Much of his theorizing on this matter is based on the conceptions of Karen Horney.

Horney, a disciple of Freud, disagreed with him on the universality of penis envy. Instead she held that the male's attempt to find a penis in the woman was an attempt to deny the existence of the intrinsically "sinister" female genitalia which represents a fear of maternal envelopment. She claimed that male homosexuals, for example, dreamed they were falling into a pit, sailing a boat in a narrow channel, and being sucked into a whirlpool, finding themselves in a cellar full of "uncanny, blood-stained plants and animals," or of being lured to death by a female. Slater found similar concepts expressed in Greek mythology and legend. To overcome this dread of the female genitalia Horney claimed that men developed two techniques, namely disparagement and idealization. By the first the male reassured himself that there was nothing to be feared from so poor and inadequate a creature, and with the second that there was nothing to fear from so saintly a being.[6] To further support the application of this thesis to Greece, Slater points to the misogynistic nature of most Greek literature and to the fact that the Greeks tended to marry barely pubescent girls and to encourage their women, and only

5. Slater, *Glory of Hera*, p. 8.
6. Karen Horney, "The Dream of Woman," *International Journal of Psychoanalysis*, 13 (1932), 348–360.

their women, to practice depilation of all body hair. Inevitably also it was the mature, maternal-type women who were the most feared and most dangerous in Greek literature.[7] But why adopt the concept of the sinister female genitalia instead of the penis-envy theory of Freud to explain ancient Greece? In fact, do either of them explain the Greeks? The real difficulty with applying any such theoretical concept to Greece is that data is conflicting and different attitudes were dominant at different time periods. Slater agrees that attitudes change but held that the increasing misogyny was due to a transition from a matriarchy to a patriarchy, something which as has been indicated elsewhere is debatable.

There were, however, other changes in Greek society which can be documented from existing sources, namely, the growth of urbanization. The Greeks pictured in Homer and Hesiod, the two earliest literary sources, were still rural, but by the fifth century B.C. they were urban. It would seem obvious that as people moved into town the nature of the family life would change. But how radical was this change? Slater argues that the role of the husband changed as he absented himself more and more and his economic role became less visible. The wife in turn became less mobile, more imprisoned within the household, thus upsetting some previous balance. In the process, he holds, there was a breakdown of the extended family system, thus throwing an emotional burden on the nuclear family which was not equipped to handle it. As ties of blood weakened, there was no corresponding strengthening of the marital bond to fill the gap, and the tensions between the sexes were simply accentuated, hence the growth of misogyny and homosexuality. It is true that women were probably less important in the city than they were in the country, where they often worked alongside their husbands, but Greek cities were not modern cities and all of the major figures in Greek life were also landholders, who commuted to their farms or if wealthy supervised from a distance. By modern standards no Greek city was large and kinship always remained important. Moreover, while the extended family was not the base unit in Athens, there were always plenty of slaves to make the Greek family different from the modern American one. Rather than the growth of urbanization in itself, it might be the rate at which the growth takes place. In periods of rapid growth there is considerable disorganization, and as growth levels

7. Slater, *Glory of Hera*, p. 12.

off there is an easing of tension as old ways are successfully modified to meet the new situation. This might have been the case in Greece, although hard data to document such a change is somewhat elusive.

On the surface, however, it would seem that social change was rapid in Athens, so rapid that it reduced the authority of the older generation and engendered what today would be called a youth culture. Though this rising youth culture, represented in the literature by the hostility of the older generation to the sophists, might have contributed to democracy, it also seemed to heighten the existing pathology. Slater would argue, for example, that to ease tensions the Athenian males turned to the source of their own pathology, pederasty and misogyny.[8] Pederasty and misogyny, however, are not necessarily the opposite sides of the same coin, although it would seem to follow that when the female is condemned the male would be exalted. On the other hand if the female is exalted too high, males tend to turn to each other also. Overlooked in such explanations is the whole socialization and acculturation patterns which have to be considered to explain the development of the Greek attitudes. On the basis of present evidence, it would seem to be much too simple to explain either homosexuality or misogyny in the terms set by Slater or by other theorists. The whole attitude toward sexuality, toward the meaning and purpose of marriage, toward the reasons for the existence of women has to be taken into consideration. The Greeks offer us much more fruitful grounds for speculation than earlier societies, but there is not enough data to arrive at any general conclusions as to why they regarded women as so inferior. In fact, we would argue, there can be no simple answer to such a question in Greece or elsewhere.

In general scholars have argued that women in the Homeric poems, probably put into final form about the ninth century B.C., had a higher position and were better regarded than later in Greek society. Samuel Butler, who is best known for his novel, *The Way of All Flesh*, a bitter and realistic study of Victorian bigotry, narrowness, and hypocrisy, was so impressed with the insight into women's character in the *Odyssey* that he felt it must have been written by a woman.[9] Though Butler has won few converts among classical schol-

8. *Ibid.*, pp. 72–74.
9. Samuel Butler, *The Authoress of the Odyssey*, new intro. by David Grene (2nd ed., reprinted, Chicago: University of Chicago Press, 1967), *passim*, but esp. pp. 105–124.

ars for his theory, it is evident that women play a more important part in the *Odyssey* than the *Iliad,* but this difference might well be due to the nature of the subject matter. The *Iliad,* to put it simply, is a story of battle, and in this activity the Greeks excluded their womenfolk. In the *Odyssey,* Ulysses, after fighting some ten years at Troy, sets out for home but is delayed some ten years through a series of adventures, mostly with women, who try to keep him from reaching his patient and devoted wife, Penelope. Penelope in the meantime is spending some twenty years anxiously awaiting the return of her wandering husband. Whether the portrayal of women is insightful or not might be left to modern readers to decide, but what becomes evident is that their menfolk treat them rather shabbily.

Scholars are in general agreement, however, that the Homeric poems reflect the attitudes and customs of the period in which they were committed to their final form, although they carry beliefs of an earlier age in which women probably had somewhat higher standing than they do in the actual poems. This higher standing, some would call it evidence of earlier matriarchy, appeared not so much in the portrayal of the mortals as in the goddesses. Among the mortals patriarchy was in full flower.[10] Matriarchy, we hold, is much too strong a term to describe the existence of earlier matrilineal and matrilocal societies. There is, nonetheless, general recognition that a feminine goddess, equated with mother nature, was very prominent in early Greek religion, and only later was supplanted by the Olympians.[11]

Zeus and his fellow Olympians came fairly late to the mythology of the Greek peninsula and never claimed to have created the world. It was Homer and Hesiod who gave final form to the Olympians, and in the process of settling into a position of dominance, Zeus took almost every local goddess as his consort. Each valley, isle, and cove seemed to have a local manifestation of a female goddess whom Zeus

10. Kaarle Hirvonen, *Matriarchal Survivals and Certain Trends in Homer's Female Characters,* in vol. 152, *Annales Academiae Scientiarum Fennicae* (Helsinki: Suomalainen Tiedeakatemia, 1968).

11. See, for example, Gilbert Murray, *Five Stages of Greek Religion* (reprinted, Garden City, N.Y.: Doubleday, 1955). The thesis was first worked out in considerable detail by Jane Harrison, *Prolegomena to the Study of Greek Religion* (reprinted, New York: Meridian Books, 1955). See E. O. James, *The Cult of the Mother Goddess* (New York: Praeger, 1959). The most fervent advocate of the theory today is Robert Graves, *The White Goddess* (New York: Farrar, Straus and Cudahy, 1948).

supplanted either by marrying or having intercourse with her, dropping children all over Greece until descent from Zeus came to be a way of authenticating heroes and founders, much as some old American families claim descent from the pilgrims on the Mayflower. By the time of Hesiod in the eighth century B.C., male dominance, which some have questioned in Homer, was no longer in doubt. Women once again, as they were in ancient Israel, were looked upon as the source of evil. In his *Theogony*, Hesiod tells the story of Pandora, the first of all women, whom Zeus had Hephaestus fashion out of clay. All the gods contributed to Pandora's beauty and charm (her name has been translated to mean "all gifts"), and Athena and Aphrodite went to great lengths to make her extremely attractive. When they had completed their task they gave her to Epimetheus, the brother of Prometheus, the hero who had stolen fire from heaven. Though Epimetheus had been warned by Prometheus against accepting any gifts from Zeus, when he saw the lovely Pandora he ignored his brother's advice. The gods had also given Pandora a box, never to be opened, as a bridal gift. Inevitably the natural "womanly" curiosity of Pandora got the best of her and soon after her arrival she opened the jar, allowing the evils and diseases which the gods had put there to swarm out and plague mankind. The only thing that remained was hope which had been caught under the lid when it was closed again, but Pandora finally allowed hope to go free also. The misogyny of Hesiod was further underlined by his emphasis upon the fact that it was from Pandora that the "deadly race and tribe of women" descended who were always troublesome to men.[12] Men were miserable whether they married them or not. Those who managed to avoid "marriage and the sorrows that women cause" reached deadly old age without anyone to tend to them and they also lacked children. Inevitably when such a man died his kinfolk would divide his possessions among themselves. Quite obviously the purpose of woman was to nurse a man in his senility and to bear him children in order that he not leave his money to distant relatives. Hesiod, in fact, thought of a wife as an expense, at best a constant drain on her husband's income, at worst a financial calamity. He cautioned his readers not to let a "flaunting woman coax

12. Hesiod, *Theogony*, ed. by M. L. West (Oxford: Clarendon Press, 1966), ll. 565–616, and Hesiod, *Works and Days*, ed. by T. A. Sinclair (Hildesheim: Georg Olms, 1966), pp. 42–105.

and decieve them" and reminded them that the "man who trusts womankind trusts deceivers."[13]

Mythology, even when it is put into didactic form, is one thing, philosophy is another, and it is for their philosophic and scientific thinking that the Greeks were raised to such a pedestal in human history. Philosophy is born when rational curiosity gets the upper hand, and men in rejecting the action of personal agents begin to seek to explain phenomena in the working out of impersonal forces. Mythical thinking, however, does not die a sudden death, and it is quite possible that it never dies. In Greek thought there was no sudden transition from a mythical to a rational mentality. Instead mythical concepts came to be dressed up in rational terms, where they gained new life in the guise of philosophic ideas. When Hesiod described the origins of the world, he posited certain powers as present in the beginning and derived others from them, and following his own experience he tried to explain things somewhat naturally. The sky married the earth and she bore the mountains and oceans as children, just as she also bore giants and gods whose form and function were purely anthropomorphic. In attributing certain characteristics to women in the myths, he and his fellow theologians were undoubtedly reflecting their own beliefs or insecurities. The same thing happened when scientific and philosophic thinking developed.

In Greece, mythological and religious explanations were unchallenged until about 600 B.C., yet by the middle of the fourth century the Greeks, or at least the educated ones, could move as easily as we ourselves do in the field of abstract conceptions and universal principles. Inevitably, however, these "scientific views" bore a strong resemblance to ideas which Greeks had before, although the basis for holding them might have changed. As far as women were concerned, the Greeks have the honor of demonstrating on a "scientific basis" that women were inferior, although there were conflicting beliefs and even considerable ambiguity. Greek philosophy and science are usually associated with the names of Plato and Aristotle, who lived and wrote in the fourth century B.C., and it was their thinking about women which most often was reflected in later scientific and philosophic writings.

Plato was considerably more ambiguous on the subject of women

13. Hesiod, *The Homeric Hymns and Homerica*, ed. and trans. by Hugh Evelyn-White (London: Heinemann, 1942), pp. 7, 9, 31, 33, 47, 53, 55, and 123.

than Aristotle. Some have even held that Plato was a feminist,[14] that is a man who argues for greater rights for women. In a sense this is true, but Plato was, if nothing else, contradictory. Part of the difficulty is in determining what Plato actually believed since the dialogue form does not always make it possible to determine what he himself felt, though in the early dialogues it would seem that Socrates acted as spokesman. Unfortunately Socrates was a rather equivocal spokesman since his own marriage left much to be desired. His wife, Xanthippe, has come to be regarded as a classical example of shrewishness, and her consistent scolding proved trying even to the exceptional fortitude of her saintly husband. In her defense it should be said that while Socrates in one sense was a saint, he was also a gadabout, who was always pestering people about truth and virtue, the very type of husband which might drive a woman to distraction. Many stories were told about Xanthippe. When Socrates, for example, was questioned as to why he continued to live with Xanthippe, he is supposed to have replied that if he could learn to adapt to her he could adapt easily to the rest of the world. When questioned by a young man as to whether or not he should marry, Socrates was supposed to have said: "On the one hand loneliness, childlessness, the dying out of your stock, and an outsider as your heir will be your destiny; on the other eternal worry, one quarrel after another, her dower cast in your face, the haughty disdain of her family, the garrulous tongue of your mother-in-law, the lurking paramour, and worry as to how the children will turn out."[15] With such a spokesman for female independence, it is no wonder that Plato's position is not at all clear.

But Plato himself was not consistent. The treatise in which women were looked upon most favorably, the *Republic*, was quite different from the *Laws*, in which he clearly made women subject to men. Since the *Laws* were written much later than the *Republic*, do the concepts presented there represent the true Plato? Did he change his ideas about women or have we read too much of an argument for equality into the *Republic*? Probably Plato was a prisoner of his own time who, though trying to solve problems, and in the process mak-

14. Gomme, *Greek History and Literature*, p. 102.
15. Diogenes Laertius, *Lives of Eminent Philosophers*, ed. and trans. by R. D. Hicks (London: Heinemann, 1959), I, 167, and Valerius Maximus, *Factorum et Dictorum Memorabilium Libri*, ed. by Karl F. Kempf (Leipzig: Teubner, 1888), VII, ii, par. 6, ext. 1, p. 327.

ing universal generalizations, reflected the reality of the Athens in which he wrote. Plato's writings date from the period after the Peloponnesian War. Athens had been defeated by Sparta, and Socrates, Plato's teacher, had been put to death by the citizens of Athens. The war had been costly, business was bad, the future uncertain, and in such conditions many men questioned the wisdom of tying themselves down with wives who, they felt, could not be trusted. Plato was concerned with meeting the problem. One solution might have been to strengthen the control of men over women. Another might have been to give women greater legal rights, including the right to an education and a place in public life. In the *Republic*, which represented an ideal state, Plato took the latter course. He argued it was absurd to divide the world into separate categories of men and women for the purpose of public affairs, of education, or anything other than the begetting and bearing of children. Such a twofold division made no more sense than it did to restrict bald-headed men to certain tasks and hairy ones to others, since the ability to grow hair had nothing to do with other abilities. Moreover, encouraging men to claim things for themselves, such as wives, created struggles between citizens: litigations, worries, anxieties, and so forth. The obvious solution was to abolish the family and hold everything in common, including lands and houses. Marriages at best were to be temporary. Women were to be sexually and socially equal to men in Plato's ideal state, to have the right to education, and even to become philosopher kings. Even in this ideal state of equality, however, Plato recognized the right of a man who was more intelligent, brave, and skilled than others to have more wives.[16]

The concepts put forth by Plato in the *Republic* do not really make him a feminist. The society he pictured in all of his dialogues was essentially masculine. Even in the *Republic* he went so far as to state that a woman's capacity to learn was less than that of man,[17] although he was enough of a scientist to recognize the existence of individual variation. Moreover, Plato believed that a woman needed a man for her own well being, but that a man did not need a woman. In his *Timaeus* he stated: "The womb is an animal which longs to

16. Plato, *Republic*, ed. and trans. by Paul Shoren (2 vols., London: Heinemann, 1935), esp. bk. 5.

17. Plato, *Republic*, 454D–456C; *Timaeus*, ed. and trans. by R. G. Bury (London: Heinemann, 1952), 42A, 90E, and perhaps also *Laws*, ed. and trans. by R. G. Bury (2 vols., London: Heinemann, 1952), 804E–806C.

generate children. When it remains barren too long after puberty, it is distressed and sorely disturbed, and straying about in the body and cutting off the passages of the breath, it impedes respiration and brings the sufferer into extreme anguish and provokes all manners of diseases besides."[18] The obvious solution to any such problem was to appease the womb by passion and love, to sow seeds that would grow and develop into a child. "Such is the nature of woman and all that is female." Plato, in effect, argued that the way to keep woman happy was, as one wit put it more crudely, to keep her barefoot and pregnant.

In his old age, Plato, who was a bachelor, rejected some of the more feminist notions expressed in the *Republic* and asserted in the *Laws* that the patriarchal family was the basic unit of state. The chief purpose of marriage was to have children, and it was wicked for a man voluntarily to deprive himself of this heritage. He nonetheless recognized that women had sexual rights, and procreation like everything else in marriage was done in partnership, although the man was clearly superior.[19] He also held that women had the right to be educated, and though the sexes were to be separated at six, their education was to be the same. Daughters, however, were not as important as sons, since it was the sons who inherited. Increasingly Plato felt that licentiousness (which he had tolerated in the *Republic*) was reprehensible. Men and women were to live in moderation and not fall to the level of the beasts. For those who were unable to abstain from all sexual acts not intended to procreate children, Plato commanded the strictest privacy in philandering to avoid scandal. For those caught in the act of sodomy, incest, or committing adultery or fornication with citizen women, or in sexual acts with slave concubines, he advocated disenfranchisement.[20] It was perhaps because of his fear of licentiousness that he idealized love, now often called Platonic love, although it seems clear that his ideal love object was a male rather than a female.

If Plato was ambiguous in his attitudes toward women, his pupil, Aristotle, must be regarded as a consistent believer in the inferiority of the female sex. It was his "scientific" proof of this subordination which tended to dominate so much of Western thinking. A belief in

18. Plato, *Timaeus*, 91C.
19. Plato, *Laws*, 783B–784B.
20. Plato, *Laws*, 839E–841E.

female inferiority entered into his physiology and biology, as well as his political, ethical, and aesthetic theories. Quite simply to Aristotle women were intellectually and morally inferior to men. All men needed to prove such inferiority to themselves was to consult the voice of nature; nature, he felt, was quite unequivocal on male superiority. Everywhere in the animal world, he held, the male of the species was demonstrably more advanced than females: larger, stronger, and more agile. So also was man, and thus male domination was the will of nature. To try to challenge nature in the name of an imagined principle of equality was quite contrary to the interests both of the individual and of the community.[21] Aristotle even believed that women had fewer teeth than men.

Key to Aristotle's concepts about the superiority of man was the overwhelming importance of the male principle in reproduction. He held there was only male semen; female semen did not exist. It was the semen which supplied the form, and the female supplied the matter fit for shaping. "If, then, the male stands for the effective and active, and the female, considered as female, for the passive, it follows that what the female would contribute to the semen of the male would not be semen but material for the semen to work upon."[22]

Some historians of science have regarded Aristotle's view as a step forward, since he at least recognized that the female supplied the substance needed for growth of the embryo, which he identified as the menstrual blood. This implied that the role of the female was important, and while not quite equal to the male, it certainly was not entirely negative. Some earlier peoples had denied physiological maternity, including, it is believed, the ancient Egyptians. If this was the case then arguments about the status of women and attitudes toward them resulting from beliefs in their part in conception can be seriously challenged. This is because the Egyptians regarded women with a less jaundiced eye than the Greeks, although they held the male totally responsible for conception. If Aristotle represented a forward step over earlier Graeco-Egyptian views, he did not give women the importance that writers of the Hippocratic corpus on

21. Aristotle, *Historia animalium*, trans. by D'Arcy W. Thompson in *The Works of Aristotle* (Oxford: Clarendon Press, 1910), vol. 4, 608B. See also Aristotle, *Politics*, ed. and trans. by H. Rackham (London: Heinemann, 1944), I, 2 (1252B), 7.

22. Aristotle, *Generation of Animals*, trans. by A. L. Peck (London: Heinemann, 1953), 729A, 25–34.

Generation did. In this work the doctrine of two seeds was advanced, with the female seed identified as vaginal secretion.[23] This would imply an equality in conception. Other Greek medical and philosophic writers followed either Hippocrates or Aristotle, but Galen who had more influence on later generations than other medical writers adopted the views of Aristotle.[24]

Aristotle used his theory of conception to argue that women were meant by nature to be passive. He regarded women as less temperate and continent than men in their desires, because women were the weaker sex. From this he concluded that a man's love was passionate and open, while a woman felt desire and was cunning. This did not mean that women lacked goodness, but only that each group in society had a different excellence and function. A woman had her special goodness, a slave his, though a woman's was less than a man's, and that of a slave was wholly inferior.[25] Aristotle explained that

> the slave has no deliberative faculty at all; the woman has, but it is without authority, and the child has, but it is immature. So it must necessarily be with moral virtues also; all may be supposed to partake of them, but only in such manner and degree as is required by each for the fulfillment of his duty. Hence the ruler ought to have moral virtue in perfection. . . . Clearly, then, moral virtue belongs to all of them; but the temperance of a man and of a woman, or the courage and justice of a man and of a woman, are not, as Socrates maintained, the same; the courage of a man is shown in commanding, of a woman in obeying.[26]

Women lacked a natural capacity for virtue but they did have other merits, such as a beautiful body and a love of work.[27]

Aristotle attempted to distinguish between the rule of a master over his servants or the father over his child, which he regarded as the superior over the inferior, and that of "citizen" rule, such as one citizen over another or of a husband over a wife. There was, however, an important distinction between the rule of one citizen over another

23. T. U. H. Ellinger, *Hippocrates on Intercourse and Pregnancy* (New York: Abelard-Schuman, 1952); Joseph Needham, *A History of Embryology* (2nd ed. rev., New York: Abelard-Schuman, 1959), pp. 31–37.

24. Needham, *History of Embryology*, pp. 69–74.

25. Aristotle, *Nichomachean Ethics*, ed. and trans. by H. Rackham (London: Heinemann, 1962), VIII, vii, 1.

26. Aristotle, *Politics*, I, 13 (1260A), 7–8.

27. Aristotle, *Rhetoric*, ed. and trans. by John Henry Freese (London: Heinemann, 1967), I (1361A), v, 6.

and the husband's rule over the wife, in that the former was temporary and the latter was permanent.[28] "For although there may be
exceptions to the order of nature, the male is by nature fitter for
command than the female, just as the elder and full grown is superior
to the younger and more immature."[29] To ensure the ability of a man
to always command his wife, Aristotle recommended marriage at
different ages. He felt women should marry when they were about
eighteen and men at thirty-seven, when both were in "the prime of
life" and the decline in their powers would coincide. Moreover if
marriage produced children it could be reasonably expected that the
children would reach their prime when the father reached his allot-
ted "three-score and ten years."[30]

Aristotle believed that "silence" was a woman's glory, although it
was not the glory of a man.[31] Quite simply it was through a certain
incapacity that the female was a female, and the female character
just had a sort of natural deficiency.[32] Since this was the case it was
only natural that women often loved and admired the male without
receiving an equivalent love in return, since Aristotle held that love
was proportionate to superiority and whoever was the superior must
receive more affection that he gave.[33]

Aristotle did not feel he was treating women badly or giving them
any less than their due. In fact, he argued that only barbarians
treated women as slaves, and he regarded himself and his fellow
Greeks as far removed from them. "But among barbarians no distinction is made between women and slaves, because there is no
natural ruler among them: they are a community of slaves, male and
female. Wherefore the poets say, 'It is meet that Hellenes should rule
over barbarians'; as if they thought that the barbarian and the slave
were by nature one."[34] Aristotle, in effect, had put the subjugation of
women on a "scientific basis." Did this reflect the reality of Greek
life?

The answer would seem to be yes since the general view of women

28. Aristotle, *Nichomachean Ethics*, VIII, vii, 1–2.
29. Aristotle, *Politics*, I, 12 (1259B), 1.
30. Aristotle, *Politics*, VII, 16 (1335A), 9–10.
31. Aristotle, *Politics*, I, 13 (1260A), 10; see also Aristotle, *Poetics*, ed. and trans.
by W. H. Fyfe (London: Heinemann, 1953) (1454B), 16ff.
32. Aristotle, *Generation of Animals*, I, xx (728A), 18–20.
33. Aristotle, *Nichomachean Ethics*, VIII, vii, 2–3.
34. Aristotle, *Politics*, I, 2 (1252B), 4.

in Greece was that legally and socially, as well as in popular estima-
tion, women occupied a fairly low place. Though, as indicated, some
doubt has been cast on this generalization, even those who question
it recognize that women had a separate sphere from the men and the
Greeks regarded the female sphere as inferior. During the rising tide
of democratic reform in Athens some of the freedom of the aristocracy to acquire wives and concubines at will or to regard whom they
would as their heir was restricted,[35] but this did not necessarily open
up opportunities for women. Even after the Peloponnesian War in
which there was a general leveling down in Athens, it was of such
overriding importance that not a breath of suspicion fall on young
girls or young wives that they were protected beyond what modern
society would regard as a reasonable degree. One Greek, for example,
praised his sister and niece because they had lived in the woman's
quarter of the house "with so much concern for their modesty that
they were embarrassed even to be seen by their male relatives."[36]
Xenophon in his treatise on domestic management emphasized that
the girl who became a bride had often lived under such strict supervision, "seeing, hearing and saying as little as possible," that "she
knew no more than how, when given wool, to turn out a cloak, and
had seen only how spinning is given out to the maids. . . . in control
of her appetite . . . she had been excellently trained, and this sort of
training is, in my opinion, the most important to man and woman
alike."[37] Wives did not go out to dinner in other houses with their
husbands and were excluded from eating with them when they were
entertaining male visitors in their own home.[38]

Women did have some legal rights and we know that they took
part in making wills, in some family councils, and that they had
organizations of their own. When this is granted, however, it still
seems that women were almost entirely dependent upon their husbands, their fathers, or male relatives. A proper woman was cut off
from a man's world, and in fact burglars and thieves were given the

35. W. K. Lacey, *The Family in Classical Greece* (London: Thames and Hudson,
1968), pp. 24–25, 151–176.
36. Lysias, *Orationes*, ed. and trans. by W. R. M. Lamb (London: Heinemann,
1957), III, 6.
37. Xenophon, *Oeconomicus*, ed. and trans. by E. C. Marchant (London: Heinemann, 1953), VII, 5–6.
38. Isaeus, *Speeches*, ed. by William Wyse (Hildesheim: Georg Olms, 1967), III,
13–14; Lysias, *Orationes*, I, 22.

death penalty, in part at least, because it was argued that it was difficult to distinguish them from adulterers and unless thieves and burglars met the same fate as adulterers, each would claim a lesser
crime.[39]

The civic necessity for female virginity ensured that girls would be
married very young, probably at fourteen, though there were some
Athenian writers who thought it should be more like the eighteen
to twenty it was said to be in Sparta. The husband was usually much
older than his wife, a sixteen- to twenty-year age differentiation was
not uncommon, and this led to a couple having little to share except
their family. It was perhaps for this reason that Aristotle in his discussion on friendship did not bother to consider the relationship of
husband and wife at all.[40] The marriage relationship was not a partnership, it was a paternalism.

Athenian girls were less educated than boys, and although many
could read and write, few received any higher education. Most of the
better educated women who are known to have lived in Athens were
either noncitizens like Aspasia (the beloved of Pericles) or else lived
in the Hellenistic age when there was some lessening of the sex barriers. Husbands and wives had little in common and Xenophon questioned whether there was anyone with whom the husband talked less
than with his wife.[41] He concluded there were few. Though it has
been argued that the meaning of Xenophon's question has been mis-
understood, he quite clearly envisioned a marriage in which an older
husband molded the younger wife to his own image of what a dutiful
helpmate should be and do.

Athenian women remained in their houses to such an extent that
it was even possible in some law cases to pretend that they did not
exist. Among the surviving speeches in the law courts are two in
which the orator had to bring evidence to prove that a woman who
had married and borne children had actually existed. This is not to
say that wives never went out, but they did so rarely, then were veiled
and accompanied by their maids. Most scholars agree that they were
excluded even from attending the theater. In short, it would seem
that the Athenians assumed a woman's life would be spent mainly at
home, probably in somewhat less than desirable circumstances, since

39. Lacey, *Family in Classical Greece*, p. 162.
40. Aristotle, *Nichomachaean Ethics*, VIII, x (1160B–1162A), 4–12.
41. Xenophon, *Oeconomicus*, III, 11–15.

townhouses were small and probably dark. During the day a wife would see little of her husband because he was usually away from home, and this meant she was largely dependent on the slaves of the household, on elderly relatives living in the house, or on her young children for companionship.[42] Girls were even brought up on a sparser diet than boys, with very little protein and scarcely any wine.[43]

Most of the information we have is about the more well-to-do women in Athens, and it is probably true that poorer women had fewer restrictions put upon them than richer ones. Some of the poorer women did work, either in the retail trade or as wet nurses. One female vase painter is known, vast numbers worked in spinning wool, and a few served as innkeepers. In the country, peasant women helped in the field.[44] Slave women also worked, mostly as domestics, but some slave and foreign women were employed as entertainers, such as flute girls. Many slaves and foreign women served as prostitutes and courtesans.

The chief purpose of women was childbearing, particularly sons, and children were regarded as essential in the Greek world. It was woman as mother who consistently was praised in the Greek world. Aristotle, for example, began his treatise on *Politics* by breaking the communities down into their parts. The smallest unit was the *oikos* (family), composed of three elements, the male, the female, and the servant. The servant by definition could be the plow ox in the case of the poor or the human slave in the case of the rich. Aristotle then added a fourth element, children, since the male and female elements had a natural instinct to procreate themselves successors. He even went so far as to state that a family without children was not fully an *oikos*.[45] A true family was to be looked upon as a living organism requiring renewal every generation to be alive, supporting its living members' need for food, and its deceased members' need for the performance of cult rituals. A childless family was visibly dying, and a child, particularly a male child, was essential to perpetuate the organism. If a man had the misfortune of having only female children it was arranged for the girls to be married to their nearest agnatic relative (a father's brother, that is, her uncle) in order to re-establish

42. Lacey, *Family in Classical Greece*, pp. 168–169.

43. Xenophon, *Lacedaemonians*, ed. and trans. by E. C. Marchant (London: Heinemann, 1925), I, 3–4.

44. Lacey, *Family in Classical Greece*, pp. 170–171.

45. Aristotle, *Politics*, I, 1 (1252A–B), 3–7.

the family in the next generation. Men without natural heirs could also adopt sons, but the adopted son could not fully inherit until he himself had begotten a son and registered him in the family of his adopted father.[46]

Most of our information on the status of women and the attitudes about them comes from Athens, and Athens was only a small part of the Greek-speaking world. In a people as diverse as the Greeks, there were obviously quite radical differences, although the source material for other parts of Greece is minor compared to that for Athens. Perhaps the opposite extreme of Athens was Sparta, a state where a small group of citizens held the vast majority of population in subjugation. Spartans, however, were often admired by the Greeks, in part because of the rigid discipline they had imposed upon themselves, and in part because of their success. The Spartans, after all, had defeated the Athenians and some have argued that Plato's *Republic* was modeled on Sparta, where women allegedly had a somewhat higher standing. Unfortunately the source material on Sparta is both scarce and difficult to interpret, since so much of it was written by Athenians who used it for hortatory purposes. It would seem, however, that while there were differences from Athens, women in Sparta were by no means equal to men. They probably had somewhat greater personal freedom if only because the military preoccupation of the Spartan state meant that they had to assume more duties. The vast numbers of slaves also freed them from the main tasks of women elsewhere in Greece, namely the making of clothes and nursing of children. Aristotle claimed that the Spartan women managed their husband's affairs,[47] but this would seem to be an exaggeration. Spartan women, however, did have somewhat greater control of their own wealth than they did in Athens.[48] Moreover, both sexes in Sparta tended to be more nearly the same age when they married, and this fact might have saved the women from some of the more obvious aspects of patriarchal domination. Women also underwent considerable training in athletics and the comparative lack of confinement led to all sorts of speculation about their morals. Euripides in his *Andromache* has a character say: "No Spartan girl/ Could ever live clean even if she wanted./ They're always out on the street in scanty

46. Lacey, *Family in Classical Greece*, pp. 24–25.
47. Aristotle, *Politics*, II, 6 (1269B), 5–7.
48. Lacey, *Family in Classical Greece*, p. 203.

outfits,/ Making a great display of naked limbs./ In those they race and wrestle with the boys too—/ Abdominable's the word. It's little wonder/ Sparta is hardly famous for chaste women."[49] The Spartan women were as militant as their men, and among the most famous of sayings attributed to them by Plutarch was that of the mother who told her son to come back from the war with his shield or on it.[50] Since it was necessary for a man to throw his shield away in order to flee from the battle the meaning is quite clear, come back dead or a hero. Aristotle naturally was upset at the power of the Spartan women and he held that Sparta had failed because the Spartans failed to control the women.[51] Still when all of this is granted, the Spartan women never had the vote and were regarded by Spartan males as quite inferior. Their position might have been somewhat better vis-à-vis the male, but the general tenor of life in Sparta was so demanding and unattractive, at least to us, that it would seem that even the freest of Spartans was a slave to the system. In fact it was this voluntary submission to such a restrictive ideal that so impressed other Greeks.

Greek literature from the poets to the playwrights was essentially misogynistic. In most of the surviving poetry from the early period, there was such sheer misogyny that one scholar was moved to comment that one of the chief purposes of Greek poetry, whether lyric, iambic, or elegaic, was to degrade the position of women. In fact the "iambic metre was invented for the express purpose of satirical calumny, and the three chief iambic poets of the Alexandrian canon, Archilochus, Simonides, and Hipponax, in their scanty fragments all agree on one point: the chief object of their lampoons is—women."[52] Archilochus, for example, called women the greatest evil that God had ever created. Even when women appeared to be most useful, they turned out to be "a curse to their owners." A man who lived with a wife could never get through a day without trouble, and even when he was on his best behavior, the woman would always find some

49. Euripides, *Andromache*, trans. by John Frederick Nims in *The Complete Greek Tragedies*, ed. by David Grene and Richmond Lattimore (Chicago: University of Chicago Press, 1959), III, 582, ll. 596–601.
50. Plutarch, *Sayings of Spartan Women*, in *Moralia*, ed. and trans. by F. C. Babbitt, vol. 3 (London: Heinemann, 1961), 241F, 16.
51. Aristotle, *Politics*, II, 6 (1269B–1270A), 5–11.
52. F. A. Wright, *Feminism in Greek Literature* (1st ed., 1923, republished, Port Washington, N.Y.: Kennikat Press, 1969), p. 29.

ground of fault.[53] In another surviving fragment Archilochus compared women to various kinds of animals and inanimate objects whom they resembled and only one in ten could bring happiness and prosperity to their husbands. He compared women to pigs because they laid about in disorder; to a fox because they were cunning; to a dog because they wanted to hear and know everything; to mud because they knew nothing; to the sea because they were so contradictory; to an ass because they proved so difficult; to a polecat because he could find nothing lovable about them; to a mare because they would not work; to a monkey because they were a mockery to man; and finally to a bee, and it was only this last type of woman working continually like an industrious bee who was regarded as a desirable wife, the best possible helpmate given to man.[54]

At least two of the early poets were women, Erinna and Sappho, and it would seem that they would give a somewhat different picture. Only a few fragments of Erinna's verse survived, mostly from a poem entitled either the "Spindle" or "Distaff." For much of history Erinna was identified as a companion of Sappho, but modern scholarship places her later, at the end of the fourth century B.C. Her chief poem was in memory of her girlfriend Baucis, who died young, and in it Erinna described their mutual girlhood. Because of this and because of the popular belief that she was a friend of Sappho, Erinna has often been identified as a homosexual. Though it might seem reasonable to suppose that women who were excluded from any kind of equality with the male sex would turn to their sisters for companionship and solace, the evidence is by no means clear. This is true even in the case of Sappho of Lesbos, from whence the terms sapphism and lebianism derive. Sappho lived in the sixth century B.C. and was apparently the head of a school for girls in Mytilene on Lesbos. The school was dedicated to Aphrodite and the Muses. Education probably took the form of a religious fellowship, where under the direction of a mistress, young girls were fashioned to conform to an ideal of beauty and feminine wisdom. They were taught dancing, the playing of musical instruments, and singing, and the school also observed a series of festivals, religious ceremonies, and banquets. In spite of the legend surrounding her, the curriculum of the school seems to have been male-oriented since there was an emphasis on

53. *Lyra Graeca*, ed. and trans. by J. M. Edmonds (London: Heinemann, 1934), I.
54. *Ibid.*

charm and coquetry. Several sayings such as "Don't ride the high horse when you are looking for a husband," and "A woman who does not even know how to lift her skirt to show her ankles," have survived.[55]

Other fragments of her poems seem to imply feelings and intimacy for other women, although even in antiquity there were doubts as to whether her love implied carnal knowledge. There is still a group of scholars who maintain that she was a woman of absolute virtue. Some scholars have even gone so far as to maintain that there were two Sapphos, one of whom was a man.[56] Nevertheless her poems were regarded as obscene in the early Christian period when most of them were destroyed. The only way in which a modern student can arrive at the real Sappho is through the surviving fragments of her poems, and from this it would seem to us that in spite of her marriage and her children, her love ideal was female.[57]

Sappho and to a lesser extent Erinna, if only because they were women, represent an exception to the misogynistic trend in Greek literature. Were there any males who defended women? The most fully drawn portraits of women appear in Greek tragedy, particularly in the plays of Euripides, and some have even regarded Euripides as a champion of rights for women. This is because women in Euripides, whether good or bad, usually seem to be more enterprising than the men; in fact, the clever woman who contrives something when the men are at a loss is almost a stock character. In spite of this, Euripides has also been regarded by some scholars as a misogynist who merely attempted to show the evil that women did and the inevitable result if the power of women continued to increase. Regardless of which attitude one adopts, it is obvious that women were not negligible creatures in his plays, and he seems to give us real insights into what women might have felt about themselves. Medea, who is often regarded as the powerful female incarnate, gave a very poignant statement about how women were looked upon.

> We women are the most unfortunate creatures.
> Firstly, with an excess of wealth it is required
> For us to buy a husband and take for our bodies

55. *Ibid.*

56. U. von Wiliamowitz-Mollendorf, *Sappho und Simonides* (Berlin, 1913); T. Reinach, *Alcée et Sapho* (Paris, 1937), but esp. the discussion by Jeannette Foster, *Sex Variant Women in Literature* (London: Muller, 1958), pp. 17–24.

57. Foster, *Sex Variant Women*, pp. 17–24.

A master; for not to take one is even worse.
And now the question is serious whether we take
A good or bad one; for there is no easy escape
For a woman, nor can she say no to her marriage.
She arrives among new modes of behavior and manners,
And needs prophetic power, unless she has learned at home,
How best to manage him who shares the bed with her.
And if we work out this well and carefully,
And the husband lives with us and lightly bears his yoke,
Then life is enviable. If not, I'd rather die.
A man, when he's tired of the company in his home,
Goes out of the house and puts an end to his boredom
And turns to a friend or companion of his own age.
But we are forced to keep our eyes on one alone.
What they say of us is that we have a peaceful time
Living at home, while they do the fighting in war.
How wrong they are! I would very much stand
Three times in the front of battle than bear one child.[58]

This isolation was one of the worst features in a Greek woman's life, and to many it could be soul-destroying. In trying to deal with her philandering husband, Jason, Medea usually lost the argument, and though she hissed her anger and threw forth her scorn, Jason kept his cool. He indicated that he had not grown tired of her bed, but that he needed money to raise their children, and this was why he needed a new wife. "But you women have got into such a state of mind/ That, if your life at night is good, you think you have/ Everything; but, if in that quarter things go wrong,/ You will consider your best and truest interests/ Most hateful. It would have been better far for men/ To have got their children in some other way, and women/ Not to have existed. Then life would have been good."[59] Later Medea seemed to submit, and apologized, "But we women are what we are—perhaps a little/ Worthless; and you men must not be like us in this,/ Nor be foolish in return when we are foolish./ Now, I give in, and admit that then I was wrong./ I have come to a better understanding now."[60] Jason responded "I approve of what you say. And I cannot blame you/ Even for what you said before. It is natural/ For a woman to be wild with her husband when

58. Euripides, *Medea*, trans. by Rex Warner in Grene and Lattimore, *Complete Greek Tragedies*, vol. 3, p. 67, ll. 231–251.
59. *Ibid.*, vol. 3, p. 77, ll. 569–575.
60. *Ibid.*, vol. 3, p. 89, ll. 889–913.

he/ Goes in for secret love. But now your mind has turned/ To better reasoning. In the end you have come to/ The right decision, like the clever woman you are."[61]

Medea was a bitter woman, discontented with her lot, and perhaps cannot be regarded as typical. At least her solution, the murder of her children, cannot. Alcestis, however, was a saint who consented to death to save her children's position. She did not do this for the love of her husband, since the husband in Greek literature often seemed to be indifferent to his wife, but because of her love for her children. It was because she did not wish her children to be left fatherless that she consented to death; the loss of the father would be a far greater tragedy than the mother.[62]

Everywhere in his plays, Euripides spoke in a contradictory voice. In spite of his portrayals of women as real flesh-and-blood creatures, with feelings and responses that a man could understand if not sympathize with, he stressed that women ought to be silent, ought not to argue with men, ought not to speak first, and ought not to speak with strangers. Sensible women were supposed to let men act for them. If Euripides was really the feminist that some believe, why such a restrictive view? To the defenders of Euripides as a feminist the answer seems obvious. The audience for his plays was male, and though Euripides might portray women with great psychological insight, he was aware of the power of the box office. This meant he also had to be careful to keep women in their place, or at least what the Greek male felt was their proper place.[63] The result is that both feminists and misogynists can find in Euripides material to fuel their cases. Still, female characters in Euripides might have been somewhat realistic because of attempts to gain greater emancipation for women. Such attempts are reflected in some of the comedies of Aristophanes, particularly *Ecclesiazousai, Thesmophoriazusae,* and *Lysistrata.* In *Ecclesiazusai,* sometimes translated as *Women of the Assembly,* women, after disguising themselves as men, seized control of the government, whereupon they enacted legislation providing a community of property in which all women were to offer their sexual favors to whom they would, and they took other actions in what might have

61. *Ibid.,* vol. 3, p. 90, ll. 908–913.

62. See Euripides, *Alcestis,* trans. by Richmond Lattimore in Grene and Lattimore, *Complete Greek Tragedies,* vol. 3.

63. Victor Ehrenberg, *The People of Aristophanes: A Sociology of Old Attic Comedy* (Cambridge: Harvard University Press, 1951), pp. 202–203.

been intended as a parody of Plato's *Republic*. Immediately women began fighting over the most desirable males. To our mind the play is left hanging; perhaps its effectiveness at that time was due to what the Greeks felt were such ludicrous ideas, ideas which only a silly woman would hold. In the *Themorphoriazusae* women tried to revenge themselves on Euripides for revealing their secrets and speaking ill of them; in the end he agreed not to do so again. Much more serious as a commentary on women is *Lysistrata*, where Lysistrata at least was depicted as a woman of true genius, determined to end the senseless killing of men in warfare. In spite of these portrayals of real live women in both comedy and tragedy, the conclusion seems to have been that women were almost entirely excluded from the ordinary life of Greece. They had separate sororities in which they had some say, but their sphere of influence was limited. Their life must have been depressing, and the countless hints in Greek comedy of woman's love of drink, however much exaggerated, probably had some real basis; wine might have been one of the only consolations they had to help them face their utter loneliness.

Though women were given to men to mother their children, marriage itself was something to be endured. Anaxadrides summed it up when he said "he who thinks to wed, aims at the fair but hits the foul instead."[64] Theophrastus, the pupil and successor of Aristotle, is sometimes credited as the author of a lost treatise on marriage which entered into the West through quotations by St. Jerome and others. "If you give her the management of the whole house, you must yourself be her slave. If you reserve something for yourself, she will not think you are loyal to her; but she will turn to strife and hatred, and unless you quickly take care, she will have the poison ready. If you introduce old women, and soothsayers, and prophets, and vendors of jewels and silken clothing, you imperil her chastity; if you shut the door upon them, she is injured and fancies you suspect her."[65] The list could go on. If she was beautiful she attracted lovers, while an ugly wife was easily seduced. Even if a man's wife was good and agreeable, a rare thing, he had to share her trials and tribulations in childbirth and worry when she was in danger.

64. Anaxadrides, in *The Fragments of Attic Comedy*, ed. and trans. by J. M. Edmonds (Leiden: Brill, 1959), vol. 2, p. 75.

65. Quoted at length by St. Jerome, *Against Jovinianus*, in *Nicene Library* (New York: Christian Literature, 1893), ser. 2, vol. 6, pp. 383–384.

Women in the Greek world were to be neither seen nor heard. They were regarded as gossipy, drunken, and immoral, as well as spendthrift. They were troublesome, but nevertheless a man needed children. The women who most often seemed to break through the barriers were the courtesans and the prostitutes, and there is a vast Greek literature about their activities. Many such women became popular heroines.[66] To enter male society, even at the level of an unequal, women had to lose status as proper women. Even Pericles, who was not exactly a conservative in his views or in his way of life, is said to have declared that a woman should not be spoken of among men, neither in praise nor blame.[67] Since Pericles is usually associated with the great courtesan Aspasia, who became his mistress and lovingly bore his child, it appears evident that the Greeks had not gone very far toward the emancipation of women. Though there are many mentions of women in surviving inscriptions, most of them picture women as wives and mothers,[68] and it was as mothers that the Greeks most honored women.[69] It was for her biological function and not for her personality that she was accepted. It was the Greeks, after all, who found philosophic and scientific reasons to justify the subjugation of women, and although Plato seemingly put in a slight dissenting vote, even he turned out to be against equality. It was the Greeks who relegated women to the house, kept them confined, and only allowed them to go out for religious festivals, a subject which will be discussed more fully later in this book. Some of these festivals were fairly exuberant, if not irrational, and this would fit in with the findings of I. M. Lewis, who has argued that in societies dominated by men, women find their compensation in demonic possession.[70] Though such possession is mostly subconscious it also has to include an element of consciousness in order to alleviate the repression. Women, however, cannot go very far since if the male is too frequently provoked his reaction is to repress the female behavior. The

66. Vern L. Bullough, *History of Prostitution* (New Hyde Park, N.Y.: University Books, 1964).

67. Thucydides, *The Peloponnesian War*, ed. and trans. by C. F. Smith (London: Heinemann, 1951–53), II, 45, 2.

68. Helen McClees, *A Study of Women in Attic Inscriptions* (New York: Columbia University Press, 1920), *passim*.

69. Hans Licht, *Sexual Life in Ancient Greece* (London: Routledge and Kegan Paul, 1932), pp. 18–19.

70. I. M. Lewis, *Ecstatic Religion: An Anthropological Study of Spirit Possession and Shamanism* (London: Penguin, 1971).

Greeks recognized the dangers of female hysteria, but adopted a male remedy and tried to keep women in control. Women, in fact, were little more than childbearers. Even romantic love was oriented more toward a male object than a female one. If society in the Greek period was undergoing transition, and men were hunting for new answers as some have said, it seems clear that women were the early victims of a search for new solutions. The Greeks not only excluded women from assisting in the search but also regarded them as a source of many of their problems.

chapter four

The "Rise" of Women and the Fall of Rome

The rise of the comparatively backward and inconsequential people from the village of Rome to eventual control of the Mediterranean seaboard is one of the great success stories of all history. Ultimately this story of triumph became one of tragedy as Rome entered into a period of decline. Since that time the fall of Rome has been the subject of all kinds of sermons with each pulpit interpreting the cause of Roman success or failure to suit its own moral. Inevitably women have been accorded a good share of the blame for the Roman fall, and moralists of today continue to use Rome as an example to women who want or demand something more out of life than subordination to their husbands.

An example of such thinking is a recent study by Charles Winick on desexualization in American life. Winick argues that Rome provided the "most tantalizing example in history of a rigid and polarized culture that became more sexually blurred." His implication is quite clear: Americans must take care not to follow the path of Rome, something he feels is a real danger as more and more women assume roles and perform tasks previously reserved for the male. Winick, to his credit, does make some qualifications and indicates that no single cause could entirely explain Roman decline. Nevertheless he still concludes that the blurring of sex roles undoubtedly facilitated a "multiplicity of developments that changed the quality of life."[1]

Winick, at least in part, is following a path blazed by a somewhat earlier investigator, the anthropologist J. E. Unwin. Unwin, as indicated earlier, argued that the cultural conditions of any society at any

1. Charles Winick, *The New People: Desexualization in American Life* (New York: Pegasus, 1968), p. 346.

time seem to depend on the amount of its mental and social energy, and this in turn seems to depend "upon the extent of the compulsory continence imposed by its past and present methods of regulating the relations between the sexes."[2] He then argued that "no society can display productive social energy unless a new generation inherits a social system under which sexual opportunity is reduced to a minimum."[3] Unfortunately, at least for those who advocate emancipation of women, Unwin believed the only way in the historical past that sexual opportunity had been reduced to a minimum was by the adoption of "absolute monogamy," a marriage relationship in which a husband had absolute power over his wife and children. According to this thesis the advance of society demanded that women be subordinate.

Unwin's ideas have been picked up and advocated by people as disparate as Winick and Pitrim Sorokin. Sorokin was convinced that a disorderly sexual life undermined the physical and mental health, the morality, and the creativity of its devotees, as well as the society in which there were any number of such individuals.[4] Inevitably the example given of a state where women gained freedom was Rome, and the decline of Rome is then attributed to this freedom. Any advocate of equal rights for women has to come to terms with what happened in Rome, and though this task sounds simple, it is not.

There are several obstacles, the most serious being that almost everything in the past has been written by men, not by women. Generally male writers have most often pictured women when they departed from the norm, when they became notorious, and only rarely when they fulfilled their expected role of wife and mother or sister. Notoriety, however, is relative, and many of the Roman writers seem to have had "tabloid mentalities."[5] They picked up and accentuated the deviant behavior and passed over that which was not headline news. Coupled with this nose for the scandalous was an obsession, present in the Roman writers from third century B.C. onward, that their own times were periods of moral degeneracy as compared to an

2. J. D. Unwin, *Sexual Regulations and Human Behavior* (London: Williams and Norgate, 1933), pp. ix–x.

3. *Ibid.*, p. 85.

4. Pitrim A. Sorokin, *The American Sex Revolution* (Boston: Porter Sargent, 1956), p. 77.

5. This is a term used by Crane Brinton, *A History of Western Morals* (New York: Harcourt, Brace, 1959), p. 113.

earlier more heroic age. Thus they pictured the women of the past as exhibiting spectacular virtue, in fact superhuman virtue, and used these mythical paragons as an example for their own "degenerate age." This attitude also forced them to exaggerate misdeeds of their own age, and to use one or two exceptions from which they made generalizations which simply are not valid. Inevitably there is the danger that modern readers will take them at their word and like a Winick, a Sorokin, or an Unwin believe everything that was said, and draw morals for our own time from extremely misleading source material.

Historians have not made the task of moralist any easier by ignoring such aspects of Roman life as courtship, marriage, and childrearing. In fact in this day of women's liberation movements, it is painful to realize the paucity of historical studies about women. J. P. V. D. Balsdon, who published his study of Roman women less than a decade ago, put it succinctly: "Intriguing as ancient Roman women may have been, they are the subject of no single work of deep and learned scholarship in English or in any other language. . . . A number of books have been written which give biographies of the most notable, or the most notorious, ladies of the imperial court but nobody, I think, has combined a historical account of Roman women, notable and notorious alike with a general description of woman's life in ancient Rome. . . ."[6] This lack of scholarly study in the past has left all participants in the debate free to generalize and to draw their own conclusions without any attempt to draw together a picture of the whole. To draw such a picture it should be kept in mind that the Romans were essentially conservative. In spite of the glories of their empire, they looked back on an idealized recreated past which never had existed. They extolled the moral outlook of the rural primitive city state of a legendary Rome where conduct had been regulated by *mos maiorum*, respect for the customs of the ancestors both in private and in public life. To men with such attitudes, change, particularly in the relationship of the sexes, was a sign of decay. Inevitably women were pictured in unflattering colors.

The best way to convey the Roman attitude is by examining the Roman writers themselves, and one of the best sources for both attitudes and information is the historian Livy (d. 17 A.D.). Livy told us that he deliberately set out to record the great achievements of the

6. J. P. V. D. Balsdon, *Roman Women* (London: Bodley Head, 1962), p. 9.

Romans, the sovereigns of the world, and to teach future generations by examples of noble conduct and virtue of their ancestors. Livy sincerely believed that no other people in history had such a long period of integrity or honor, and inevitably he tried to contrast the past virtuousness with what he regarded as the self-indulgence and corruption of his own time. In his preface, Livy wrote: "I hope everyone will pay keen attention to the moral life of earlier times, to the personalities and principles of the men responsible at home and in the field for the foundation and growth of the empire, and will appreciate the subsequent decline in discipline and in moral standards, the collapse and disintegration of morality down to the present day. For we have now reached a point where our degeneracy is intolerable—and so are the measures by which alone it can be reformed."[7] It should perhaps be added that Livy was writing during the lifetime of Augustus, an epoch now regarded as the "Golden Age" of Rome. This was followed a short time later by the period which the eighteenth-century historian Edward Gibbon, famous for his book on the *Decline and Fall of the Roman Empire*, called the most happy and prosperous age in all of human history.[8] Quite clearly Livy was a pessimist, but it is this attitude which has so influenced most commentators on the status of women.

Livy's stories (they seem to be more legend than history) emphasized the old virtues, courage against odds, soldierly obedience, individual heroism, simplicity of manners, *gravitas* (dignity and seriousness), *pietas* (loyal respectful feelings toward the established moral order), and in the case of women, virtue and submissiveness. Inevitably many of his tales sound like that of George Washington and the cherry tree, symbolic of an ideal with which he wished to indoctrinate his readers, but not necessarily true. It should also be said that in spite of these limitations Livy is still one of the best and most reliable guides to Roman history.

If Livy's attitude reflected that of the dominant Roman class, and there is no reason to doubt that it did, then any change in what the mythological status of women had been would be regarded as a

7. Livy, *Ab urbe Condita Libri*, ed. and trans. by B. O. Foster, Evan T. Sage, F. G. Moore (London: Heinemann, 1936), intro., p. 9.
8. Edward Gibbon, *Decline and Fall of the Roman Empire*, ed. by J. B. Bury (reprinted, New York: Heritage Press, 1946), p. 61.

threat to the moral structure of Rome, even if that mythological woman had never existed. In their study of the sociology of sex differentiation the Vaertings hypothesized that a sex which had regarded itself as dominant would tend to see any increase in the power of the opposite sex as a threat to the very fabric of society.[9] Without subscribing to all their ideas, this particular thesis seems to have applicability to Rome, since Livy and other masculine writers inevitably tended to see their society threatened by any slight change in the status of women, and even by the most charitable measure they have to be labeled as misogynists. It is their misogynistic views, however, which appear so often in some of the current explanations for the decline of Rome.

Coupled with a respect for a legendary and mythical past was the ability of the Romans to engage in self-deception, perhaps inevitable in a people who though they conquered the Mediterranean world always argued that they went to war reluctantly and not with any imperialistic gains in mind. Even after the conquests and booty of an empire brought them great riches, they liked to believe that they were living a very simple life. Their definition of what constitutes a simple life seems quite incredible to most modern readers. This can best be illustrated with the cast of the first century A.D. philosopher, Seneca, who described what he called a simple pastoral trip. In his letter recounting the trip Seneca was quite proud of the utter simplicity in which he traveled and emphasized how he roughed it by taking only one carriage load of slaves, sleeping on the ground with the Roman equivalent of air mattresses, and taking only an hour to prepare the "simple" noonday meal.[10] The Romans were also extremely patriotic, tending to think of Rome as embodying all virtues and of other peoples as inferior. Even the sophisticated Cicero (d. 43 B.C.) claimed that after the Romans had surveyed all other peoples, they would find that "there is no social relation among them all more close, none more dear than that which links each one of us with our country. Parents are dear; dear are children, relatives, friends; but one native land embraces all our loves; and who that is

9. Mathilde and Mathias Vaerting, *The Dominant Sex: A Study in the Sociology of Sex Differentiation*, trans. by Eden and Cedar Paul (London: Allen and Unwin, 1923).

10. Seneca, *Epistolae Morales*, ed. and trans. by Richard K. Gummere (London: Heinemann, 1920), I, 17 (57).

true would not hesitate to give his life for her."[11] Anything that was extraneous, that threatened to undermine the Roman concept of the past, was dangerous, a basic threat to existence. Women who attempted to challenge the old ways were a threat to Rome, regardless of the fact that the mythological old ways had never really existed. Since the Roman experience has been so influential, it means that whenever women attempt to change their status to work for equality, part of the mythology they have to fight is the burden of the fall of Rome, a story written for the most part by men, and with a male view toward the female sex.

Rome itself was very much a man's world. Its government was run by men, for men, and its history was written by men, for men. Like Greek women, Roman women were to be wives, mothers, and daughters, but they were always to observe decorum and never gain notoriety, except for their virtue. In fact, until fairly late in Roman history women even lacked individual names in the proper sense of the term. Claudia, Julia, Cornelia, and Lucretia were merely family names with a feminine ending, like calling a girl whose family name was Drew, Drusilla. Sisters had the same name and could be distinguished from one another only by the use of such identifying terms as the "elder," or the "younger," or the "first," or the "second." In the not uncommon case of marriage between paternal cousins, mothers and daughters would have the same name. No doubt this led to considerable confusion, but the Romans apparently were unconcerned, since it would not have taken any great genius to think up the idea of giving every girl a personal name, as was done with boys.

In point of fact the whole Roman system was designed to suggest that women were not, or ought not to be, genuine individuals, but only a fraction of a family, specifically anonymous and passive fractions. The virtues stressed were decorum, chastity, gracefulness, an even temper, and the ability to bear children. Inevitably all of this was seen from a male point of view, as even a woman's tombstone testifies. "Friend, I have not much to say; stop and read it. This tomb, which is not fair, is for a fair woman. Her parents gave her the name of Claudia. She loved her husband in her heart. She bore two sons, one of whom she left on earth, the other beneath it. She was pleasant to talk with, and she walked with grace. She kept the house and

11. Cicero, *De Officis*, ed. and trans. by Walter Miller (London: Heinemann, 1951), I, 17 (57).

worked in wool. That is all. You may go."[12] Girl children were not even listed on their mother's tombstone.

Roman tradition emphasized the family, but family did not mean the same to the Romans as it does to us. Originally the term included all persons under the authority of the head of household, all descendants from a common ancestor, all one's property, as well as all of the servants of the household. The emphasis was on a power structure and not on biology or intimacy. The head of the family was the *pater familias*, the father of the family. He had absolute and uncontrolled power over his wife, his sons and daughters, his son's wives and children, his slaves, and property. In effect women in the family relationship were little more than another piece of property.

With such a masculine orientation it is not surprising that the Romans would manage to exclude women from any active role in the legends of their founding. It is true that Aeneas, from whom the Romans claimed descent, was the son of the goddess Venus, but there were no recognizably human female ancestors who were given much formal recognition. It was the descendants of Aeneas, Romulus and Remus, who founded Rome. The only female involved in their lives, however, was a wolf (*lupa*) and it was the she-wolf which gave them their earliest tastes of mother-love. It is worthy of comment that the word *lupa* can mean prostitute as well as wolf, but the Romans chose to extol the animal female over the human. From at least as early as 296 B.C. there has been a monument in Rome of children being suckled by a wolf, and it is this symbol which has continued to be observed by the Romans up to this day. The implications seem clear. Any real change from the unseen and unknown woman to a real live one with ambitions, frustrations, hopes, and desires caused trouble to the Romans.

Women, however, were needed as sexual mates, if only to give birth to children so that Rome could grow. Unfortunately Romulus and Remus who founded the new colony of Rome in 753 B.C. had not brought any women with them. Moreover their new neighbors were reluctant to give their daughters in marriage to the young men who had apparently acquired a reputation as being uncouth barbarians. To solve the problem the founders of Rome decided to hold a feast for all the neighboring peoples. At a signal from Romulus every

12. This is found in R. Lattimore, *Themes in Greek and Latin Epitaphs* (reprinted, Urbana: University of Illinois Press, 1962), p. 271.

Roman seized the most attractive woman he could find and hurried her away while the other guests, unprepared for such an assault, either fled or were killed.

According to tradition, again recorded by males, the Romans treated the young women, mostly Sabines, with great delicacy for the night. The next morning the captives were awakened to hear a lecture by Romulus on the superiority of the marriage institutions which he proposed for his new state. A woman, he explained, was to be under the absolute power of her husband, and if she was unfaithful or took to drinking (an activity which might lead to unfaithfulness), she would be punished. The sole judges of her activities were to be her husband or her male relatives. However, if a wife observed decorum, respected her husband, and bore him children (preferably male), she was to be regarded as mistress of the house during her husband's lifetime and he would keep his interference in the household to the minimum. If he died before she did, she was to share his property with the children or if there were no children and he had made no other disposition of his property, she inherited the whole of his estate. The Romans then took their captives to wife.

The Sabines in the meantime had returned home, armed themselves, and took the offensive. After a series of encounters the Sabine women, now pregnant, intervened to separate the combatants on the grounds that they had lost one set of husbands and did not want to lose another. Peace was made, with the Sabines and Romans joining together to form a single community. In return for the loyalty of their new-found wives, the Romans promised never to make them grind corn or cook for them, a promise which, if ever made, was soon forgotten.[13]

Though the Romans apparently did not see anything wrong with stealing wives from other men who were not Romans, they were extremely upset if anyone dared to touch their own womenfolk. This point is best illustrated by the legendary Rape of Lucretia, again told from the man's point of view. In the Roman tradition it was this incident which led to the overthrow of the last of the kings of Rome, the Etruscan Tarquinus Superbus. As recounted by Livy, the Roman army was in the field some twenty-three miles from Rome when several of the officers became involved in a discussion of the virtue of

13. *Livy*, I, 4, 11–13; Dionysius of Halicarnassus, *Roman Antiquities*, ed. and trans. by Ernest Cary (London: Heinemann, 1950), I, 76–79; II, 25, 30, 38–46.

the women they had left behind. Generally the discussion must have been fairly misogynistic, as such discussions often are, but one of the participants, Collatinus, held that his wife would be hard at work, anxiously awaiting his return. Nobody believed him, and to prove him wrong several men, including Collatinus and the son of the Etruscan king, Sextus Tarquinius, rode back to check on their wives. They first spied on the wife of Tarquinius and found her at a splendid banquet. Then they went to investigate Lucretia, wife of Collatinus. They found her spinning away with her handmaidens, anxiously awaiting her husband's return. Sextus paid off on the wager they had made but now thoroughly enamored of Lucretia, he decided to pay her a visit himself. Lucretia, who knew him as a kinsman of her husband, welcomed him to the house, as was the tradition. In the dead of night he entered her chamber with a drawn sword demanding that she sleep with him. When she refused he threatened not only to kill her but a male slave as well and to leave both bodies naked in her bedroom in order to prove to the world that he had caught her in the act of adultery. Since as a male kinsman he had the right to kill an adulterous female relative, Lucretia yielded to his wishes. When Sextus rode off the next morning Lucretia quickly summoned her husband and father. They found her in the agony of sorrow for having betrayed them, and after telling them what had happened and why she had to submit, she enjoined them to avenge her dishonor and then stabbed herself to death, the only suitable ending for a wife who had disgraced her husband. Her body was carried to the Roman forum where the account of her death so inflamed the Romans that they successfully rebelled against the king.[14]

Most other stories told about women in early Rome emphasize the same kind of concern for their virtue, their self-sacrifices for their menfolk and for the Roman state. Women in 390 B.C. are said to have given their hair for bowstrings when the Gauls besieged the city and this event was commemorated by a statue erected to a bald Venus (Venus Calva).[15] Roman women at a later date are also said to have presented the state with their gold ornaments and other jewels in order to bribe the invading Gauls to quit the siege of their city.[16]

14. Livy, I, 57–60.
15. Balsdon, *Roman Women*, p. 31.
16. *Diodorus Siculus, History*, ed. and trans. by C. H. Oldfather (London: Heinemann, 1933), 14, 116, 9.

The purpose of such stories was quite obviously to impress a later generation with the docile and virtuous women who were their ancestors. Whether they were based upon truth or entirely upon myth is unimportant. It was the ideal that the Romans wanted to inculcate. The unreality of this ideal was exemplified during the second Punic War (218–201 B.C.) when Hannibal invaded Italy. In their determination to defeat Hannibal the Romans turned to consulting oracles, trying to perform any religious or magical ceremony which would lead to a change in their fortunes. One prophecy foretold that Hannibal would be forced to leave Italy if the cult of the Great Mother (*Magna Mater*) was imported from Asia Minor to Rome. The Romans, never ones to be satisfied with half-steps, took action to bring the statue of the goddess to Rome from Asia Minor. The ship carrying the goddess ran aground near the mouth of the Tiber River, and in spite of all their efforts, the Romans were unable to move the boat. At this juncture Claudia Quinta stepped forward and proclaimed that the boat would follow her if her chastity, about which there perhaps had been some speculation, was unsullied. Then calling to the ship to follow her, she marched into Rome. Miraculously the ship followed her, emphasizing again that in Rome, at least as far as females were concerned, chastity was the only power that really counted.[17]

Roman history becomes somewhat more believable at the beginning of the second century B.C., and from this time on it seems that women were less compliant and much more lifelike. It was from this time also that the Roman misogynist attitude began to grow and spread, although it is only by comparison with the earlier mythological period that there can be said to have been any radical change in the relationship between the sexes. There were some minor changes. The so-called "free" marriage had developed, and some have equated this with growing female emancipation. These marriages, however, were not free in the sense that a wife had the free choice of a partner but rather that the marriages were free from some of the ancient rituals and formalities. Moreover the wife retained some kind of control over her property after marriage, but this con-

17. *Suetonius*, "Tiberius," *De Vita Caesarum*, ed. and trans. by John C. Rolfe (London: Heinemann, 1951), 2, 3; Ovid, *Fasti*, ed. and trans. by Sir James Frazer (London: Heinemann, 1929), iii, p. 241.

trol was always under the supervision of a male guardian. Previously the wife had passed out of the authority of her father and owed almost total submission to her husband, but under the new conditions her father, by giving her some property, could give her some independence. Husbands could also give their wives property, a practice which was encouraged by the fact that a wife could not be sued in court since a woman had no standing before the law. Such practices protected many a Roman investment. Marriage was still negotiated by the heads of the families, and girls could be married as soon as they reached the age of twelve. Divorce and remarriage were also possible under free-marriage contracts, although the woman could not take any legal punitive action against an unfaithful husband but a husband could against such a wife.[18]

As the riches of conquest and empire flowed into Rome, many well-to-do Romans began decorating their wives and daughters with visible signs of their wealth. Some wives even became rich in their own right. With their new wealth a few of the previously repressed wives and mothers were less willing to be the docile and meek creatures they had been taught to be. Inevitably some tried to assert an independent personality. Nevertheless there was a growing denunciation of women by those male writers who believed that the only true state of female existence should be a masculine-dominated one. It seems that the more insecure the male feels vis-à-vis the female, the more power he attributes to her, and in the light of historical reality, he has greatly overestimated the real power of women.

The most obvious male reaction to a change in woman's state is seen in a diatribe of Cato the Censor at the beginning of the second century B.C. Cato, to put it charitably, was a Roman reactionary. As a stern upholder of Roman morals he felt that woman's place was in the home, cowering before her husband, and he did not accept any of the new-fangled notions about women's rights for which some men argued. He particularly opposed the repeal of the Oppian law which had passed in 215 B.C. during the stresses of the second Punic War. Among other things the law had forbidden women to use ornaments, wear multicolored dresses, or ride in chariots. When discussion over repeal of the law started in 195 B.C. many women demonstrated in the forum in favor of repeal. Cato, naturally, led the

18. Balsdon, *Roman Women*, pp. 216–221.

unsuccessful fight to have the law retained; the speech which he gave on the occasion was recreated by the historian Livy. It was standard practice for classical writers to use speeches to convey an idea, and while the words might not have been Cato's they undoubtedly represented the thoughts of a great many men of his day:

> If each of us citizens, had determined to assert his rights and dignity as a husband with respect to his own spouse, we should have less trouble with the sex as a whole; as it is, our liberty, destroyed at home by female violence, even here in the Forum is crushed and trodden underfoot, and because we have not kept them individually under control, we dread them collectively. . . . For myself, I could not conceal my blushes a while ago, when I had to make my way to the Forum through a crowd of women. . . . Our ancestors permitted no woman to conduct even personal business without a guardian to intervene in her behalf. . . . Give loose reign to their uncontrollable nature and to this untainted creature and [you cannot] expect that they will themselves set bounds to their license; unless you act, this is the least of things. . . . It is complete liberty or, rather complete license they desire. If they win in this, what will they not attempt? . . . The moment they begin to be your equals, they will be your superiors. . . .[19]

This fear of women, whether real or imagined by Cato, is an important factor in assessing woman's place in Rome, since the so-called "new woman" became the scapegoat for much of Roman criticism and has led many modern writers to overemphasize the independence of woman, and ultimately to equate some lessening of restrictions against women with equality. Roman women never achieved equality, and in fact never approached it. Any slight gain was the subject of such diatribes that careless readers of the classics might think that Roman women had actually gained some power.

In spite of Cato's diatribe, the Oppian laws were repealed, but the criticism of women continued. Sallust (d. 35 B.C.) claimed that "women offered their chastity for sale,"[20] while Horace chimed that marriage became defiled as maidens learned the art of love and

19. *Livy*, XXIV, ii–iii, 3, with some modifications by me. Some scholars dispute whether this is a real speech of Cato's since stylistically it is unlike any of his other extant speeches. It seems, however, that it is a good example of an attitude which was extremely influential in Rome, and Livy had some justification in using Cato to symbolize the attitude.

20. Sallust, *War with Catiline*, ed. and trans. by J. C. Rolfe (London: Heinemann, 1960), 13.

sought out lovers at the expense of their husbands.[21] Part of the difficulty in assessing these writings is that the sources themselves are misleading. No Roman woman ever wrote anything, at least that has survived. Though many Roman women (at least of the upper classes) were literate, nothing they might have written is extant today. For example, Cicero (d. 43 B.C.) wrote to his wife and daughter but no letter that they wrote to him exists today. Some seven women were included among the correspondents of Pliny the Younger (d. c.114 A.D.), but only his letters and not their replies survived.[22] Moreover most extant information is of the upper and not the lower classes. Poorer women may well have had somewhat greater freedom than their upper-class sisters, but this can only be conjectured. By the end of the second century a large proportion of the free population was being drawn from ex-slaves, and if nothing else the experience of the slave women with their male masters would have been enough to give them, as well as their menfolk, a somewhat different attitude toward the accepted, traditional, upper-class values. Add to this such things as economic necessity, slum conditions, the fact that their work was serious, and not a pastime, and it seems reasonable that they might well have different attitudes toward men and men different attitudes toward them.[23]

Since the literature was inevitably written from a male point of view, it would seem natural that women would be blamed for many of the ills of society. Any historian of the last years of the Republic would be forced to note that divorce was quite common, but it does not necessarily follow from this that women were to blame. *Marriages de politique* in fact were almost the norm among the upper-class men ambitious to move ahead. Men chose, or youths had chosen for them, wives who would bring a rich dowry or bring advantageous connections. There is little to indicate that women had much say in the matter. In the first century B.C., for example, the generals Sulla and Pompey each married five times. Sulla, seeking to

21. Horace, *Odes*, ed. and trans. by C. E. Bennett (London: Heinemann, 1960). III 6.

22. Cicero, *Epistulae ad Familiaries*, ed. and trans. by W. Glynn Williams (London: Heinemann, 1958), XIV, and Pliny, *Letters*, ed. and trans. by W. M. L. Hutchinson (London: Heinemann, 1957), I, 4; II, 4; III, 3, 10; IV, 19; VI, 4, 7; VII, 5, 14; VIII, 11.

23. M. I. Finley, *Aspects of Antiquity* (New York: Viking Press, 1968), pp. 136–138.

attach Pompey to his cause, persuaded the young man to put away his first wife and marry Amelia, Sulla's stepdaughter, who was already pregnant by an earlier husband. Caesar later married his daughter, Julia, to Pompey as part of the triumviral alliance which he made with Pompey and Crassus. Augustus, who was greatly concerned with Roman "immorality," used his daughter Julia as a fisherman uses bait, marrying her in turn to each of his chosen heirs. Undoubtedly such practices weakened marriage as an institution, but rather than face the base cause, the Romans complained of female immorality and misogynist historians and poets romanticized a past where female virtue alone had mattered and a woman such as Lucretia would kill herself because she had betrayed her husband.

Once Augustus had consolidated his power at the end of the first century B.C. he took steps to reintroduce the morals of a fabled antiquity. In a series of laws he tried to make certain that all men between twenty-five and sixty and all women between twenty and fifty should be married. Mothers of three or more children were granted greater independence in the administration of their property, while fathers of three or more children were privileged to advance more expeditiously through the necessary stages for a pubic career. Bachelors were penalized, as were childless widows and divorcées.[24] The masculine orientation of the legislation, with the exception of the penalties imposed on bachelors (which were never enforced), is evident from the fact that it apparently never entered Augustus's mind to include the abolition of concubines, mistresses, and brothels, an end to sleeping with one's female slaves, or a redefinition of adultery to extend it to extramarital intercourse by a married man, or even to prohibit politically motivated marriages as necessary to his program of moral regeneration.

Even under Augustus the slave girl who attracted her master had little choice, if he was married, but to become his mistress, or one of his many mistresses. Most slaveholders had slave girls, and some of the girls even earned their freedom by serving their master. Cato, the same guardian of public morals mentioned earlier, was greatly surprised to find that his son and daughter-in-law were irritated by the fact that he had kept a slave girl as a mistress while his wife was still

---

24. For details of Augustan moral legislation see Hugh Last, "The Social Policy of Augustus," *Cambridge Ancient History* (New York: Macmillan, 1934), vol. 10, esp. pp. 441–455.

alive. This, after all, was a matter of custom, not of morals. When Cato's contemporary Scipio Africanus died, his bereaved widow enfranchised his favorite slave girl and even found a freedman to marry her. Since marriage was supposed to be along class lines, and brides were supposed to furnish dowries, there were a great many relationships which were not legally classified as marriage. Concubinage was especially popular with soldiers who were forbidden to marry during their service, and with girls who could not raise the dowry to become wives. Concubines, however, were found at all levels of the social ladder. For example, the Emperors Vespasian, Marcus Aurelius, and Antoninus Pius all took concubines after their wives had died. Marcus Aurelius claimed he did so because he did not wish his children to suffer from a stepmother, although in his *Meditations* he had written that he was most happy he had managed to avoid overlong contact with his grandfather's concubine. Commodus at the end of the second century rid himself of his wife, but rather than marrying again took a concubine. The Emperor Constantine was the son of his father's concubine Helena, and his father, Constantius, probably was the son of the concubine of his father. Noble women, however, were not free to engage in such illicit relationships, since the Romans practiced a double standard. A Roman woman who wanted to free a slave in order to marry him was forbidden to do so unless she herself had recently been freed and her prospective husband had been a slave with her. The Emperor Septimus Severus forbade such alliances altogether.[25] Nevertheless there undoubtedly were a few freewomen who lived in concubinage with slaves, since the Senate in 52 A.D. passed a law reducing a freewoman to slavery if she lived in concubinage with a slave without his master's knowledge; if the master approved she was debased to the rank of freedwoman (that is, exslave). The children of such unions were in either case to rank as slaves.[26]

Some of the moralists who try to equate women of today with those of ancient Rome tend to argue that women in Rome began to assume roles that previously were filled by males. There is, however, no evidence for this. Throughout Roman history it was woman as wife and mother whom the Romans extolled, and it was only through her informal power that a woman gained a place in Roman society.

25. Balsdon, *Roman Women*, pp. 230–234.
26. *Ibid.*

It can be argued, nevertheless, that when woman's formal power is greatly limited, as it was in Rome, then her informal power will grow. Informal power, however, means that a woman has to work through someone else, rather than in a direct way. During the first and second century A.D. there seemed to be many women who did exercise this kind of power, but they were never free to act in their own name and suffered condemnation for their lust for power. This does not mean that women were usurping roles reserved to males but only that they were utilizing their own position to manipulate their husbands and sons. The wife of Augustus, Livia, seemed to have considerable influence over him, and Claudius, one of his successors, seemed to have great difficulty with his wives. One of them, Agrippina, who was also his niece, was so anxious to have her son (by another husband) succeed Claudius that she allegedly had him killed. Though Agrippina did exercise power through her son for a time, as soon as he tired of her he had her executed.

The real place of woman is evident from a discussion carried on in the Senate during this same period. The debate was over allowing wives to accompany their husbands when they left Rome for an administrative post, something which traditionally had not been allowed. Here the role taken by Cato in an earlier period was assumed by Severus Caecina, who argued that there was great wisdom involved in the earlier tradition of leaving the wife behind. He said that if a wife was allowed to accompany her husband she would insist on being entertained in peacetime and if war did break out she could only interfere with its efficient conduct. The trouble with women, he claimed, was not only that they were weak, but if discipline over them was the least bit relaxed they were also inclined to be cruel and to scheme to get power in their own hands. In fact, he added, if women were legally allowed into the provinces there would not be one government but two, the second controlled secretly by the wife. The senators, to their credit, ignored his arguments by pointing out that even though women were naturally weak, this was only added reason why they should not be deserted by their husbands where they could become victims to the temptation of their own flesh and the lusts of other men.[27]

27. Tacitus, *Annals*, ed. and trans. by John Jackson (London: Heinemann, 1956), III, 33f.

If women never competed with men, from where did the myth of the power of women come? The answer to this question seems to be from the literary misogynists, such as Juvenal, who wrote in the second century A.D. Juvenal sincerely believed that all women were lustful and anxious to dominate men. Conjugal love for him was synonymous with submissiveness by the husband, and it inevitably led to henpecking. "If you are honestly uxorious and devoted to one woman, then bow your head and submit your neck ready to bear the yoke. Never will you find a woman who spares the man who loves her; for although she be herself aflame, she delights to torment and plunder him." Women not only browbeat their husbands but if allowed they would display unwomanly tendencies by entering traditional masculine preserves either directly or indirectly. Juvenal alleged that they surreptitiously planned their own legal cases, practiced fencing, attended political meetings, spoke boldly to public officials, and worst of all even affected learning. "I hate a woman who is for ever consulting and pouring over the 'Grammar of Palaemon,' who observes all the rules and laws of language, who like an antiquary quotes verses that I never heard of, and corrects her unlettered female friends for slips of speech that no man need trouble about: let husbands at least be permitted to make slips in grammar." Juvenal simply did not like women, and even the perfect woman who might be beautiful, charming, rich, fertile, of noble descent, a chaste wife, a prodigy as "rare upon the earth as a black swan," he found distasteful simply because who could endure a wife that possessed all perfection. His whole sixth satire was a catalog of female vices.[28]

Because Juvenal justified his own hostility toward women by disparaging them, however, is no reason why moralists of today need to adopt his attitudes as historically accurate descriptions of women. It would seem natural that a society which denied women any role but wife and mother would justify the subjugation of women by insisting that they were weak in mind and character, incapable of directing themselves. On a deeper level, the man who does so has to allay his fear that woman is naturally more powerful than man (perhaps an inheritance from his biological dependency during infanthood) by reassuring himself of her unimportance in the more important affairs

28. Juvenal, *Satires*, ed. and trans. by G. C. Ramsay (London: Heinemann, 1957), sixth satire.

of the world. Juvenal is a good example. There were undoubtedly scheming women in Rome, but it was only through manipulation that a woman could operate on the larger scene at all.

It is not only satirists such as Juvenal who give such a sad picture of women but the lyric poets of the first century who popularized the concept of romantic love. These writers managed to make their love affairs sound full of misery and paint their women in the long run as unworthy of male affection. Though their sentiments were in part directed by convention, their choice of a mistress rather than a wife and mother as the subject of their poems permitted them an overt expression of hostility which would not have been acceptable in marriages. The Clodia of Catullus, the Nemesis of Tibulus, and the Cynthia of Propertius are all berated for their faults, and from these mistresses the authors generalized about women. Their conclusion was that love (and women) inevitably brought misery to man.[29]

A possible explanation for this can be found in the philosophical poet Lucretius, who was writing about the same time as the erotic poets. Lucretius, who agreed that love made one miserable, had a rational solution, namely the eradication of love. The first sign of love had to be lanced with quick incisions; the best way to free a male of the course of the disease was to destroy the romantic overestimation of his beloved. In effect Catullus, Tibulus, and Propertius were all doing just that, attempting to deny that women even in love had any real reason for asserting any control over man. Lucretius went so far as to say that in the rare case that a mistress might be faultless, unlikely but not impossible, a man could still free himself from the pangs of love by reflecting that in her physical nature his love object was not different from all other women. Still he ended with a charitable acceptance of woman, that if the lady was good-hearted and void of malice, it was up to the man to accept her imperfections.[30] He should continually remind himself of these so that she could not get too great a hold on him.

Ovid, another contemporary, built up the charms of love and women in his *Art of Love*, but in his *Remedies of Love* he showed how to counteract the attractions of a mistress, however lovely. Though Ovid claimed to preserve the illusions of a woman's beauty

---

29. See Catullus, Tibulus, and Propertius in the Loeb library.

30. Lucretius, *De Rerum Natura*, ed. and trans. by W. H. D. Rouse (London: Heinemann, 1924), III, 894–899.

to enhance the delights of love, his *Remedies* indicated a real delight in ridiculing and degrading woman. His evaluation of woman was entirely consistent; though women might have been attractive, they were frail, foolish, and greedy, and their lust was uncontrollable. A man always had to be extremely wary of them.[31]

Inevitably Romans came to think that man would be better off if he were free of woman. Soranus of Ephesus, one of the most famous of Roman physicians of the second century A.D., argued that "permanent virginity" could be healthful and that intercourse was harmful in itself.[32] It was this attitude which was picked up by the Christian writers, who were even more misogynistically inclined than the Romans. With such attitudes, it was perhaps inevitable that Roman women were blamed, without much justification, for all of the ills of Rome.

The Romans, however, were much less misogynistic than the Greeks. Compared to women in Greece, women in Rome were emancipated. They did not need to go veiled, they were not entirely isolated from their husband's company, and they could even enjoy the company of the opposite sex. Women could go out of the house to shop, to visit the baths, to pay social calls, to worship at temples, and to attend a public function. During the Republican period men and women were allowed to intermingle at the games in the circus and in the amphitheaters, but later they were forced to sit apart in separate blocks of seats. Some women, probably widows, engaged in business, and there were a few women physicians, probably midwives or with practices limited to treat other women. Their emancipation, however, was only relative. Roman women did not play any particularly important place in the religious life of Rome, nor did they have much of a say about their own home. In today's world the furnishing and decorating of a house is usually regarded either as the wife's responsibility and interest, or a shared responsibility with her husband. In Roman times furniture was a male extravagance, and wives preferred to see the money spent on jewels for themselves. Ordinary housewifely chores were done for most Romans by slaves, and it was necessary to go to a very low level in society

31. Ovid, *Ars Amoris*, ed. and trans. by J. H. Mogley (London: Heinemann, 1962).
32. Soranus, *Gynecology*, ed. and trans. by O. W. Temkin (Baltimore: John Hopkins Press, 1956), I, vii (32).

to find a housewife, as the term is defined today. Before the second century B.C. the wife was said to have baked the bread, but after this time bakeries were started, and in the richer houses chefs became the norm. The mistress of the house undoubtedly supervised the menu and oversaw the household slaves. There was even a sex differentiation in attitudes on drinking, something which women of the better classes were cautioned to avoid. Dislike of an intoxicated woman was almost an obsession with the Romans.

It was as wife and mother that the woman had a place in Roman society, and as the mother of sons that she earned her reputation. The Romans seldom vilified respectable mothers, but they took out their hostility toward the female sex on their mistresses, the objects of their erotic love. Romantic love was considered degrading since it brought men into the irresistible power of women—something to be avoided at all costs. Hence the hostility in the erotic poets. The Romans were much too male-centered to allow themselves to fall under the sway of any woman, at least publicly, and erotic love had to be separated from conjugal love. When a satirist like Juvenal took on women in general, it is easy for modern moralists who are perhaps paternalistically oriented to see all women at fault and to claim there was confusion of sexual roles in ancient Rome. This obviously was not the case, and there is no real evidence for such a statement. Women might have been unhappy in Rome, but they quite clearly knew their place. A few might have rebelled, but even they had to rebel through a male. The most powerful women in Rome, the four women named Julia who were the power behind the throne at the beginning of the third century A.D., all had to depend upon their sons for their influence. Rome was a man's world and women never mounted much of a threat to the citadel of masculine prerogatives. Rome fell, but women had little to do with the fall, or for that matter with its climb to prominence. They gave birth to sons who fought and died, and they shed tears and suffered, perhaps they even attempted to use "feminine wiles" once in a while, probably even successfully. Nonetheless they clearly realized, and their menfolk always emphasized, that Rome was a man's world and women's purpose was to serve men.

chapter five

Christianity, Sex, and Women

Christianity has been one of the dominating forces in shaping Western civilization. It has permeated our institutions, given us the moral basis for our laws, formed our ideals, and until recently the church itself controlled our education. Though Christians have always been split into different groupings, and these have a considerable variation in doctrine, all look with reverence upon the teachings of Jesus and the interpretation of these teachings which appears in the various parts of the New Testament and in the early church fathers. Attitudes expressed in these sources about women were bound to effect Western attitudes, even though the reality of a particular society or culture might have led to variations.

Traditionally Christianity has been regarded as a religion of love and charity, but it is equally a religion of asceticism and renunciation of the things of this world. Asceticism quite early was equated with sexual celibacy, and at times the sexual aspects of holiness have seemed to eclipse all other issues. Morality, in fact, became identified with sexual purity, a definition which has not quite been lost in our day. St. Athanasius went so far as to claim that the appreciation of virginity and of chastity was the supreme revelation and blessing brought into the world by Jesus.[1] Sexual continence became both one of the chief virtues and chief doctrines of the Christian faith, the first and indispensable condition of righteousness.[2] Tertullian argued that

---

1. Athanasius, *In passionem et crucem Domini*, XXXX, in J. P. Migne, *Patrologie cursus completus, Series Graeco Latina*, vol. 28 (Paris, 1887). The attribution of this work to Athanasius is perhaps dubious.

2. Ambrose, *Commentaria in Epistolam S. Pauli and Corinthos Primam*, cap. v, Migne, *Patrologie Latina*, vol. 27 (Paris, 1879).

a stain upon one's chastity was even more dreadful "than any punishment or any death."[3]

Sex in the early Christian church was usually equated with women, and again it was women who were looked upon as the source of all male difficulties. The problem was accentuated because in his Sermon on the Mount Jesus stated that "every one that looketh on a woman to lust after her hath committed adultery with her already in his heart,"[4] which was interpreted to mean that even the stirrings of sexual feeling were sinful. To put it simply, women kept reminding men of sex desires that they tried to forget. As St. John Chrysostom put it: "How often do we, from beholding a woman, suffer a thousand evils: returning home, and entertaining an inordinate desire, and experiencing anguish for many days. . . . The beauty of women is the greatest snare."[5] Sometimes it almost seems as if the church fathers felt that woman's only purpose was to tempt man from following the true path of righteousness. Though the demands of sexuality vary greatly from individual to individual, and some men and women can remain celibate without great emotional costs to their personalities, others have a much more difficult time. Many of the church fathers seemed to find it difficult to follow their ascetic ideals and obviously felt the task would have been somewhat simpler if women did not exist. Though it is possible to sympathize with these ascetic-minded and sexually tormented men who blamed all their difficulties on the female, Christianity would probably have had a somewhat different attitude toward women if women themselves had had a major role in formulating Christian doctrine. It is possible that they would have blamed men for their sexual difficulties, but even if this was not the case, Christianity might have had less of a tradition of misogyny.

Though religion is usually regarded as representing man's striving toward the better life and higher good, man has always had a tendency to identify his own attitudes with those of the gods. The nature of the human hand in the formulation of Christian attitudes

3. Tertullian, *Apology,* L, 12, trans. by Sister Emily Joseph Daly, in vol. 10, *The Fathers of the Church* (New York: Catholic University of America, 1950), p. 125.

4. *Matthew* 5:28. (Quotations unless otherwise stated are from the King James translation.)

5. St. John Chrysostom, *Homilies sur les statues,* in vol. 3, *Oeuvres,* ed. and trans. by M. Jeannin Bar-le-Duc (Nantes: L. Guérin, 1866), homily xv.

toward women is evident when it is emphasized that Jesus, who is regarded by Christians as the messiah, was never reported by any writer of the canonical Gospels as having derogatory attitudes toward women. There is, for example, no warning from him about the wiles of women, no intentional reference to them as inferior creatures. We know that women formed an important part of his following, although in the Gospels most of the women remain anonymous. In his dealings with women Jesus refused to be bound by the shackles of petty convention. For example, he discussed his mission with a Samaritan woman at the well even though it was considered improper for him both as a Jew and a male to converse with her because she was a hated Samaritan and an inferior woman. When his disciples heard of the conversation they marveled that "he talked with the woman: yet no man said, What seekest thou? or Why talkest thou with her."[6] Several women emerge in greater focus including the two sisters, Mary and Martha, and Mary Magdalene, the reformed prostitute.[7]

One critic of the traditional position of women in the Christian church emphasized that though there is no recorded speech of Jesus concerning women, in those "passages describing the relationship of Jesus with various women, one characteristic stands out starkly: they emerge as persons, for they are treated as persons, often in such contrast with prevailing custom as to astonish onlookers."[8] Another writer has gone so far as to claim that Jesus not only gave women an important place in his kingdom, but also recognized that their faith, purity, and tenderness were to be the fountains of spirituality.[9] From a cursory reading of the New Testament it appears that women in fact played an important part in the emerging Christian church. They were among the earliest and most faithful converts,[10] they displayed charismatic gifts,[11] they devoted themselves to charity,[12]

6. *John* 4:27.

7. See William E. Phipps, *Was Jesus Married* (New York: Harper and Row, 1970), pp. 61–67.

8. Mary Daly, *The Church and the Second Sex* (New York: Harper and Row, 1968), p. 37.

9. Sarah Parker White, *A Moral History of Woman* (Garden City, N.Y.: Doubleday, Doran, 1937), p. 143.

10. *Acts* 16:14–15; 17:4, 12, 34.

11. *Acts* 21:9.

12. *Acts* 9:36–42.

dispensed hospitality,[13] labored in the tasks of evangelism,[14] and imparted instruction in the faith.[15] Some of these tasks, such as extending hospitality, were the traditional roles of women, but in other respects women seemed to have assumed new importance.

Biblical specialists usually emphasize that Jesus himself, at least from his extant teachings, did not proclaim a new code of sexual conduct or a new idea of sexual relationships, but was building upon the Jewish code of the time. This is also true of his statements on marriage and divorce,[16] although he attempted to apply the same standards on adultery, divorce, and remarriage to men as traditionally had applied to women. The nature of this departure from the norm is evidenced by the fact that his disciples complained about the severity of this teaching and contended it might be better for men not to marry if it was enforced. Jesus replied in a somewhat ambiguous way. "All men cannot receive this saying, save them to whom it is given. For there are some eunuchs, which were so born from their mother's womb; and there are some eunuchs which were made eunuchs of men: and there be eunuchs, which have made themselves eunuchs for the kingdom of heaven's sake. He that is able to receive it, let him receive it."[17] This statement has been the basis of the Christian doctrine of celibacy and a mandate to observe a self-imposed continence. Occasionally in the early Christian period it was interpreted literally. Origen, for example, castrated himself.[18] There were others who followed a similar practice, but by the fourth century such acts of self-mutilation had been forbidden by the church councils.[19]

In spite of the fact that the teachings of Jesus might have offered a higher conception of woman and given new meaning and potential to the relationship between man and woman,[20] they were soon

13. *Acts* 12:12; 16:15, 40; *Romans* 16:2.

14. *Romans* 16:1, 3–4, 6, 12; *Philippians* 4:2–3.

15. *Acts* 18:26.

16. *Matthew* 5:31–32; 19:3–9; *Mark* 10:11–12.

17. *Matthew* 19:11–12.

18. Eusebius, *Ecclesiastical History*, ed. and trans. by Kirsopp Lake (London: Heinemann, 1926), VI, viii.

19. Derrick Sherwin Bailey, *Sexual Relation in Christian Thought* (New York: Harper, 1959), p. 72, fn. 11.

20. *Ibid.*, p. 17; Roland H. Bainton, *What Christianity Says about Sex, Love and Marriage* (New York: Association Press, 1957); White, *Moral History of Woman*, pp. 171–173.

modified to conform to the traditional views that society had of women. Woman's new assertiveness, or at least her prominence, created tensions between the progressive and reactionary elements in early Christianity, a tension which was only relieved by the reassertion of the traditional masculine view of the position of women. Even taking the most positive view of the statements about women contained in the writings of the various evangelists and church fathers it would seem that they believed woman should be confined to her traditional role in the house, in the family, and in the church, but in no case was she to assert herself as an equal. Though there was a recognition that women were equal in spirit to men, this fact was usually relegated to the background and the emphasis was on keeping them in their place here on earth. Thus while women were recognized as "joint heirs of the grace of life," they were also called the "weaker vessel who were to remain in subjugation to their menfolk."[21] While there was "neither Jew nor Greek," neither "bond nor free," neither "male nor female," in the Kingdom of God,[22] man was the image and glory of God. Women on the other hand were "the glory of man. For the man is not of the woman: but the woman of the man. Neither was the man created for the woman; but woman for the man."[23]

Women were forbidden to teach in the church[24] and were ordered to keep silent. If they had questions or wanted to learn anything, they were to ask their husbands at home.[25] In their homes they were to learn in all quietness and subjection, making sure that they did not usurp authority over the man.[26] There were almost continuous admonitions for women to obey their husbands.

> Wives, submit yourselves unto your husbands, as it is fit in the Lord. Husbands love your wives, and be not bitter again them.[27]

> . . .

> Wives, submit yourselves unto your own husbands, as unto the Lord. For the husband is the head of the wife, even as Christ is the head of the Church: and he is the savior of the body. Therefore as the church

21. *I Peter* 3:1–7.
22. *Galatians* 4:28.
23. *I Corinthians* 11:4–9.
24. *I Timothy* 2:12.
25. *I Corinthians* 14:34–36.
26. *I Timothy* 2:11–12.
27. *Colossians* 3:18–19.

is subject unto Christ, so let the wives be to their own husbands in everything. Husbands, love your wives, even as Christ also loved the church, and himself for it.[28]

. . .

Likewise, ye wives, be in subjection to your own husbands; that, if any obey not the word, they also may without the word be won by the conversation with the wives.[29]

Woman was, after all, the creature who had beguiled Adam into transgression, although it was said that sin would be redeemed in childbearing if all women continued in faith, charity, holiness, and sobriety.[30] It was wicked women who had provoked God to send the flood,[31] and St. Paul felt their seductive powers were so great that they could cause even angels to sin.

Quite clearly men would be better off if they could ignore women altogether. St. Luke said that a man must hate his own wife and children in order to be a disciple of Jesus,[32] although other gospel writers tended to use a term that can be translated as "leave" rather than hate.[33] This might only mean that man must sacrifice everything, even his wife and children if necessary, to achieve salvation, but it also indicates a growing trend toward asceticism and misogyny. Adding further ambiguity was the statement about the second coming, "woe unto them that are with child, and to them that give suck in those days."[34]

St. Paul emphasized the higher good of celibacy:

> Now concerning the things whereof ye wrote unto me: It
> is good for a man not to touch a woman.
> Nevertheless, to avoid fornication, let every man have his
> own wife, and let every woman have her own husband.
> Let the husband render unto the wife due benevolence:
> and likewise also the wife unto the husband. . . .
> For I would that all men were even as I myself. But every
> man hath his proper gift of God, one after this manner,
> and another after that.

28. *Ephesians* 5:22–25.
29. *I Peter* 3:1.
30. *I Timothy* 2:15.
31. *I Corinthians* 11:10.
32. *Luke* 14:26.
33. *Matthew* 10:37, 19:29; *Mark* 10:29.
34. *Mark* 3:17; *Luke* 21:23.

I say therefore to the unmarried and widows, It is good
for them if they abide even as I.
But if they cannot contain, let them marry: for it is better
to marry than to burn."[35]

Some modern commentators, anxious to defend Paul from charges
of misogynism, have gone so far as to claim that he advocated an
ethic of mutual obligation in sexual relations. Instead of regarding
coitus as a detached and peripheral veneral function involving little
more than an exercise of the genital organs, it is said he insisted that
it was an act which, by reason of its nature, engaged and expressed
the whole personality in such a way as to constitute a unique mode of
self-disclosure and self-commitment.[36] While occasionally emphasizing this rather mystical aspect of sexual intercourse, St. Paul quite
clearly regarded celibacy as an ideal and marriage and sexual intercourse as reluctant concessions to human frailty. Though marriage
was not sinful, married people had "trouble in the flesh: and are
overly concerned with worldly things."[37] Nevertheless he held that
forbidding a person to marry constituted heresy,[38] emphasizing that
marriage was in honor among all.[39] The most misogynistic statements
in the scriptures appear not in the epistles of Paul but in the Apocalypse, the author of which saw the procession of the redeemed as a
company of virgins "not defiled with women."[40] St. Paul, however,
gave unprecedented emphasis to the sin of Adam and Eve, although
this might have been due in part to his own belief that without the
fall there would have been no need for redemption by Jesus. Still it
was woman who was at fault, since "Adam was not deceived, but the
woman being deceived was in the transgression."[41]

The hostility with which some of the early Christians looked upon
sex is indicated by the fact that only unmarried Christians could be
baptized into the Syrian church.[42] There were even some bishops

35. *I Corinthians* 7:1–12.
36. Bailey, *Sexual Relations in Christian Thought*, p. 10.
37. *I Corinthians* 7:28, 32–34.
38. *I Timothy* 4:3.
39. *Hebrews* 13:4.
40. *Revelations* 14:4.
41. *I Timothy* 2:14.
42. See the discussion by A. Vööbus, *Celibacy, a Requirement for Admission to
Baptism in the Early Syrian Church* (Stockholm: Estonian Theological Society in
Exile, 1951.)

who advocated compulsory continence,[43] but in general rationality seemed to have prevailed, if only because it was difficult to deny the positive statements about marriage in the Bible. Since marriage had been instituted and blessed by God, as well as sanctified by Jesus, it could not in itself be either impure or evil. In fact in the Epistle to the Ephesians, which probably reflected the thoughts of the misogynistic St. Paul, marriage was regarded as "the great mystery" by which Christ's union with the church was signified.[44] The solution of the dilemma of asceticism vis-à-vis the worldly marriage was to recognize marriage as good but to claim celibacy a higher good. Through this concept of the good versus the better, the church fathers managed to uphold the superiority of the virgin state and the higher merit of continence.

Some have tended to put the blame for misogynistic attitudes which appear in scriptures and in the church fathers upon Paul, but this is much too simple an answer. Paul appears to have been a fairly open-minded man who preferred celibacy for himself, recognized that marriage might be the way of God, and felt that women were essential for propagation of the species, but rather wished that they were not around. In fact the general tenure of early Christian views would probably best be summed up in the words attributed to Methodius, Bishop of Olympus, who felt that while women were the daughters of Satan, it was man's Christian duty to take them out of the clothes of sin and lead them on the right path, preferably that of virginity.[45]

Religious teachings do not usually appear in a vacuum and Christianity was but one of several competing religions in the Roman empire. It survived perhaps because it had greater truth, but also because it had greater insights into human needs and eventually had the strongest political backing. Generally the writers of the Patristic period emphasized asceticism, which included sexual continence. This demand must have struck a responsive chord in Western intellectual thought, or else there would not have been such widespread agreement. The trouble with ascetic life is that man is often reminded of his sexual urges by women, and inevitably Christian

43. Eusebius, *Ecclesiastical History*, IV, 23, 7–8.

44. *Ephesians* 5:22–23.

45. Richard Lewinsohn, *A History of Sexual Customs*, trans. by Alexander Mayce (New York: Harper, 1958), p. 99.

asceticism was associated with misogynism. Perhaps the most remarkable manifestation of sexual asceticism in the early church was the phenomenon known as *syneisaktism* (also *agapetae*), or spiritual marriage. This was the cohabitation of the sexes under conditions of strict continence. A couple often shared the same house, the same room, even the same bed, but yet conducted themselves as if there was no sex difference.[46] In part this was an attempt to show that one could withstand temptation at closest quarters, but while the spirit was strong the flesh was often weak. Inevitably this led to further denunciations of women. Where did these concepts of sex as evil come from and what were their implications for attitudes toward women?

Christian concepts came not only from the teachings of Jesus but also from Jewish, Roman, and Greek beliefs. Much of the New Testament and many of the early church fathers wrote to refute certain pagan ideas, or to explain how Christianity fitted in with pre-Christian concepts. In the process Christianity became much less dependent upon its Jewish background, and adopted more of the ideas and attitudes of Greece and Rome. As far as sex was concerned some scholars have gone so far as to argue that Christianity sexually was orphaned from Judaism prior to its coming of age, and it was this sudden independence that made it so vulnerable to hostile views of the body and misogynistic attitudes toward women.[47]

Emil Brunner, one of the most influential theologians of the twentieth century, held that the conception of sex as something which was low and unworthy of intelligent man penetrated the early Christian church from the Platonic-Hellenistic ideas floating around the Mediterranean world. The concept was in absolute opposition to the biblical idea of creation.[48] Brunner felt that the major task of the modern generation of scholars should be to take up opposition to what he felt was the false non-Christian view of marriage, of sex, and of women, which has dominated and still dominates much of Christian thinking. Morton S. Enslin put it more succinctly: "Chris-

46. Bailey, *Sexual Relations in Christian Thought*, p. 33.

47. See Joseph Ward Swain, *The Hellenic Origins of Christian Asceticism* (New York, 1916, a privately printed Ph.D. thesis from Columbia University), *passim*, and Johannes Leipoldt, *Griechische Philosophie and Frühchristliche Askesse* (Berlin: Akademie Verlag, 1961), pp. 31ff., 60ff.

48. Emil Brunner, *The Divine Imperative*, trans. by Olive Wyon (Philadelphia: Westminster Press, 1947), p. 364.

tianity did not make the world ascetic; rather the world in which Christianity found itself strove to make Christianity ascetic."[49]

Key to these concepts was the dualism which developed in Greece as the old Olympic gods proved unacceptable to enlightened persons. This was further accentuated by the political failure of the Greek world which culminated in the Roman conquest. In their disenchantment with this world and in a search for certainty the Greeks turned to other-worldly asceticism. In their search they tended to ignore man in the flesh and to look upon him as a soul lost and imprisoned in a body. This dichotomy between spirit and flesh became more and more influential in the pagan world, and as this dualism seeped into the emerging Christian religion, it broke down the psychosomatic characteristics of the biblical view of man. One Christian scholar claims that it contaminated Christianity, "sterilized its sense of creation, perverted its confession of evil, and limited its hopes of total reconciliation to the horizons of a narrowed and bloodless spiritualism."[50] Inevitably it also led to somewhat extreme misogynistic views.

Scholars have traced the origin of these concepts to the cult of the god Dionysius and the legendary Orpheus, although today there is still considerable confusion about the relationship of the Orphic cult with Dionysius. The story itself is simple. Orpheus was the famed musician who so charmed Hades, the god of the underworld, that he was allowed to bring back his wife Eurydice from the dead providing he did not look back. The temptation proved too much for him, and when he did look back Eurydice had to return to Hades.[51] This simple myth was grafted on to the cult of Dionysius and resulted in a religion which taught the possibility of attaining immortality. This, however, required purity both in ritual and as a way of life. Within each individual was a divine soul undergoing punishment for sin. Immortality consisted of loosing the soul from its bodily prison. In effect there was a concept of soul and purity on one hand and body (or material) and evil on the other.

The Orphics erected a theology which emphasized this two-fold

49. Morton S. Enslin, *The Ethics of Paul* (New York: Harper, 1930), p. 180.

50. Paul Ricoeur, "Wine, Eroticism, and Enigma," *Cross Currents*, 14 (1964), p. 135.

51. One of the pioneer investigators of this was Jane Harrison, *Prolegomena to the Study of Greek Religion* (reprinted, New York: Meridian Books, 1955), but esp. chaps. 9, 10, and 11.

nature of man, good and evil. To realize eventual divinity man had to cherish and cultivate the divine and purge away the evil. Man's purpose on earth was to suppress the evil and achieve the good by periodic rituals, the nature of which is unknown to us today, but most important, by living an Orphic life.[52] Life on earth was regarded as a conflict between an essentially "higher" and an essentially "lower" nature, a radical departure from traditional Greek religious and moral thought which emphasized that the difference between virtue and vice was not one of kind but of degree and direction.

The Orphic mysteries were never incorporated into the state religions of classical Greece but they exercised considerable influence on those aspects of Greek thought which most influenced Christianity. Though Greek attitudes toward women have already been examined, this other aspect of Greek thinking was important in the context of Christianity because it was here that it had its greatest influence on modern attitudes. The line can be traced from the Orphics, to the Pythagoreans, to some teachings of Plato, to the neo-Pythagoreans and neo-Platonists in Alexandria, and then into Christianity and its rival religions.

Pythagoras taught that the universe was ultimately divisible into two opposing principles, the Limited and the Unlimited, and this was reflected in the opposition of light to darkness, odd to even, one to many, right to left, male to female, good and bad, and so forth. Limited, light, odd, male, good were all in the same category while unlimited, dark, even, female, bad were in another. Women in the dualistic thought had already been identified as evil. Salvation to the Pythagoreans could only be achieved through *catharsis*, which required the observance of rigid taboos. The soul, the higher principle, was imprisoned in a mortal body which was governed by evil passions. Man must not, however, be a slave of his own body but must improve and save his soul by escaping from the domination of flesh. Sexual consummation was considered the prime pandering to the indwelling Furies, and every passion, every symbol, related to it had to be repudiated. Though Pythagoras himself did not advocate total abstinence, one of his fifth-century B.C. disciples, Empedocles, did.[53] This

52. W. K. C. Guthrie, *The Greeks and Their Gods* (Boston: Beacon Press, 1950), p. 311.

53. See Aristotle, *Metaphysics*, ed. and trans. by Hugh Tredennick (London: Heinemann, 1936), I, v, 3–7 (968A).

and similar denunciations have led scholars to conclude that sexual asceticism not only originated in Greece but also was carried by "a Greek mind to its extreme theoretical limit."[54] The implication is also evident that the Greeks not only held that women were inferior from a scientific view but also from a religious view.

Plato, whose attitudes toward women have already been discussed, rejected the cultic aspects of a religion but elevated the dualism inherent in the Orphic cult and Pythagoreanism into philosophical ideals. He postulated two universal principles, Ideas and Matter, which he equated with the intelligible and the sensible worlds. Ideas were eternal and immutable, present always and everywhere, self-identical, self-existent, absolute, separate, simple without beginning or end. They were complete, perfect existence in every respect. Matter or the material world of sensible objects existed only so far as it caught and retained the likeness of the idea, but in any case was almost an imperfect imitation. The soul, an immaterial agent, was superior in nature to the body, and was hindered by the body in its performance of higher psychic functions of human life. Reality for Plato had two components, the changeable world of bodies which man could know through sense perception, and the Ideal, the timeless essence or universal realities, which could be known only through the *nous*, the mind of the soul which perceived it. Though the soul had been born with true knowledge, the encrustation of bodily cares and interests made it difficult to recall the truth which was innately and subconsciously present. Love also was conceived in dualistic terms, the sacred and profane, the one occupied with the mind and character of the beloved, the other with the body. It was only through the higher love, the nonphysical, that true happiness could be found. True love was the mutual attainment of the self-mastery that cured the disease of physical craving. Physical love was inferior to true love, and copulation itself lowered a man to the frenzied passions characteristic of beasts.[55] This is the essence of Platonic love, and the implication is clear that true lovers would be celibate.

The center of Greek philosophical thinking and speculation

54. E. R. Dodds, *The Greeks and the Irrational* (Boston: Beacon Press, 1957), p. 155.

55. See Plato, *Symposium*, ed. and trans. by W. R. M. Lamb (London: Heinemann, 1953), *passim*, but particularly 211B, and the *Phaedrus*, ed. and trans. by Harold North Fowler (London: Heinemann, 1953), 246–247, 250–253.

moved from Athens to Alexandria, and it was in Egypt that the fullest expression was given to growing asceticism and misogynism went from philosophy into the various competing religious creeds. One of the transitional figures was the philosopher Philo, the Alexandrian Jew born in the last quarter of the first century B.C. Philo accepted the Jewish concept of the divine command to procreate and replenish the earth, but he held the only goal of marriage was to procreate legitimate children for the perpetuation of the race. Those who had intercourse for pleasure were compared to pigs and goats.[56]

In spite of his need to justify marriage, Philo thought that the highest nature of man was asexual. It was only the irrational part of the soul which contained the categories of male and female and existed in the realm of the sexual. It was the original sin of Eve and of Adam which had resulted in sexual desires and this marked the "beginnings of wrongs and violations of the law." Philo defined the female as inferior to the male since the female represented sense perception, the created world, while the male on the other hand represented the rational soul. Progress meant giving up the female gender, the material, passive, corporeal, and sense perceptible, for the active, rational, incorporeal, more akin to mind and thought. Woman could become most like the male by remaining a virgin, and the words virgin, virginity, ever virginal occur continually in Philo's references to women.[57]

Philo himself seems to have had no immediate disciples of any note, although he had great effect on Christian thinking. More immediately influential were the neo-Pythagoreans and neo-Platonists who taught that redemption was a flight of the soul from the fetters of the body and the senses. Though they did not necessarily advocate celibacy, they insisted that sexual relations not be motivated by the promptings of nature but only by a regard for propagating the species. A neo-Pythagorean treatise of the first century B.C. stated "we have intercourse not for pleasure but for the purpose of procreation."

56. Philo, *On the Special Laws*, ed. and trans. by F. H. Colson (London: Heinemann, 1958), III, 113.

57. Richard A. Baer, Jr., *Philo's Use of the Categories Male and Female* (Leiden: Brill, 1970), pp. 46, 51, and see also Philo, *On the Creation*, ed. and trans. by F. H. Colson and G. H. Whittaker (London: Heinemann, 1963), pp. 69–70, 151, 162, and *Questions and Answers on Genesis*, ed. and trans. by Ralph Marcus (London: Heinemann, 1961), I, 40.

Sexual organs were given to man only for the "maintenance of the species," and not for sensual pleasures.[58]

Numenius of Apamea, a second century A.D. writer, indicated the ability of the Alexandrian scholars to patch together various philosophic and religious teachings into one system. Numenius taught that Pythagoras and Plato were interpreters of a kind of universal wisdom which could be found in the teachings of the Brahmans, the Magi, the Egyptians, and the Jews. With him dualism was carried to its logical conclusion. God, representing good, the ideal, was so high and so remote that he was out of contact with the world as man knew it and in fact had nothing whatever to do with its creation. Instead the universe was the work of a "second God," derived from an inferior deity, while the universe itself was a third God. Thus there were really three gods, the father, the creative agent generated by him, and the creative world. The second and third gods both had dual natures since they contained matter and spirit. Matter was the evil principle which opposed the divine soul. Salvation represented an escape from the corporeal and sensible existence, a reabsorption of the soul into its divine source. This was accomplished by the means of a series of reincarnations, but in the meantime man was to cultivate his reason in order to commune with God. Individual salvation consisted in the abandonment of sexual activity, which act of renunciation served to liberate the soul from passion and thereby gain mystical ecstasy.[59]

The correlation of religion with philosophic thought becomes even more apparent in the writings of Plotinus, who lived and wrote in the third century A.D. Plotinus taught that the goal of life was to merge with the universal spirit. The path of redemption was long and gradual, but in the end the soul would be united with the divine in an indescribable ecstasy. To prepare for this ultimate union required long and rigorous discipline, both moral and intellectual. The core of human virtue lay in detachment from worldly goods, from evil, which required an indifference to the caresses and stings of material life. Once this "apathy" from the material world was attained the soul was free to turn its attention upon the intelligible world, to

58. The treatise is usually erroneously attributed to Ocellus Lucanus and can be found in Ocellus Lucanus, *De universi natura*, text and commentary by Richard Harder (Berlin: Weidmann, 1926), sec. 44, pp. 121–126.

59. W. K. S. Guthrie, *Numenius of Apamea* (London: George Bell, 1917), p. 133.

identify with the path toward Divine Reason on which truth could be found.[60] Abstinence from sex was one of the requirements, and Porphyry, a disciple of Plotinus, condemned sexual intercourse under any condition.[61]

Christianity and other religions of the time were greatly influenced by such teachings. Since Christianity was competing with various other redemptive cults for supremacy, it was influenced by what its rivals said or taught, either positively or negatively. Within any particular Christian community the attitudes toward sex and women seemed, in fact, to be dependent upon the practices of its leading rivals, and sexual concepts ranged from permitting copulation if motivated by a desire for children to an outright demand for celibacy of all church members. At times it seemed that Christians tried to gain status if not adherents by outdoing the pagan rivals at ascetic practices.

As far as sexual practices and attitudes toward women were concerned, the most influential rival of Christianity was Gnosticism and its offshoots. Like Christianity it represented a syncretism of various religious and philosophical movements and was both pre-Christian and Christian, independent of yet still dependent upon it. Scholars feel that much of the New Testament was written in reaction to the influence of Gnosticism, and the earliest sources of Gnostic teachings are the writings of the early Christians who militantly opposed the rival movement. Central to Gnostic speculation was the conception of the dualistic world so essential to the Alexandrian philosophical and religious teaching. Man had elements of both good and evil, of the spiritual and the material in him, and the key to salvation was the escape of the spirit from its material body. To cscape required a stringent asceticism, in particular an abstinence from sex. This has led some writers to label Gnosticism a special mixture of Christian theology and sexual morality,[62] although there were variations in Gnosticism and some Gnostics went so far as to say that no human action was subject to moral law because it only involved the material body.

60. Plotinus, *The Enneads*, ed. and trans. by Stephen MacKenna, rev. B. S. Page (London: Faber and Faber, 1956), V, 3, par. 1–9; V, 9, par. 1.
61. Porphyry, *Abstinence from Animal Food*, trans. by Thomas Taylor (London: Thomas Rodd, 1823), I, 45; IV, 8, 20; there are other references.
62. John T. Noonan, Jr., *Contraception: A History of Its Treatment by Catholic Theologians and Canonists* (Cambridge: Harvard University Press, 1966), p. 58.

The Gnostics looked to various teachers including Simon, Saturninus, and Marcion. The interrelationships between Christianity
and Gnosticism are evident from the fact that Simon Magus was
preaching in Samaria when St. Peter was there.[63] In the Apocalypse
there is a fierce denunciation of the Nicolaites who were seen by the
second-century Christians as Gnostics.[64] One of the most important
of the Gnostic leaders was Marcion, a church reformer who after
being excommunicated by the Christian church in Rome in 144 A.D.
set up a competing organization and hierarchy. Clement of Alexandria (second century) reported that the Marcionites felt nature
was evil because it had been created out of evil matter and that they
abstained from intercourse and marriage.[65] Sex, evidently, was associated with evil, as was the whole process of reproduction and growth.
Marcion was accused by the Christians of denying the very birth of
Jesus in order that he might not have to admit the flesh of Jesus.[66]
Instead Marcion portrayed Jesus as descending from heaven as a fully
formed adult without undergoing birth, boyhood, or temptation.[67]

Another Gnostic leader, Saturninus, believed that God had fashioned two kinds of people: the wicked and the good, with men
representing the good and women the evil. Satan, the god of evil,
advocated marriage and reproduction as a means of continuing evil,
and through this, women, the evil, were able to dominate men. Jesus
had come to restore the spark of godliness in man, to destroy the
works of the female, to bring marriage and reproduction to an end.[68]
The evilness of women was a consistent theme in ascetic Gnosticism
although Gnosticism had another strain. Some Gnostics felt that
they were not bound by the ordinary law of men but instead were
free to go nude, commit adultery, and engage in other sexual activities with impunity. Still another group believed they had the power
to commit sin because of their perfection.

63. Acts 8:9–24.
64. *Revelations* 2:6, 14–15.
65. Clement, *Stromata*, bk. 3, cap. 3 (12) in vol. 2, *The Ante Nicene Fathers*, ed.
and trans. by Alexander Roberts and James Donaldson, American ed. A. Cleveland
Coxe (reprinted, Grand Rapids: Eerdmans Publishing, 1961). It is worth a comment
that the editors hesitated to translate this section and left it in Latin. There is, however,
an English translation of the third book in John E. L. Oulton and Henry Chadwick,
Alexandrian Christianity (Philadelphia: Westminster Press, 1954).
66. Tertullian, *On the Flesh of Christ*, cap. 1 in vol. 3, *The Ante Nicene Fathers*.
67. Tertullian, *Against Marcion*, bk. 4, cap. 7 in vol. 3, *The Ante Nicene Fathers*.
68. Robert M. Grant, *Augustus to Constantine: The Thrust of the Christian Movement into the Roman World* (New York: Harper and Row, 1970), p. 123.

Christians as a whole rejected this so-called immoralist school of Gnosticism, but they were strongly influenced by the ascetic one. One of the transmitters of this Gnostic concept was Justin Martyr, a convert to Christianity. He described approvingly a Christian youth who asked surgeons to emasculate him as a protection for bodily virtue and pointed with pride to those Christians who renounced marriage in order to live in perfect continence.[69] He associated virtue with sexual abstinence and argued that Mary was undefiled, conceived as a virgin, and was the antitype to Eve, the wicked woman, with whom he associated sexual intercourse.[70] His disciple Tatian, the leader of a group of Christians known as the Encratites (the self-controlled), taught that marriage was corruption, and prohibited sexual intercourse, intoxicants, and meats to his followers.[71] He referred to wedlock as a "polluted and foul way of life" and urged the faithful to replace the tree of carnal appetite with the tree of the cross.[72] Tatian's greatest influence was on the Syrian church, which apparently never considered him a heretic, and it was probably from his teachings that Christians in Syria seemed to believe that Christianity could only be compatible with a life of virginity.[73]

Inevitably with such attitudes toward sex, the Gnostics would have a low opinion of women with whom they associated sex. In the Gnostic Gospel of Thomas, it was held that women could only be saved by becoming men or at least asexual creatures. Women were held not to be worthy of becoming Christians by the Gnostics, unless they became males: "For every woman who makes herself male shall enter the kingdom of heaven."[74] This was usually interpreted to mean that women could only be saved by denying their sex, remaining virgins.

By the end of the second century Gnosticism was generally looked

69. Justin Martyr, *Apology*, bk. 1, cap. 29 in vol. 1, *The Ante Nicene Fathers*.

70. Justin Martyr, *Dialogue with Trypho*, 100 in vol. 1, *The Ante Nicene Fathers*; see also Erwin R. Goodenough, *The Theology of Justin Martyr* (reprinted, Amsterdam: Philo Press, 1923).

71. Eusebius, *Ecclesiastical History*, IV, cap. 29; Irenaeus, *Against Heresies*, bk. 1, cap. 28 in vol. 1, *The Ante Nicene Fathers*.

72. *Acts and Martyrdom of Andrew* in vol. 8 of *The Ante Nicene Fathers*, p. 512, and *Acts of Thomas* in vol. 8, *The Ante Nicene Fathers*, p. 537.

73. Arthur Vööbus, *History of Asceticism in the Syria Orient* (Louvain: Corpus Scriptorum Christianorum Orientalium, 1958), vol. 1, p. 69.

74. The gospel can be found in various editions but the one used here is in an appendix to Jean Doresse, *The Secret Books of the Egyptian Gnostics*, trans. by Philip Mairet (London: Hollis and Carter, 1960), *Gospel of Thomas*, V, 22.

upon as a distorted expression of Christianity. The organizing ability of the more orthodox Christian had begun to win the war between the conflicting groups. By insisting upon the importance of the community as opposed to individuals, by emphasizing the scriptural antecedents of Christianity, yet incorporating pagan philosophy, Christianity eventually succeeded in overcoming Gnosticism and other rivals. In the process, however, the Christian church became thoroughly Hellenized and its attitudes toward sex came to be more like the ascetic Gnostics than the more earthly Jews. Inevitably women were the victims.

Clement of Alexandria, while recognizing that women were endowed with the same human nature as man and capable of attaining the same degree of perfection, taught that men were usually better at everything than women.[75] He also emphasized the importance of continence in marriage, and urged that intercourse be undertaken only for purposes of procreation.[76] This was a somewhat more moderate stand than Tertullian, an avid opponent of the Gnostics, who stopped just short of condemning intercourse and seemed to be uncertain why God had ever permitted it.[77] He undoubtedly felt as did Athenagoras that while Christians might have to have children it was best if they experienced no desire at all.[78]

Tertullian requested all women to remember that each one of them was an Eve, the devil's gateway, the unsealer of the forbidden tree, "the first deserter of the divine law; you are she who persuaded him whom the devil was not valiant enough to attack. You destroyed so easily God's image, man. On account of your desert—that is, death —even the Son of God had to die."[79] Though Tertullian was married, he was deeply sorrowful that this was the case. In attempting to dissuade his wife from remarriage if he should predecease her, he felt her only possible motives for wanting to be married were her natural lust or her desire to rule another man's household and to spend her husband's hard-earned money.[80] He urged women to refrain from

75. Clement of Alexandria, *Paedagogus*, bk. 1, iv in vol. 2, *The Ante Nicene Fathers*.
76. Clement, *Stromata*, bk. 2, cap. 7.
77. *Ibid.*, caps. 8 and 19.
78. At least this seems to be the implication of Athenagoras in *A Plea for Christians*, caps. 32–34 in vol. 2, *The Ante Nicene Fathers*.
79. Tertullian, *On the Apparel of Women*, bk. 1 in vol. 4, *The Ante Nicene Fathers*.
80. Tertullian, *To His Wife*, iv, v, vi in vol. 4, *The Ante Nicene Fathers*.

enhancing their appearance, to conceal and neglect any signs of natural beauty. Physical beauty was not a crime since it came from God, but it was to be feared. Every woman should wear a veil or else all (men) would be put in peril by the sight of her.[81]

A good Christian girl was to be kept in strict seclusion until the time of her marriage,[82] and this meant that women as a whole were denied opportunities for education, excluded from active participation in church affairs. St. John Chrysostom argued that a man was ordained to regulate woman and his duty was to mold and form her while she was young and tame her so that she would later submit and obey.[83] He cautioned fathers to keep their sons away from all women, except possibly some charmless old maidservant, and to take as much care to shield a young man from a young woman as a child from the fire.[84] He felt it was the female sex which had caused David's adultery and Solomon's apostasy. If any man stopped to "consider what is stored up inside those beautiful eyes and that straight nose, and the mouth and the cheeks, you will affirm the well-shaped body to be nothing else than a white sepulchre; the parts within are full of so much uncleanness. Moreover when you see a rag with any of these things on it, such as phlegm, or spittle, you cannot bear to touch it with even the tips of your fingers, nay you cannot even endure looking at it; you are in a flutter of excitement about the storehouses and depositories of these things."[85]

Though marriage had been instituted by God for the generation of children it was a concession to the inordinate desires of fallen humanity and a refuse for those weaker souls who could not bear the discipline of celibacy. The church fathers never hesitated to remind their readers that marriage at best was a painful affair, with the trials of pregnancy, the pains of childbirth, the anxieties of parenthood,

81. Tertullian, *On the Veiling of Virgins*, xvi and *passim* in vol. 4, *The Ante Nicene Fathers*.

82. St. Jerome, *Letters*, in *Select Letters*, ed. and trans. by F. A. Wright (London: Heinemann, 1933), cvii (A Girl's Education), and cxxviii (Feminine Training).

83. St. John Chrysostom, *Commentaire sur l'epitre aux Ephesiens*, in vol. 10, *Oeuvres*, xii, and xiii, homily 10.

84. St. John Chrysostom, *Address on Vainglory and the Right Way for Parents to Bring Up Their Children*, in M. Laistner, *Christianity and Pagan Culture* (Ithaca, N.Y.: Cornell University Press, 1951), chap. 53, pp. 109–110.

85. St. John Chrysostom, *An Exhortation to Theodore after His Fall*, in vol. 9, *Nicene and Post Nicene Fathers*, ed. by Philip Schaff and Henry Wace, ser. 2 (New York: Christian Literature, 1893), p. 346.

and the distractions brought about by wives, children, and family life. Gregory of Nyssa in the fourth century dismissed marriage as a sad tragedy.[86] St. John Chrysostom did much the same thing.[87]

St. Jerome, the one church father who seemed to enjoy the company of women, argued that there could be no cause for shame in associating with the sex from which the Virgin Mary had come. He enjoyed teaching the Gospel to women, had several women as close friends, but his admiration had limits and was restricted to virgins and widows, women who were only spiritual companions. He expressed active distaste for women as sexual objects. His views on marriage appeared in an oft-quoted passage: "I praise marriage and wedlock, but I do so because they produce virgins for me. I gather roses from thorns, gold from the earth, the pearl from the shell."[88] He saw nothing attractive in motherhood and considered pregnant women a revolting sight. He could not imagine why anyone would want children, a brat to crawl upon his breast and soil his neck with nastiness.[89] St. Ambrose called marriage a galling burden, urging all those contemplating matrimony to think about the bondage and servitude into which wedded love degenerated.[90] In sum the fathers argued with monotonous regularity that the wedded state was not as good as the single.

With the Gnostic threat on the wane, Christianity should have been able to reassess its position and tone down some of its more misogynistic and antisexual statements. This did not happen. In the first part of the fifth century Christianity, at least Western Christianity, put renewed emphasis upon ascetic ideas toward sex. This was due mainly to the influence of St. Augustine, who was responding to a new threat to Christianity, Manicheanism, a kind of Gnostic synthesis. Manicheanism was based upon the teachings of the prophet Mani (216–277 A.D.), who lived and was crucified in southern

86. Gregory of Nyssa, *On Virginity*, trans. by Virginia Woods Callahan in vol. 58, *The Fathers of the Church* (Washington, D.C.: Catholic University of America, 1948).

87. St. John Chrysostom, *Commentaires sur l'evangile selon Saint Matthieu*, lii, in vol. 7, *Oeuvres*, and *Commentaire sur l'epitre aux Ephesiens*, in vol. 10, homily 15.

88. Jerome, *Letters*, XXII, 20.

89. *Ibid.*, LIV, and CVII, and *Against Helvidus*, trans. by John N. Hritza, vol. 53, *The Fathers of the Church* (Washington, D.C.: Catholic University of America, 1948), 8aff.

90. St. Ambrose, *De Vidius*, in vol. 7, *Omnia Opera*, ed. by D. A. B. Caillau (Paris: Paul Mellier, 1844), 11, lxix; 13, xxxi; 15, lxxxviii; and *De Virginitate*, 6 in vol. 7.

Babylonia. Mani incorporated the teachings of the Gnostics, the Christians, the Zoroastrians, and the Greeks, and his teachings spread rapidly. Like Gnosticism Manicheanism was a dualistic religion in which there was a struggle between Light and Darkness, between good and evil. Originally, the Manicheans believed, the two realms had existed without intermingling, but history began when the Prince of Darkness, attracted by the splendor of the light, invaded the Kingdom of Light. In this original invasion the forces of light had been vanquished, then eaten by their opponents. In this way light had come to be imprisoned in the material world of darkness. The God of Light had rescued primordial man from this condition but man still retained a mixture of light and darkness. Adam and Eve were the result of a union between a son and daughter of the Prince of Darkness. Adam, however, had more light than Eve. Recognizing the miserable state of man the God of Light had sent Jesus in the form of the Incarnate Word to warn Adam that Eve was the tool of darkness and as a result Adam refused to sleep with her. The powers of darkness countered this refusal by teaching Eve the necessary witchcraft by which she seduced Adam so that he became her mate and together they propagated the world. Jesus had been sent again to accomplish the redemption of the Elect. Procreation was an act of evil since it kept the light imprisoned. The purpose of man was to gain the light, and light could be released by eating bread, vegetables, or fruit containing seeds since the light was in the seed. The seed of man also contained light, but sexual intercourse between male and female chained the soul to Satan, denying it progress into the Kingdom of Light. Marriage was a sin, procreation the defiling birth of the divine substance. Sin consisted both in the overt act of sex and in the impulse to have sex.[91] The true Manichean remained celibate, observed strict vegetarianism, never engaged in trade, never killed anything. Not all adherents of Manicheanism, however, were expected to follow its rigid principle, only the Elect. Below the Elect were the Auditors, who as yet could not contain themselves but in

---

91. See Henri-Charles Puech, *Le Manicheisme* (Paris: Civilisations du Sud, 1949). The best source for the teachings of the Manicheans is in the writings of St. Augustine. The continued existence of these ideas is evident in the *Register of the Sciences* of Muhammad ibn Ishaq ibn al-Nadim written in the tenth century in Arabic. It was edited and translated into English by Bayard Dodge, *The Fihrist of al-Nadim* (2 vols., New York: Columbia University Press, 1970). See also Noonan, *Contraception*, pp. 107–130.

the meantime supported the Elect. There was also a third group, the completely sensual members of society who, totally lost in wickedness, rejected the gospel of Mani.

St. Augustine was an adherent of the Manichean religion for some eleven years but never reached the Elect stage, in part because of his difficulties with sex. He remained an Auditor, living with a mistress, uncomfortable about his inability to control his lustful desires. Though he eventually rejected Manicheanism, his writings still conveyed the idea that sexual intercourse was the greatest threat to spiritual freedom. "I know nothing which brings the manly mind down from the heights more than a woman's caresses and that joining of bodies without which one cannot have a wife." [92] St. Augustine, however, could not quite reject marriage since it clearly had biblical sanction. He solved his dilemma by equating original sin with concupiscence (the unbidden motion of the genitals) and veneral emotion. This allowed him to hold that the act of coitus in theory was good, since it was of God, but also to claim that every concrete act of coitus was intrinsically evil and every child was literally conceived by the sinful actions of their parents. Marriage had only been sanctioned by God to moderate venereal desire, which it did by diverting it to the task of procreation. Intercourse for any other purpose was a sin. [93] Celibacy was the highest good. Intercourse was little more than an animal lust and only justified by procreation, and then only in marriage.

Since the church fathers were male, and many of them became conscious of the physical desires of their bodies when in the presence of women, misogynism became engrained in Christianity. Marriage and motherhood were recognized, but they were not as important as the women who denied their sex. It was woman as virgin, as a sexless creature, who was most admired. The ideal woman is a virgin, detached from the world, preoccupied with spiritual things. She

> fasts, maintains vigils, meditates on the Scripture. Her attire is mean, poverty is the way of her life. She is joyous but has the gift of tears. She is simple but prudent. She is serene and innocent and sweet. From her interior purity, recollection, and devotion emanate the

92. St. Augustine, *Concerning the Nature of Good*, trans. by A. H. Newman in *Basic Writings of St. Augustine*, ed. by Whitney J. Oates (New York: Random House, 1948), cap. xviii, p. 455.

93. St. Augustine *Soliloquies*, trans. by Thomas F. Gilligan in vol. 1, *Fathers of the Church* (New York: Cima Publishing, 1948), p. 10 (17).

sweet odor of prayer and good works. . . . Everything about her exterior manner bespeaks her angelic holiness—her dignified bearing, her modest decorum, the comely pallor of her sober countenance, the pure, virginal blush of her modesty, the chaste restraint of her downcast eyes, and the silence of her closed lips. When obliged to speak, her voice is gentle, her words prudent. If she must walk among men, she walks as through a desert, oblivious to all about her.[94]

Undoubtedly such a life is possible for a few women just as celibacy is desired and accepted by some men. The problem was that this was the standard applied to everyone and quite simply most of us fail to meet these standards, even some who have striven mightily to do so. It is when the male who is striving to be chaste becomes conscious of women's power to arouse his sexual desires that he is most likely to lash out at them, to blame them for his own failings. Inevitably Christian teachings became misogynistic to a degree unequaled in the Western world before or since, although there was always the mitigating factor that Christians had to admit women as spiritually equal to men. The antagonism to the female reached the point that some felt it necessary to explain why Jesus had associated with such a wicked and inferior sex. The acceptable answer to this query was that if Jesus had refused, the sin-laden female could never have hoped for redemption.

Christianity was a male-centered, sex-negative religion with a strong misogynistic tendency. The very fact that it was male-centered and suspicious of sex would lead to a suspicious attitude toward women as any kind of sexual creature. Christianity almost went so far as to adopt the view that sexual life was unclean, but ultimately managed to repress those elements which overstressed this point of view. These ideas of the early Christian fathers about the evilness of sex and the dangers of women were carried over into the mainstream of Western thought. While the ordinary Christian man seldom achieved celibate life, he nevertheless was influenced by this negative attitude toward sex and tended to regard those who could repress their sexuality with awe and wonder, and indirectly to blame his own inability to do so on women.[95] Somewhat hesitatingly Western man

94. Sister M. Rosamond Nugent, *Portrait of the Consecrated Women in Greek Christian Literature of the First Four Centuries* (Washington: Catholic University of America, 1941), p. 107.

95. See the discussion by A. D. Nock, *Conversion* (reprinted, Oxford: Oxford University Press, 1952), pp. 218ff. and *passim*.

endorsed the view of women as temptress. It was not woman as mother who originally achieved the highest respect in Christianity, although there was always the example of Mary, but woman as "man," as an asexual virginal creature. This Christian attitude was added to the attitudes of general inferiority of women present throughout the Mediterranean world. The result was to classify women as inferior to men not only upon scientific and philosophic grounds, but to set them apart legally and socially as inferior, and with Christianity to recognize them as morally inferior. Though Christianity always recognized that the soul of the female had the potential of being equal to the male, on this earth at least they were quite clearly below the level of man.

chapter six

Byzantium: Actuality Versus the Ideal

In spite of the extreme misogynism of the church fathers, the attitudes toward women probably changed for the better in the Christian Roman empire over the pagan Roman empire. This contradiction emphasizes an essential difference between Christianity as an ideal and Christianity as reality. When Christianity became first a legal religion and then the official religion of the Roman state, it had to deal with the problems of power. As part of the establishment it could still work for change but if it was to remain in power it could no longer attempt to deny the right of the establishment to rule.

Early Christians had regarded themselves more or less as sojourners on earth, unconcerned with the problems of power. Some Christians even regarded the imperial Roman government as the work of Satan, although the majority probably accepted it as ordained of God. All, however, viewed it as an external power alien to themselves. When the government became Christian, or at least Christian-oriented, Christians found themselves in a dilemma when they attempted to reconcile the obligations imposed by participation in government with their personal belief. Christians placed in a position of secular authority had to face moral problems which they had not been prepared to face since official obligations required them to act contrary to Christian beliefs. In the fourth century, for example, St. Basil held that Christianity was incompatible with military service and any soldier who killed a man in the course of duty was to be regarded as excommunicated for at least three years.[1]

1. At least he was to be denied the sacrament for three years, and this was equivalent to excommunication. St. Basil, *Letters*, in vol. 28, *The Fathers of the Church*, trans. by Agnes Clare Way (New York: Fathers of the Church, 1955), Letter 188, par. 3.

Rome, however, was faced with powerful military pressures, and no Roman government would countenance the excommunication of its soldiers by officially subsidized clergy. Moreover, the army itself was a potent political force, and included vast numbers of men, many of whom wanted to believe in the Christian god. The result was compromise. By the fifth century, Innocent I, Bishop of Rome, ruled that people who had to execute citizens in their line of duty should not be excommunicated since the powers of the state "had been granted by God and the sword had been permitted for the punishment of the guilty."[2]

As Christianity made its adjustment to the realities of power, it also provided an alternative in the form of monasticism for those who felt any kind of compromise with secular government was dangerous to the soul. Monasticism, which developed in Egypt in the third century A.D., was a logical extension of the emphasis upon asceticism and celibacy so evident in early Christian life. It allowed the institutionalization of the higher ideal of celibacy and at the same time permitted ordinary Christians to have families and deal with the secular world, content in the belief that they were doing their best.

Monasticism also had important implications for women, since originally it started out as a lay movement, open to men and women alike. The acceptance of holy orders, an act which was first restricted to men, was regarded by many if not most of the early ascetics as a hindrance to a monastic career. This meant that within the monastic movement both men and women were equal, and both could inflict upon themselves austerities to rival the sufferings of the martyrs of the past. Some of the early monks and nuns tried to emphasize their ascetic abilities by living together, but as monasticism became more and more organized there was a strict separation of the sexes. Organization also implied that certain social ideals, such as charity, were incumbent upon those who embraced the ascetic ideal. Women in convents were allowed to give free rein to their organizing abilities with comparatively little masculine interference. Thus the convent became the major institution outside of the home in which women could exercise authority, and not surprisingly a number of women managed to leave their imprint upon history from the seclusion of the convent.

2. Innocent, *Epistolae et Decreta* in vol. 20, *Patrologiae Latina*, ed. by J. P. Migne (Paris, 1845), *Epistola*, VI, cap. 111.8.

Equally important in forming attitudes toward women was the fact that when Christianity became part of the Roman state, it found itself conforming to Roman law. Roman law stated that women had the right to own property and her property was not to be confused with that of her husband. She was also qualified to serve as a guardian in her own right. In the Greek East, the adoption of Roman law had made an essential distinction between the women of ancient Athens and the Byzantine women, while the possibilities of economic independence gave them somewhat higher status. This does not mean, however, that women were equal to men; they were still very restricted in their activities. In the Eastern Roman or Byzantine empire, no respectable woman ever appeared unveiled in the streets, and even in her house she never dined with a stranger. Nor did she enter into the presence of a strange man except silently and with downcast eyes. Nonetheless by emphasizing the spiritual equality of women, the Christian church offered a way for Byzantine women to be active in society through ministering to the poor and the unfortunate.

The influence of Roman law was demonstrated most effectively in the matter of divorce and remarriage, a subject on which the Church fathers had strong opinions. In general the Christian church took over the pre-Christian Roman marriage rites with only slight changes. Episcopal approval was not necessary for marriage, nor was there any necessity for any ecclesiastical rites or blessings. Traditional ceremonies remained the same, save for the omission of the auspices of the augurs and similar more obvious aspects of paganism. The church orders contained no Christian marriage rite, nor was there any reference to one in the literature of the period. Even in the Western part of the empire where the church had somewhat greater say over such matters, it was not until the ninth century that there was any detailed account of the rite of Christian matrimony. At that late date it was still identical with the old nuptial ceremony of pagan Rome, except for the substitution of eucharist for pagan sacrifice and divination.[3]

Since marriage was essentially a civil affair, a contractual relationship established by consent, it was voidable like any other contract.[4]

3. See O. D. Watkins, *Holy Matrimony* (London: Rivington, Percival, 1895), *passim*, and Derrick Sherwin Bailey, *Sexual Relation in Christian Thought* (New York: Harper, 1959), pp. 64–80.

4. *Digest*, L, xvii, 30, in *Corpus Juris Civiles* (3 vols., Berlin: Weidmann, 1959).

Divorce was a private act, not particularly juridical, although it did have to take place in the presence of seven adult citizens. Usually divorce was by mutual agreement, but a man could divorce his wife without her consent for quite arbitrary reasons.[5] Though some Christian emperors tried to restrict the wide grounds for divorce both husband and wife still retained considerable freedom to separate themselves from their marriage contracts.[6] Generally the church condemned remarriage during the lifetime of the partner dismissed,[7] but this was not written into law, and if the example of the emperors has any merit, they were unable to enforce any such prohibition. Christianity also quite clearly developed a double standard. Concubinage, for example, was recognized.[8] St. Basil of Caesarea held somewhat reluctantly that greater indulgence ought to be shown toward the husband who strayed from his marriage vows than to the wife.[9] In fact, the husband who failed to divorce an adulterous wife and also neglected to prosecute her paramour could be charged with the crime of pandering. The wife had no such right. Christianity, in effect, institutionalized the double standard.

One other factor, however, seemed to strengthen the position of women, namely, the power of the empress. The Roman empire in the third and fourth century had suffered from a series of military usurpers. Perhaps in an attempt to lessen the possibility of usurpation, the empress in the Byzantine state was given special powers. She had to be specially crowned and acclaimed, and many of the court and imperial ceremonies could not be conducted without her presence. Technically there was no constitutional bar to a woman acting as ruler in her own right, although most women who served as head of the state acted in the name of their sons. The exception was the Empress Irene (797–802), who deposed and blinded her

5. *Digest*, XXIV, i, 60, 61, 62; ii, 4, 9; iii, 22, par. 7.

6. Under the Emperor Justinian, *Novella*, xxii (536), mutual consent still sufficed to effect divorce although *Novella*, cxxiv (556), prohibited divorce by consent and allowed it only on specific grounds. There were considerable other changes as the law changed back and forth over the next few centuries. See Watkins, *Holy Matrimony*, pp. 291–293.

7. Bailey, *Sexual Relations in Christian Thought*, pp. 835–885; Watkins, *Holy Matrimony*, p. 418. A good example of this inability was the case of Leo VI and his wife Theaphano.

8. A. A. Vasiliev, *History of the Byzantine Empire* (Madison: University of Wisconsin Press, 1952), pp. 395–396.

9. St. Basil, *Letters*, clxxxviii, 9; ccxvii, 58, 59, 77.

own son in order to rule. She was called by the masculine term, emperor, in official documents, but there apparently was no constitutional bar to her rule. Her ultimate failure was due more to her ill health than her sex. Later two other empresses, Zoe and Theodora, jointly exercised sovereignty for a brief period in the eleventh century. When Zoe appointed Constantine IX Monomachus as emperor, the two ladies turned over power to him, but after his death and that of Zoe, Theodora herself returned to full power.[10]

One of the most remarkable women was another Theodora, the wife of the Emperor Justinian in the sixth century. Theodora's great reputation is dependent almost entirely upon an account of her by the historian Procopius, who tried to blacken her character in no uncertain terms. His portrait of her has been called the most scandalous record ever left by any notable historian of the past,[11] and apparently there was no love lost between Procopius and the empress. He indicated that she had started out as a prostitute, and though she was not a particularly good flute player, or harpist, or even a trained dancer she proved effective as a burlesque comedienne.[12] After her marriage to Justinian, Theodora settled down into respectability, but Procopius still resented her. Her moment of greatest power came during the Nika riots of January 532 A.D., which almost cost Justinian his throne. In this crisis Theodora addressed the mobs, calming them down. Procopius did not preserve her speech but reported the essence of it, and it was indicative of attitudes toward women in general that Theodora started out by stating that many would feel it was wrong for a woman "to put herself forward among men or show daring where others are faltering." Though conscious of woman's place, Theodora argued that the present crisis made such questions irrelevant, and that during such a period of peril even a lowly woman had to make the best of the immediate situation.[13]

In spite of their comparative emancipation, the empresses lived in separate quarters from their menfolk, and the same pattern of

10. For biographical portraits of thirteen of the empresses see Charles Diehl, *Byzantine Empresses*, trans. by Harold Bell and Theresa de Kerpely (New York: Knopf, 1963).

11. Percy Neville Ure, *Justinian and His Age* (Harmondsworth, Eng.: Penguin, 1951), p. 197.

12. Procopius, *Anecdota*, trans. by H. B. Dewing (London: Heinemann, 1940), IX, 12–13.

13. Procopius, *History of the Wars* (London: Heinemann, 1914–28), I, xxiv, 33–37.

segregated living was true on lesser levels of Greek life. The exception might be the peasant women whose houses were not large enough to permit rigid segregation. The empresses were kept cloistered in the *Gynaeceum*, guarded by armed eunuchs, and other than their immediate family only women, eunuchs, and priests were permitted to visit them. When they appeared in public they were veiled to keep them from being seen. Within the *Gynaeceum* women were free to act as they chose, and the sanctity of their quarters from male invaders, even the emperor, is illustrated by the case of Anthemius and Theodora. Theodora's greatest disagreement with Justinian was over the question of whether or not the Monophysites should be treated as heretics. Justinian, who considered himself a theologian, regarded the Monophysites, the forerunners of the modern Copts, as heretical and had deposed one of their powerful sponsors, Anthemius, the patriarch of Constantinople. After his deposition Anthemius disappeared, his whereabouts unknown, until twelve years later when Theodora died Anthemius emerged from the empress's quarters where Theodora had kept him hidden among her women.

Unmarried girls, at least from the more well-to-do families, were kept in strict seclusion and most never saw their husbands until their marriage. Mothers of sons inevitably had considerable say in choosing a wife for their offspring. It was not uncommon for the empress to choose a wife by holding a bride show. When the Empress Irene, for example, decided to find a wife for her son, Constantine, she sent messengers up and down the empire seeking out desirable girls of a specific age, height, and size in shoes. Why the shoe size was so crucial is unknown, but this particular episode might have served as a basis for an early version of the Cinderella story. Whether the power of the empress vis-à-vis the emperor was matched by the power of ordinary women and their husbands is perhaps debatable, but in all cases it was woman as mother who was highly respected.

One of the most celebrated encomiums to motherhood in all literature is that by Michael Psellus, a eleventh-century Byzantine historian. He gives us a unique and charming picture of family life. His mother is pictured as a high-minded, hard-working woman of strong principle who governed her house, her parents, her children, and her husband with relentless but kindly exactitude. She lulled her children to sleep with biblical tales and refused to allow them to be terrified by stories of demons and hobgoblins with which the servants attempted to frighten them. Though averse to displays of affection, she would kiss them tenderly when she thought they were asleep. Her dominating energy marked her son throughout his life.[14] Psellus's mother was unique in the existing portrait of her, but probably a great many other Byzantine women had similar influence on their children. It was perhaps because of his admiration for his mother that Psellus emphasized the importance the empresses had in molding character.[15]

Intellectually also the Byzantine women seemed to be somewhat more important than women of earlier times, both because of their position in the convent and in the imperial court. One of the first women intellectuals was Eudocia, wife of an Athenian teacher, who had studied rhetoric, literature, philosophy, astronomy, and geometry. She wrote poetry, and even made a public speech to the Senate. Her sister, Pulcheria, also had a reputation as a learned woman. Damascius, a Syrian who lived in the sixth century, dedicated one of his books to his pupil, Theodora, whom he called learned in philosophy, poetry, and letters. In the ninth century there was the learned nun Cassia (also called Cassiana or Kasia) to whom verbal tradition ascribed several poems. The Empress Eudocia Macrembolitissa, wife of the eleventh-century Emperor Constantine X, was also credited with several poems and learned treatises. There were others, but all of them were apparently privately tutored since there is no mention of girl pupils in any of the schools.

A most remarkable woman intellectual was Anna Comnena, the daughter of Alexius I, the emperor who ruled in Constantinople during the time of the first crusade. It is in the writings of Anna, called by some the greatest woman historian, that we find how much women themselves had adopted the idea they were inferior. Though by denigrating other women Anna might have an unconscious desire to exalt herself by contrast, it seems more likely she was merely reflecting the prevailing masculine opinion of women. Anna believed that women were best at serving as mourners, where their liability to tears and other emotions served as an attribute. Women were also good as penitents, but on most other matters the woman most likely

14. Michael Psellus, *Encomium*, ed. by K. N. Sathas in *Bibliotheca Graeca Medii Aevi* (7 vols., Venice and Paris, 1872–94), vol. 5.

15. Michael Psellus, *The Chronographia*, trans. by E. R. A. Sewter (New Haven, Conn.: Yale University Press, 1953).

to succeed was the woman who best acted and thought as a man. In speaking of the Empress Irene's fears, for example, Anna said that even though the empress was terrified, she "kept her fear in the recesses of her heart, and showed it neither in words nor in gestures. For she was *manly* and staunch in mind, like that woman sung of by Solomon in Proverbs, and showed no *womanly* and cowardly feelings, such as we mostly see *woman* experience when they fear something alarming."[16] Most women, according to Anna, were leaky vessels who could not be trusted to keep the secrets confided in them by their husbands. Her ideal woman was someone like her mother who preferred not to appear in public, but rather to stay at home, read the books of the saints, do good deeds, and perform acts of charity.

> And when she had to make herself public for some urgent need as Empress, she was filled with modesty and straightway blossomed out in a blush on her cheeks. The wise Theano (pupil of Pythagoras) on one occasion, when her forearm had been bared and some said to her justingly, "Beautiful in the forearm," replied, "But not public." So the Empress my mother, image of dignity, resting place of holiness, not only did not love to make her forearm and glance public but did not even wish that her voice should be sent forth into unfamiliar ears. Such a great and wonderful portent of modesty was she. But since, as they say, "not even the gods fight against Necessity," she was compelled on the Emperor's frequent campaigns to go with him. For on the one hand her innate modesty tended to keep her inside the Palace, and on the other hand her devotion to the Emperor and burning love to him drove her all reluctant out of Palace for various reasons, and first because the disease of the feet [gout] which had attacked him required the greatest care.[17]

When her mother was serving her last hours as empress, Anna was particularly proud of the way she acted in keeping her feminine weakness in bounds.

> Always in former perils also the Empress had a manly mind, but especially on this occasion did she play the man. Though deeply moved by the feeling of grief, she stood like an Olympic victor wrestling against those keenest pains. For she was pierced in soul and troubled in heart by the sight of the Emperor's state, yet she braced

16. Anna Comnena, *Alexiad*, trans. by Elizabeth A. S. Dawes (London: Kegan Paul, Trench, Trubner, 1928), XV, 2 (italics mine).
17. *Ibid.*, XII, 3.

herself and stood firm against trials. And though she received mortal wounds and the pain of them entered into her marrow, yet she resisted.[18]

The ideal wife was one with feminine soft-heartedness combined with the manly qualities of watchfulness, sharpness, activity, and who remained steadfast in faith willing to offer good counsel. It was the woman with the manly mind Anna admired, but she believed that even the best of women could only be a lesser man. Still, she felt there were compensations for this biological inferiority in woman's position as mother, and her account is full of the influence of mothers and the devotions of their sons, even those sons who became rulers.[19]

Anna Comnena is important because she wrote down her attitudes toward women in such detail. During most of the earlier eras covered in this study there are ideas about what men felt about women, and sometimes what men thought women felt about themselves, but women writers who left extant works about their feelings were almost nonexistent. It becomes significant, if also somewhat disappointing, to note that Anna's attitudes toward women seem not to differ from the attitudes of the men around her. She seems to have accepted all of the stereotypes of her culture in regards to women. When she wanted to bestow the highest praise on a woman she called her manly—not womanly. All of the bad qualities seem to have been the feminine ones, while the good qualities were masculine. Moreover, she seems to have accepted without question the helpmate role of the ideal woman.

Anna's attitude was not an isolated one, and numerous later women held similar attitudes. This is an indication that women themselves were an important force in their own repression. Women have been convinced of their own inferiority and in the inferiority of others of their sex. Recent experimental research tends to suggest that these prejudices remain deeply ingrained. Even when the work of men and of women is of identical quality, women tend to value the work of men more highly. In a study conducted by a group of psychologists, college girls were given a set of six short scholarly articles to rate. The names of the supposed authors of the articles

18. *Ibid.*, XV, ii.
19. Georgina G. Buckler, *Anna Comnena: A Study* (London: Oxford University Press, 1929), pp. 121–123.

were so manipulated that for each article half of the subjects thought the author was a man and the other believed it had been written by a woman. For example, half saw the name of John T. McKay on the first article while the other half saw Joan T. McKay. The subjects were asked to rate the authors for writing style, professional competence, professional status, and ability to sway the reader. Invariably articles which carried the names of male authors were rated significantly higher. The researchers compared the ratings to see if the subject matter of the article might make a difference, since it was hypothesized that in those fields which are traditionally regarded as female, women authors might be more readily accepted. Only in one of the fields, art history, did the articles supposedly written by female authors rate slightly higher than the ones labeled with male names. In dietetics, education, city planning, linguistics, and law, male authors received significantly higher ratings.[20] The women evaluators were unwilling to accept other women as equal to men, even in those fields where women outnumber men, such as dietetics and education.

In a similar study another group of female college students were shown a series of modern paintings for evaluation. Again half of the group saw a brief biographical sketch listed under a male name while the other half saw a similar sketch under a female name. Those pictures with a man's name attached were judged better than the others unless the painter in the biographical sketch was presented as a top winner of an art contest; only in this proven situation were the "women's" paintings judged equal to the "men's."[21] Most other studies show similar results.

Why do women so consistently devalue their own performance and believe the cultural stereotypes about their inferiority to men? This is not an easy question to answer, but the question itself has important implications for this book. It seems likely that some of the same dynamics are involved in this type of prejudice as are demonstrated in other kinds of prejudice. Other minority group members, for example, also tend to adopt the attitudes of the dominant group toward themselves. Gordon W. Allport in his study of prejudice

20. Philip Goldberg, "Are Women Prejudiced against Women?," *Transaction* (April, 1968), pp. 28–30.

21. Gail I. Peterson, Sara B. Kiesler, and Philip A. Goldberg, "Evaluation of the Performance of Women as a Function of Their Sex, Achievement and Personal History," *Journal of Personality and Social Psychology*, 19, 1 (July, 1971), 114–118.

called this phenomenon "identification with the aggressor."[22] In a study of similar attitudes among Jews the phenomenon was labeled by Kurt Lewin as "self-hatred."[23] This apparently deep tendency for minority group members to endorse negative stereotypes about themselves is the mechanism which supports the power of any dominant group in a society, in this case, males, and prevents rebellion of the inferior minority (majority?), women. To be effective in preserving the status quo, the stereotype must include a belief that the minority group is incapable of rebellion or other independent action. This is obviously what has happened to women in the past, and Anna is one of the first witnesses we have to this phenomenon.

A historian cannot easily answer how the stereotype of female inferiority was established in the first place. Once instituted, the stereotype continued to be accepted by women because of the rewards society gave to those women who did not quarrel with it. Women, for example, have been protected and do not need to take part in major decisionmaking activities. This avoids conflict, and it is much easier for a woman to live with a man who feels that she is inferior if they both agree on that point. When the minority group member disagrees about his own inferiority, conflict is likely to follow, and the laws and institutions were designed to punish the women who did not go along. Identification with the aggressor at least helped to create stability in a household or society. It might well be that this was the only way women could keep their sanity in a society which treated them as second-class citizens.

Ordinary people do not think through their reasons for adopting an attitude or even critically survey the attitudes they hold. They acquire their attitudes in the socialization process, most of which occurs in childhood years. This means that those who rear the young hold great power over attitudes, and since women have always had some hand in this activity they turn out to have been an effective force in creating negative stereotypes about themselves. Children acquire an image of themselves in their early years and usually well before the age of five they have a clear idea of their sexual identity, as well as some idea about their social status in the society. This self-

22. Gordon W. Allport, *The Nature of Prejudice* (Cambridge: Addison-Wesley, 1958).

23. Kurt Lewin, "Self-Hatred among Jews," *Resolving Social Conflicts* (New York: Harper, 1948), pp. 186–200.

image includes not only the facts about who they are, but the evaluative overtones of that identity. Giving strength to such a hypothesis is a significant body of research about the racial attitudes of young American children. Both white and Negro children, for example, tend to consider Negro children inferior, just as men and women consider women inferior. When Negro children were presented with dolls of different colors or crayons to fill in a picture, they tended to choose the light-skin colors as prettier, nicer, and more desirable. Their comments indicated that they had not only learned that they were dark-skinned, but they also accepted the negative stereotypes that accompanied such an identity. Other research demonstrated the same findings. In sociometric tests children were asked to select the child they would most like to sit next to or play with, and inevitably they tended to select the white or light children.[24] Hopefully this research was done before the current "black is beautiful" movement had a chance to be felt, but such deeply felt prejudices are difficult to change and will probably to some extent hold for some time in the future. Put in their context the findings are still significant because they show the mechanism by which the negative self-image of the minority group is arrived at through the socialization process.

Byzantium, in effect, did not have a much different attitude toward women than did the Romans, and in many ways was as restrictive on the activities of women as were the Greeks. The misogynism so inherent in the church fathers had been toned down, although occasionally it broke through, as in Procopius's denunciations of the Empress Theodora. Women, however, had adopted the idea they were inferior, and if women themselves believed it, the task of emancipation would seem to be formidable. Anna was one of the first women witnesses to woman's belief in her own inferiority, and while Anna believed that women had special compensations, her emphasis on manly women and manly qualities made it clear that at best she still felt women were inferior. Before examining Western

24. Bruno Lasker, *Race Attitudes in Children* (New York: Holt, 1935); Mary Ellen Goodman, *Race Awareness in Young Children* (Cambridge: Addison-Wesley, 1952); Kenneth B. and Mamie K. Clark, "The Development of Consciousness of Self and the Emergence of Racial Identification in Negro Preschool Children," *Journal of Social Psychology,* 10 (1939), 591–599; Kenneth B. Clark, *Prejudice and Your Child* (Boston: Beacon Press, 1955); Harold Proshansky and Peggy Newton, "The Nature and Meaning of Negro Self-Identity," in *Social Class, Race and Psychological Development,* ed. by Martin Deutsch, Irwin Katz, and Arthur Jensen (New York: Holt, Rinehart, and Winston, 1968), pp. 178–218.

Christian attitudes toward women, it is necessary to look at another segment of the Roman empire which by the end of the seventh century had fallen sway to a new emerging religious identity, that of Islam.

chapter seven

Sex Is Not Enough: Women in Islam

If Christianity is classified as a sex-negative religion then Islam must be regarded as a sex-positive one, but with strong misogynistic tendencies. In fact, the change in attitudes toward sex changed neither the attitudes toward women nor their status. In comparing Christianity with Islam it becomes evident that regardless of what a religion teaches about the status of women, or what its attitudes toward sex might be, if women are excluded from the institutions and positions which influence society, a general misogynism seems to result. In spite of some generalized statements in the Koran about sexual equality, women in Islam were subjugated and regarded as inferior beings.

Before the appearance of Muhammad and the rise of Islam in the seventh century A.D., the Arabs were a male-centered tribal people who practiced polygamy and held women to be inferior. In spite of the reform of Muhammad, this attitude remained. Islam had no organized priesthood and the lack of an all-male priestly caste in theory should have permitted greater influence for women. It did not. This is because the legal interpreters of Islam were primarily men, while prophecy, leadership in public prayer, and saintship were in general reserved for men. Though in early Islam it was regarded as incumbent upon every Muslim man and woman to seek learning, any woman who tried to do so soon attracted the hostility of learned men who looked upon scholarship as their own prerogative. Some later Muslim commentators even went so far as to argue that most of the inhabitants of Hell were women because of their unbelief, in spite of the fact that such teachings were contrary to the Koran.[1] In many

---

1. Reuben Levy, *The Social Structure of Islam* (Cambridge: Cambridge University Press, 1965), p. 130.

areas of the Islamic world women were even prevented from attending the mosque, or could attend only under conditions where men could not see them.

Richard Burton, the nineteenth-century explorer and linguist, who translated the *Thousand and One Nights* into English, argued that women in Arab countries had legal rights in inheritance and in law which were not given to English women until 1882.[2] From this he argued that women in Islam had a higher status than in the West, but this does not follow. Protection of rights by law does not necessarily mean equality, nor does it mean a high status. It simply means that women have certain rights which men cannot take away from them. Burton claimed that "women all over the world are what men make them," but no feminist could accept such a definition of women's place. Nevertheless, until women become not just what men make them but what they make themselves there can be no semblance to equality. To exercise this influence women have to have access to the decisionmaking influence-generating institutions in society. In Islam they never had such influence, and they lacked even the convent which gave women some independence in the West. The masculine bias inherent in Islam was evidenced by the fact that even sex was defined primarily from a male point of view. Woman was a sexual object of the man as well as a somewhat helpless pawn to her own passions. The prophet Muhammad himself emphasized this in his supposed advice to his male followers: "Coition is one of the causes of the preservation of health. Let him among you who is in a condition for having sufficient copulation marry; marriage gives moderation of the gaze and more obligatorily turns one away from incest and adultery."[3]

Almost up to the birth of the Prophet (c. 570 A.D.), the Arabs were classed as a preliterate people, though there had been a great outpouring of poetry in the sixth century. This first great age of Arabic literature seemed to spring into existence almost overnight

2. Richard Burton, "Terminal Essay," sec. 4, "Social Conditions," in *The Book of the Thousand Nights and a Night*, trans. and annotated by Richard Burton (6 vols. in 3, reprinted, New York: Heritage Press, 1934), pp. 3739–46.

3. Omer Haleby, *El Ktab or the Sex Laws of Mohammad*, trans. by A. F. Niemoeller (Girard, Kansas: Haldeman-Julius, 1949), p. 10. Niemoeller's translation, unfortunately, was not from the Arabic but from a French version made by Paul de Regia which was not available to me. Haleby himself, however, only wrote in the nineteenth century. There were various similar books of earlier date. See Burton, *The Thousand Nights*, pp. 3745–46.

without any precursors and involved complex and elaborate meters. Later the extant poems were committed to memory, transmitted by oral tradition, and ultimately written down in the Muslim era. Though modern critical research makes it evident that numerous modifications were made to bring this poetry into accord with the spirit of Islam, it is perhaps significant that women in them remained very much erotic creatures.

According to tradition many of the early poems were hung up in the *Ka'ba*, the holy of Arabic holies from whence they were called *Mu-allaqat*, literally the "hung up" or "suspended" poems. The oldest and most famous of the poets in the *Mu-allaqat* group was Imra'al-Quais, whose description of the erotic female creature seemed particularly attractive to the men of his time.

> I twisted her side-tresses to me, and she leaned over me; slender-waisted she was, and tenderly plump her ankles, shapely and taut her belly, white-fleshed, not the least flabby, polished the lie of her breastbones, smooth as a burnished mirror. She turns away, to show a soft cheek, and wards me off with the glance of a wild deer of Wajr, a shy gazelle with its fawn; she shows me a throat like the throat of an antelope, not ungainly when she lifts it upward, neither naked of ornament; she shows me her thick black tresses, a dark embellishment clustering down her back like bunches of a laden date-tree—twisted upwards meanwhile are the locks that ring her brow, the knots cunningly lost in the plaited and loosened strands; she shows me a waist slender and slight as a camel's nose rein, and a smooth shank like the reed of a watered bent papyrus. . . .[4]

This erotic portraiture of women was carried over into Islam, but it was at the same time a very limited concept. For example, the interest of the poets was on the object of woman rather than on the emotional experience with her. Moreover, the amatory prelude so touching and colorful at first sight was actually limited to less than half-a-dozen motive sequences, each with its own phraseology and imagery.

The "woman" was always of high social status in tribal society and by and large conformed more to the fleshy females of the age of Rubens than to modern American concepts. When the poet spoke of love inevitably it was always of bygone days and lost hopes. Later

4. Translated by A. J. Arberry in *Arabic Poetry* (Cambridge: Cambridge University Press, 1965), pp. 13–14.

Islamic social custom supported this same kind of female imperson-
ality, since a family would feel disgraced if one of their womenfolk
was mentioned by a poet as the object of his affections. It was bad
manners to use other than fictitious names in erotic verse, however
modest. Slave girls might be named but ladies never. The rigor of
convention was occasionally relaxed, but just when a victory for
genuineness in the portrayal of passion and affection seemed near, a
fatal tendency toward rhetorization always set in which stifled the
warmth of personal feelings.[5] In essence then it was the female as an
erotic creature, with sex-positive tones, which captured the Arabic
and later Islamic imagination, but woman as an individual remained
unimportant.

Islamic literature represents an amalgam of Arabic, Jewish, Greek,
Roman, Persian, Babylonian, and Indian source materials, but a
unique Arabic literature resulted which was united by the spirit of
Islam as a whole. The key to any understanding of attitudes toward
women were the revelations of God (Allah) to the prophet Muhammad which compose the *Koran*. Like Judaism and Christianity,
Islam emphasized that men were in charge of women because God
"made the one of them to excel the other, and because they spend
of their property [for the support of women]. So good women are the
obedient, guarding in secret that which Allah hath guarded. As for
those from whom ye fear rebellion, admonish them and banish
them to beds apart, and scourge them. Then if they obey you, seek
not a way against them."[6] Nevertheless, women were erotic creatures, continually giving trouble to man. To avoid this Muhammad
advised them to lower "their gaze and be modest, and to display of
their adornment only that which is apparent, and to draw their veils
over their bosoms, and not to reveal their adornments save to their
own husbands or fathers or husband's fathers, or their sons or their
husband's sons, or their brothers or their brothers' sons or sisters'
sons, or their women, or their slaves, or male attendants who lack

5. Gustave E. von Grunebaum, *Medieval Islam* (Chicago: University of Chicago
Press, 1946), pp. 262–263.
6. *Koran*, IV (Women), 34. There are various translations of the *Koran* into
English, none of them official since it is forbidden to translate it. In this section most
of the translations have been taken from "exploratory" translations of Mohammad
Marmaduke Pickthall because of its wide distribution in the English-speaking world
(New York: New American Library, 1953). In some cases other versions are used
because they seem to better express the meaning of the original Arabic.

vigour, or children who know naught of women's nakedness. And let them not stamp their feet so as to reveal what they hide of their adornment."[7] When male visitors came into their homes, women were advised to stay behind a curtain, both in order that their guests could remain purer in heart and so the woman herself could remain pure.[8] Women were only allowed to speak freely with their male kinsmen, other women, or slaves; when they went out of their homes they were to draw their cloaks close around them in order that they neither be recognized nor annoyed.[9] Traditionally this provision has been interpreted to justify the veiling of women, although some dispute this. The whole body of a free woman was regarded as pudendal; no part of her was to be seen by anyone except her husband or close kin.[10] Men were advised never to look at the body of a strange woman but only her face, hands, or feet.[11]

Where early Christianity considered marriage good but celibacy better, Islam accepted marriage as the highest good, ordained by God: "He created for you helpmeets from yourselves that ye might find rest in them, and He ordained between you love and mercy. Lo, herein indeed are portents for folk who reflect."[12] Or again: "He hath made for you pairs of yourselves, and of the cattle also pairs, whereby he multiplieth you. Naught is his likeness; and He is the Hearer, the Seer."[13] Muhammad went so far as to state that marriage was incumbent upon all who possessed the ability,[14] and many should "marry of the women, who seem good to you, two or three or four; and if ye fear that ye cannot do justice [to so many] then one [only] or [the captives] that your right hand possess. Thus it is more likely that ye will not do injustice."[15] Women, like other property, were to

7. *Koran*, XXIV (Light), 30.

8. *Koran*, XXXIII (The Clans), 53.

9. *Ibid.*, p. 59.

10. Reuben Levy, *Social Structure of Islam*, p. 126.

11. Alī ibn Abī Bakr, Burhan al-Din, al-Marghīnānī, *The Hedaya or Guide: A Commentary on the Mussulman Laws*, trans. by Charles Hamilton and ed., with a preface and index, by Standish Grove Grady (4 vols. in 1, reprinted, Lahore: Premier Book House, 1957), IV, 598–599, or bk. xliv, sec. 4.

12. *Koran*, XXX (The Romans), 21.

13. *Koran*, XLII (Counsel), 11.

14. *The Sayings of Muhammad*, collected and trans. by Allama Sir Abdullah al-Mamun al-Suhrawardy (London: John Murray, 1941), no. 297, p. 95.

15. *Koran*, IV (Women), 4.

be treated with care and kindness, and Muhammad regarded a virtuous wife as a man's best treasure.[16]

Obviously these verses reflect a male point of view. Women were recognized as sexual companions for the male, and it was quite permissible for pious Muslims to praise God for having created women in all their beauty. It was God who formed the female body with all the charms that awakened desire, who made woman's hair so silky, who made the precious curves of her breast. Though Muhammad emphasized that both men and women could achieve paradise, even the portrait of paradise seemed to reflect masculine wish fulfillment rather than any sign of equality for the female. The good Muslim in paradise would enjoy the society of ever virgin houris, dark-eyed damsels with swelling breasts and shy, retiring glances. Paradise was also material. Its inhabitants reposed on luxurious couches, were clad in the richest raiment, enjoying exquisite food, drinking from gold and silver vessels, smelling heavenly scents, and quaffing celestial wine.[17] According to Islamic tradition it was believed that many men had reached perfection, but only four women had,[18] although Muhammad himself stated that there were several women who were outstanding.[19]

On earth, where God had made man superior to woman, women were to be subject to their nearest male relative whose right over them was similar to his right over any of his other property. In Islamic tradition the wife's honor was in the hands of her husband, and it was his business to see that she was not violated. Women were meant to be guarded, and if a man failed in his duty it was not necessarily the woman's fault if she strayed from the straight and narrow. There were few legal sanctions to enforce the subservience of a wife

16. *The Sayings of Muhammad*, nos. 411–418, pp. 115–116.

17. There are numerous descriptions of Paradise in the *Koran*. See for example XXXVI (The Poets), 55; XLVII (Muhammad), 16–17; LXXVI (Time of Man), 11–22; LXXVII (Emissaries), 31–37; LXXXIII (Defrauding), 21–28; LXXXVIII (The Overwhelming), 8–16; LXXVI (Time of Man), 11–22; LVI (The Event), 22–24; and LXXVII (Emissaries), 31–37. The last three refer to the ever virgin nymphs and the eternal boys. The women of Paradise were said to have been created and their virginity preserved; *Koran*, LV (The Beneficient), 72, and they are kept in secluded pavillions.

18. Abu abd Allah Muhammad ibn al-Bukhari, *Sahīh*, trans. from the Arabic by Muhammad Asad (Lahore: Arafat Publications, 1938), L, xxxiii, vol. V, p. 98.

19. *Ibid.*, L, liii, vol. V, p. 128.

to her husband, but custom itself emphasized that this was the normal and honorable way of life for a woman. If a man from another tribe seduced a married woman, he committed no unlawful or dishonorable act; poets in fact constantly boasted of their stolen loves.[20]

Sexual intercourse was a good religious deed for the Muslim male. The Koran stated that women were a field for men to cultivate, and men were advised to cultivate them as often and as frequently as they would.[21] Men were cautioned, however, to seek women out for "honest wedlock," not debauchery.[22] Women also had rights, and in this respect Muhammad initiated far-reaching reforms. Since these rights, nonetheless, were guarded by institutions from which women were excluded, it was not too difficult to manipulate Muhammad's teachings against them. Muhammad, for example, emphasized that women were to be allowed to keep their rights to their dowry,[23] that all wives in a multiple marriage were to be treated equally, and that it was forbidden to turn away from one, leaving her in suspense.[24] This has usually been interpreted to mean that coitus interruptus or other forms of birth control were not to be practiced without the woman's consent. Muhammad also stipulated that wives and daughters were to inherit, but the portion of a male child was to be twice that of the female, indicating his own attitudes toward women as lesser beings.[25] Wives were allowed to leave legacies,[26] and no man could inherit a woman's estate against her will.[27] Divorced wives (divorce for men in Islam was easy) were allowed to keep their dowries. A former husband was not supposed to impede their remarriage.[28] Widows who had been in mourning for four months and ten days could remarry.[29]

20. Levy, *Social Structure of Islam*, p. 94; Muhammad, however, *Koran*, IV (Women), 24, forbade intercourse with all married women except captives.
21. *Koran*, II (The Cow), 223.
22. *Ibid.*, IV (The Women), 24–25.
23. *Ibid.*, 4.
24. *Ibid.*, 129.
25. *Ibid.*, 11.
26. *Ibid.*, 12.
27. *Ibid.*, 23. Pickthall's translation is not clear on this point and in his version the verse is numbered 19.
28. *Koran*, II (The Cow), 231–232.
29. *Ibid.*, 234.

No legal age was set by Muhammad for marriage, but as a general rule girls were not to be handed over to their husbands until they were fit for intercourse. A man who had intercourse with a girl before she had menstruated was subject to punishment.[30] Marriage (*Nikāh*) literally meant sexual intercourse, although it was used in the Koran to also mean contract. If there was doubt about a girl's readiness for marriage, two matrons were appointed to examine and report on her. Usually a girl was married at twelve or thirteen; a girl of nineteen was already regarded as an old maid. In most cases the bridegroom was older than the bride.[31]

Divorce, for the male, was easily arranged. For a woman it was difficult. A man could divorce a wife twice and take her back once but before he could marry her for a third time she had to be married and divorced (or widowed) from another husband. After a divorce a woman was to wait until three successive menses had passed to leave her divorced husband's house. This waiting period was to ensure that she was not cast onto the streets pregnant. If she was pregnant her husband was supposed to take care of her until after the delivery. Usually he kept any male children, but she usually kept the female. If it was mutually agreeable to a husband and his former wife, she could remain in his house after divorce. If she was sent away her husband had to restore her dowry. In those cases where the woman had persuaded her husband to divorce her, however, the husband could claim part of her dowry.[32] If a husband divorced a wife before the marriage was consummated he had to return her dowry and pay half of the marriage fee agreed upon.[33]

Traditionally it is accepted that Muhammad limited the number of wives to four, although Muhammad himself married several wives, probably fourteen in all, and several prominent early rulers of Islam also had more than four. This was in part because the Koranic prohibition of four was not so clear-cut, and also because no limit was ever set on the number of concubines. The essential difference between concubinage and marriage was that marriage entailed a union with a freewoman while concubines were slaves. To marry a slave it

30. al-Marqhīnānī, *The Hedaya or Guide*, II, 186, bk. VII, chap. 2.
31. Levy, *Social Structure of Islam*, p. 17.
32. *Koran*, II (The Cow), 237; XXXIII (The Clans), 49.
33. *Ibid.*, LVIII (She that Disputeth), 4.

was necessary that she be emancipated. Concubines, however, were not to be selected from married women unless they were captives.[34]

Muhammad's first wife, Khadijah, was a widow around forty years old and when he married her he was twenty-five. Their relationship was very close and at her death Muhammad seemed inconsolable. His friends advised him to marry again in order that he might more easily overcome his grief, but the prophet was reluctant to do so. Finally he married Ayesha, a young girl of six or seven. It was said that just watching the girl play with her dolls proved a consolation to the prophet. The marriage was not consummated for several years. Most of his other wives Muhammad took for political reasons, formalizing in the process alliances with tribes and cementing their support. Many of them were widows for whom marriage provided a kind of social security. Tradition has it that Muhammad was scrupulously fair with his wives, sleeping with each in rotation. The fact that all of his children save one were by his first wife indicates either that most of the prophet's wives were past the childbearing age or the prophet himself was troubled by impotency, had become sterile, or perhaps had his mind on other activities.

It was Ayesha who, once she grew into a happy, fun-loving woman, gave Muhammad the most trouble. She remained his favorite, often accompanying him on campaigns. On such expeditions she observed purdah by being carried in a heavily curtained litter so that no man would gaze upon the wife of the prophet. Tradition has it that on one occasion Ayesha vanished from her litter and was nowhere to be found when the caravan arrived at its stopping place for the night. The next morning she arrived with a handsome young soldier, a fact which caused considerable tongue-wagging among the faithful. She reported that during a rest stop she had gone to perform her ablutions but after returning to the hoogah she noticed she had left her jewelry behind at the well. Without thinking to tell anyone she ran back to the well in order to retrieve it, but before she returned the expedition had moved on. She then waited for someone to come back and rescue her; soon after the gallant young soldier had appeared. Few of Muhammad's followers believed her story and various derogatory rumors about her character circulated through the camp. Muhammad defended her, thundering against her accusers: "Why did they not pro-

34. *Ibid.*, LXX (The Ascending Stairway), 29–31; XIII (The Believers), 5–7; IV (The Women), 3, 24f. or in some 28f.

duce four witnesses? Since they produce not witnesses, they verily are liars in the sight of Allah. Had it not been for the grace of Allah and His mercy unto you in the world and the Hereafter an awful doom had overtaken you for that whereof ye murmured. When ye welcomed it with your tongues, and uttered with your mouths that whereof ye had no knowledge ye counted it a trifle. In the sight of Allah it is very great."[35] Thereafter to accuse a woman of adultery it was necessary to produce four witnesses, something that was unlikely to happen with any great frequency. Without four witnesses such an accusation amounted to slander, a crime, and the gossip quickly ceased. The requirement for four witnesses entered into the Koran and it became a safeguard for Muslim women, although some later commentators held that a husband could meet the requirement by swearing four times. Ayesha never forgave those who failed to accept her innocence, among whom apparently was Ali, Muhammad's son-in-law and one of his successors. She later conspired to bring about the ruin of Ali and his family, the murder of his two sons, Hassan and Husein, and helped split Islam into two major camps, the Sunni and Shi-ite. While Ayesha's escapade was still fresh in people's minds, the principal parties in the spread of gossip against her were punished with eighty lashes.

One of the contradictions of the Muslim attitude about the sexuality of women is that female circumcision is widespread in the Muslim world. Since Islam teaches that the clitoris is the source and well of all passion in women, the excision of the clitoris is quite obviously a deliberate attempt to make women less sensuous. One Sudanese recently justified the practice on the grounds that "circumcision of women releases them from their bondage to sex, and enables them to fulfill their real destiny as mother. The clitoris is the basis for female masturbation; such masturbation is common in a hot climate; the spiritual basis of masturbation is fantasy; in fantasy a woman broods on sexual images; such brooding inevitably leads a woman to spiritual infidelity, since she commits adultery in her heart, and this is the first step to physical infidelity, which is the breaker of homes."[36] To their credit the Muslims are consistent, they practice male circumcision as well, but the erotic effect of male circumcision

35. *Ibid.*, XXIV (Light), 13–15.
36. Quoted by George Allgrove, *Love in the East* (London: Gibbs and Philipps, 1962), pp. 128–129.

is much less than female. The excision of the clitoris apparently does not remove all ability to have an orgasm but it makes it next to impossible unless intercourse is carried out for a long time. This has apparently led women to encourage their husbands to use hashish and other such drugs to slow down their performance.[37] The Koran itself does not provide for female circumcision but neither does it provide for male circumcision. Both are accepted in the Islamic world, and male circumcision is considered obligatory for a pilgrimage to Mecca; doubtful pilgrims are sometimes inspected to see that they meet the requirement.

As far as reproduction itself was concerned, Muhammad recognized that there was both a male and female element with the vaginal secretion equated with the semen of the male. He taught that the sex of the child depended upon which one of the parents had the strongest seed. If the female had the stronger seed the child was female, if the male, a male child resulted. Occasionally, though one seed determined the sex, the other seed was strong enough to effect the individual characteristics.[38] Not surprisingly this belief had important implications on the attitudes a father would hold toward his children. Male children would be proof that the man dominated the woman, a desirable characteristic in Muslim society. Thus sons were very much more desired than daughters, if only to prove the masculinity of the father.

One of the institutions which relegated women to an inferior position in society was the harem. Scholars today do not agree when the harem system and the seclusion of women came to exercise such great influence in Islam, but it seems to have developed fairly early. Many of the interpreters of the Koran were men from Persia, where women had long been secluded, and it was probably their authority in Islam which made itself felt fairly early. The Greeks also secluded their women, and Christian churches of the East still separate men and women, as did Judaism, so that it is perhaps going too far to overemphasize the Persian influence. By the time of Harun al-Raschid, a century and a half after the death of the prophet, the harem system was fully established. In fact it was so widely accepted that pious visitors to other lands were shocked when they saw free

37. During our stay in Egypt it was widely believed that one of the reasons Nasser was interested in abolishing female circumcision was to curtail the illicit drug traffic.

38. *Koran*, XXIV (Light), 33.

social intercourse between men and women.[39] Harem intrigues furnished a major theme in Islamic history. This was because women in the harem could gain status if their sons emerged as rulers, and thus almost anything they did to encourage the advancement of their sons became justified. The harem had strong political overtones, and was not merely a romantic menage of women.

It was women's very position as sexual objects which caused so much trouble in Islam. As Vis, the heroine of an Islamic romance, was made to confess by her male author:

> in women desire is stronger than modesty and wisdom. Among created beings woman is imperfect, and in consequence capricious and of ill repute, hazarding this world and the next for the sake of a moment's desire, losing all reason when her desire is fulfilled. . . .
> Many wiles are within a woman's skill, but she is ever disposed to accept fair words from a man. Man instinctively sets a thousand traps through which his desire will be fulfilled: always, woman is the game he hunts, and it costs him small pains to run her down. . . .
> Then the wretched woman is contemptible in the eyes of the man who has seduced her, and who now turns away from her.[40]

There were numerous sayings which indicate a gut-level hostility to the "weaker" sex:

> I have not left any calamity more detrimental to mankind than woman.

> A bad omen is found in a woman, a house, or a horse.

> Look to your actions and abstain from the world and from women, for verily the first sin which the children of Israel committed was on account of Women.

Countering these were ambiguous statements such as

> The world and all things in it are valuable, but more valuable than all is a virtuous woman.[41]

Not any woman but a virtuous woman, one who had been seen only

---

39. Levy, *Social Structure of Islam*, p. 127.

40. Robert Surieu, *Sarv-é naz: An Essay on Love and the Representation of Erotic Themes in Ancient Iran*, trans. by James Hogarth (Geneva: Nagel Publishers, 1967), p. 65. The quotation comes from the story of Vis and Ramin by Gurgani in the eleventh century.

41. All of these quotations can be found in *A Dictionary of Islam*, ed. by Thomas Patrick Hughes (reprinted, Clifton, N.J.: Reference Books, 1965), pp. 620–621.

by her husband and male relatives, one who in effect bought the idea that women were inferior creatures:

> If you have a daughter, entrust her to kindly nurses and give her a good nurture. When she grows up, entrust her to a preceptor so that she shall learn the provisions of sacred law and the essential religious duties. But do not teach her to read and write; that is a great calamity. Once she is grown up, do your utmost to give her in marriage; it were best for a girl not to come into existence, but being born she had better be married or buried . . . as long as she is in your house, treat your daughter with compassion.[42]

Muslim men were cautioned about women and told that God would "reward the Muslim who, having beheld the beauties of a woman, shuts his eyes." They were warned not to visit the houses of their men friends when "they are absent from their homes, for the devil circulates within you like the blood in your veins. It was said 'O Prophet in your veins also.' He [Muhammad] replied, 'My veins also. But God has given me power over the devil and I am free from wickedness.' " Some teachers went so far as to advise two women not to sit together "because the one may describe the other to her husband, so that you might say the husband has seen her himself."[43]

The devotional literature of Islam prepared for women urged them to help their neighbors in need, to spin for their own husbands and make clothes for their children, to remain obedient always to their husband, never to be angry with their menfolk, and if their husbands were angry toward them, to try to appease them, not to go out without their husband's permission, not to uncover themselves to anyone but their husbands, and to always beatifically smile at their husbands and never deny them their sexual privileges.[44] The ideal woman in fact:

> speaks and laughs rarely, and never without a reason. She never leaves the house, even to see neighbours of her acquaintance. She has no women friends, gives her confidence to nobody, and her husband is her sole reliance. She takes nothing from anyone, excepting her

42. Kai Kā'ūs Iskander, *A Mirror for Princes* (The Qābūs Nāma), trans. from the Persian by Reuben Levy (London: The Cresset Press, 1951), chap. 27, p. 125.

43. Hughes, *Encylopedia of Islam,* pp. 620–621.

44. Muhammad Mustafā al-'Adawī, *Qissat ar-Rahā li's-Sayyida Fātima az-Zahrā or the Story of Fātima's Hand Mill,* ed. and trans. by Arthur Jeffery in *Islam: Muhammad and His Religion* (New York: Liberal Arts Press, 1958), pp. 217–222. This was a little eight-paged pamphlet used for devotional reading in feminine circles.

husband and her parents. If she sees relatives, she does not meddle with their affairs. She is not treacherous, and has no faults to hide, nor bad reasons to profer. She does not try to entice people. If her husband shows his intention of performing the conjugal rite, she is agreeable to his desires and occasionally even provokes them. She assists him always in his affairs, and is sparing in complaints and tears; she does not laugh or rejoice when she sees her husband moody or sorrowful, but shares his troubles, and wheedles him into good humour, till he is quite content again. She does not surrender herself to anybody but her husband, even if abstinence would kill her. She hides her secret parts, and does not allow them to be seen; she is always elegantly attired, of the utmost personal propriety, and takes care not to let her husband see what might be repugnant to him. She perfumes herself with scents, uses antimony for her toilets, and cleans her teeth with *souak* [i.e., the bark of the walnut tree]. Such a woman is cherished by all men.[45]

On the other hand the contemptible woman was garrulous, fond of gaming and jesting, constantly laughing out loud, always running to her neighbors, meddling with matters that were of no concern to her, plaguing her husband, leaguing herself with other women against him, playing the grand lady, accepting gifts from everybody. Also despised was the woman who was somber, frowning, light-headed in her relations with men, contentious, fond of talebearing, unable to keep her husband's secrets, prolific in talk.[46]

These same values appeared in that vast catalog of Islamic attitudes and beliefs known as the *Thousand and One Nights*. Women in the *Nights* appeared to be either governed by impulse, blown about by passion, stable only in instability, constant only in inconstancy, falsely ascetic, perfidious, and murderous, or on the other extreme, as dutiful daughters, devoted wives, perfect mothers, saintly devotees, or model lovers. The whole basis of the *Tales* dealt with women's perfidy. Shah Zaman Samarkan received an invitation to visit his older brother, the Emperor Shahryar. He departed almost immediately but half-way through the night he remembered he had forgotten something and hastened back alone. He found his wife making love to a cook. He killed them both, then proceeded on his

45. Sheik Nefazi, *The Perfumed Garden*, trans. by Richard F. Burton, ed., with an intro. by Alan Hull Walton (New York: Putnam's, 1964), chap. 2, "Concerning Women Who Desire to Be Praised," p. 97.
46. *Ibid.*, chap. 4, "Women Who Are to Be Held in Contempt," pp. 119–120.

journey, troubled by his wife's perfidy. When his brother Shahryar went out to hunt, Zaman stayed behind accidentally looking down into the courtyard of the harem. He found that only ten of the twenty girls in the harem were really girls, the rest were men. They immediately paired off as soon as the king had left. The queen herself kept a lover hidden in the tree. The moral obviously was to "Rely not on women;/ Trust not to their hearts,/ Whose joys and whose sorrows/ Are hung to their parts!/ Lying love they will swear thee/ When guile ne'er departs. . . ."[47] Shahryar solved his problem by inventing a new mode of marriage. Everyday for three years he took a new virgin as wife, deflowered her at night, then decapitated her at dawn. This went on till the city was all but empty of nubile girls. Finally Sheherazade, the daughter of his wazir, volunteered to marry him. In order to preserve herself from beheading Sheherazade told her husband an incomplete story which she then finished the next night, then started another. In the process of telling her tales for a *Thousand and One Nights* Sheherazade became the mother of three boys. When she concluded she requested her children be brought to her and then said: "O King of the age, these are thy children and I crave that thou release me from the doom of death, as a dole to these infants; for, if thou kill me, they will become motherless and with none among women to rear them as they should be reared."[48] The king immediately pardoned her because he had found her chaste, pure, ingenuous, and pious. The story ended happily with Zaman marrying Dunyazad, Sheherazade's sister.

Throughout the *Nights*, women were pictured as followers of impulse. They were called offal, but as Sheherazade stated, it was not the case that "women are always bad." A feature of the stories about women was their combination of sensuality with genuine affections. The good girl might be chaste but she knew that sexual pleasures were good, and she spoke with a frankness which is sometimes alien to the West. Burton quotes a Muslim contemporary of his as stating that the Arabs think that when a man has a precious jewel "tis wiser to lock it up in a box than to leave it about for anyone to take."[49]

47. *The Book of the Thousand Nights and a Night,* "The Story of King Shahryar and His Brother," I, 13.
    48. *Ibid.,* "Conclusion," VI, 3634.
    49. *Ibid., Terminal Essay,* secs. IV, VI, 3743.

This in essence reflects a typical Islamic view, a sex-positive one. Women like jewels are admired and sought after, but should be protected and guarded lest they be stolen. They are property, valuable property, but really not persons, and must not take upon themselves the prerogative of persons who are after all exclusively male.

Farīd al-Dīn 'Attār, a biographer of Sufi saints, included an account of the learned woman follower of Sufism, Rābi'a, in his account, but felt he had to justify himself. "If anyone should ask me why I note her amongst the ranks of men, I reply that the master of all prophets has said, God looks not to your outward appearance. Attainment of the divine lies not in appearance but in [sincerity of] purpose . . . it is possible to learn some of the truth of religion from one of her handmaidens. Since a woman on the path of God becomes a man, she cannot be called a woman."[50] There are a few women saints in Islam but their place in the pantheon was not as strong as it was in Christianity. There were also some early women intellectuals such as Shuhda bint al-Ibari, "the pride of womankind," whose reputation rested on her knowledge of *hadīth*, the collection of the teachings of Muhammad in which Ayesha also played an important part. By the tenth century, however, the woman scholar was no more. Though indirectly women in the harem and behind the throne exercised influence, it was rarely acknowledged outside. Sitta Zubayda, wife of Hārūn al-Rashīd, acquired such renown that the faithful erroneously believed a tomb was built to mark her remains. Somewhat later the mother of Caliph Muqtadir, an incompetent, ruled the empire in her son's name but the names of such women appeared infrequently enough to excite comment when they did. In both of these cases it was woman as wife and mother who was important, and the Muslim mother probably had considerable influence in the home, particularly over her children, her servants, and her slaves, but not necessarily over her husband.

In general Islamic literature made no mention of any grand loves where a lone woman ruled the lover, and the lyric poets knew nothing of the idealized heroines of Western romantic poetry. There were, of course, such verses as Omar Khayyam's famous one: "a Loaf of Bread beneath the Bough, / A Flask of Wine, a Book of Verse—and Thou / Beside me singing in the Wilderness—/ And Wilderness is Paradise

50. Quoted by Levy, *Social Structure of Islam*, p. 132.

enow."[51] The beloved, however, was nameless and could have been male or female. There was another aspect of Islam which had implications for attitudes toward women, namely the concept of unattainable love, where the lover was a martyr of love; in this genre the chaste lover who died of or for his love gained paradise. This concept was a unique contribution of Islam and had great influence on Western chivalric literature.

Particularly influential in propagating such an ideal were the teachings of the Arab mystics, the Sufis.[52] Some sects of the Sufis taught that femininity and saintliness were related because "woman is considered in many instances holy, as being the mother of mankind, carrying no arms, and often suffering beating, baking the bread, and entering the oven."[53] Often among the Sufis, the mystical love of the universal self was expressed in terms of masculine and feminine, with God being expressed in feminine form.

> Until then I had been enamoured of her, but when I
>   renounced my desire, she desired me for herself
>   and loved me,
> And I became a beloved, nay, one loving himself; this
>   is not like what I said before, that my soul is my
>   beloved.
> Through her I went forth from myself to her and came
>   not back to myself: one like me does not hold the
>   doctrine of return.[54]

The beauty which inspired love, though expressed in beings of flesh and blood, was the beauty of divinity; love itself passed beyond the impulses of flesh and the heart to become a spiritual discipline and one of the paths which led to mystical union. The erotic metaphors employed by the Islamic poets, particularly of the so-called Medinese school, were strikingly akin to the romantic poets of the later Middle

51. This is a famous translation of the *Rubaiyat of Omar Khayyam* by Edward Fitzgerald which, though it probably represents more Fitzgerald than Omar Khayyam, in this case represents the intent of the original. This is the eleventh quatrain. There are numerous editions.

52. Philip J. Baldensperger, "Orders of Holy Men in Palestine," *Palestine Exploration Fund Quarterly Statement* (London, 1894), p. 38. See also Frederick J. Bliss, *The Religions of Modern Syria and Palestine* (New York, 1912), p. 254.

53. Raphael Patai, *Sex and Family in the Bible* (Garden City, N.Y.: Doubleday, 1959), p. 173.

54. Translated by Reynold Alleyne Nicholson, *Studies in Islamic Mysticism* (Cambridge: Cambridge University Press, 1921), p. 217.

Ages. Though undoubtedly many of the Arabs who followed the ideal like their Christian counterparts were not averse to actual physical love, it was chaste love which was the most consuming and most desirous. Courtly love was a delicate game, and the play was more important than the goal.[55] Women's sexuality kept men from realizing their ideal of chaste love, and rather than blame their own sexuality, they inevitably blamed women.

The inferior position of women was effectively demonstrated by Islamic folklore about the evil eye. As befit a society which put a premium upon men, the evil eye was more attracted to boy babies than girls. Thus the way for boy children to avoid being harmed by the evil eye was to dress them as girls. Though this might have had some traumatic effect on the males, they could always emphasize they were better than mere girls. The purdah requirements of Islam also encouraged the appearance of numerous male transvestites who in public acted the parts of women on the stage, or danced at formal occasions. Thus we have the spectacle of a society which prized women as sexual creatures denying women the chance to really appear in public as such. Women quite simply had to be protected from themselves, and were much too valuable a property to be put into the public arena, this in spite of the fact that Muhammad himself had forbidden women's clothes to men, and condemned men who put them on.[56] The male-run society would rather put men into women's clothes than run the risk of women assuming any real importance, even as sexual creatures, outside of the home.

In sum a positive attitude toward sex was not enough to change negative attitudes toward women. The more sexually secure Muslim writers did not differ in essentials in their attitudes toward women from the sexually fearful Christian church fathers. With purdah, polygamy, concubinage, and the harem there was both a shortage of women for the majority of males and a real lack of opportunity for men to become acquainted with anyone of the opposite sex, other than their mothers or sisters, and even then the conditions were often not conducive to establishing close relationships. When men raised

55. See von Grunebaum, *Medieval Islam*, pp. 315–318; Gustave E. von Grunebaum, "Avicenna's Risala fi l Isq and Courtly Love," *Journal of Near Eastern Studies*, 11 (1952), 233–238. Von Grunebaum feels, however, that Avicenna's concepts were not known to the European middle ages, although others were. See also A. J. Denomy, *The Heresy of Courtly Love* (New York: D. X. McMullen, 1947), pp. 29–32.

56. al-Marghīnānī, *The Hedaya or Guide*, bk. LIV, sec. 2, IV, 597.

in these conditions grew into positions of control in Islamic institutions, their own repressive ideas grew and became dominant. Women had no effective voice in countering them. There was no institution she could call her own and all she could be was the myth of the male creation, a sexy senseless creature who made an interesting and troublesome possession, but was necessary to have children.

chapter eight

On the Pedestal: The Beginning
of the Feminine Mystique

Early medieval society has been broken down into three groups: those who fought, those who prayed, and those who worked. Since women were regarded as unable to fight, were prohibited from the priesthood, and only seldom allowed into the monastic life, the only thing they could do was work; even in this, however, they were subordinate to their menfolk. Nevertheless toward the end of the Middle Ages, women, or at least aristocratic women, also became love objects, and it was this development of the chivalric love mystique as much as anything else that ultimately led to a different attitude toward women. Even then it had to go through several phases and well into the period of modern history before any meaningful attitudinal change resulted.

Medieval society in the West represented a fusion of Roman, Christian, and Germanic attitudes and institutions, but the addition of the German element did not necessarily lead to any improvement in the status of women, nor to any radical change in attitudes. This is important to emphasize because our first literary description of the German woman is misleading. Our source for the misinformation is the Roman historian Tacitus (c. 55 to 117 A.D.), a conservative who was unhappy at the changing family structure in Rome and with Roman morals in general. To him German women served as an example for their Roman sisters to follow. He emphasized their subservience to their husbands and rhapsodized over their virtue and purity, pointing out the rarity of adultery among them.[1]

Whether Tacitus was recording reality or creating a new mythology of the perfect woman has often been debated, but the evi-

1. Tacitus, *Germania*, trans. by Sir William Peterson (London: Heinemann, 1946), caps. 18f.

dence would seem to support the latter. German women might well have been more virtuous than Roman women at the time of Tacitus but this was not because they were made of finer fabric. It was because the consequences of any misstep were so disastrous. Germanic custom gave the husband the right to execute a wife and her lover if she was caught in an adulterous relationship, and it was the duty of all male relatives to protect the virtue of their female ones. Female chastity had property value and women were, to put it simply, the property of their menfolk. They were always under the protection of some male: father, brother, son, or some other near male relative. Theoretically the justification for this was the physical inferiority of the female. Since women were held to be constitutionally unable to bear arms it was felt essential she be protected by a relative who wore a sword and could draw it if necessary to defend her.

That this might be necessary is evident from some of the provisions of the various Germanic legal codes. The laws of the Alemanni, for instance, provided that if a man met a free woman in the country and deprived her of all that she wore above the waist, he had to pay a penalty of six *solidi*. If he stripped her entirely, the fine was doubled, and if he raped her, he had to pay forty *solidi*.[2] Women were valuable and had to be protected. The laws of the Ripuarian Franks set the penalty for killing a free woman between the age of puberty and her fortieth year at 600 *solidi*, while the death of a young girl cost 200. The code estimated 600 *solidi*, to be the equivalent of 300 cattle or fifty male horses, and so severe was the penalty that provisions were made to pay it in installments extending over three generations.[3]

At first a woman could not appear in the judicial assembly, could not inherit in her own right, and if she inherited through others, she could neither administer nor dispose of her property without permission of male guardians.[4] Later women under some conditions were able to appear in court, to make a contract, and even to make a will in the manner of men. This, however, never meant that a woman could freely dispose of her property since such an action would conflict with family rights, but only that she could have some say in what

2. *Leges Alamannorum*, ed. by Karl Lehman in *Monumenta Germaniae historica, Leges nationum Germanicarum*, vol. 5, pt. 1 (Hanover: Hahn, 1888), p. 115.

3. *Lex Ribuaria*, ed. by Rudolph Sohm, *Monumenta Germaniae historica, Legum*, vol. 5 (Hanover: Hahn, 1875–79), pp. 216, 231.

4. See Jean Brissaud, A *History of French Private Law*, trans. by Rapelje Howell (reprinted, Boston: Little, Brown, 1969), pp. 221–223.

was going to take place. The Germans followed the custom of *mundium* (from *munt,* meaning hand), which meant that when the woman passed from her father's house she came into her husband's hand, and he then exercised control over her. She took his name, lived according to his station, acquired his nationality and his domicile. She also lost all right to inherit from her relatives, although she might have been given a share of the inheritance as a dowry. The husband had the right to beat his wife, and this was true throughout the medieval period, but he was not supposed to mutilate or kill her. The only limitation in a wife's submission to her husband was her necessity to observe her duties to God, and in theory no husband could force a wife to act contrary to the Christian religion. In all other matters, however, the husband was almost the sole judge of her action.

In spite of these obstacles a few women managed to become politically powerful, although the inevitable result was resentment. In the Anglo-Saxon kingdom of Wessex, for example, Eadberg, the wife of Beorthtric, so antagonized her subjects that the title of queen was abolished. Instead after her reign the king's wife was known as the Lady, and his mother, "naturally but perhaps less happily, as the Old Lady."[5] Even when women began to gain more rights, there was almost a total lack of statute law and only very little interpretative legal writing dealing with her status. This was because, according to the standard text on English law, "private law with few exceptions put women on a par with men; public law gives a woman no rights and exacts from her no duties, save that of paying taxes and performing such services as can be performed by deputy."[6] A woman could never be outlawed simply because she was never in the law. She could, however, be declared a waif, and this waiving of the law had most of the effects of outlawry since it removed all the protections she had under the law. Even in private law her position was not as good as it might appear since the law demonstrated a preference for males over females in the right of inheritance, as well as in most other matters. Even when women were given the theoretical right to inherit, only a few became major landowners. In the *Domesday Book,*

5. Doris Mary Stenton, *The English Woman in History* (London: Allen and Unwin, 1957), p. 3.

6. Sir Frederick Pollock and Frederick William Maitland, *The History of English Law* (2nd ed., Cambridge: Cambridge University Press, 1952), p. 482.

the census of English property compiled by William the Conqueror in the eleventh century, only a minute proportion of place names, some thirty in the more than 10,000, bore names that indicated they were held or had been held by women.[7]

Another way to examine the status of women and societal attitudes toward them was their position in marriage. In general it was not particularly high. A wife was expected to be chaste, but she had no control over her husband, and the marriage could be easily dissolved if he wanted. Concubinage was widespread and polygamy was not unknown. Several of the early Frankish kings were polygamists,[8] and one of them, King Clotaire (d. 561), who had seven wives, was married to two sisters at the same time. The sixth-century Gregory of Tours explained that this had come about because Inagunda, Clotaire's first wife, had approached her husband about her unmarried sister Aregunda: "My lord hath done with his handmaid according to his pleasure, and taken her to his bed; now to make my reward complete, let my lord hear the proposal of his servant. I entreat him graciously to choose for his servant my sister an able and rich husband, that I be not humbled but exalted by her, and thus may give thee yet more faithful service." Clotaire, in order to please his wife, summoned his sister-in-law and after looking her over decided that rather than finding a husband for her he would marry her himself. He reported his decision to Inagunda: "I have done my best to procure for thee the reward which thy sweetness asked of me. I sought a man wealthy and of good wit, whom I might give in marriage to thy sister, but I found none better than myself. Know therefore that I have taken her to wife, which I believe will not displease thee." As a devoted wife should, Inagunda meekly replied: "Let my lord do that which seemeth good in his sight; only let his handmaid live in enjoyment of his favour."[9]

Charlemagne, the most famous of the Frankish rulers, managed to have either two or four wives at the same time, as well as a number of concubines. Charlemagne also refused to allow his daughters to get

7. F. M. Stenton, "The Historical Bearing of Place Name Studies: The Place of Women in Anglo Saxon History," Royal Historical Society, *Transactions*, 4th ser., 25 (1943), 1–13.

8. Gregory of Tours, *History of the Franks*, trans. by O. M. Dalton (Oxford: Clarendon Press, 1927), IV, 26, 28.

9. *Ibid.*, IV, 3.

married, on the grounds that he "could not part with their company. . . . What he found charming in one was the sweetness of her voice, in another the freshness of her smile, in this one the grace of her bearing, in that one her rebelliousness." It might well be, however, that Charlemagne was fearful that the would-be husbands of his daughters would become powerful by marrying them, and eventually challenge his power. At any rate he had no objection to their establishing informal alliances, and several of his grandchildren were born out of wedlock.[10]

The problem of a religious vocation for women proved a troublesome question in the masculine-oriented society of the early Middle Ages. Many of the early women who turned to the ascetic life had been forced to disguise themselves as men in order to follow their vocation.[11] This changed as convents were founded but few women ever had the opportunity to choose a religious vocation. Girls were commonly married at thirteen or fourteen and widows were expected to marry again without undue delay. Still there were exceptions, and medieval society found it necessary to make provisions for girls who could not or would not marry and for those powerful widows who did not want to marry again. The main purpose of the convents, however, was to provide a retreat for the widows and daughters of the great; only a few lesser women entered them in the medieval period. It was in the convent that women were most free of male domination, although it was not easy for society to accept this. The Frankish King Clotaire II (584–629), for example, felt compelled to warn his subjects that

> no maidens, holy widows or religious persons who are vowed to God, whether they stay at home or live in monasteries, shall be enticed away, or appropriated, or taken in marriage by making use of a special royal permit. And if anyone surreptitiously gets hold of a permit, it shall have no force. And should anyone by violent or other means carry off any such woman and take her to wife, let him be put to death. And if he be married in church and the woman who is appropriated, or who is on the point of being appropriated, seems to be a

10. Richard Winston, *Charlemagne: From the Hammer to the Cross* (Indianapolis: Bobbs-Merrill, 1954), pp. 234–235.

11. See the case of Papula in Gregory of Tours, *History of the Franks*, (introduction), I, 356. See also Vern L. Bullough, "Transvestism in the Middle Ages," *American Journal of Sociology* (in press, 1973).

consenting party, they shall be separated, sent into exile, and their possessions given to their natural heirs.[12]

Some of the most famous names in early English and Frankish monastic history were nuns of royal descent, Hilda at Whitby, Etheldreda at Ely, Radegunde at Poitiers, Bathild at Chelles, and there is no doubt that they were masterful and formidable women. In spite of the fact that they were nuns such women never forgot that they belonged to a ruling class. Often these early nunneries had colonies of monks attached in order to provide the necessary sacraments and temporal administration, but both the male and female communities were ruled with an iron hand by their abbesses.

In theory convent life was a means by which women could deny their sex and thus follow the suggestion of some of the church fathers to become more like men. It was much more difficult for a woman to become a nun than a man a monk, with the result that compared to the number of men who took monastic vows there was only a handful of women who managed to do so. Many of the convents seemed to be a place for older rather than younger women, and even the famous convent at Arles founded by Caesarius, Bishop of Arles (501–573), refused for a time to admit a woman until she was in her fortieth year.[13]

One of the most famous convents in the early medieval period was that of Gandersheim, founded in the middle of the ninth century by the Duke of Saxony, whose progeny eventually became holy Roman emperors. Duke Liudolf, the founder, was persuaded by his wife to establish the convent, and all of his daughters were attached to it, at least for a time, and one of his daughters, Hathumod, was its first abbess. As the dukes of Saxony rose in power and influence, they continued to send their daughters to be educated at the convent, and for a time it was probably the center of female learning in western Europe. Gandersheim was a free abbey, that is to say its abbess held it direct from the king and her rights of overlordship extended far beyond the walls of the convent; she had her own law courts and sent her own men at arms into the field. She even had the right to a seat in the imperial diet, and coins bearing her portrait are extant. Some of the nuns were quite exceptional women, and probably the

12. Quoted by Lina Eckenstein, *Woman under Monasticism* (reprinted, New York: Russell and Russell, 1963), p. 72.
13. *Ibid.*, p. 49.

most famous was Hroswitha (c. 932–1002), one of the few early medieval female writers whose works survive. Hroswitha was a poet, as well as a dramatist, although her plays were obviously written more to be read than acted. She claimed Terence as her master, but she used him as a base for moral contrast rather than for his literary style. Where Terence's comedies almost invariably dealt with the frailty of women, Hroswitha just as invariably emphasized her heroine's heroic adherence to chastity. Though her six plays varied somewhat in their story line, the motive was always to glorify uncompromising fidelity to the vow of virginity. As suited a woman of that period, Hroswitha began by apologizing for writing at all:

> Although prosody may seem a hard and difficult art for a woman to master, I, without any assistance but that given by the merciful grace of Heaven (in which I have trusted, rather than in my own strength), have attempted in this book to sing in dactyls. I was eager that the talent given me by Heaven should not grow rusty from neglect, and remain silent in my heart from apathy, but under the hammer of assiduous devotion should sound a chord of divine praise.[14]

> Yet if my work is examined by those who know how to weigh things fairly, I shall be more easily pardoned on account of my sex and my inferior knowledge, especially as I did not undertake it of my own will but at your [her abbess] command.[15]

> To you, learned and virtuous men, who do not envy the success of others, but on the contrary rejoice in it as becomes the truly great. Hrotswitha [*sic*], poor humble sinner, sends wishes for your health in this life and your joy in eternity. . . . You have, however, not praised me but the Giver of Grace which works in me, by sending me your paternal congratulations and admitting that I possess some little knowledge of these arts the subtleties of which exceed the grasp of my woman's mind. . . .[16]

In short a woman might well write but she had to be properly humble about it and not pretend to be equal to the male.

The period of Hroswitha's residence at Gandersheim represented a peak of women's influence in monastic life, and during the eleventh and twelfth centuries convent life entered a period of decline. The institution of double monasteries, particularly the influential

14. Hroswitha, *The Plays of Hroswitha*, trans. by Christopher St. John (London: Chatto and Windus, 1923), pp. xxxii–xxxiii.

15. *Ibid.*, p. xxv.

16. *Ibid.*, pp. xviii–xxix.

position of women in them, came under attack, and the new and exacting conception of monastic duty associated with the Cluniac reform movement gave emphasis to the priestly role of monks. Though there were hundreds of monasteries founded or associated with Cluny, only one of them was for women. This was at Marcigny and it was founded specifically to provide a retreat for women whose husbands had become monks. These women were not to direct their own affairs, which were under the direction of a prior appointed by the abbot at Cluny.

In spite of the attempts to limit women's independence in convents, the religious revival associated with the twelfth century led to thousands of women attempting to take orders or to follow the life of a dedicated chaste bride of God. The Premonstratensians in particular attracted such large numbers of women that the clergy grew fearful. By the end of the twelfth century the general chapter of Premontré had decreed that no more women were to be admitted into the order, and one of the abbots, a certain Conrad of Marchtal, put the reason for rejecting women in these words: "We and our whole community of canons, recognizing that the wickedness of women is greater than all the other wickedness of the world, and there is no anger like that of women, and that the poison of asps and dragons is more curable and less dangerous for men than the familiarity of women, have unanimously decreed for the safety of our souls, no less than for that of our bodies and goods, that we will on no account receive any more sisters to the increase of our perdition, but will avoid them like poisonous animals."[17]

The Cistercian reform movement also attracted large numbers of women, largely to the discomfort of its great champion, Saint Bernard of Clairvaux (1090–1153). St. Bernard saw every woman as a threat to his chastity and worried about the vast and nameless dangers in the easy association of men and women, even those committed to a religious life. "To be always with a woman and not to have intercourse with her is more difficult than to raise the dead. You cannot do the less difficult: do you think I will believe that you can do what is more difficult."[18] A number of Cistercian convents, nonetheless, were founded, but since they had no formal place in the organi-

17. The quotation was translated by R. W. Southern, *Western Society and the Church in the Middle Ages* (London: Penguin, 1970), p. 314.
18. *Ibid.*, pp. 314–315.

zational structure of the order, the nuns had considerable freedom. Some nuns went so far as to hear confessions and preach in the pulpit, much to the scandal of the male clergy. Fearful about what such strong-willed nuns might try to do next, the general chapter of the Cistercian order finally drew up regulations insisting that the so-called Cistercian nuns receive no visitors without permission and make their confession only to a confessor appointed by the supervising abbot, and also prohibited the establishment of any more nunneries. The nuns objected to this high-handed way of attempting to limit their independence, and in the period 1242 to 1244 there was a series of rebellions against such attempts to curtail their independence. The abbess and nuns of Parc-aux-Dames in northern France, for example, shouted and stamped and walked out of the chapter house when the official male visitors told them of the recent legislation. Though there was an attempt to discipline the ringleaders of this female rebellion, some of the most offensive passages in the legislation were eventually rescinded.

It was upon this background that the movement known as the *beguines* appears, a women's religious movement independent of any male impetus or direction. The name *beguine* had been attached to the movement by its opponents in a smear campaign to link its adherents with the Albigensian heretics, but it proved difficult to make the charge of heresy stick. The movement which began in the thirteenth century originally had no organization or constitution, promised no benefits, sought no patrons, and insisted its adherents continue their ordinary work in the world. Many of the women lived in their family homes, others lived together in houses, but it was not where they lived but how they lived which the *beguines* thought was important. Historians tend to agree that the movement was primarily urban and was probably influenced by the fact that in many of the medieval cities at that time there was a significantly higher proportion of women to men due to the large number of men who followed a religious vocation and the male mortality figures associated with war and work. The unmarried and widowed women in these cities individually were often unable to fend for themselves but collectively they could, and it was this group that was attracted to the *beguines*. Normally the *beguines* renounced marriage and took an oath of chastity, but the oath was not irrevocable and it was possible for a *beguine* to later change her mind and be married. The main theme of the *beguine* was dedication to God, but this entailed not only prayer but work, and it was essential that the women devote time and energy to doing good work in the hospitals, in homes for the elderly, or in weaving and embroidery, as well as in praying and meditating. There was a strong ecstatic and visionary aspect in the *beguines*, but there was also a kind of naive sexuality. The *beguines* were not particularly learned, and in fact did not concern themselves with such matters, but instead contended themselves with living "religiously." Nevertheless some of them composed hymns, prayers, and poems which give insight into their beliefs. The erotic nature of their religious commitment might be demonstrated by the following poem about the conflict between soul and body.

> My body is in great distress.
> My soul is in highest bliss,
> for she has seen
> and thrown her arms around
> her Loved One all at once.
> Poor thing,
> she is distressed by him:
> he so draws and delights her,
> she cannot withhold herself,
> and he brings her into himself.
>
> Then the body speaks to the soul:
> "Where have you been? I cannot bear it any more."
> I want to be with my beloved;
> You will never enjoy me any more—
> I am his joy; he is my distress—
> Your distress is, that you can no longer enjoy me:
> You must put up with this distress
> for it will never leave you.[19]

The *beguines* were often associated with the friars, the Franciscans and Dominicans, who were also founded in the thirteenth century and who proved to be their chief supporters. As the *beguines* grew in numbers, however, the church attempted to bring them into organized religious life, and again the criticism against them was their refusal to follow the traditional role of women in religion. A Council of Vienne in 1312 makes this clear:

We have been told that certain women commonly called Beguines,

19. *Ibid.,* p. 327.

afflicted by a kind of madness, discuss the Holy Trinity and the divine essence, and express opinions on matters of faith and sacraments contrary to the catholic faith, deceiving many simple people. Since these women promise no obedience to anyone and do not renounce their property or profess an approved Rule, they are certainly not "religious," although they wear a habit and are associated with such religious orders as they find congenial. . . . We have therefore decided and decreed with the approval of the Council that their way of life is to be permanently forbidden and altogether excluded from the Church of God. . . . In saying this we by no means intend to forbid any faithful women from living as the Lord shall inspire them, provided they wish to live a life of penance and to serve God in humility, even if they have taken no vow of chastity, but live chastely together in their lodgings.[20]

Soon afterward the *beguines* were forced to integrate into orders approved by the pope, and by the fifteenth century those women living under the cloak of religion without a definite rule were sought out and their convents destroyed. The *beguines*, however, left a charitable heritage in the vast number of hospitals and homes for the aged which existed into modern times.

The ambiguity and even hostility to women in religious life was symptomatic of the position of women in secular life. From the information we can gather about the feudal noble in the medieval period it would seem that his chief interest was in his fief (his land) which he had built up or maintained. His great desire was to have an heir worthy to succeed him in his estates, and it was a common belief that a father's traits would be passed on to his heir. It was this belief which probably influenced the laws to regard a wife's adultery, particularly with a social inferior, as a heinous offense. Cowardly and weak barons were believed to be the products of their mothers' adulteries with lesser men. Even if the woman committed adultery with a social equal the biological theories of the day held small hope for the offspring of such unions. This was because it was believed that a child was produced from the merging blood of fathers and mothers. If the wife committed adultery a third element would be added, with the resulting offspring a mixture of the legal father, the mother, and her

20. *Ibid.*, p. 330. For further discussion of the *beguines* see E. W. McDonnell, *The Beguines and Beghards in Medieval Culture* (New Brunswick, N.J.: Rutgers University Press, 1954), and Robert E. Lerner, *The Heresy of the Free Spirit in the Later Middle Ages* (Berkeley and Los Angeles: University of California Press, 1972).

lover, and bound to grow up to become a worthless man not fit to be an heir. The confused concepts about sex were even more obvious in the treatment of sexual relations between Jews and Christians. The law for German Jewry stipulated: "If a Christian lies with a Jewess, or a Jew with a Christian woman, they are both guilty of superharlotry, and they shall be laid one upon the other and be burned; for the Christian has denied the faith."[21] This was one of the rare instances in which the male was punished equally with the female. It was this kind of thinking which strengthened the traditional inclination on the part of the nobles to demand virginal brides, although this never prevented an ambitious noble from marrying a rich widow.[22]

The need for a wife to provide an heir led childless nobles either to dissolve unproductive marriages or to bring in another wife. During much of the medieval period the Christian church fought the customary law which allowed men to divorce their wives with ease, but it was not until the eleventh century that there was any degree of success. Concubines were endemic in the early part of the Middle Ages, and this was perhaps inevitable in a time when wives, particularly noble wives, were chosen for their family connections, marriage portions, and ability to give heirs. Beauty, charm, or compatibility rarely entered into the matter. Inevitably a nobleman was inclined to satisfy his lust where he found the process most pleasant, and concubinage was a matter of course. Male adultery did not have the same social or biological implications as female, and the result was a large number of bastards, some of them quite famous, such as Charles the Bastard and William the Bastard, who are better known as Charles Martel and William the Conqueror. Quite simply women as individuals were not particularly important to the males, and the term "love," in our sense, was almost totally absent in the early medieval period. The favorite stories of the nobility were not of how a man married or failed to marry a woman, but how a holy man went to heaven or how a brave man went to battle. The *Song of Roland,* one of the earliest *Chansons de Geste,* reflected this attitude in its coverage of Alda, the betrothed of Roland, who was only briefly

21. Guido Kisch, *The Jews in Medieval Germany: A Study of Their Legal and Social Status* (reprinted, New York: Ktav Publishing House, 1970), p. 204.
22. Sidney Painter, *French Chivalry* (Baltimore: Johns Hopkins Press, 1940), pp. 98–99.

mentioned. Roland and his loyal supporters killed mountainous heaps of Muslims, but eventually he too was killed, and Charlemagne, his lord, returned to France in sorrow. When Charlemagne entered his palace

> Alda, a lovely maiden, comes to him there.
> She asks the king: "Where is the chieftain count,
> Roland, who swore that I would be his wife?"
> Charles, as she speaks, is overcome with grief;
> Tears fill his eyes, he pulls at his white beard:
> "Sister, sweet friend, I can't bring back the dead.
> But I will give you one better in his place.
> You'll marry Louis—that's all that I can do—
> He is my son, and he shall rule my realm."
> Alda replies, "Your words seem to me strange.
> The saints and angels, and God above forbid
> That I live on when Roland has been slain!"
> Her color fades, she falls down at Charles' feet,
> And dies—may God have mercy on her soul![23]

Quite clearly she was of marginal interest. Roland did not think about her on the battlefield, and her figure was shadowy, and Charlemagne, recognizing her right to a husband, promised her even a better one. The deepest signs of affection in the poem, as well as in similar ones, appear in the love of man for man, the mutual love of warriors who die together fighting against odds, and the affection between the vassal and the lord or within the church, between two clergy, usually an older and a younger.

The feudal male was chiefly absorbed in war and the chase. His wife bore him sons, his mistresses satisfied his momentary lusts, but beyond this women had no particular place in his life, and he was not particularly interested in them as individuals. When they appeared in the feudal literature, at least in the literature prior to the twelfth century, they were pictured either as sex objects or as noble and virtuous wives and mothers, nursing their children, mourning their slain husbands, and exhorting their sons to brave and often cruel deeds. If they dared to confront a male in any other role they were resented and vilified. One of the chansons dealing with the adventures of the sons of Garins indicates how Garins's son Girart was

23. *Song of Roland*, vss. 3708–21. This is from the translation by Patricia Terry (Indianapolis: Bobbs-Merrill, 1965).

affronted by the boldness of a woman. Girart, who became a loyal knight of Charlemagne, was to be rewarded for his services by being given the widowed Duchess of Burgundy as a wife, and this would make his heirs dukes of Burgundy. Before the marriage was finalized, however, Charlemagne himself visited the widow and was so impressed with her and her property that he decided to take her for his own wife. The duchess, in spite of Charlemagne's great reputation, preferred the younger and handsomer Girart, and when he came to see her she had the temerity to request that he hurry and marry her else there would be a long dispute with the king. Girart replied: "Our age begins to be a dreadful one when women go asking men to marry them! On the faith I owe to God, who has us all to save from perdition, from this day onward two years shall pass before I am seen marrying either you or anyone else. So, hunt for another husband— if you can find one. You will never have me, and I tell you that to your face. Do you doubt me?"[24] The duchess prayed to God to give her Girart as husband, but without his positive reaction in demanding her as wife she had to become the wife of the Emperor Charlemagne. Inevitably Girart was upset at her perfidy, but Charlemagne appeased him by giving him the city of Vienne. When Girart went to the bridal chamber to give his thanks for this fief, Charlemagne was already in bed, and when Girart bent over to kiss the foot of his emperor, the duchess, now queen, still enamored of Girart, extended her own from beneath the covers and he kissed it instead. This, when it became known, was not regarded as a sign of affection but as a personal insult to Girart and he went to war with Charlemagne over the matter. The storyteller, naturally, blamed all of Girart's difficulties on the Duchess of Burgundy rather than on his hero's arrogant rudeness.

Sex, nonetheless, was of interest to the feudal noble, and in the epics there were often beautiful and sensual young girls of exalted rank, both Muslim and Christian. Muslim princesses were generally much more suitable for such poems because they not only could rescue their handsome Christian captives from their father's dungeons but could eventually become converted. The baptism of a fair Saracen gave scope to some of the best lyrical efforts of the poets, since the lady could be undressed and her charms and their effect on

24. This is a translation by Norma Lorre Goodrich, *The Ways of Love* (Boston: Beacon Press, 1964), p. 37.

her knightly sponsor described in great detail all with the pious and worthy object of recounting a solemn religious ceremony. There were also a fair number of nubile Christian girls which considerably upset Leon Gautier, one of the nineteenth-century historians of chivalry, who was firmly convinced that the feudal epics mirrored medieval life and yet also was convinced that no proper French girl would act in the way described in some of the epics. He satisfied his conscience by holding that the authors of such poems had very little knowledge of young girls.[25] Without maligning the virtuous character of French medieval womanhood, it seems readily apparent that the poets were not so much dealing with reality as with male erotic dreams. The medieval knight, no less than the modern male, thought erotic thoughts and dreamed erotic dreams, but the medieval knight was nothing if not practical. Only rarely were any of these Christian girls married to the knights on whom they lavished their favors, but instead they were either deserted or passed on to secondary characters. Even fiction seemed to emphasize that marriage was quite a different matter than erotic dreams.

Tied into this concept of erotic thought was the legendary *jus primae noctis* or *droit du seigneur*, stories of which have intrigued the male imagination since medieval times. In popular theory, the *jus primae noctis* was the right of the noble knight to spend the first night with the brides on his estates. Known under various terms, *culagium, jambage, cuissage, gambada, derecho de pernada,* and less accurately as *jus cunnagii, jus cunni, jus coxae locandae, jus coxae luxandae,* it has often been the topic of popular literature from Voltaire to Sir Walter Scott to George Bernard Shaw. The stories were probably derived from references to *culagium,* which was a request for permission to marry. This required that a *marchet* or *merchet* (also *marchetta, marquetta*), a fine, be paid. The fine had originated from the fact that a woman moved into the house of her husband, leaving the jurisdiction of one noble for another. Since such a move technically deprived the lord of part of his property, his human stock, he required indemnification for this loss. Even within a manor it was customary to have the lord's permission to marry, and this often also entailed a fine. In addition, in some dioceses the husband had to pay his bishop or ecclesiastical authority for the privilege of sleeping with his wife on the first night or first few nights of their

25. Leon Gautier, *La chevalerie* (Paris: Victor Palme, 1884), pp. 377–379.

marriage. This, however, was not so much a compensation for the relinquishment of a right but payment for a dispensation, since the medieval church urged newly married couples to observe chastity on their wedding night, and set three nights of chastity as an ideal. In effect the fine was a sort of penance for not observing the rules. Kings Philip VI and Charles VI of France both made efforts in the fourteenth century to induce the Bishops of Amiens to give up their customs of demanding a fine for granting every newly married couple permission to have conjugal intercourse during the first three nights of their marriage.[26] Some authorities, however, persist in arguing that in some areas there was also legal justification for the *jus primae noctis* and that it was a holdover custom from pre-Christian Europe. The center of the controversy gathers around the Celtic populations of Europe, particularly Scotland, where the *Chronicle* of Boecus reported that King Ewen III (about 875 A.D.) established the right of *jus primae noctis*: "Ane othir law he maid, that wiffis of the commonis sal be fre to the nobilis; and the lord of the ground sal have the madinheid of all virginis dwelling on the same." Boece, however, wrote at the beginning of the sixteenth century and his history included many fabulous narratives, of which this was probably one. There are, nevertheless, some authors who believe the account. One investigator concluded: "After weighing all the evidence, it is difficult to avoid the conclusion that the *Jus primae noctis* was the custom, at any rate in some parts of Scotland, in early times. There is no authority to the contrary, nor have any facts inconsistent with such a right ever been advanced by those who challenge it."[27]

In spite of such arguments, it seems to us that the "right of the first night" must be classified as legend rather than fact. The legend, however, still reflects an attitude toward women which was not too far removed from the actual position of many women. In the early medieval period many women had a status little above a slave, and like slaves could be violated more or less with impunity by their lords. Even when slavery had declined in the later medieval period, the more powerful often slept with the less powerful without paying much attention to the legal niceties. It was an honor to be a king's

26. For a discussion of it see Edward Westermarck, *The History of Human Marriage* (3 vols., 5th ed., New York: Allerton Book, 1922), vol. 1, pp. 177–179.

27. Hector MacKechnie, article on the *Ius Primus Noctae, Juridical Review*, 43 (Edinburgh, 1930), pp. 303–311.

mistress, or a king's whore, and while the honor was somewhat less for being a mistress to lesser nobility, there was still prestige attached to the position. The mother of a royal or noble bastard stood to gain too much to reject the advances of a lord or a prospective lord, and even if she herself might suffer, her family could benefit. A lascivious lord, or even a lascivious abbot, and there were a few of these, quite clearly could have the pick of a whole flock of possible companions without resorting to any legendary right of the first night.[28] As far as noble women were concerned, one of the fundamental tenants of feudal law was that the lord would respect the wife of his vassal, and several kings, including John of England, got into trouble when they attempted to ignore such prohibitions.

The Middle Ages were contradictory, and while women them-selves were often treated with little respect or devotion, this was not true of the Virgin Mary. During part of the Middle Ages the exalta-tion of Mary reached such an extent that she became almost the fourth person of the Trinity, and in the popular mind she incorpo-rated the Trinity. In the early Middle Ages there was a tendency to frighten men into heaven, and in the process God became almost a relentless prosecutor while Jesus became Christ the Judge. There was an obvious need for a mediator, and it was Mary who assumed the role. She was the grieving sorrowful mother, sorry that her chil-dren had strayed, but loving them still, regardless of what they had done. In the eyes of most men Jesus was too sublime, too terrible, too just, to deal with effectively, but even the weakest of humans could approach his mother and she could exercise her influence on her son. A Franciscan author of the fourteenth century compared the inter-cession of Mary with the intervention of a queen. He said that when a man sought to turn aside a king's anger:

> He goes secretly to the queen and promises a present, then to the earls and barons and does the same; then to the free men of the household, and lastly to the footmen. So when we have offended Christ, we should first go to the Queen of heaven and offer her, in-

---

28. The best discussion and an invaluable bibliography can be found in Edward Westermarck, *The History of Human Marriage*, I, chap. 5, pp. 166–206. A good brief dicussion of it can be found in Samuel Putnam, "Jus Primae Noctis," in *Encylopaedia Sexualis*, ed. by Victor Robinson (New York: Dingwall-Rock, 1936). Somewhat less accurate is the pamphlet by A. F. Niemoeller, *The Right of the First Night* (Girard, Kansas: Haldeman-Julius, 1948).

stead of a present, prayers, fasting, vigils, and alms; then she, like a mother, will come between thee and Christ, the father who wishes to beat us, and she will throw the cloak of mercy between the rod of punishment and us, and soften the king's anger against us. . . .[29]

Mary, however, remained very feminine and was very much a noble woman with womanly moods and caprices. She loved grace, beauty, ornament, her toilette, robes, jewels, and she demanded attention. She protected her friends and punished her enemies. Though Mary had always been important in medieval Christiandom, some see her as a Christian counterpart to the pagan Isis, and the statues of Mary and Jesus were originally often the same ones representing Isis and Horus. It was with the monastic revival of the eleventh century that she moved to the forefront. This emphasis on Mary then coincided with antagonism to women in the religious life, and one of the great advocates of the Virgin was the very same St. Bernard who basically was so hostile to women. The Cistercian order, founded in 1098, put all of its churches under the special protection of the Virgin, and the result was a vast number of cathedrals dedicated to her, including Notre Dame de Paris (Our Lady of Paris). According to a twelfth-century tradition, which the artist Murillo later utilized as a subject for a famous painting, St. Bernard, a leader of the Cistercians, had once been praying before the statue of the Virgin when the image, pressing its breast, dropped on his lips three drops of the milk from the breast which had nourished the Saviour. Thereafter Bernard was devoted to the Virgin. It was not only the priests and the poor who asked for her assistance but also the nobles. Her attribute was humility; her love and pity were infinite. "Let him deny your mercy who can say that he has ever asked it in vain" was the prayer, and apparently few ever did. Though a woman and not a warrior, she protected warriors, and the favorite battle cry of each side in the various wars of the latter Middle Ages was to Our Lady, Notre Dame. The "Fighting Irish" of Notre Dame emphasize this contradiction on the football field today. Saint Bernard, although condemning womankind, chanted hymns to her:

> O saviour Virgin, Star of Sea,
> Who bore for child the Son of Justice,

---

29. This is quoted in G. G. Coulton, *Five Centuries of Religion* (Cambridge: Cambridge University Press, 1929), vol. 1, p. 140.

The source of Light, Virgin always
>   Hear our praise!

Queen of Heaven who have given
Medicine to the sick, Grace to the devout
Joy to the sad, Heaven's light to the world
>   And hope of salvation;

Court royal, Virgin typical,
Grant us cure and guard,
Accept our vows, and by prayers
>   Drive all griefs away![30]

Not only was the Son absorbed into the Mother, or represented as under her guardianship, but the Father fared no better, while the Holy Ghost nearly disappeared. Some of the poets regarded her as the temple of the Trinity, the church itself, and in the building of a church the Trinity as represented by the triple aisle was absorbed in her. Undoubtedly part of this elevation of the Virgin was due to a masculine tendency to feminize things such as ships, institutions such as the church, and buildings such as cathedrals. The priest was married to the church, and it was much easier to visualize this in feminine form than in masculine, but the interesting thing is that women as a whole benefited so little from this emphasis upon Mary.

In fact the very opposite tended to happen. The growth of a romantic and devotional literature extolling women only strengthened the belief in the moral and social dangers of feminine wantonness. The emphasis on virginity tended to create in many minds an almost hysterical aversion to the state of matrimony. In the devotional literature it was Mary as Virgin who was elevated. Though she was a mother figure, she was also an immaculate mother figure who not only remained a virgin but had herself been conceived without sin, which, in medieval terminology, meant without intercourse. Women might be of the same sex as Mary but they were also the same as Eve, and it was as Eve that woman kept reminding the religious man of his sinfulness, of his desire to have sex. Lust itself was a sin, and sexual intercourse, except for the purpose of procreation, was regarded by the church as a sin equal to murder and heresy. Some of

---

30. The translation is by Henry Adams and appears in his *Mont Saint-Michel and Chartres* (reprinted, Boston: Houghton Mifflin, 1933), pp. 93–96. The whole book is devoted to a discussion of the Virgin in medieval life.

the early penitentials, guidelines for giving penances, went so far as to prohibit intercourse between married couples during and shortly after menstruation, on Sundays, feastdays, and in any other position but face to face.[31] Woman made man aware of his bodily responses. "He who loves a woman in his mind shall seek pardon from God; but if he has spoken [to her], that is, of love and friendship, but is not received by her, he shall do penance for seven days."[32] As the medieval church put more and more emphasis on celibacy for the priesthood, women came to be more and more condemned. Part of the reason for this was that though some men apparently came easily to the celibate life, many found it a traumatic experience to fight off sexual temptation. This was woman's fault: "If a presbyter kisses a woman from desire, he shall do penance for forty days. Likewise if a presbyter is polluted through imagination [has orgasm] he shall fast for a week."[33] Even close association could lead to a need for penance:

> But if one of the clerical order is on familiar terms with any woman and he has himself done no evil with her, neither by cohabitating with her nor by lascivious embraces, this is his penance: For such time as he has done this he shall withdraw from the communion of the altar and do penance for forty days and nights with bread and water and cast out of his heart his fellowship with the woman, and so be restored to the altar. If, however, he is on familiar terms with women and has given himself to association with them and to their lascivious embraces, but has, as he says, preserved himself from ruin, he shall do penance for half a year with an allowance of bread and water, and for another half year he shall abstain from wine and meat and he shall not surrender his clerical office; and after an entire year of penance, he shall join himself to the altar. If any cleric lusts after a virgin or any woman in his heart but does not utter [his wish] with lips, if he sins thus but once he ought to do penance for seven days with an allowance of bread and water. But if he continually lusts and is unable to indulge his desire, since the woman does not permit him or since he is ashamed to speak, still he has committed adultery with her in his heart. It is the same sin though it be in the heart and not in

31. *The Penitential of Theodore*, XIV, 19, 20, 21, in John T. McNeill and Helena M. Gamer, eds. and trans., *Medieval Handbooks of Penance* (New York: Columbia University Press, 1938), p. 197.
32. *Ibid.*, II, 22, on p. 186.
33. *Ibid.*, VIII, 2–3, on p. 191.

the body; yet the penance is not the same. This is his penance: let him do penance for forty days with bread and water.[34]

With such fear of women engrained in the clergy, it was perhaps inevitable that the clergy would condemn them, while at the same time admire them through the Virgin. The contradictory nature of these feelings is demonstrated by the fact that the height of Virgin worship came in the thirteenth century at the same time that clerical celibacy became the law of the church. The elevation of the Virgin could only be accomplished by comparing her with the characteristics of ordinary women, and the more she was exalted, the more ordinary women failed to come anywhere near the ideal and the more they could be condemned for their failures.

As the Wife of Bath in Chaucer's *Canterbury Tales* said: "By God, if women had but written satires/ Like those the clergy keep in oratores,/ More had been written of man's wickedness/ Than all the sons of Adam could redress."[35] It was the male view which appeared in writing, particularly in clerical literature, so much so that the Wife of Bath claimed that she could find no cleric who would speak well of women. Salimbene, the thirteenth-century Franciscan, collected several sayings about women in his autobiography, and some of these phrases were published by G. G. Coulton, who felt they were typical of medieval clerical attitudes about women.

With flames of fire doth a woman sear the conscience of him who dwelleth by her.

Where women are with men, there shall be no lack of the devil's birdlime.

Wouldst thou define or know what woman is? She is glittering mud, a stinking rose, sweet poison, ever leaning towards that which is forbidden her.

Woman is adamant, pitch, buckthorn, a rough thistle, a clinging burr, a stinging wasp, a burning nettle.

Man hath three joys—praise, wisdom, and glory: which three things are overthrown and ruined by woman's art.

34. *The Penitential of Finnian* (sixth century), pars. 14–17 in McNeill and Gamer, *Medieval Handbooks*, pp. 89–90.
35. Geoffrey Chaucer, *The Canterbury Tales*, trans. into modern English by Nevill Coghill (Baltimore: Penguin, 1952), "The Wife of Bath's Prologue," vs. 693–696, pp. 300–301.

What else is woman but a foe to friendship, an inevitable penance, a necessary evil, a natural temptation, a coveted calamity, a domestic peril, a pleasant harm, the nature of evil painted over with the colours of good; wherefore it is a sin to desert her, but a torment to keep her.

Woman was evil from the beginnings, a gate of death, a disciple of the servant, the devil's accomplice, a fount of deception, a dogstar to godly labours, rust corrupting the saints; whose perilous face hath overthrown such as had already become almost angels.

Lo, woman is the head of sin, a weapon of the devil, expulsion from Paradise, mother of guilt, corruption of the ancient law.[36]

This from a man who worshiped the Virgin Mary and had many women under his spiritual guidance.

The official attitudes of the church can be found in the writings of the great thirteenth-century doctor of the church, St. Thomas Aquinas. Aquinas approached the subject of women from the point of view of one who believed in clerical celibacy and held that virginity was preferable to marriage. From this it almost inevitably followed that "venereal pleasures above all debauch a man's mind," and nothing "so casts down the manly mind from its height as the fondling of a woman." To love a woman too ardently, even if she is one's own wife, constituted adultery to the good Saint Thomas.[37] Still he recognized that women were human and had a right to exist, although he felt a need to justify her existence since according to Aristotle woman was only a "misbegotten male," and "nothing misbegotten or defective should have been in the first production of things." Aquinas felt Aristotle was wrong. Woman, he argued, was not misbegotten but included in nature's intentions in order to continue the works of generation. She was, however, naturally subject to man. "For good order would have been wanting in the human family if some were not governed by others wiser than themselves. So by such a kind of subjection woman is naturally subject to man, because in man the discretion of reason predominates." Woman in fact had been cre-

36. Translated in G. G. Coulton, *From St. Francis to Dante: A Translation of All that Is of Primary Interest in the Chronicle of the Franciscan Salimbene (1221–1288)* (London: David Nutt, 1906), pp. 91–92.
37. St. Thomas Aquinas, *Summa Theologica*, ed. and trans. by the Fathers of the English Dominican Province (3 vols., New York: Benzinger, 1947), vol. 2, pt. 2, ques. 152, "Of Virginity," art. 4, ques. 153, "Of Lust," arts. 1, 2, and ques. 154, "Of the Parts of Lust," art. 8.

ated as a helper to man, "not, indeed, as a helpmate in other works, as some say, since man can be more efficiently helped by another man in other works; but as a helper in the works of generation. . . . Among perfect animals the active power of generation belongs to the male sex, and the passive power to the female. . . ." This was why the first woman was created from man, rather than following the normative principle of generation and having man born of woman. Thus just as "God is the principle of the whole universe, so the first man, in likeness to God, was the principle of the whole human race. . . . Secondly, that man might love woman all the more, and cleave to her more closely, knowing her to be fashioned from himself. . . . Thirdly, because . . . man is the head of woman . . . it was suitable for woman to be made out of man. . . . Fourthly, there is a sacramental reason for this. For by this is signified that the Church takes her origin from Christ." But why was woman created from Adam's rib? "First, to signify the social union of man and woman, for the woman should neither use authority over man, and so she was not made from his head; nor was it right for her to be subject to man's contempt as his slave, and so she was not made from his feet." By delegating the power of gestation to females, God also left men freer to pursue a higher aim, namely, intellectual tasks.[38]

Aquinas's chief task was to incorporate the concepts of Greek science and philosophy into Christian thinking, and in this he also had to come to terms with Greek biology. Aristotle, for example, had said that the father provided a child's soul while the mother supplied only formless matter. Christians, on the other hand, believed that the soul came from God, and this belief would have left the earthly father with no contribution at all. To solve this problem St. Thomas concluded that "the father is principle in a more excellent way than the mother, because he is the active principle, while the mother is a passive and material principle. Consequently, strictly speaking, the father is to be loved more . . . the mother supplied the formless matter of the body; and the latter receives its form through the formative power that is in the semen of the father. And though this power cannot create the rational soul, yet it disposes the matter of the body to receive that form."[39] St. Thomas had observed that women often

38. *Ibid.*, vol. 1, pt. 1, ques. 92, "The Production of Women."
39. *Ibid.*, vol. 2, pt. 2, ques. 26, "Whether a Man Ought to Love His Mother More than His Father," art. 10.

led men to lust, and this led him to wonder whether the tendency of women to adorn themselves constituted mortal sin. He concluded that a married woman might adorn herself somewhat to please her husband, "lest through despising her he fall into adultery," but for a woman without a husband to do so only gave lustful pleasure to men who saw them. Thus "if women adorn themselves with the intention of provoking others to lust they sin mortally; whereas if they do so from frivolity, or from vanity for the sake of ostentation, it is not always mortal, but sometimes venial. And the same applies to men."[40] St. Thomas, however, recognized the right of people to distinguish their estate by their clothing and also to disguise a disfigurement. When a costume or disguise went to excess, became fantastic, or excited lust, then it was to be regarded as sinful.

Even an unadorned woman had dangerous seductive properties, and medieval clerics attempted to overcome their desires by denying that the female body was attractive at all. A thirteenth-century writer compared a woman who let herself be seen by men to a person who uncovered a pit for people to fall into: "The pit is her fair face, and her white neck, and her light eye, and her hand, if she stretch it forth in his sight . . . all that belongs to her, whatsoever it be, through which sinful love might the sooner be excited."[41] Moreover a woman who either consciously or unconsciously tempted a man to sin should be held responsible for his lost soul on the day of judgment. Nevertheless women should remember that their bodies were hardly enticing: "what fruit doth thy flesh bear in all its apertures? Amidst the greatest ornament of thy face; that is, the fairest part between the taste of mouth and smell of nose, hast thou not two holes, as if they were two privy holes? Art thou not formed of foul slime? Art thou not always full of uncleanness? Shalt thou not be food for worms?"[42]

Johann Herolt was a fifteenth-century Dominican and only one of many[43] who believed that women were more likely to suffer the fires of Hell than men because

40. *Ibid.*, vol. 2, pt. 2, ques. 169, "Whether the Adornment of Women Is Devoid of Mortal Sin?," art. 11.

41. *The Ancren Riwle (Rule for Anchoresses)*, ed. and trans. by James Morton in Camden Society, *Publications*, 57 (1853), p. 59.

42. *Ibid.*, p. 277.

43. See G. R. Owst, *Literature and Pulpit in Medieval England* (Oxford: Blackwell, 1961), pp. 375ff.

most women belie their catholic faith with charms and spells, after the fashion of Eve their first mother, who believed the devil speaking through the serpent rather than God Himself. . . . Even nowadays, the most part of women imitate Eve in pride and unbelief; for it is well known that a girl of nine years old will go more curiously apparelled than a boy of eighteen; and when she is too old to dare to adorn herself, then will she follow pride and vainglory in tricking out her daughter or her niece. So also will she busy herself more than a man in unbelief and enchantments; for any woman by herself, knows more of such superstitions and charms than a hundred men.[44]

Why did women put up with such libelous characterizations? Probably because they did not know the full extent of them. Clerical misogyny was often intended only for clerical listeners, and public statements on the subject were only uttered by some of the more extreme members of the celibate priesthood.[45] The church leaders had to keep in mind that occasionally women, too, might have money or power and could endow convents, monasteries, churches, or colleges. While women might be more susceptible to sin than men, they could not be condemned entirely, and in their public utterances some clerics exercised considerable caution. Humbert de Romans, a thirteenth-century master general of the Dominican order, for example, left a sermon which he intended as a model for other friars to use when they preached to women. It gave a somewhat different view of women than usually expressed by clerics. He said that

God gave women many prerogatives, not only over other living things but even over man himself, and this (i) by nature; (ii) by grace; and (iii) by glory. (i) In the world of nature she excelled man by her origin, for man He made of the vile earth, but woman He made in Paradise. Man He formed of the slime, but woman of man's rib. She was not made of a lower limb of man—as for example of his foot—lest man should esteem her his servant, but from his midmost part, that he should hold her to be his fellow, as Adam himself said: "The Woman Whom Thou gavest as my helpmate." (ii) In the world of grace she excelled man, for God, Who could have taken flesh of a man, did not do so, but took flesh of a woman. Again, we

44. Coulton, *Five Centuries of Religion*, vol. 1, p. 180.
45. Eileen Power, "The Position of Women," in *The Legacy of the Middle Ages*, ed. by G. C. Crump and E. F. Jacob (Oxford: Clarendon Press, 1926), p. 403.

do not read of any man trying to prevent the Passion of Our Lord, but we do read of a woman who tried—namely, Pilate's wife—to dissuade her husband from so great a crime because she had suffered much in a dream because of Christ. Again, at His Ressurection, it was to a woman He first appeared—namely, to Mary Magdalen. (iii) In the world of glory, for the king in that country is no mere man but a mere woman is its queen [Mary]. It is not a mere man who is set above the angels and all the rest of the heavenly court, but a mere woman is; nor is anyone who is merely man as powerful there as is a mere woman. Thus is woman's nature in Our Lady raised above woman's in worth, dignity, and power; and this should lead women to love God and to hate evil.[46]

Even when the clergy spoke favorably of women, however, they emphasized that women were always to be subject to men. "Woman is subject to man on account of the frailty of nature, as regards both vigor of soul and strength of body. After the resurrection, however, the difference in those points will be not on account of the difference of the sex, but by reason of the difference of merits."[47] It was this state of subjection which kept her from holding the priesthood. "Since it is not possible in the female sex to signify eminence of degree, for a woman is in the state of subjection, it follows that she cannot receive the sacrament of order."[48] A man's duty was to provide for the things of the house and it was woman's duty to attend to the affairs of the family of the house. As an Italian writer of the fourteenth century in his advice to women put it: "The seventh commandment is that thou shalt not do any great thing of thine own accord without the consent of thy husband, however, good reason there seem to be unto thee for doing it: and take care thou dost on no account say to him, 'My advice is better than thine,' even though truly it was better, for by so doing thou couldst easily drive him into great anger against thee and great hatred."[49] In this respect royal women were not different from lesser women, and Louis IX (1214–1270), the saintly king of France, wrote to his daughter, Isabella, Queen of Navarre, on the role she should play. "Dear daughter, because I think you hearken more to my words than anyone for the

46. Bede M. Jarrett, *Social Theories of the Middle Ages* (reprinted, New York: Ungar, 1966), pp. 72–73.
47. St. Thomas Aquinas, *Summa Theologica*, supp. ques. 81, "Of the Quality of Those Who Rise Again," art. 3, reply obj. 2.
48. *Ibid.*, supp., ques. 39, "Of the Impediments to This Sacrament," art. 1, obj. 3.
49. Quoted by Jarrett, *Social Theories of the Middle Ages*, p. 75.

love you bear me, I propose to give you some advice. . . . Accustom yourself to confess frequently and select always confessors of holy life and good education. . . . Obey your husband humbly and your father and mother also in all that is pleasing to God. You must give to each of them your due for the love that you have for them and still more you should do it for the love of Our Lord."[50]

Though the typical woman was probably wife and housekeeper, subject to her husband, marriage was not the lot of every woman in the Middle Ages. In many areas of Europe, if not all, adult women were in excess of men. Though medieval population estimates were often inaccurate, there is some indication of sex ratios in the fourteenth- and fifteenth-century censuses taken in some of the German towns. Frankfort, for example, had 1,100 women for every 1,000 men in 1385, and Nuremberg in 1449 had 1,246 women for 1,000 men. Though the figures might be misleading since many widows from the country retired to the towns, the various wars and feuds took a higher toll of males than females. The vast number of unmarried clergy and monks helped create a surplus of unmarried women, since there were only comparatively few nuns, most of whom were from aristocratic families. Even at the lowest level of medieval society, on the manors, there were women without husbands, some of them widows but many of whom had never married. This unmarried status was not such an obstacle since there was plenty of work to do on estates and women engaged in almost every kind of agricultural labor with the exception of plowing. Though the tasks assigned to women varied from manor to manor and within the manor according to their status, they always had control of the dairy, the poultry, and the vegetable garden. In the cities, also, they carried on a variety of trades. Most craft guilds had provisions for widows to follow their husbands' occupation, and some occupations were reserved to women. Throughout Europe they dominated the manufacture of beer and much of the processes of textile manufacture. In fact, the very word "spinster" would indicate that spinning was not only the regular occupation of all women but also the habitual means of support for many of the unmarried. Still many craft regulations excluded females, and when they did work they often did so at wages lower than that of the man.[51]

50. *Ibid.*, pp. 75–76.
51. Power, "Position of Women," pp. 410–412.

Nevertheless Roman and Germanic tradition had always been opposed to confining women in a harem under the custody of servants, and regardless of their economic status women always had considerably more personal freedom than their sisters in the East. Even though the noble woman was completely subject to her husband, she was still mistress of the household. She supervised the performance of household tasks and the younger children received their training from her. When the nobility of Europe went forth to do battle it was their wives who managed their affairs at home, superintended the farming, interviewed the tenants, and saved up money for their husband's next expedition. A good and loyal wife was the best and strongest support a man away on a crusade or a war could leave behind. She not only administered his estates but also provided hospitality for wandering travelers, and it was probably her ability to be mistress at home which was an influential force in helping change some of the literary portraits of women.

Literature is molded by the type of audience it has. In much of the past the audience that counted most was male. It was the men who had the money to hire poets to sing their praises and to recount the epic stories of war. When prose developed it was men who were usually literate since so many obstacles were put into the path of women who wanted to be educated. During the Middle Ages the most literate group was of course the clergy and in their literature women, as indicated, had very little place. Women, even if they could not read, could still be patrons of literature, and it was this right of patronage which led to the development of romantic love.

Sidney Painter speculated that the whole thing started one day when a hungry minstrel who was wandering about the duchy of Aquitaine came to a castle where he hoped that his tales of battles and his tumbling tricks would earn him a good dinner. The lord of the castle, however, was absent and the lady who acted as his hostess found his endless stories of battles rather tiring and boring, and could care less for his tumbling. It somehow occurred to the poet that his stay in the castle would not be very long nor would his meals be particularly enjoyable unless he managed to gain her attention. Being very inventive he composed a song in praise of the lady's beauty and virtue and described their effect on him in rather glowing terms. Naturally he found the lady was quite pleased, and she rewarded him with a better bed and more ample food. Soon other minstrels followed his example and it was not long before the baronial halls of southern France were ringing with songs in praise of ladies who were able to dispense lavish hospitality, and any lady who did not have a minstrel singing her virtues felt definitely out of fashion. On this scene came William IX, count of Poitous and duke of Aquitaine, who thought such songs might prove a pleasant accompaniment to his numerous triumphs over feminine virtue and with which he could entertain his companions. The duke's accounts of his amorous adventures not so surprisingly proved as interesting to his friends as his stories of battles, and with the example of a powerful prince who ruled a third of France to spur them, the fashion grew and expanded. Those barons who were unable to sing or write could hire someone to do so.[52]

Scholars have spent a good deal of time and energy in trying to trace the sources of romantic love to Islamic lyric poetry, to Greek Platonism, to Ovid—apparently all contributory factors—but it was probably the ability of women to act as patrons which was the cement that bound together these various elements. Romantic love was associated with knighthood and chivalry, and in poems and literature love was pictured as a despairing and tragic emotion which drove the lover to accomplish great deeds of derring do for his beloved and the Christian God. In theory true love was unattainable love, that is, it was not to be consummated by sexual intercourse; in fact, the female object of the love was usually married to a man other than her beloved. This theory undoubtedly reflected the real situation of the noble ladies who acted as patrons. Adultery probably occurred in some cases where reality coincided with theory, but the medieval poet usually condemned any such amorous interludes. The theory of romantic love espoused first by the eleventh-century French poets eventually spread throughout Europe and "effected a change which has left no corner of our ethics, our imagination, or our daily life untouched and they erected impassable barriers between us and the classical past or the Oriental present."[53] Our code of etiquette with its rule that women always have precedence is based upon the concepts of romantic love, and the concept of the gentle courteous male,

52. Sidney Painter, *French Chivalry* (Baltimore: Johns Hopkins Press, 1957), pp. 111–112.

53. C. S. Lewis, *The Allegory of Love* (New York: Oxford University Press, 1958), p. 4.

the housebroken male if you will, is part and parcel of the whole tradition. In a sense romantic love represents a break from the Christian tradition which emphasized that all love, or at least any such thing as passionate love, was more or less wicked unless it was directed to God. Thus it does not seem to arise so much from the worship of the blessed virgin as it does from a parody of the religious teachings of the Middle Ages.

In the chivalric literature love was the emotion produced by the unrestrained adoration of a lady. Love might be rewarded by smiles, kisses, or still other favors, but the presence or absence of these was not supposed to have any effect on the love itself. The male in love lost interest in food and drink, scarcely noticed whether it was hot or cold outside, and concentrated every fiber of his being on his love for his lady. Love encouraged the development of *preux*, skill and knightly honor, and made a cowardly man valiant, a brave man braver. In fact, according to the chivalric literature, it was even doubtful whether a man who did not adore a lady could ever be a true knight. Though a woman could not fight, she gave man courage, skill, and honor—in short, she had ennobling qualities. Thus was born the myth of feminine mystique which raised woman to a pedestal. The true lady was a sort of passive goddess who was adored whether she wished to be or not, and while the knight was expected to serve his adored one with every fiber of his body, the service primarily consisted of fidelity and worship. Love was not to be mutual. The lady might or might not reward him, but at first in any case she was not to feel any great passion. She was a vision of love and like the Virgin Mary she was unattainable.

There were, however, some modifications in this ideal during the course of the later Middle Ages. As troubadour poetry moved northward, sexual intercourse became an integral and sometimes necessary part of the conception of love; knights also felt called upon to make themselves attractive to ladies. How often did the love end in ultimate consummation? The answer was dependent on the poet's or hero's status. When the poet was a great lord he was undoubtedly rewarded by sharing the bed with his lady love; if he was just a humble knight praising the wife of a great baron, he kept his distance.

One of the great patrons of the chivalric poets was Eleanor of Aquitaine (c. 1122–1204), one of the most remarkable women in medieval history. She was the granddaughter and heir of Duke William of Aquitaine who helped formulate the concepts of chivalric love, and her possession of Aquitaine made her the most desirable of brides. She became the wife first of Louis VII, the king of France, and then, after her divorce, to Henry II of England. She was the mother of Richard the Lionhearted and King John of Magna Carta fame, but even she could not exercise power directly, only through attempting to manipulate the men around her. She spent most of the last part of her life in enforced confinement while her husband spent his time with his mistress. Even queens had to know their place and it was Eleanor's misfortune that she did not.[54] Eleanor's position as patroness of the new romantic concepts of love and womanhood was assumed by her daughters, Marie, countess of Champagne, and Alix, countess of Blois. The *minnesingers* of Germany and the poets of Italy spread the concepts eastward and southward. The original ideas were refortified by the translation of Ovid's *Ars Amoris* into the vernacular by Chretien de Troyes, one of the great poets of the new love lyrics. A philosophy of love developed and the new amalgam appeared in the writings of Andreas Capellanus, a member of Marie's household, and author of *The Art of Courtly Love.*

Love to Andreas was a passion which came from looking at and thinking too much about the body of a member of the opposite sex; it could only be satisfied by embracing and fulfilling love's commands, in other words, by sexual intercourse. Love, however, was still separate from marriage. Marriage was a contractual obligation while love was entirely voluntary. True love might well become adulterous but it need not end up that way. The fact that he might really be sanctioning adultery or at least fornication troubled Andreas, and his book is full of ambiguities. How much his concepts might have modified attitudes toward women is evident from the last section of his book entitled "The Rejection of Love," which is little more than a diatribe against the female sex. Why he wrote the book if he felt this way is unclear, but he cleansed his hands of all blame when he concluded by saying that it was all woman's fault that she was so sexual, and she, not man, should take the blame.[55] Andreas's concept of love was, nonetheless, limited only to the upper

54. See Amy Kelly, *Eleanor of Aquitaine and the Four Kings* (Cambridge: Harvard University Press, 1950).

55. Andreas Capellanus, *The Art of Courtly Love*, trans. by J. J. Parry (New York: Columbia University Press, 1941), bk. 1, chaps. 1–4, and final section.

classes. He wrote that it was very unlikely that the lower classes would have the necessary virtues for love. If a man desired a peasant woman so strongly he could not resist temptation, Andreas felt he should rape her on the spot since a courteous approach would only be wasted on a woman who could not possibly feel love.[56]

The dualism so evident in Andreas appeared also in the classic, thirteenth-century *The Romance of the Rose*, written by Guillaume de Lorris and Jean de Meung. Within a framework of courtly love, the poem contained a satire on women's artifice, folly, and greed, although in this case the two contradictory elements were contributed by different authors. In the original segment of the poem by Guillaume de Lorris the poet was conducted to the Palace of Pleasure where he met love and her companions Sweet-Looks, Riches, Jollity, Courtesy, Liberality, and Youth, who spend their time in dancing, singing, and other amusements. Eventually the poet reached a bed of roses and while he was attempting to pluck one, an arrow from Cupid's bow pierced him and he fell fainting to the ground. Upon his recovery he found himself alone, far removed from the rose bed, and he set out on a quest to find his beloved rose. Just as he again found it and touched it with his lips, he was taken prisoner and the key to the castle door was given to an old hag. As the poet was mourning over his fate the original poem ended. In the second part, Jean de Meung then mounted his vendetta against women and it is at least worthy of note that he chose to express his misogynistic ideas within the framework of a romantic allegory.[57] Woman might well be placed on a pedestal of love but her position at best was rather precarious.

The *Romance of the Rose* represented a kind of reaction to the sensuousness of some of the romantic literature. A century later, with Sir Thomas Malory's *Le Morte d'Arthur*, the classical summary of the Arthur legends and romantic love, virginity was firmly in the saddle. Malory emphasized that the sin which prevented some Knights of the Round Table from achieving a vision of the Holy Grail was desire for women. Only Sir Galahad and Sir Percival were "like maidens clean and without spot," while one other, Sir Bors de Banis, had only once trespassed and after that had "kept himself so

56. *Ibid.*, bk. 1, chap. 11.
57. Guillaume de Lorris and Jean de Meung, *The Romance of the Rose*, trans. by F. S. Ellis (London: J. M. Dent, 1900).

well in chastity that all is forgiven him."[58] In the course of the quest, two of the successful knights, Percival and Bors, were tempted by devils in the guise of beautiful women, and Percival punished himself for almost yielding by stabbing himself deeply in the thigh. Galahad, however, was not even tempted, presumably because he was so pure and holy he was immune to sexual attraction. In the end, after the destruction of the Round Table, all the surviving knights became hermits which perhaps can be regarded as a symbolical rejection of women. Malory continually showed women ruining men. Morgan le Fay, for example, tried to destroy her virtuous and devoted brother, King Arthur, as well as to undermine virtue in general. Morgan hated all men but particularly Arthur because he was the most eminent of her kin; she stole his sword, replaced it with a brittle replica, and sent him a mantle intended to burn him to death. She also tried to lead Lancelot and Tristam, the best of knights, into fatal ambushes. Guinevere, the wife of King Arthur, through her spiteful behavior to Lancelot brought about the ruin of the Round Table.[59]

In the fourteenth-century story of *Gawain and the Green Knight*, it was also woman as temptress who emerges, indicating that in spite of the chivalric ideal the view of women was slow to change. Gawain had managed to pass a whole series of tests of his courage and chastity in part through the gift of a life-saving girdle by the wife of his host. He felt guilty for concealing this gift from his host, who in fact had ordered his wife to tempt Sir Gawain. It was the woman who was blamed for all Sir Gawain's troubles, and he departed with a burst of invective:

> But no marvel it is for a fool to act madly,
> Through woman's wiles to be brought to woe.
> So for certain was Adam deceived by some woman,
> By several Solomon, Samson besides;
> Delilah dealt him his doom; and David
> Was duped by Bath-sheba, enduring much sorrow.
> Since these were grieved by their guile, 'twould be
>   great gain
> To love them yet never believe them, if knights could.

58. Sir Thomas Malory, *Le Morte d'Arthur*, ed. by A. W. Pollard (reprinted, New Hyde Park, N.Y.: University Books, 1961), bk. XVI, chaps. 1, 3.

59. *Ibid.*, VI, iii; IX, xli, xlii.

For formerly these [men] were most noble and fortunate,
More than all other who lived on earth;

And these few
By women's wiles were caught
With whom they had to do.
Though I'm beguiled, I ought
To be excused now too.[60]

Even in the Robin Hood literature it was a woman who was to blame
for Robin Hood's death. Robin Hood, seeking help from his cousin,
the Prioress of Kirkly Abbey, was bled to death by her, and by the
time he realized what was happening he was too weak to escape. He
managed to blow a blast on his horn and Little John came running,
begging for permission to get revenge by destroying the nunnery.
Robin Hood as he lay dying forbade this since he said he had never
hurt a woman in his life.[61] Women were to be protected but they
could not be trusted. A true lady was a fine creature but one never
found out who was a true lady until too late.

Late medieval literature in fact remained full of misogynous portraits of women. One of the most virulent assaults upon women was
by John of Salisbury, who collected almost every possible example
of troublesome women in history, mythology, and literature from
Diana, goddess of hunt, to his own time. John considered hunting
self-indulgent and vicious and he claimed that the Greeks had only
put a woman as patron because they did not wish to degrade their
gods by making them sponsors of such a degrading pastime. Cleopatra was another one of his subjects, and he regarded her suicide a
worthy death for a poisonous courtesan who tried to corrupt the
character and virtue of noble men. John felt that though matrimony
might be justified because it excused lustful pleasure, in all cases
single loneliness was much better than marital bliss.[62] Women were
frivolous, passionate, cruel, and immodest.

John was a cleric but this was not simply a continuation of clerical

60. "Gawain and the Green Knight," trans. by T. H. Banks in *The Age of Chaucer*,
ed. by William Frost (Englewood Cliffs, N.J.: Prentice Hall, 1950), 11, 2414–28,
p. 317.
61. See Katharine M. Rogers, *The Troublesome Helpmate* (Seattle: University of
Washington Press, 1966), pp. 59–60.
62. John of Salisbury, *Frivolities of Courtiers and Footprints of Philosophers*, trans.
from portions of the *Policraticus* by J. B. Pike (London: Oxford University Press,
1938), pp. 355, 358, 360, 363.

misogyny, since most books were written by antifeminist writers. It might even be that books were regarded by some as a replacement for women. Richard de Bury, the fourteenth-century Bishop of Durham, said it was woman, which men should "flee more than the asp and the bailisk," who make it plain that "we [books] alone of all the furniture in the house are superfluous and complains that we are worthless for any service of the household. Soon she advises that we be exchanged for costly caps, for muslim and silk, for twice-dyed purple, for robes, and silver-colored furs, and for wool and linen. . . ." Nonetheless it was only books which could offer salvation and not women.[63] Women merely detracted men from the higher causes. Walter Map (fl. 1200) in his *Courtiers' Trifles* attacked marriage with a vengeance. "Even the very good woman, who is rarer than the phoenix, cannot be loved without the loathsome bitterness of fear and worry and constant unhappiness . . . and many maladies interrupted by the alternation of health are less painful than one illness which affecteth us with incurable pangs. . . . My friend, may the omnipotent God grant thee power not to be deceived by the deceit of the omnipotent female, and may He illuminate thy heart, that thou wilt not, with eyes bespelled, continue on the way. . . ."[64]

The late Middle Ages were caught up in contradictions. Officially, at least as represented by the clerical and scientific writers, the concept that sex was bad and that sexuality was sinful was accepted. Yet at the same time the cult of courtly love, emphasizing the erotic, was elevated, and the idea that the love of woman was the force that improved man's character and elevated his spirit was advanced. Unfortunately love also led to sex and even to adultery, and this was always the fault of women. Women were praised on the one hand and damned on the other. They were the butt of satire, some of it good-natured and some of it malicious: "For take my word for it, there is no libel/ On women that the clergy will not paint,/ Except when writing of a woman-saint,/ But never good of other women, though."[65] This is the complaint of Chaucer's Wife of Bath. Women were still essential if a man was to have children, and economically

63. Richard de Bury (Aungerville), *The Philobiblon*, with intro. by Archer Taylor (Berkeley: University of California Press, 1948), pp. 23–24, *passim*.

64. Walter Map, *De Nugis Curialium (Courtiers' Trifles)*, ed. by Frederick Tupper and Marbury Bladen Ogle (London: Chatto and Windus, 1924), pp. 186–198.

65. Chaucer, "The Wife of Bath's Prologue," vs. 688–692, *Canterbury Tales*, pp. 300–301.

wives in most cases were not only helpful but also an asset. Still marriage at best was a kind of partnership, and partnerships often prove troublesome. In a society in which marriage was rated as the second-best thing, as it was in the medieval period, it would seem that large numbers of men might rebel against the limitations put upon them by marriage, and blame much of their difficulty on their wives, particularly on wives who did not keep their place. The ideal wife appeared in the story of Griselda, recounted by Chaucer in English, by Boccaccio in Italian, by Petrarch in Latin, and probably elsewhere. Though such a person as Griselda never existed, she was the ideal by which other wives were measured, and inevitably all came up short, subject to criticism. The theme of the story was simple. A nobleman, anxious to continue his line, hunted for a wife. He examined all prospects but finally agreed to marry one of his own serfs, Griselda, providing that she would promise to cheerfully comply with his every wish and never show the slightest dissatisfaction. She agreed, and much to his surprise she became a model wife, pleasing him in every way and fulfilling all her duties and functions. He, nevertheless, continually tested her submissiveness. When she gave birth to a daughter he told her that he must have the child killed. The pluperfect Griselda replied: "My child and I are your possession/ And at your pleasure; on my heart's profession/ We are all yours and you may spare or kill/ What is your own. Do therefore as you will." Though pleased with the answer, he had the child removed. Griselda never even sighed, although she did beg the man who came to take the child to bury the little body unless her lord objected. When she gave birth to a second child, a boy, he too was taken away. Again Griselda remained calm and peaceful, adhering to her husband's orders. Still he was not satisfied. To test her still further he announced to her that she must go back to her father since he had decided to take another wife. Griselda obediently responded: "My lord, I know as I have always done/ That, set against your high magnificence,/ My poverty makes no comparison./ It cannot be denied, and I for one/ Was never worthy, never in my life,/ To be your chambermaid, much less your wife." After she cheerfully returned to her father's hovel, her husband was satisfied with her true obedience. He finally revealed to her that his new bride was really her daughter, that her son was also alive, and she remained his wife. He had just devised these innocent schemes to test her.

On hearing this Griselda fell in a swoon
In piteous joy, but made recovery
And called her children to her and they soon
Were folded in her arms . . .
"All thank to you, my dearest lord," said she,
"For you have saved my children, you alone!
Were I to die this moment I have known
Your love and have found favor in your sight,
And death were nothing, though I died to-night. . . ." [66]

Griselda has to be an exaggeration, but the medieval male believed in the subjugation of women. Philippe de Novaire, a thirteenth-century writer, held that women "have a great advantage in one thing, they can easily preserve their honour if they wish to be held virtuous, by one thing only. But for a man many are needful, if he wish to be esteemed virtuous, for it behoves him to be courteous and generous, brave and wise. And for a woman, if she be a worthy woman of her body, all her faults are covered, and she can go with a high head wheresoever she will; and therefore it is in no way needful to teach as many things to girls as to boys." [67] Philippe then logically concluded that it was not necessary to teach girls to read. Virtue and virtue alone counted.

Chaucer's Wife of Bath was the opposite extreme to Griselda. In the prologue to her tale, Chaucer revealed that she had had five husbands. Her first three, all since dead, had been chosen because they were old and rich and she rather quickly had gained their love and their property. Once she gained mastery she did not even have to bother to be nice to them, although she treated them with affection when they gave her presents. Her fourth husband, a rake, had been a mistake, but she had managed to cure him by making him jealous. Her last husband, and the one with whom she was still living, she had married for love. He was much younger than she and also at first had proven to be difficult, but she had found his weakness when she had pretended to be dying after he had hit her. In effect a determined woman could find the weakness of any man. After telling about herself in the prologue, the Wife of Bath recounted the adventures of a knight who set out to find what women really wanted most. Though some had responded to the knight that women wanted

66. *Ibid.*, "The Clerk's Tale."
67. Power, "Position of Women," p. 404.

wealth and treasure, others jollity and pleasures, some gorgeous clothes, others fun in bed, and still others to be gratified and flattered, he himself had discovered that what women really desired was "the self same sovereignty/ On husbands as they on those that love them,/ And would be set in mastery above them;/ That is your greatest wish."[68]

There was, however, a limit to how far medieval misogyny could go. This was simply because though the clerics might condemn women, and the secular writers might make ribald jokes about them, the church still recognized that sex existed, and heterosexuality was much preferable to homosexuality. Helping to emphasize this crisis was the revival of Platonism in the late medieval period. To Plato and the neo-Platonists love was the desire of beauty; it began on the individual level, extended to a recognition of the kinship of all physical beauty, and concluded with the recognition that beauty was an intangible spiritual essence. Love in effect was a means of achieving the highest spiritual cognition. Plato, however, had conceived of love primarily as between two men or between a man and a youth, and this to the medieval church was anathema. When the study of Plato was intensified in fifteenth-century Italy, many writers were concerned with avoiding the charge of homosexuality. They could do this either by attributing only an intellectual and moral fervor to those who loved members of the same sex or they could attribute to women, not men, the personal beauty which excited men to love and impelled the lover to seek the higher forms of beauty.[69] If these were the alternatives the course of the Christian church was clear. The contradictions of medieval views of sexuality were never more evident than in the fact that it was the very antisexuality and fear of sex which led Christianity to elevate women. The more materialistic concepts of courtly love were reinforced with the spiritual aspects of Platonic love. It was through the ennobling love of woman that man could attain the contemplative state which led by degrees to a desire for things divine. Still the argument could not be carried too far and Leon Battista Alberti (c. 1390–1472) could still write that women were "crazy and full of fleas."[70]

68. Chaucer, "The Wife of Bath's Prologue," and "The Wife of Bath's Tale."

69. John Charles Nelson, *Renaissance Theory of Love* (New York: Columbia University Press, 1958), p. 78.

70. Maurice Valency, *In Praise of Love: An Introduction to the Love Poetry of the Renaissance* (New York: Macmillan, 1958), p. 3.

Even though chastity came to be emphasized, there was still considerable mistrust of women, and it was during the fifteenth century, the so-called Renaissance period, that chastity girdles appeared. If it was the virtuous woman who was going to be admired, some husbands were going to take all efforts to ensure the chastity of their wives and daughters, even if it meant enclosing them in barbaric contraptions. How widespread such contraptions were is debatable, but the first authenticated picture of one dates from 1405. It is believed that it was in Italy that they reached the height of their development and where they existed for several centuries.[71] Women had to be controlled, whether in chastity belts or otherwise, and the fourteenth-century Geoffrey, the knight of La Tour Landry, in a book compiled for the instruction of his daughters, held that a gentleman in a rage could strike his wife. He kept emphasizing to his daughters to take "hede how all good women owe to be humble, curteis, and seruisable vnto her hosbondes."[72] Bourgeois literature which had not yet incorporated the chivalric ideas was essentially misogynistic and the henpecked husband was a suspiciously favorite theme.

Perhaps the only way the picture could be changed was for women themselves to write from their point of view, and women wrote very little. Heloise in her love letters to Abelard was perhaps an exception, but when most women did write they either ignored the topic of woman's place or accepted the male stereotypes.[73] Countess Beatrice de Die and Marie de France, both poets, did not picture women in their work any differently than did male poets. The only real medieval exception to this statement was Christine de Pisan, a fifteenth-century woman who might be regarded as an early feminist voice. Christine, at best, was a cautious advocate of woman's rights, careful not to antagonize the male. Instead of trying to argue that women were equal in intelligence, culture, or education to men, she accused

71. The subject is somewhat controversial, but probably the best account in English is by Eric John Dingwall, *The Girdle of Chastity* (reprinted, New York: Macaulay Company, n.d.). There has been some attempt to find evidence for the custom during the crusades, and though this is the legendary tradition of its beginning, there is no hard evidence for such an assumption.

72. Geoffrey de la Tour-Landry, *The Book of the Knight of La Tour-Landry*, ed. and trans. by Thomas Wright for Early English Text Society (rev. ed., New York: Greenwood Press, 1969), LXXV, p. 98.

73. See for example Louise Collis, *Memoirs of a Medieval Woman: The Life and Times of Margery Kempe* (New York: Crowell, 1964).

those who attacked women as guilty of ingratitude. After all, she pointed out, woman had been the ever present servant of man, the nurse of infancy, the mourner at his burial, and his true helpmate. To call such a servant faithless, cruel, inconstant, vain, and worthless was not only rude but also demonstrated a lack of common courtesy. Moreover it was simply poor logic to lump all women together. Some were bad, just as some men were bad, but some were good, and men unfortunately labeled all women as one group. She emphasized that God had created woman in his own image and had chosen her to be the mother of Jesus while an ordinary man had not been chosen as the father. Woman was made of finer material than the simple dirt out of which man had been created, and this obviously meant that woman was more noble than man. Woman was also created in Paradise while man was not. She cited a whole series of women from Medea to Dido to Penelope who remained constant to their men even when the men had deserted them. For these reasons, as well as others, men should prize, cherish, and love women. No man could be without a mother; it was women alone who were the mothers, as well as the sisters, daughters, and friends of man. While she admitted that she was only a woman and not particularly important, she could claim the right to defend her sex on the grounds that a small knife could make a big hole in a sack and a very small rodent could assault and put a lion to flight. Christine also argued that women should be educated; no amount of learning could ever prove injurious to a virtuous woman. She would concede, however, that woman's education should be different from man's because there were sexual differences and woman should not be expected to occupy all the positions of men.[74] This moderate attack was the first assault by a woman on the misogyny of the Middle Ages, and one of the first to survive from any period.

There were a few men who sided with Christine. At first glance her most unlikely ally was Giovanni Boccaccio, whose *Decameron* sometimes seemed to be a catalog-listing of cuckolded husbands and scheming wives. Boccaccio, however, also wrote *De Claris Mulieribus* (*Concerning Famous Women*), a collection of biographies of

74. See Lula McDowell Richardson, *The Forerunners of Feminism in French Literature of the Renaissance* (Baltimore: Johns Hopkins Press, 1929), pp. 12–34; Marguerite Favier, *Christine de Pisan* (Lausanne: Editions Recontre, 1967); and M. Laigle, *Le livre des trois vertus de Christine de Pisan, Bibiotheque du XV siecle,* XVI (Paris, 1912).

some 104 women, the first collection of women's biographies ever written. It was from the pages of Boccaccio that Christine took some of her ammunition to deal with the misogynistic critics of women. Though Boccaccio's stories covered all types of women from those who betrayed and tricked men to those who served their menfolk loyally and devotedly, the emphasis was more on the latter than the former. Boccaccio, nonetheless, was still somewhat ambiguous about the female of the species. The highest praise he could offer to woman was to call her "manly," and he used the adjective repeatedly. Women to become great had to overcome the obstacles of their bodies because nature had not created them equal to men. He recognized that women could become great scholars, rulers, and painters, and he encouraged them to do so, but he also feared that they would encroach on the rights of men.[75] Ambivalence, however, was better than hostility, and Boccaccio represented a step forward over most of his contemporaries.

Women for the most part were still regarded as inferior to men at the end of the Middle Ages, as they were at the beginning. Leon Battista Alberti summed up the expected role of women in the fifteenth century:

> The character of men is stronger than that of women and can bear the attacks of enemies better, can stand strain longer, is more constant under stress. Therefore men have the freedom to travel with honor in foreign lands, acquiring and gathering the goods of fortune. Women, on the other hand, are almost all timid by nature, soft, slow, and therefore more useful when they sit still and watch over our things. It is as though nature thus provided for our well-being, arranging for men to bring things home and for women to guard them. The woman as she remains locked up at home, should watch over things by staying at her post, by diligent care and watchfulness. The man should guard the woman, the house, and his family and country, but not by sitting still. He should exercise his spirit and his hands in brave enterprise, even at the cost of sweat and blood.[76]

In spite of Alberti's view, it seems clear that attitudes toward women were undergoing some modification at the end of the medieval peri-

75. Giovanni Boccaccio, *Concerning Famous Women*, trans. by Guido A. Guarino (New Brunswick: Rutgers University Press, 1963).

76. Leon Battista Alberti, *I Libri della Famigilia*, trans. under the title of *The Family in Renaissance Florence* by Reneé Neu Watkins (Columbia, S.C.: University of South Carolina Press, 1969), bk. 3, pp. 208–209.

od. The change, however, was ambiguous as indicated by the growth of romantic love. There was a tendency to place some women on a pedestal, restricting this elevated position to the most noble women and denying it to women of the lesser classes. Attitudes toward women were still tied up with attitudes toward sex, but the church recognized that sex was part of human existence and vastly preferred that its members engage in heterosexual rather than homosexual activities. Quite clearly women remained subordinate to men, although the nature of this subordination was being redefined to meet changing conditions. The vast majority of women, even those such as Christine de Pisan who challenged some of the masculine assumptions, were primarily mothers, and it was either as mothers or as chaste exemplars of virtue that women had respect. Though few women probably enjoyed the pedestal that the concepts of romantic love put them on, most of them thought that at least temporarily it was better than the gutter, and the myths of the female mystique appealed to them. The difficulty with the pedestal, however, was that it was hard to remain there without falling.

chapter nine

The More Things Change, the More
They Remain the Same

If the view of women during the medieval period was heavily colored by a clerical emphasis on the need for celibacy, it would seem logical that the appearance of Protestantism with its denial of the virtue of celibacy would lead to a change in attitude toward women. Logic, as should be evident by this point in the book, had little place in man's attitudes toward women, and though the advent of married clergy probably curtailed some of the worst excesses of clerical misogyny, it did little to elevate the status of women. In fact, one observer, G. Rattray Taylor, in his sometimes brilliant but always highly opinionated study of *Sex in History*, labeled the advent of Protestantism as a "desperate attempt by patrists to restore patrist ideals."[1] This seems to be an exaggeration, although it is true that Protestants in general condemned the courtly lover's worship of women as disgusting effeminacy.

Most of the leaders of mainstream Protestant thought from Martin Luther to John Calvin regarded the physical superiority of the male as a sign from God of man's superiority in the household. They looked upon the husband-father as the ultimate authority within the home, the breadwinner, the pastor and priest to the family. It was only by submission to her husband that a woman could atone for Eve's transgression.[2] Martin Luther, who was often rather earthy in

1. G. Rattray Taylor, *Sex in History* (New York: Vanguard Press, 1954), p. 141.
2. E. Troeltsch, *The Social Teachings of the Christian Church* (2 vols., London: Allen and Unwin, 1931), vol. 1, p. 546, and Luther, *Table Talk*, no. 5538, in *Luther's Works*, ed. and trans. by Theodore G. Tappert (Philadelphia: Fortress Press, 1967), pp. 449–450.

his expressions, and whose *Table Talk* was more or less accurately recorded by various disciples, put the matter of women's submission rather bluntly: "Men have broad shoulders and narrow hips, and accordingly they possess intelligence. Women have narrow shoulders and broad hips. Women ought to stay at home; the way they were created indicates this, for they have broad hips and a wide fundament to sit upon [to keep house and bear and raise children]."[3] Luther regarded marriage as an effective means of curing sin, although women were necessary in other ways as well. He wrote: "many good things may be perceived in a wife. First, there is the Lord's blessing, namely offspring. Then there is community of property. These are some of the pre-eminently good things that can overwhelm a man. Imagine what it would be like without this sex. The home, cities, economic life, and government would virtually disappear. Men can't do without women. Even if it were possible for men to beget and bear children, they still couldn't do without women."[4]

After his break with Rome, Luther gradually arrived at the conclusion that clerical celibacy was wrong because it had originated from what he regarded as the false belief that divine favor could be won by performing self-imposed tasks. The key to his religious thought was that salvation came from faith, not good works, and thus chastity which had been regarded as a good work could no longer be so regarded. For Luther the gift of continence came only from God. Luther was positive that sex in and of itself did not involve man in any more sinful conduct than other potentially sinful acts. Wedlock, in fact, was God's gift to mankind, a state of life approved by God and possessing the authority of His sanction. Marriage was inherent in the very nature of man, had been instituted in Paradise, confirmed by the fifth commandment, and safeguarded by the seventh. It was a true, heavenly, spiritual, and divine estate.

Once Luther arrived at an idea he tended to act upon it, and so at forty-two he married the ex-nun, Katherine von Bora, who was then twenty-seven. Soren Kierkegaard, the great theologian of the nineteenth century, said Luther might as well have married a plank as Katherine, since he felt that Luther had nothing more in mind by his marriage than to demonstrate his approval of clerical marriage. Any woman might have suited his purpose and Katherine's only

3. Luther, *Table Talk*, no. 55, p. 8.
4. *Ibid.*, no. 1658, pp. 160–161.

claim to fame was that she was Luther's wife.[5] In part because of Luther's garrulousness, and in part because Luther took to marriage like a duck to water, we know something about Katherine. Luther put strong emphasis upon marital love, upon the home as a school for character not only for children, but also for the husband and wife as well. Though Luther was always the magistrate within his house, he recognized the difficulties of two human beings living together as man and wife and came to marvel at the patriarchs who had been able to stick out marriages which lasted for several hundred years. He once wondered how often Eve must have said to Adam, "You ate the apple," and Adam had retorted, "You gave it to me." He could feel only compassion for Abraham, who in his old age was caught in a cross fire between two jealous women, and he sympathized with the blind Isaac who had nothing to do in his declining years but listen to the wrangling of Rebecca with the wives of Esau.[6] Luther still had a somewhat jaundiced view of the female, but in many ways he looked upon the opposite sex as a kind of friendly rival and he lacked the fear of some of his clerical predecessors. He wrote:

> When one looks back upon it, marriage isn't so bad as when one looks forward to it. We see that our mothers and our fathers were saints and that we have the divine commandment, "Honor your father and your mother." When I look beside myself I see my brothers and sisters and friends, and I find that there's nothing but godliness in marriage. To be sure, when I consider marriage, only the flesh seems to be there. Yet my father must have slept with my mother and made love to her, and they were nevertheless godly people. All the patriarchs and prophets did likewise. The longing of man for a woman is God's creation—that is to say, when nature's sound, not when it's corrupted as it is among Italians and Turks.[7]

> You can't be without a wife and remain without sin. After all, marriage is an ordinance and creation of God. Therefore it is not Satan's idea when a man desires to marry an honorable girl, for Satan hates this kind of life. So make the ventures in the name of the Lord and on the strength of his blessing and institution.[8]

5. Roland H. Bainton, *Women of the Reformation* (Minneapolis: Augsburg Publishing House, 1971), p. 23.
6. Roland H. Bainton, *What Christianity Says about Sex, Love and Marriage* (New York: Association Press, 1957), p. 82.
7. Luther, *Table Talk*, no. 1659, p. 161.
8. *Ibid.*, no. 233, p. 31.

Men, no matter how antagonized they might be by the female, should always keep in mind that women are also God's creation. Luther felt called upon to upbraid the Archbishop of Mainz who had been quoted as condemning the "stinking, putrid, private parts of women."

> That godless knave, forgetful of his mother and his sister, dares to blaspheme God's creature through whom he was himself born. It would be tolerable if he were to find fault with the behavior of women, but to defile their creation and nature is most godless. As if I were to ridicule man's face on account of his nose! For the nose is the latrine of man's head and stands above his mouth. As a matter of fact, God himself must allow all prayer and worship to take place under this privy.[9]

Luther, in general, was opposed to ridiculing women in public. "Girls and women ought not to be censured in public pamphlets, even if there is reason to suspect them, but ought to be rebuked in private or reported to the magistrate. There are many imperfections in the female sex—as the proverb puts it, 'If all girls are good, where do wicked women come from?' " In the privacy of his own home, however, he sang some words of caution about beautiful woman since "A red apple may look good and inviting,/And yet worminess hide:/ So a girl with the worst disposition/ May be pretty outside." Though Luther felt there were defects in everything, the poets, having learned from experience, could still nonetheless only lament that woman was such a "weak vessel."[10]

The good wife was the one who kept her place. Once after an argument with his wife Katherine, whom Luther affectionately called Katie, he stated rather plaintively: "You convince me of whatever you please. You have complete control. I concede to you the control of the household, provided my rights are preserved. Female government has never done any good. God made Adam master over all creatures, to rule over all living things, but when Eve persuaded him that he was lord even over God she spoiled everything. We have you women to thank for that! With tricks and cunning women deceive men, as I, too, have experienced."[11] In the home the husband should be master over his womenfolk, although he could delegate

9. *Ibid.*, no. 2807b, p. 171.
10. *Ibid.*, no. 3523, p. 221.
11. *Ibid.*, no. 2847b, pp. 174–175.

certain tasks to his wife in order to devote himself to higher and more important things.[12] Luther regarded himself as master in his own home, at least most of the time, was quite possessive of his wife and children, and also rather happy and content. "I am rich, God has given me my nun and three children; what care I if I am debt, Katie pays the bills. . . . George Kark has taken a rich wife and sold his freedom. I am luckier, for when Katie gets saucy, she gets nothing but a box on the ear."[13] Luther strongly believed that women were inferior to man. This belief was a contradiction, since he also believed there was a universal priesthood of all believers and that God did not distinguish between men and women in this respect. He still, nonetheless, excluded women from the ministry on the grounds of the necessity for preserving order and decency and because of the inferior aptitudes inherent in the female sex. He recognized, however, that exceptions might be made in time of necessity.[14] Luther was willing to make an occasional exception, but women in general were inferior to the male. This might be regarded as a slight gain for women, but any concessions to women were to be made on male terms by the men themselves.

John Calvin put less emphasis upon the subordination of women than Luther did, and he also put less emphasis upon their tasks as childbearers. Instead he taught that the primary purpose of marriage was social rather than generative. Woman had not been created simply to be man's helper in procreation, nor was she just a necessary remedy for his sexual needs caused by the corruption of human nature by the Fall, but rather the female had been created as man's inseparable associate in life as well as in the bed chamber.[15] Calvin agreed that the scriptures emphasized males instead of females, but questioned whether it should be concluded that "women are nothing." Instead he held that generally women were included under the generic term "men" and it was obvious that men could not have children without women. Though the family name rests in the pos-

12. *Ibid.*, no. 154, pp. 22–23.
13. Quoted in *Sex and the Church*, ed. by Oscar E. Feucht and other members of the Family Life Committee of the Lutheran Church (St. Louis: Concordia Publishing House, 1961), p. 84.
14. See Derrick Sherwin Bailey, *Sexual Relation in Christian Thought* (New York: Harper, 1959), p. 173.
15. John Calvin, *In Genesis*, ii, 18, in *Opera*, eds. G. Baum, E. Cunitz, *et al.* (Brunswick and Berlin: C. A. Schwetschke, 1863–1900), vol. 1, p. 14.

session of the males rather than the females, Jesus himself had been born from a woman.[16] Nevertheless Calvin held, as did Luther, that the subjugation of woman to man was part of God's law, although it was not this in itself which made her incapable of serving in the ministry of the church. Rather the ministry of woman was motherhood, and this prevented her from assuming positions in the church which in turn deprived her of authority to preach publicly. Ultimately Calvin concluded that a woman should not be allowed to speak in the church, to baptize, to offer, and could not claim for herself the function of any man, much less the priest. Calvin said he was well "aware of the answer of those who think otherwise: that there is a great difference between common usage and an extraordinary remedy required by dire necessity. But since Epiphanius declares that it is a mockery to give women the right to baptize and makes no exception, it is clear enough that he condemns this corrupt practice as inexcusable under any pretension."[17] We know little about Calvin's wife, Idelette, except that he had a high opinion of her. When she died he wrote to a friend: "I have been bereaved of the best companion of my life, who, if our lot had been harsher, would have been not only the willing sharer of exile and poverty, but even of death. While she lived, she was the faithful helper of my ministry. From her I never experienced the slightest hindrance."[18]

Thomas Hooker, the American Puritan and follower of John Calvin, went much further than Calvin in expressing his feelings about women: "The man whose heart is endeared to the woman he loves, he dreams of her in the night, hath her in his eye and apprehension when he awakes, museth on her as he sits at table, walks with her when he travels and parlies with her in each place where he comes.... That the husband tenders his spouse with an indeared affection above all mortal creatures: This appears by the expressions of his respect, that all he hath, is at her command, all he can do, is wholly improved for her content and comfort, she lies in his bosom and his heart trusts in her, which forceth all to confess, that the stream

16. John Calvin, *Institutes of the Christian Religion*, 2, chap. xiii, par. 3, trans. by Ford Lewis Battles in vols. 20 and 21, *Library of Christian Classics*, ed. by John T. McNeill (Philadelphia: The Westminster Press, 1960), 1, pp. 479–480.

17. *Ibid.*, 4, chap. xv, 21; 2, 1321–22.

18. Williston Walker, *John Calvin* (reprinted, New York: Schocken Books, 1969), p. 236.

of his affection, like a mighty current, runs with full tide and strength...."[19]

The Calvinist acceptance of woman depended on her knowing her place in a male world. When it appeared that two queens Mary Tudor and Mary Guise might rule in England and Scotland, and that these two women were also Catholic, the Protestant misogyny which lay under the surface burst into the open. Probably the most notorious attack on women by the Protestant reformers of the sixteenth century was that issued by John Knox under the title of "The First Blast of the Trumpet against the Monstrous Regiment of Women" in 1558. Knox, who was living as an exile in Calvin's Geneva, wrote that to promote a woman to a position of rule, superiority, or dominion, over any city, realm, or nation, was repugnant not only to nature but also to God. God, he claimed, had not only deprived woman of the right to any such authority or domination, but man himself had seen why this denial of female rule was necessary. "For who can denie but it is repugneth to nature, that the blind shall be appointed to leade and conduct such as do see? That the weake, the sicke, and impotent persons shall norishe and kepe the hole and strong? And finallie, that the foolishe, madde, and phrenetike shal governe the discrete, and give counsel to such as be sober of mind. And such be al women, compared unto man in bearing of authoritie. For their sight in civile regiment is but blindness; their strength, weaknes; their counsel, foolishnes; and judgment, phrensie, if it be rightlie considered."[20]

God had plainly denied woman any authority over man, although Knox recognized they did have certain legal rights to inheritance. This right, however, even in the case of queens, could never be construed as the right to rule.[21] Knox had projected a second and third blast of his trumpet against women, but these were never written, probably because some of his more prudent colleagues persuaded him that a female ruler sympathetic to Protestantism (Elizabeth I) might soon ascend the throne of England. Knox never recanted his

19. Quoted in Edmund S. Morgan, *The Puritan Family* (rev. ed., New York: Harper and Row, 1966), pp. 61–62.

20. John Knox, "The First Blast of the Trumpet against the Monstrous Regiment of Women," in *The Works of John Knox*, collected and ed. by David Laing, vol. 4 (Edinburgh: Bannatyne Club, 1855), p. 373.

21. *Ibid.*, p. 409

views on women and later after Elizabeth was on the throne, he wrote to her minister William Cecil giving reverence for the miraculous work of God in comforting His afflicted by such an "infirme vessell," namely a female ruler. Knox was only willing to support Elizabeth's right to rule if she would confess that the "extraordinary dispensation" of God's mercy had made lawful unto her that "which both nature and Godes lawe denye" to other women.[22] It was these attitudes which made him *persona non grata* to Mary Queen of Scots, although he was not alone in his hostility to female rule. Two of his colleagues, John Ponet and Christopher Goodman, wrote tracts with similar themes.

Even the "defenders" of rights for women found it hard to justify the right of a female to rule. John Aylmer, for example, who wrote a refutation to Knox, maintained not that women were fit to rule but only that God occasionally chose to work his way through a weak instrument. If God chose to place in authority a "woman weake in nature, feable in bodie, softe in courage, unskilfull in practise, not terrible to the enemy, no shilde to the frynde," it was because God could work through the weak as well as the strong, through a woman as well as a man. Even though women might occasionally rule, however, Aylmer held that they could never be ordained as clergy because the female lacked the mental and moral virtue indispensable for a clergyman. In general Aylmer regarded women as "fond, folish, wanton, flibbergibbes, tatlers, triflers, wavering, witles, without counsell, feable, careless, rashe, proude, deintie, nise, talebearers, eavesdroppers, rumor raisers, evell tonged, worse minded, and in every wise doltified with the dregges of the Devils dounge hill."[23] Excluded from this general category of females was Elizabeth, whom he praised lavishly if only because at the time he very much desired a career in the church of England. As Katharine M. Rogers in her invaluable study of misogyny in literature remarked, "it is not hard to see, however, why she kept him waiting a long time for his bishopric."[24]

22. For a discussion of this see James E. Phillipps, "The Background of Spenser's Attitude Towards Women Rulers," *Huntington Library Quarterly*, 5 (October, 1941, and July, 1942), 5–32, 211–234, esp. 19–20.

23. Quoted in S. R. Maitland, *The Reformation in England* (London: J. Lane, 1906), pp. 209, 214–215.

24. Katharine M. Rogers, *The Troublesome Helpmate* (Seattle: University of Washington Press, 1966), p. 137.

Separate and distinct from the Lutheran wing and the Calvinist wing of Protestantism was the Anglican, the success of which ultimately was due to the policies of Queen Elizabeth. Nevertheless, in spite of this, the Anglicans made but few concessions in their attitudes toward women. William Tyndale (d. 1536), who died long before Elizabeth ascended the throne, insisted upon women's subordination in marriage. Women, he held, were put under men in order to keep female lusts and wanton appetites under control. Later, however, Thomas Becon paid tribute to woman's wisdom and prudence and to her competence, while Jeremy Taylor in the seventeenth century went to some effort to disassociate himself from those morose cynics who deemed women unfit for man's friendship. Still the Anglican writers with almost uniform monotony expounded the basic principle of male headship and credited men with superior understanding and reasoning. Women, on the other hand, were said to have been so constituted that they required guidance, control, and protection. "They are intrinsically inferior in excellence, imbecile by sex and nature, weak in body, inconstant in mind, and imperfect and infirm in character; yet in spiritual capacity it is allowed they are equal to their lords, having 'as good an interest in the promise of God, and as fair a title to that eternal life which the divine grace bestows upon us.' "[25] The subordination of women was regarded as inherent in nature itself, an integral part of the divine hierarchical ordering of the universe, proof of which could be found in the nature of the feminine defects, namely, the action of God in creating woman after, out of, and for man, and the fact that women first fell into sin. The good woman was the wife who was ever vigilant in conforming to the wishes of her husband, diligent in the discharge of wifely duties, compliant in manner, interested in domestic affairs, ready to obey, and always good humored. Any wife should be treated by a husband as he would a child, which a woman was at heart, and his control over her was to be paternal and friendly, not magisterial nor despotic. By delegation from him woman was to have authority over the nursery and to the offices of domestic employment.[26]

Those women who did speak publicly on religious issues were usually rebuked by the males. For example, when Katherine Zell, whose ex-priest husband was one of the leaders in the Protestant

25. Bailey, *Sexual Relation in Christian Thought*, p. 201.
26. *Ibid.*, p. 202.

movement in Strasbourgh, defended the right of priests to marry, she was immediately reminded of St. Paul's injunction for women to be silent in the church. Katherine, however, knew her Bible and she effectively replied: "I would remind you of the word of this same apostle that in Christ there is no longer male nor female and of the prophecy of Joel: 'I will pour forth my spirit upon all flesh and your sons and your daughters will prophesy.' I do not pretend to be John the Baptist rebuking the Pharisees. I do not claim to be Nathan upbraiding David. I aspire only to be Balaam's ass, castigating his master."[27] Another woman, Argula von Grumbach, defended Luther by writing a letter of protest to the faculty at the University of Ingolstadt. She, however, immediately adopted the humble demeanor of a proper woman: "I am not unacquainted with the word of Paul that women should be silent in church but, when no man will or can speak, I am driven by the word of the Lord when he said 'He who confesses me on earth, him will I confess and he who denies me, him will I deny,' and I take comfort in the words of the prophet Isaiah, 'I will send you children to be your princes and women to be your rulers.' "[28]

Protestantism, by its emphasis upon the scriptures, encouraged women to read, and the development of the printing press in the fifteenth century further stimulated literacy in both men and women and made reading material far more accessible. The greatest gains in equality appeared in some of the minor Protestant groups. Many of these were much more willing to accept women on the basis of near equality than a Luther or Calvin. John Comenius, a seventeenth-century minister of the church of the Brethren (Moravian church), sympathized with women's complaint that they had to live under the rule of men even though they formed one-half of the human race. He felt that neither sex should try to rule one another, although he felt that men should rule the community and women the home, and this might mean that women sometimes would also have dominance over men. He could see no good reason why women should be excluded from the pursuit of knowledge and argued that women were often endowed with a greater sharpness of mind as well as a capacity for knowledge than men. He also wanted them to be well educated

27. Quoted in Bainton, *Women of the Reformation*, p. 55.
28. *Ibid.*, pp. 97–98.

since the more learning they have stuffed into their minds "the less will the folly that arises from emptiness of mind find a place."[29]

Catholicism reaffirmed the doctrine of clerical celibacy in the sixteenth century, and though there was a series of rather remarkable women religious leaders, there was little change in the clerical attitude toward women. This lack of change is most evident in the writings of St. Theresa of Avila (1515–82), one of the most remarkable women of any period. In spite of her sainthood she once wrote that the "very thought that I am a woman is enough to make my wings droop."[30] Like her famous predecessor, St. Katherine, she wondered whether Saint Paul was right in his misogynistic dismissal of women, and through her mystical vision she felt she arrived at new truths. She held that while the church should be guided by the teachings of St. Paul, all the scriptures should also be followed, and if this occurred there would be a radical change in attitudes toward women. St. Theresa recognized the physical weakness of women as compared to men, but stated this was not enough to justify their subordination.

When thou wert in the world, Lord, thou didst not despise women, but didst always help them and show them great compassion. Thou didst find more faith and no less love in them than in men. . . . We can do nothing in public that is of any use to thee, nor dare we speak of some of the truths over which we weep in secret, lest thou should not hear this, our just petition. Yet, Lord, I cannot believe this of thy goodness and righteousness, for thou art a righteous Judge, not like judges in the world, who, being after all, men and sons of Adam, refuse to consider any woman's virtue as above suspicion. Yes, my King, but the day will come when all will be known. I am not speaking on my account, for the whole world is already aware of my wickedness, and I am glad that it should become known; but, when I see what the times are like, I feel it is not right to repel spirits which are virtuous and brave, even though they be the spirits of women.[31]

In spite of such a plaintive cry, clerical attitudes changed but little. Cardinal Cajeta (1469–1534), the sixteenth-century commentator on St. Thomas Aquinas, expressed agreement with the great doctor's

29. John Edward Sadler, *J. A. Comenius and the Concept of Universal Education* (New York: Barnes and Noble, 1966), pp. 177–178, 193–194.

30. Quoted in Mary Daly, *The Church and the Second Sex* (New York: Harper and Row, 1968), p. 56.

31. *Ibid.*, p. 57.

view on women, although he did admit that there were many things which a woman might do better than a man. St. Ignatius Loyola (1491–1556), the founder of the Jesuits and one of the leaders in the Catholic reform movement of the sixteenth century, thought he detected a similarity between women and Satan: "The enemy conducts himself as a woman. He is a weakling before a show of strength, and a tyrant if he has his will." The Spanish Dominican, Dominic Soto (1495–1560), held that the female sex was a natural impediment to the reception of holy orders, and after echoing St. Paul's views on women, added that nature demonstrated it would be absurd for women to hear confessions, for even if by chance there were some women who were prudent, the female sex in general manifested a poverty of reason and a softness of mind.[32]

The best they could do was go along with St. Francis de Sales (1567–1622), who, in his *Introduction to the Devout Life*, urged men not to be provoked by the weakness and infirmities of the bodies and minds of their wives, but instead to preserve a tender, constant, and heartfelt love. "Woman was taken from that side of the first man which was nearest his heart, to the end that she might be loved by him cordially and tenderly. The weakness and infirmity of your wives, whether in body or in mind, ought never to provoke you to any kind of disdain, but rather to a mild and affectionate compassion. God has created them such, to the end that they should depend upon you and you should receive from them more honor and respect. It is also that you should have them for your companions in such manner that you should still be their heads and superiors." He cautioned wives to "love tenderly and cordially the husbands whom God has given you, but with a love respectful and full of reverence. God indeed created them of a sex more vigorous and commanding and was pleased to ordain that the women should depend upon the man, being bone of his bone and flesh of his flesh, and that she should be made of a rib taken from under his arm, to show that she ought to be under the hand and guidance of her husband. All Holy Scripture strictly recommends this submission to you. . . ."[33]

In spite of the assaults of Protestantism upon Catholicism, the Catholic church attempted to limit women's careers in the religious

32. *Ibid.*, pp. 58–59.
33. St. Francis de Sales, *Introduction to the Devout Life*, ed. and trans. by John K. Ryan (Garden City, N.Y.: Image Books, 1955), pt. 3, xxxviii, pp. 215–216.

life by imposing strict enclosures upon all religious women, forbidding them to enter the world in the fashion of the Franciscans or Jesuits or Dominicans once they had taken their vows. These prohibitions which probably had been originally promulgated against the *beguines* in the thirteenth century were renewed in the sixteenth century at the Council of Trent and confirmed by Pope Pius V, who held that women who took solemn vows must accept cloister. Not all women were willing to abide by such strictures but few were able to overcome them. Angela Merici (1474–1540), the founder of the Ursulines, insisted during her lifetime that her followers not be bound by the cloister, wear a habit, or even live together. Their only vow was to be one of chastity, and her followers were to live a life of consecrated virginity while laboring as apostles in the world. After her death, however, church officials forced her companions back into the old monastic mold. A similar fate was imposed upon the Sisters of Visitation, established by Francis de Sales and Jeanne de Chantal. Only St. Vincent de Paul seemed to be successful in having his Daughters of Charity break away from the past strictures, and they became particularly influential in the emergence of modern nursing.[34]

The extent of clerical hostility to any change in the role of women within the Catholic church is evident in the case of Mary Ward (1585–1645), the founder of the "English ladies." A Catholic in Protestant England, Mary Ward wanted her ladies to work in the world, conducting schools for girls, subject only to the pope, independent of all other bishops and men's orders. For her time she was a strong advocate of greater freedom for women, and she planned to teach girls Latin as well as various secular subjects up to this time reserved largely for men. She wrote "there is no such difference between men and women that women may not do great things, as we have seen by the example of many saints. . . . For what think you of this word, 'but women'? As if we were in all things inferior to some other creature which I suppose to be man. . . . And if they would make us believe we can do nothing, and that we are but women, we might do great matters."[35] She was, however, a far cry from being a

34. See Vern and Bonnie Bullough, *Emergence of Modern Nursing* (2nd ed., New York: Macmillan, 1969), pp. 70–72.

35. Daly, *The Church and the Second Sex*, p. 62. See also Margarita O'Connor, *That Incomparable Woman* (Montreal: Palm Publishers, 1962).

revolutionary. She accepted the duty of wives to submit to their husbands, believed that men were to be head of the church, and agreed that women could not administer the sacrament or preach in public churches; the clergy, nonetheless, still condemned her. Some of the Catholic leaders in England wrote to Pope Gregory XV in 1621 in an effort to have her congregation dissolved on the grounds that women were "soft, fickle, deceitful, inconstant, erroneous, always desiring novelty, liable to a thousand dangers." They claimed such weaknesses were accentuated in the case of Mary Ward because she would not submit to cloister and insisted on her right as well as those of her followers to speak freely on spiritual matters. This led to erroneous teaching by her female followers; moreover, their ability to travel freely and visit the homes of the faithful could only cause a scandal, while their apostolic work would make them the subject of ridicule. Mary Ward appealed to Pope Urban VIII in 1624, who ordered her case reviewed by a board of cardinals. The board concluded that it was doubtful any organization of women such as she contemplated could do any good. Her order was suppressed in 1629, and when she disregarded the order of the suppression because she thought it had been falsified, she was arrested as a heretic and schematic. The wording of the bull suppressing her order issued by Pope Urban VIII effectively reveals the clerical attitude. "Certain women, taking the name of Jesuitesses, assembled and living together, built colleges, and appointed superiors and a General, assumed a peculiar habit without the approbation of the Holy See . . . carried out works by no means suiting the weakness of their sex, womanly modesty, virginal purity . . . works which men most experienced in the knowledge of the sacred scriptures undertake with difficulty, and not without great caution."[36] In short, religious attitudes toward women did not change much during the rise of Protestantism or the coming of Catholic reform. Protestantism by emphasizing the virtue of marriage had eliminated some of the clerical misogyny, but a woman, whether she was Protestant, Catholic, Jewish, or Muslim, was not to assert any authority over the male. She was clearly subordinate, even if by some chance she might even become a ruling monarch.

Although religious officials had not basically changed their view of women during the sixteenth and seventeenth centuries, there were quite radical changes in the field of education, particularly about the

36. Daly, *The Church and the Second Sex*, p. 64.

importance of female education. These changes were not so much the result of any change of attitude toward women as a change in the concepts of education. During much of the medieval period the aim of education had been religious, to train priests and theologians. This concept was modified somewhat in the twelfth and thirteenth centuries by the development of universities, but the students in such institutions, even those studying medicine and law, were still regarded as clerics. In fact, throughout much of Europe almost any male charged with a crime could claim benefit of clergy and if he could read Latin he was entitled to be tried under church law instead of secular law. Since women were prohibited from becoming clerics they were automatically eliminated from any possibility of attaining a university education. The development of professionalization in the university thus excluded heretics, schismatics, and Jews, as well as women, from becoming lawyers or physicians, and this had long-run implications for the status of women, since increasingly the professions moved into the university and without the opportunity to attend such schools women were severely handicapped.[37] Girls in the later Middle Ages, however, could attend "song" schools, schools run by "chantry" priests who were paid to say masses for the dead and who usually ran a school on the side. Girls were also taught by casual tutors, but they were excluded from the formal grammar schools which were regarded as preparatory schools for the university. If parents or guardians wanted their daughters to learn more than simple reading they had to hire tutors; this sometimes caused difficulty, as the famous love affair between Heloise and Abelard exemplified. In the larger noble households girls were sometimes taught by chaplains, but their learning took place in their home and the emphasis was on matters of domestic utility, including the teaching of manners, the enhancement of personal beauty and charm, and how to dress well. In theory women who wanted to have more education might turn to a convent, but increasingly there was suspicion about educated nuns and few dared to go beyond elementary Latin. In fact it came to be assumed that nuns did not know Latin, with the result that visiting bishops talked with them in the vernacular.

Though Protestantism by its emphasis on scriptures probably gave some impetus to education for girls, and the invention of the print-

37. For a discussion of this see Vern L. Bullough, *The Development of Medicine as a Profession* (Basle: Karger, 1966).

ing press made reading much more important, the key to the change
was the growth of humanism, an intellectual movement which
started in Italy during the fourteenth century and from there spread
throughout much of Europe. At this time Italy politically was over-
shadowed by the growing states to the north and west of it, while the
papacy, the medieval glory of Italy, was located at Avignon in what
is now France. In these circumstances the Italians turned to their
past glories and rediscovered their Roman heritage. To restore the
magnificance of Roman culture, the virtue and power inherent in
Rome came to be the inspiring aim of the Italians. They regarded
themselves as the true possessors of the culture not only of Rome
but also of Greece, and they avidly sought to import the classical concepts into their own day. This effort was marked by an assertion of
individuality, an emphasis upon *virtu*, manly self-expression and vir-
tuosity, activities which Jacob Burckhardt said led to the Renaissance.[38] In the process of reviving the glories of the past the nature of
education was changed since the humanist scholars came to believe
that the secret of the wisdom of Alexander or the virtue of a Trojan
lay in the way they had been educated in their youth. Education was
thus the key to virtue, and as this concept caught the fancy of the
Italian ruling classes, humanists came to be in great demand as teachers, both for boys and for girls. Though at first educated girls were
few, attitudes gradually changed until by the sixteenth century the
education of woman was an important subject, both for literary discussion and in actual practice.

Some observers of the Italian Renaissance have much exaggerated
this new emphasis upon female education. Burckhardt, for example,
held that "women stood on a footing of perfect equality with men."
Such a statement must be regarded as strictly ahistorical, although
Burckhardt undoubtedly meant something different by equality than
might be accepted today.

> There was no question of woman's rights' or female emancipation,
> simply because the thing itself was a matter of course. The educated
> woman, no less than the man, strove naturally after a characteristic
> and complete individuality. The same intellectual and emotional
> development which perfected the man, was demanded for the per-

38. Jacob Burckhardt's, *The Civilization of the Renaissance in Italy,* originally published in 1860, developed this concept. The book has often been reprinted, and the
first English translation was made by S. G. C. Middlemore in 1878.

fection of the woman. Active literary work, nevertheless, was not expected from her, and if she were a poet, some powerful utterance of feeling, rather than the confidences of the novel or the diary, was looked for. These women had not thought of the public; their function was to influence distinguished men, and to moderate male impulse and caprice.[39]

Women, at least upper-class women, might well have become somewhat better educated in the Renaissance than earlier but she had to be careful not to assert herself very much. Probably even more important than the humanist emphasis on learning in encouraging education for women was the fact that women played an important role on the political scene in the sixteenth century in their own right. That they were able to do so is indicative of some change in societal attitudes. Earlier women like the Empress Matilda, mother of Henry II of England, and Eleanor of Aquitaine, his wife, had tried to rule independently of their husbands, but they had been severely handicapped and in the long run unsuccessful. At the end of the fifteenth and beginning of the sixteenth centuries, however, there were a number of women who were important as rulers in their own right or as regents. Isabella of Castille was a queen of Spain, while in England Mary and Elizabeth were reigning monarchs. In France Catherine de Medici fought like a tiger to see to it that her minor sons succeeded to their inheritance. The influence of these women rulers is evident from the fact that they were instrumental in forcing a reassessment of education of women. Catherine, the wife of Henry VIII, had hired her fellow Spaniard, Luis Vives, to serve as tutor for her daughter Mary. In an effort to prove his qualifications Vives wrote *Instruction of a Christian Woman* (1523), which he felt was the first treatise to ever deal with the subject. Vives stated that while Zenophon, Plato, and Aristotle had said many things about a woman's function, and saints such as Cyprian, Jerome, and Augustine had discussed maids and widows, he was the first to really write a treatise on female education.[40] Though Vives perhaps exaggerated his own importance in the area since Francesco Barberino, for example, had written a treatise on the subject in the thirteenth century, Vives marked a new beginning for what came to be a long tradition.

39. *Ibid.*, p. 294, in the Modern Library edition (New York: Random House, 1954).
40. Foster Watson, ed., *Vives and the Renascence Education of Women* (London: Edward Arnold, 1912), chap. 4, pp. 54–56.

By no stretch of the imagination could Vives be called a feminist. A girl, he felt, should be taught to read in order to study holy books, but she should also learn the domestic arts, needlecraft, spinning, and weaving, in order to better serve her parents and her husband. Though Vives believed that intelligent girls should go on to study he felt their field should be severely restricted: "Let a woman learn for herself alone and her young children, or her sisters in the Lord. For it neither becometh a woman to rule a school, nor to live amongst men, or speak abroad, and shake off her demureness and honesty. . . . Therefore, because a woman is a frail thing, and of weak discretion, and that may lightly be deceived . . . a woman should not teach lest when she hath taken a false opinion and belief of any thing, she spread it unto the hearers, by the authority of mastership and lightly bring others into the same error, for the learners commonly do after the teacher with a good will."[41] Good Christian women were to be secluded from the world for fear that they would develop a taste for misbehavior; they should be taught by example never to use unclean words or uncomely gestures; and they must not be allowed to read romances written by idle men, but only uplifting kinds of literature. Vives seemed to believe that if a woman was left to herself she would instinctively read dangerous nonsense, and thus it was essential girls go to wise and learned men for guidance. He held that unmarried virgins were to pass their time in company of other girls, reading and discussing holy books, resisting the temptation to talk about feasting and dancing. No girl should be encouraged to sit alone in her room and muse, for although her thoughts at the outset might be good and pious, a "woman's mind is unstable and abideth not long in one place."

Royal princesses were special women, requiring special treatment, and Vives made a *Plan of Studies* for the young Princess Mary. He felt she should study all that was best in classical literature from Plato to Cicero and Plutarch, the works of the Christian fathers, and also the writings of some of his contemporaries, particularly Sir Thomas More and Desiderus Erasmus, his friends. Both More and Erasmus were important in helping to modify societal attitudes toward educated women. More was the father of three daughters who were probably the most learned women in England. He had carefully supervised their education, and during his various absences from

41. *Ibid.*, chap. 10, quoted p. 86.

home had corresponded with their tutors. He wrote to one of them: "it mattereth not in Harvest Time whether the Corn were sown by a Man or a Woman, and I see not why Learning in Like Manner may not equally agree with both Sexes: for by it Reason is cultivated, and as a Field, sown with wholesome Precepts, which bring forth good Fruit."[42] More's daughter Margaret, who married William Roper, was said to have acquired a "perfect mastery of Greek and Latin," together with some knowledge of philosophy, astronomy, physic, arithmetic, logic, rhetoric, and music. Though More's example had great influence upon both Vives and Erasmus, others felt that allowing women to study Latin and Greek would encourage them to become too independent. Richard Hyrde (or Hart), another one of the tutors that More hired, argued that this could not possibly be true since English and French literature had the same kind of information as Latin and Greek, but not everyone believed him.[43]

Erasmus went further and argued that learning was not particularly dangerous to the moral fiber of a woman; instead the real dangers were idleness or triviality of interests. A girl cooped up with a "foolish and empty-headed" woman was more likely to learn mischief than if she read good books, and those men who felt that a learned woman was twice a fool, were themselves ignoramuses. A learned woman would make a better wife than an ignorant one since intelligence implies reason and there is nothing so hard to control as ignorance where reason and argument are of no avail. Erasmus, unlike some of his contemporaries who thought as he did, gave few rules for the education of girls, partly because as a celibate priest he had little experience upon which to draw, but also because he felt that circumstances varied from individual to individual. The first duty of an educator was to train his students, male or female, to exercise their free will to make rational choices in the affair of life. He compared the educated women with the uneducated woman, much to the advantage of the former. The uneducated women began their day "with hair-dressing and rouging; formal attendance at public worship follows, for the sake of seeing and being seen: then comes breakfast. Gossip and the lightest of 'literature' fill up the morning until dinner. The afternoon is occupied by promenades, and, for the young

42. Quoted in Josephine Kamm, *Hope Deferred: Girls' Education in English History* (London: Methuen, 1965), p. 40.

43. *Ibid.*, p. 43.

people games sadly lacking in decorum. Then more gossip and supper. It is no better when the family moves to the country, where amid idle days, the crowds of retainers, lackeys, and serving-girls, is a standing influence of evil. How different is such an environment for a young girl from that careful supervision which Aristotle commands."[44]

Richard Mulcaster, the first headmaster of Merchant Taylors' School in London, agreed that both young boys and girls should be educated but he, like most of those who advocated education for girls, believed boys should have priority. This was because the "male is more worthy, and politikely he is more employed," and the bringing up of young maidens "in any kynd of learning, is but an accessary by the waye...."[45] Most educational writers held that the purpose of female education was to inculcate in women a love of goodness, particularly of chastity, and a hatred of evil. They should be taught "reading well, writing faire, singing sweet, playing fine," but they were not to be regarded as professional, only "honest perfourmers and vertuous livers." Some of the male writers wondered if women should be taught to read at all since there were dangers in books, and most of those who did believe girls should read felt that their reading should be censored. In general girls were to be closely confined to the home where they could be kept away from public entertainments, and some went so far as to urge that they be kept from windows in order that they not see the evil of the world. Though it was necessary for girls to venture outside occasionally for various purposes, such as going to church, it was recommended that they be escorted by older persons who would try to select the nearest and shortest ways possible without encountering the reality of evil. In every way they were to be guarded from learning unclean words, acquiring uncomely gestures, or making lascivious movements of the body. The first things to teach girls were submission and obedience. Educational theory did not divide women into two groups, the ruler and the ruled, as it did men, but instead held that all women were to be ruled. While books addressed to boys were filled with discussions of various occupations, those aimed toward a female audience recommended only one occu-

44. Quoted by William H. Woodward, *Desiderius Erasmus Concerning the Aim and Method of Education* (Cambridge: Cambridge University Press, 1904), p. 152.

45. Richard Mulcaster, *Positions* (reprinted, London: Longmans, Green, 1888), chap. 36, pp. 133–134.

pation, housewifery. The purpose of education for a lady was to ensure proficiency in domestic affairs, to give her moral and religious
training to help her remain chaste, obedient, and run a well-managed
household. The so-called "female" virtues of chastity, humility, obedience, constancy, patience, piety, temperance, kindness, prudence
in household management, and fortitude under affliction were emphasized. Someone has called these the Christian virtues. If this were
true the virtues most admired in males were the pagan ones, namely
self-expansion and realization. The male was to develop to the up-
most every power he had and direct every action to enhance his authority. Women were to suppress and negate themselves. Women
were also urged to marry early in order to increase their chances of
being virgins at marriage, but also to curtail their opportunities for
education and to force them to turn to the problem of attending to
children.[46]

A significant portion of sixteenth- and seventeenth-century literature dealt with what the French call *Querell des femmes,* or the debate over woman. In a sense this was a continuation of the medieval
discussion associated with chivalric love, but it received new emphasis with the publication of Baldesar Castiglione's *Book of the Courtier* in 1528. The influence of the book was emphasized by the fact
that 100 different printings were made in the sixteenth century and
it was translated from Italian into Latin, German, Spanish, English,
and French during this same period. The end of the second section
and the whole of the third were devoted to the questions of what was
woman, what was her essence, what was her destiny? The book was
in dialogue form and included a discussion between Count Gaspar
Pallavicino and Agostino Fregoso, who generally represented the
standard misogynistic views, and Giuliano de Medici, who defended
the fair sex. Fregoso and Pallavicino argued that women were very
imperfect creatures, inferior in every respect to man, whose only
destiny was to guarantee the continuation of the human species
through childbearing. Since woman was all body, whoever possessed
a woman's body was master of her mind, and feminine sexual morals
were bridles imposed upon them by men in order to insure the
legitimacy of their children.

46. For a discussion of this see Ruth Kelso, *Doctrine for the Lady of the Renaissance* (Urbana: University of Illinois Press, 1956), esp. p. 36, where this summary is
found.

Giuliano replied to all of these arguments. "For just as no one stone can be more perfectly stone than another as regards the essence of a stone, noe one piece of wood more perfectly wood than another —soe one man cannot be more perfectly man than another; and consequently the male will not be more perfect than the female as regards its essential substance, because both are included in the species man, and that wherein the one differs from the other is an accidental matter and not essential. . . . Again, if you examine the ancient histories . . . you will find that worth has continually existed among women as well as among men; and that there have even been those who waged wars and won glorious victories therein, governed kingdoms with the highest prudence and justice, and did everything that men have done. . . . Do you not remember having read of many women who were learned in philosophy? Others who were very excellent in poetry? Others who conducted suits. . . ."[47]

One of the most effective defenses of women was in Erasmus's *Colloquy* entitled "The Abbot and the Learned Lady." This was a short dialogue between Antronius, an abbot, and Magdalia, a learned lady. Antronius, who was visiting in the lady's apartment, remarked that the room was unbecoming both to a "young miss and a married woman" because it was so "filled with books." Magdalia questioned him as to whether he had ever seen books in a lady's house before:

> Antronius: Yes, but those were in French. Here I see Greek and Latin ones.
> Magdalia: Are French books the only ones that teach wisdom.
> Antronius: But it's fitting for court ladies to have something with which to beguile their leisure.
> Magdalia: Are court ladies the only ones allowed to improve their minds and enjoy themselves?
> Antronius: You confuse growing wise with enjoying yourself. It's not feminine to be brainy. A lady's business is to have a good time.
>
> . . .
>
> Magdalia: What if I enjoy reading a good author more than you do hunting, drinking or playing dice? You won't think I'm having a good time?
> Antronius: I wouldn't live like that.

47. Baldesar Castiglione, *The Book of the Courtier*, trans. by Leonard Eckstein Opdycke (New York: Scribner's, 1903), III, 12–13, pp. 182–183.

Magdalia: I'm not asking what you would enjoy most, but what
ought to be enjoyable. . . .
Antronius: You strike me as a sophistress, so keenly do you
dispute.
Magdalia: Isn't it a wife's business to manage the household
and rear the children.
Antronius: It is.
Magdalia: Do you think she can manage so big a job without
wisdom?
Antronius: I suppose not.
Magdalia: But books teach me this wisdom. . . .
Antronius: I've often heard the common saying, "A wise woman
is twice foolish."
Magdalia: That's commonly said, yes, but by fools. A woman
truly wise is not wise in her own conceit. On the other
hand, one who thinks herself wise when she knows nothing,
is indeed twice foolish.
Antronius: I don't know how it is, but as packsaddles don't
fit an ox, so learning doesn't fit a woman.
Magdalia: But you can't deny that packsaddles would fit an ox
better than a miter would fit an ass or a swine.[48]

There were other defenders. Henry Cornelius Agrippa von Nettesheim published a defense of women in 1529. He recognized that
there were differences between men and women, but these were only
physical, and since the soul had no sex, there could be no difference
in this respect. Although he granted that women occupied a decidedly subordinate position in society, he said this subjection was
not proof for the incapacity of women but rather the usurpation by
men of women's natural right. Little more could be expected of
women who were shut up in the house from the time they were born,
given nothing serious or worthwhile to do, treated as if they were incapable of a real action, forced to make the needle and thread their
sole occupation.[49]

Women, however, could also speak for themselves. One of the

48. Erasmus *Colloquies*, trans. by Craig R. Thompson (Chicago: University of
Chicago Press, 1964), pp. 219–223. Erasmus, however, in his *Council of Women,
Colloquies*, pp. 441–447, made fun of feminine vanity but he was not so hostile as
many of his contemporaries.
49. See Lula McDowell Richardson, *The Forerunners of Feminism in French Literature of the Renaissance* (Baltimore: Johns Hopkins Press, 1929), pp. 63–64.

leading literary figures of the sixteenth century was Marguerite de
Navarre, author of the *Heptameron*. Marguerite also composed a
book of letters to defend her sex against unjust charges, and though
her defense of women is no longer extant, it was analyzed by Pierre
de l'Escale in 1612 and from his summary we can get the basis of her
ideas. Marguerite held that woman was the masterpiece of God since
she was formed after man and was God's last work. Because women
had intuitive powers lacking to men they were also more intelligent,
and woman should have been able to command more effectively because she was more willing to listen and was therefore more reasonable. In fact Marguerite held that women had originally commanded
men until men had usurped power, which made her an early advocate
of the theory of matriarchy. Inevitably, however, those who wanted
to complement Marguerite on her intelligence and ability held that
she had a manly heart in a woman's body, and that she surpassed the
rest of her sex in intelligence.[50]

The great feminist of the period was Marie de Gournay (1565–
1645), one of the intellectual leaders of France during her lifetime
and friend and correspondent of most of the major literary figures,
particularly the great Michel de Montaigne. Marie fought hard for
the emancipation of women and against the conviction that women
were inferior to men. She entered the battle for women's rights in
1594 and continued in it up to her death. She personally suffered
more than most other women of her time because of her refusal to
follow the custom of submissiveness for women, but instead openly
displayed her learning, both in her writings and in her social contacts. Inevitably she also alienated many women, particularly those
"ladies" who were becoming important for their salons where they
invited leading intellectual figures to discuss the issues of the day.
These women, though important societal figures, had different aims
in life than Marie. Marie felt that the salon ladies strived only to
perfect the social graces and to act in the proper submissive role of
women as helpmates for the more superior males. Marie, however,
could not condemn them since she believed that women by their
early environment, habit, and climate in which they lived could do
little else. It was this condition she worked to change. The human
animal for her was neither man nor woman, and although there were
physical differences these were only for purposes of propagation. She

50. *Ibid.*, p. 112.

emphasized this by the statement that "nothing so resembles a male cat on the window sill as a female cat." Her own feelings of alienation appear in the introductory sentence to one of her books: "Happy are you, Reader, if you do not belong to this sex to whom all good is forbidden, since to us liberty is proscribed . . . so that the sole joy and sovereign virtue allowed us is to be ignorant, to play the dullard, and to serve."[51]

Renée of Ferrara, daughter of King Louis XII of France, put the prejudice toward women rather bluntly: "Had I had a beard I would have been the king of France. I have been defrauded by that confounded Salic law." This was a reference to an ancient Frankish law which prevented women from ruling in France. Even when women did get to rule, as they did in England, they had difficulties. Such simple things as marriage caused difficulties in a period in which women were legally and conventionally subject to men. For a queen to marry meant conferring kingship either upon a native social inferior or upon a foreign equal. To do the first was to compromise internal peace, and to do the second was to jeopardize national independence. In England Queen Elizabeth evaded the dilemma by remaining single, but her half-sister Mary fell into the marriage trap. By the Act of Succession which placed Mary upon the throne she was to be succeeded by her sister Elizabeth if she died without heirs. Since Elizabeth was the daughter of Anne Boleyn, whom Henry had married at least in part to get a male heir, and this marriage had forced a break with Rome, it was essential that Mary have an heir in order to make certain that Catholicism was maintained in England. There were, of course, other ways of preventing Elizabeth's succession, and some of them were contemplated by advisers to Mary, but Mary would have no part in them. The only impeccable and infallible way to retain Catholicism and prevent Elizabeth from succeeding was for Mary to have an heir. For her husband she chose King Philip of Spain and of the Netherlands, a somewhat natural choice since the Tudors and Hapsburgs had long been allies, and England's commercial interests were closely tied to the Netherlands. Mary recognized this and the marriage agreement stated that if Mary and Philip had a child he would be Philip's heir in the Netherlands and Burgandy as well as Mary's in England, thus giving England

51. See Marjorie Henry Isley, *A Daughter of the Renaissance* (The Hague: Mouton, 1963), pp. 207, 210, 216.

political control over an area to which they were so strongly tied commercially. Great care was taken in drawing up the marriage agreement in order to ensure Mary's rights. Though Philip was called King of England and was to assist in the government, Mary alone was to bestow and only Englishmen were to be appointed to fill offices in church and state. If Mary died without an heir Philip had to renounce all claims to the English throne.

In spite of such safeguards, as well as the potential advantages to England of control over the Netherlands, Mary's marriage was greeted with considerable hostility. Hatred of the foreigner was particularly rampant at this time in England and much of the success of Henry VIII had been due to his ability to exploit and foster such hatred. Even while the treaty was under negotiation there was a rebellion led by Thomas Wyatt, whose motives were in part religious, hostility to the return of the Catholic faith, but mostly political, the threat of a Spanish king. Mary managed to put down the rebellion and her throne was saved by the loyalty of the citizens of London, but the hostility to Philip remained. Some of this hostility was transferred to Mary herself by her executions of Protestants who refused to accept her Catholic appointees, and though the numbers were not so great in total the average of some ninety a year caused increasing antagonism toward her. The growing domestic discontent was further complicated by Mary's involvement in the wars of her husband with France which led to the loss of the last British outpost, Calais, on the European continent. Unfortunately, also, Mary, in spite of all her ambitions for the future and her genuine affection for her usually absent husband, proved unable to conceive a child. The first English experiment with a woman ruler proved to be little short of disastrous.

Elizabeth, on the other hand, was much more successful. In fact, she turned out to be a political genius and much of her success was due to her ability to remain unmarried, not subordinate to a husband. It was not enough to remain unmarried; Elizabeth also had to avoid having an illegitimate child. Her ability to do this meant that she either was sterile or that she remained a virgin since there were no effective birth control pills and abortion was dangerous. Her countrymen believed she remained a virgin and this belief is commemorated in the American state of Virginia and its offshoot West Virginia, dedicated to the virgin queen. Though it seems clear that Elizabeth, with the example of her sister Mary before her, had probably decided not to marry, she did not publicly commit herself to spinsterhood and for some twenty years she was one of the most courted women in all history.

The very success of Elizabeth, and at least one indication of the way in which women were regarded, is the fact that even as late as the nineteenth century there were some "historians" who felt that Elizabeth must have been a man in disguise. These people argued that Elizabeth, following the execution of her mother, was more or less neglected, isolated from the court, and lodged in the countryside. Here she became ill and died, but her guardians, fearful of telling the king of the death of his daughter, and knowing that he probably would not recognize her anyway, scoured the countryside for a replacement of the right age. Unable to find a suitable girl child they utilized a boy. This, it was said, explained Elizabeth's somewhat masculine features in her old age, including a tendency to baldness, as well as her "masculine ability" in ruling. Naturally it explained her reluctance to marry.

Though it is easy to be cynical about the reputed intellectual accomplishments of the rich and powerful, Elizabeth obviously was intelligent and she had a very real love of learning. She must be regarded as one of the great rulers of England, and her abilities were early attested to by her teacher, Roger Ascham, who wrote to his friend that it was difficult to say

> whether the gifts of nature or of fortune are most to be admired in my distinguished mistress. The praise which Aristotle gives wholly centers in her; beauty, stature, prudence, and industry. She has just passed her sixteenth birthday and shows such dignity and gentleness as are wonderful at her age and in her rank. Her study of true religion and learning is most eager. Her mind has no womanly weakness, her perseverance is equal to that of a man, and her memory long keeps what it quickly picks up. She talks French and Italian as well as she does English, and has often talked to me readily and well in Latin, moderately in Greek. When she writes Greek and Latin, nothing is more beautiful than her handwriting. She delights as much in music as she is skillful in it. . . . I am inventing nothing, my dear Strum; there is no need.[52]

52. Quoted in J. E. Neale, *Queen Elizabeth: A Biography* (Garden City, N.Y.: Doubleday, 1957), pp. 14–15.

The success of Elizabeth leads one to question how many other able women were denied chances to succeed. The numbers must have been legion. Elizabeth's reign, however, led to little change in the status of women, although it seems likely that at least some women wondered whether it was not unreasonable to subject themselves to such stringent male controls while a queen was ruling England. There was considerable controversy over the nature of women's role which perhaps grew out of Elizabeth's reign,[53] but women remained firmly under control of their husbands. The legal status of women in England is evident in the case of Frances Coke, the younger daughter of Sir Edward Coke, the famed champion and exponent of the common law. Frances was a daughter of Coke's second marriage to Elizabeth Haton, which was not a particularly happy alliance. Coke, anxious for support at court, arranged for Frances, then fourteen, to marry Sir John Villiers, the eldest brother of the king's favorite, the Duke of Buckingham. Villiers unfortunately was mentally defective and inclined to spells of insanity. Lady Elizabeth felt that her daughter could expect a better match and tried to secrete her in a cousin's house. Coke, however, seized Frances by force and when her mother attempted to complain about his conduct to the Star Chamber, she found herself put into custody, unable even to attend her daughter's wedding. Frances's husband took the name of Lord Purbeck after the property he hoped to receive from his wife, but apparently he had other things wrong with him than defective intelligence. When Frances gave birth to a child, she was suspected of adultery, and was sentenced to pay a heavy fine, sent to prison, and had to do public penance wearing a white sheet. She eventually managed to escape her imprisonment but her money and property went to her husband.[54]

If women were asserting themselves somewhat more during the sixteenth century, which is at least debatable, the self-assertive woman and even the educated one faced growing hostility in the seventeenth. King James I of England, for example, was particularly hostile to female pretensions. When a learned young lady was pre-

---

53. See Louis B. Wright, *Middle-Class Culture in Elizabethan England* (Chapel Hill: University of North Carolina Press, 1935), chap. 13, "The Popular Controversy over Women."

54. Doris Mary Stenton, *The English Woman in History* (London: Allen and Unwin, 1957), p. 67.

sented to him at court with a comment on her ability in Latin, Greek, and Hebrew, he is said to have replied: "But can she spin?"[55] In 1620 he urged the clergy of his kingdom to "inveigh vehemently against the insolence of our women." James was also known for his belief in witchcraft which in some ways seemed to institutionalize a fear of women.

The period from 1450 to 1750, in fact, was the great age of witchcraft, and Europe went berserk in seeking out witches. Some areas were worse than others. In general the witchcraft trials were restricted to France, Germany, Scotland, England, and to some extent Italy. Holland, the Scandinavian countries, Ireland, and Spain were virtually free from the delusion, as was most of eastern Europe. Until almost the thirteenth century the official position of the Christian church was that acts associated with witchcraft were all illusions or fantasies originating in dreams and that belief in the actuality of witches was a pagan and heretical custom. This idea was challenged in the writings of St. Thomas Aquinas, who held that even though witches might be illusions or dreams they were no less real. The key document in changes toward witchcraft, however, was a papal bull of Innocent VIII in 1484 designed to assist in eradicating witchcraft in Germany. Appointed to carry out the search for witches were two Dominicans, Heinrich Kramer and Jakob Sprenger, who between them wrote a manual, *Malleus Maleficarum* or the *Hammer of Witches*, first printed in 1486. The manual had the merit, or perhaps fault might be a better term, of codifying all the folk belief about black magic and witchcraft into church dogma and in the process it opened up the floodgates of hysteria. Before 1520 the book had gone through thirteen editions and it continued to be published during the sixteenth century. The authors argued that witches were more likely to be female than male, because women knew no moderation whether in goodness or in vice, and they quoted a whole catalog of church fathers and other misogynistic writers to prove that women were the sources of all evil, that they had defective intelligence, inordinate passions, weak memories, and tried to dominate men.[56]

The root of the fear of witches lay in the social tensions of the

55. Eva Figes, *Patriarchal Attitudes: Women in Society* (London: Faber and Faber, 1970), p. 69.
56. See Jakob Sprenger and Heinrich Kramer, *Malleus Maleficarum*, English trans. ed. by Montague Summers (limited ed., London: Pushkin Press, 1948).

time, marked by the growth of heresy, by the appearance of Protestantism, by challenges to old defined dogmas, but also by the changing social scene in which women were challenging some of the old assumptions. Witchcraft could explain not only what seemed mysterious and dangerous, but also even the odd and the deviant. One reason that Joan of Arc, for example, was condemned was because she wore men's clothing and fought like a man; such a form of deviant conduct could only be due to witchcraft. Once the Protestant movement appeared, both Catholics and Protestants turned to hunting witches with equal abandon. In a sense the belief in witches was a clerical phenomenon foisted upon a somewhat reluctant public, and it reflected all the hostilities of the clergy, including their traditional misogyny. When the new science of Galileo, Kepler, and Newton effectively challenged some of the basic assumptions upon which Christianity said witchcraft worked, both the fear of witchcraft and the power of the clergy were weakened.[57]

Though both men and women could be witches, it was women by far who were most often accused. In England six times as many women were indicted as men, and contrary to popular impression, twice as many married women were charged as were spinsters or widows.[58] Germany suffered the most from the persecution and some 100,000 people were executed, the vast majority of whom were women. In 1631 Cardinal Albizzi on a trip to Cologne wrote: "A horrible spectacle met our eyes. Outside of the walls of many towns and villages, we saw numerous stakes to which poor, wretched women were bound and burned as witches."[59]

How much the threat of being accused as a witch kept a woman in her place is difficult to determine historically, but there was a concerted effort in the seventeenth century to reassert masculine prerogatives. In England this appeared most obviously in the Puritan

57. See H. R. Trevor Roper, *The European Witch Craze of the Sixteenth and Seventeenth Centuries and Other Essays* (New York: Harper and Row, 1969), pp. 90–192.

58. Wallace Notestein, *A History of Witchcraft in England* (reprinted, New York: Russell and Russell, 1965), pp. 114–115.

59. For the most comprehensive treatment of the subject see Russell Hope Robbins, *The Encyclopedia of Witchcraft and Demonology* (New York: Crown Publishers, 1959), p. 100, from whence this quotation is derived. See the article "Witchcraft in Germany." Since this book went to press a new study of witchcraft in the Middle Ages has appeared which is invaluable, Jeffrey Burton Russel, *Witchcraft in the Middle Ages* (Ithaca: Cornell University Press, 1972).

marriage relationships. Though the wife was the husband's friend and companion, she was also his servant, deriving her authority from him. The nature of the wife's subordinate status in Puritanism has been the subject of much discussion,[60] mostly erroneous, but the best literary representation of this tendency is found in the works of John Milton. Milton, while emphasizing that the wife was something more than a sexual vessel, also claimed that she was less than a man. It was because Adam did not maintain his authority over Eve that he fell, and everywhere Milton insisted that women must be subject to man's sway.[61]

Giving further impetus to the need to keep woman in her place were the medical writings of the sixteenth century, most notably in those of Francois Rabelais, who was a physician as well as author of the *Gargantua* and *Pantagruel*. Rabelais was expressing standard medical beliefs when he wrote that nature had placed in female bodies,

> in a secret and intestinal place, a certain animal or member which is not in man, in which are engendered, frequently, certain humours, brackish, nitrous, voracious, acrid, mordant, shooting, and bitterly tickling, by the painful prickling and wriggling of which—for this member is extremely nervous and sensitive—the entire feminine body is shaken, all the senses ravished, all the passions carried to a point of repletion, and all through thrown into confusion. To such a degree that, if Nature had not rouged their foreheads with a tint of shame, you would see them running the streets like mad women, in a more frightful manner than the Protides, the Mimallonides, or the Bacchich Tyades on the day of their Bacchanalia ever did; and this, for the reason that this terrible animal I am telling you about is so very intimately associated with all the principal parts of the body, as anatomy teaches us.[62]

60. For a discussion see James T. Johnson, *A Society Ordained by God: English Puritan Marriage Doctrine in the First Half of the Seventeenth Century* (Nashville: Abingdon Press, 1970).

61. See Allan Gilbert, "Milton on the Position of Women," *Modern Language Review*, 15 (1920), 7–27, 240–264. See also the various works of John Milton, particularly *Paradise Lost*, IV, 295–308, 635–638, 750–770; VIII, 551–556; IX, 1183–84; X, 145–156, 889–908; XI, 163–165, 629–636 in *Complete Poetry and Selected Prose*, ed. by E. H. Visiak (Glasgow: Nonesuch Press, 1948). See also the various citations in Rogers, *Troublesome Helpmate*, pp. 151–159.

62. François Rabelais, *Pantagruel* in the *Portable Rabelais*, trans. and ed. by Samuel Putnam (New York: Viking Press, 1946), pp. 477–478.

The only way women could control this internal animal (the womb), for Rabelais said it was an animal because it moved by itself, was by absorption in other activities, by subordination to the male. "I shall not go any further into this dispute. I merely would say to you that those virtuous women who have lived modestly and blamelessly, and who have had the courage to rein in that unbridled animal and to make it obedient to reason, are deserving of no small praise indeed. And I may, in conclusion, add that once this same animal is glutted, if glutted it can be, through that alimentation which Nature has prepared for it in man, then all these specialized motions come to an end, all appetite is satiated and all fury appeased."[63]

It was during the sixteenth century, at the same time the concept of a lady was being developed, that clothes became a sign of status. Inevitably confining clothes developed which limited women's abilities to engage in any real activity. The result was that the very women who were writing and thinking the most about the role and status of women were among those who were being forced to confine themselves to corsets and limit their action by yards and yards of material. In general prior to the fifteenth century woman's costume had followed the natural configuration of the body, with no artificial or confining shaping. By the end of the fifteenth century, however, two items of female apparel appeared which tended to limit their freedom of activity, namely the "busc" and the "farthingale," both of which were also known under various other terms. The "busc" was an early form of corset. It was made from two pieces of linen, stiffened by paste, stitched together, and shaped to the waist at the sides. To keep the front part really rigid a piece of wood, horn, whalebone, metal, or ivory (busc was the technical term) was inserted between the layers, thick at the top and tapering toward a point at the waist. Shoulder straps were attached to hold these "pair of bodys" or stays in place since they were not shaped to the breasts, and they were laced together. The effect must have been like a tight waistcincher which also held the breasts in, since illustrations and literary references indicate that the ideal woman in the last part of the sixteenth and first part of the seventeenth centuries was one with a small waist.

To further accentuate the waist farthingales were developed. The term comes from the Spanish *Verdugos* (saplings). They were

63. *Ibid.*, pp. 478–479.

basically a kind of hooped petticoat, probably originally made from saplings. At the beginning of the sixteenth century the farthingale was cone-shaped by a series of graduated hoops, giving the required shape, but they were bolstered by adding extra padding to the hips to give a more rounded shape. Some of them required enormous amounts of material to complete and as much as fifty yards of whalebone and buckram to construct. The difficulties of wearing one were indicated by an epigram of the sixteenth century: "Alas, poor verdingales must lie in the street,/To house them no doore in the citee made meete,/ Syns at our narrow doores they in can not win,/ Send them to Oxford, at Brodegates to get in."[64] The Venetian ambassador to the court of France described the French women in 1577 as having "inconceivably narrow waists: they swell out their gowns from the waist downwards by whaleboned stuffs and vertugadins, which increases the elegance of their figures. Over the chemise they wear a corset or bodice, that they call a 'corps pique' which makes their shape more delicate and more slender. It is fastened behind which helps to show off the form of the bust."[65] By the seventeenth century, the French-type farthingale had replaced the Spanish. The hooped petticoat remained tub-shaped but it was stretched out from the sides by means of a thick bolsterlike bustle commonly known as "a bum roll," a sort of doughnut open at one end and tied around the waist. Anne, the wife of King James I, wore one so expansive that she was four feet wide at the hips.[66]

With such a costume the lady became ever more handicapped in her movements, and more and more activities were denied to her. Perhaps the most ludicrous denial of rights to our mind was the ability to play women's parts on the stage. On the stage a woman was not a female but a male. This was not so much the case in Italy as in England, but the custom was widespread. In a sense the Europeans were simply following the Greek custom, but there were additional reasons which emphasized the subordinate and protected status of women. Modern drama originated in the late Middle Ages from two sources, groups of strolling players who were at first offi-

64. Quoted in C. Willett Cunnington and Phyllis Cunnington, *The History of Underclothes* (London: Michael Joseph, 1951,) p. 48.
65. Quoted in Norah Waugh, *Corsets and Crinolines* (London: B. T. Batsford, 1954), p. 27.
66. Cunnington and Cunnington, *History of Underclothes*, p. 51.

cially classed as rogues and vagabonds and from church dramas. Both excluded women. Women who appeared in the strolling groups would have been despised as shameless and scorned as prostitutes, and since women could play no active part either in the services or offices of the church, they were usually prohibited from serving as actresses in religious drama. As the dramatic art took on new luster in the sixteenth century, men continued to play the heroines. Actors were formed into companies, each under the patronage of a wealthy member of the aristocracy, and younger boys were apprenticed to leading actors from whom they learned their art. Many of them would start out playing female roles as well as the smaller male parts. Some became quite famous for their impersonations.[67]

It seems difficult for us to imagine males playing female roles in some of the juicier female parts in Shakespeare's plays, but this was the custom and the playwrights adjusted to it. It might well be that some of the female roles were written more masculine than they might otherwise have been. The controversial modern drama critic, Kenneth Tynan, for example, has gone so far as to suggest that Lady Macbeth was basically a man's role and it would be a mistake to cast a woman in the role at all. This might well be another example of male chauvinism, twentieth-century chauvinism if you will, in denying that women could be or should be as dominating a personality as Lady Macbeth. We know the names of some of the men and boys who played the Shakespearean roles. The first Ophelia is thought to have been Nathaniel Field; the first Desdemona, the famous Richard or "Dickie" Robinson. Lady Macbeth was probably originally played by Alexander Cooke, while the ambitious role of Rosalind was played by Willie Ostler. Robert Gough or Goffe was the first Juliet and possibly the first Cleopatra. Perhaps the difficulty boys and men had in impersonating women in their early twenties and thirties was one reason Shakespeare's female roles were primarily for older women or young girls. The French included actresses in their dramas somewhat earlier than the English but when a French troop with women actresses ventured on to the English stage in 1632, the women were jeered and pelted with apples. It was only in the last

67. See Roger Baker, *Drag: A History of Female Impersonation on the Stage* (London: Triton Books, 1968), and C. J. Bulliet, *Venus Castina: Famous Female Impersonators* (reprinted, New York: Bonanza Books, 1956).

part of the seventeenth century that female actresses made their appearance in England.

In sum the sixteenth and seventeenth centuries, although many women were unhappy with their role, saw little effort to change. To be a good wife and mother was the end for which every young girl in the seventeenth century was carefully trained from early child-hood. To be a true housewife then as now was not an easy occupation, and it required that the woman run the house efficiently, beautify it with the work of her hands, and spiritually make it a place of peace and happiness for those who lived in it. The good housewife was to "be of chaste thought, stout courage, patient, untired, watch-ful, diligent, witty, pleasant, constant in friendship, full of good Neighbourhood, wise in Discourse but not frequent therein, sharp and quick of speech, but not bitter or talkative, secret in her affairs, comfortable in her counsels, and generally skillful in the worthy knowledge which do belong in her Vocation."[68] We might add that she was to be subordinate to her husband and to males in general. There had been some changes but the more things changed the more they seemed to be the same, at least as far as women were concerned.

68. Quoted in Christina Hole, *The English Housewife in the Seventeenth Century* (London: Chatto and Windus, 1953), p. 99.

chapter ten

China and India: Inferiority
Is Not Only Western

Though this book concentrates on Western civilization, it is important to realize that a belief in women's inferiority and her subordination was not just confined to the West. This belief was present in Eastern civilization as well. To do justice to the East it would be necessary to write as lengthy a treatment as we have devoted to the West, but some indication of these attitudes can be seen by a brief survey of attitudes in India and in China.

Women in India, as in the West, were completely under the subjugation of males. There are some indications that the level of subordination was not as severe in very early Indian history as later, and in fact some historians believe they have found evidence of an early matrilineal system. Many of the early tribes in India, for example, were named after women, such as the Kādravey, descendants of Kadrū, the Vinateya of Vinatā, the Daitya of Diti, and the Dānavas of Danu. Some investigators have claimed that there is evidence of an early matriarchal system since originally the female divinity, at least in some parts of India, took precedence over the male, as among the Sāktas, and in the dual form of divine names the goddess was almost always named first, as in Lakshmī-Nārāyan, Gaurī-Sankar, Rāha-Krishna. There are also surviving legends of states ruled by women which at least indicate that the Indians did not think female rulers were beyond the realm of probability. With the appearance of the Aryans, an Indo-European speaking people in the second millennium B.C., however, patriarchy was firmly established, and in the religious pantheon the female became, if she had not always been, subordinate to the male. She was not, however, as subordinate as she later became.

The earliest extant literature of these Indo-European invaders are the *Veda*, and these indicate that women, though clearly subordinate, still held an important function in the religious rituals, a function which only gradually was taken away from them. During the Vedic period most religious rites and ceremonies were open to them, and women took an active part in the various rituals. Certain sacrifices were restricted to women. The Vedic age also produced at least a score of eminent female scholars, poets, and teachers, and a number of hymns included in the *Rig-veda*, composed some time between 1500 B.C. and 900 B.C., were attributed to women. By the time the first Hindu law codes emerged around 100 A.D., however, women had lost more ground vis-à-vis the male.[1]

Hindu law was not based on the decree of a sovereign or political body but rather on sacred scriptures believed to be divinely inspired and unalterable. It assumed a metaphysical foundation of universal regularity and order in the whole cosmic process, and from this concept came the notion of *dharma*, which means law, religion, morality, and in effect the universal laws of nature that upheld the cosmos. The earliest and most famous of these laws was that of Manu, which dated from about 100 A.D., although according to orthodox Hindu tradition the laws coincided with the appearance of man himself. The purpose of the code seems to have been to give divine sanction to the institution of caste, to make caste supreme in India, and the brāhmin supreme among the castes. In these laws women were put under the control of men:

> By a girl, by a young woman, or even by an aged one, nothing must be done independently, even in her own house.
>
> In childhood a female must be subject to her father, in youth to her husband, when her lord is dead to her sons; a woman must never be independent.
>
> She must not seek to separate herself from her father, husband, or sons; by leaving them she would make both [her own and her husband's] families contemptible.
>
> She must always be cheerful, clever in [the management of her] household affairs, careful in cleaning her utensils, and economical in expenditure.

1. For a summary see M. A. Indra, *The Status of Women in Ancient India* (Banaras: Motilal Banarasidass, 1955).

> Him to whom her father may give her, or her brother with the
> father's permission, she shall obey as long as he lives, and when he
> is dead, she must not insult [his memory].[2]

Men must be continually watchful of their womenfolk. "Day and
night women must be kept in dependence by the males [of their
families], and if they attach themselves to sensual enjoyments, they
must be kept under one's control. . . . Women must particularly be
guarded against evil inclinations, however trifling [they may appear],
for, if they are not guarded, they will bring sorrow on two families.
Considering that the highest duty of all castes, even weak husbands
[must] strive to guard their wives."[3] Women by their very nature
were wicked creatures.

> It is the nature of women to seduce men in this [world]; for that
> reason the wise are never unguarded in [the company of] females.
> For women are able to lead astray in [this] world not only a fool,
> but even a learned man, and [to make] him a slave of desire and
> anger.
> One should not sit in a lonely place with one's mother, sister, or
> daughter, for the senses are powerful, and master even a learned
> man.[4]

> [When creating them] Manu alloted to women [a love of their]
> bed, [of their] seat and [of] ornament, impure desires, wrath, dis-
> honesty, malice, and bad conduct. For women no [sacramental] rite
> [is performed] with sacred texts, thus the law is settled; women [who
> are] destitute of strength and destitute of [the knowledge of] Vedic
> texts [are as impure as] falsehood [itself], that is a fixed rule.[5]

For women who accepted their status and obeyed their masters there
were rewards.

> Women must be honoured and adorned by their fathers, brothers,
> husbands, and brothers-in-law, who desire [their own] welfare.
> Where women are honoured, there the gods are pleased; but
> where they are not honoured, no sacred rite yields rewards.
> Where the female relations live in grief, the family soon wholly
> perishes; but that family where they are not unhappy ever prospers.

2. *Laws of Manu*, 5, pp. 147–151 in *Sacred Books of the East*, ed. by G. Bühler,
vol. 15 (reprinted, Delhi: Motilal Banarasidass, 1964).
3. *Ibid.*, 9, pp. 2, 5–6.
4. *Ibid.*, 2, pp. 213–215.
5. *Ibid.*, 9, pp. 17–18.

The houses on which female relations, not being duly honoured, pronounce a curse, perish completely, as if destroyed by magic."[6]

Yet in spite of this the slaying of a woman was not a particularly serious crime, since as Manu says, "stealing grain, base metals, or cattle," having "intercourse with women who drink spirituous liquor," or slaying a woman, are "all minor offences, causing loss of caste."[7]

Other lawgivers generally reflected Manu's biases, although Yāj-navalkya, who denounced brāhminical avarice, has been regarded as less misogynistic, but only to a slightly less degree. Yājnāvalkya also taught that the ideal woman spent all her greatness and goodness in maintaining a happy home and husband, and always obeyed the men in her family. Woman's duties included "Learning to arrange furniture and being expert, cheerful and frugal, she should worship the feet of her both parents-in-law, and be devoted to her husband. She whose husband is away from home, should abandon playing, beautifying the body, joining societies, and festivities, laughing and going to another's home. Devoted to the pleasure and to the good of her husband, of good conduct with subdued passions, [such a wife] obtains renown in this world, and after death attains the best end."[8]

Until recently in India, it was often held that being born a girl was a penalty for some sin committed in a previous incarnation. In many areas of the subcontinent the birth of a girl was not announced, or it was merely stated that "nothing" had been born. The friends awaiting the birth of a boy then went away "grave and quiet."[9] Females were regarded as an encumbrance and a burden from birth. They were an impediment in war; they had to be protected in time of peace; they were unclean and dangerous during their menses, pregnancy, and childbirth; they had to be provided with a dowry when they married; they were of no use to anyone as widows. The father of daughters, even though his position was as exalted as a king, had to put up with insults not only from equals but from inferiors as well. Even when the father succeeded in selecting a good son-in-law, his

6. *Ibid.*, 3, pp. 55–58.
7. *Ibid.*, 11, p. 67.
8. Sudhakar Chattopadhyaya, *Social Life in Ancient India* (Calcutta: Academic Publishers, 1965), pp. 110–111.
9. David and Vera Mace, *Marriage: East and West* (Garden City, N.Y.: Doubleday, 1960), p. 263.

anxiety did not end, for he still had to wait to find out whether the marriage was a happy one. Inevitably female infanticide was practiced on a wide scale from earliest times and the casting away of children, of unmarried mothers of unwanted girl babies, and the destruction of the fetus, were mentioned in the Vedic texts. The *Yajur-veda* told of girls being exposed when born, a custom that continued down through the centuries with little effort to modify it. In Bengali a woman might drown her child in fulfillment of a vow; in western India female infants were strangled or smothered; among the Rajputs parents often used to kill their unwanted children, usually girls, either by refusing proper nourishment or sometimes simply poisoning the nipples of the mother's breasts.[10] Those who try to find some justification for such a callous disregard of girl children indicate that perhaps it was not so much a hatred of the female sex as an anxiety to see that the daughter was well placed so that she could live in comfort and happiness,[11] but this seems a rather far-fetched apology.

Women, nevertheless, had their place, and in the religious rituals of Hinduism they were indispensable since certain ceremonies could not be performed by a Brahman unless his wife was with him.[12] She was, however, to be clearly subordinate to her husband. Unmarried daughters were to live in chastity and obedience toward their father, mother, and other kinfolk. Marriage was not only a necessity for girls but a religious sacrament as well, since it was believed that a female virgin could never attain spiritual enlightenment in this world, or reach the abodes of bliss in the next. Marriages were arranged by the father, and if he died his role was to be taken over by a girl's brothers. Brotherless maidens were believed to be exposed to all kinds of danger so that a girl with brothers was preferred as a bride.[13] The absolute necessity of acquiring a husband led Indian parents to marry their daughters at younger and younger ages, and also led to a widespread discrepancy between the age of the bride

10. R. C. Majumdar, H. C. Raychaudhuri, and Kalikinkar Datta, *An Advanced History of India* (London: Macmillan, 1953), p. 822.

11. A. S. Altekar, *The Position of Women in Hindu Civilization* (Banaras: Motilal Banarasidass, 1956), pp. 5–6.

12. R. N. Dandekar, "The Role of Man in Hinduism," in Kenneth W. Morgan, *The Religion of the Hindus* (New York: Ronald Press, 1953), p. 140.

13. P. S. Sivaswamy Aiyer, *Evolution of Hindu Moral Ideals* (Calcutta: University of Calcutta, 1935), pp. 57–59.

and groom. Marriage was so important to a girl that at times formal marriage ceremonies were performed over corpses of girls who had died before they had been married.

In the Vedic period when the emphasis on marriage was not so overwhelming, girls were usually married at fifteen or sixteen years of age. By the period 500 to 1000 A.D. many of the writers were urging that girls be married before the age of ten, the age at which it was believed they reached puberty. Certain factions argued for even younger marriages, and five- and six-year-old brides were not unknown. Early marriages helped the parents secure a guardian for the daughter in the case that the father died.[14] As younger marriages came more and more into vogue, women's educational accomplishments deteriorated. In turn this lack of education lessened women's importance in Hindu religious ceremonies, leaving them less and less independence. Inevitably women were relegated to the home where they were out of sight if not out of mind. While some of the girls in the cultured and rich families still acquired some learning, it was increasingly the outcast girl who managed to maintain any degree of independence. As in Greek society when women had been so subordinated, men turned to prostitutes and dancing girls for entertainment and companionship, and India developed a special class of prostitutes to entertain the male.[15] Woman in general, however, had no independence in virtue, religion, or law; they did not even have the freedom to dispose of themselves. As one modern Hindu woman lamented, the only place a woman could be free of the male was "in hell."[16]

Often the difference in ages between a man and his child bride was very great, and it was not unusual for a man of fifty or sixty to marry a girl of five or six. Even if the husband died before consummation, which was not usually attempted until the girl was about ten, the child was regarded as a widow and could not remarry. Some children were even married in embryo. In such cases two pregnant women underwent the formalities of a marriage ceremony, and this

14. Altekar, *Position of Women*, pp. 33, 55–61.

15. *Ibid.*, pp. 17–19, and J. A. Dubois, *Hindu Manners, Customs and Ceremonies* (Oxford: Clarendon Press, 1906), p. 337.

16. Johann Jakob Meyer, *Sexual Life in Ancient India* (New York: Barnes and Noble, 1953), p. 346, n. 1. Meyer's account relies heavily on two Hindu epics, the *Rāmayāna* and the *Mahābhārata*, and includes long extracts from them. I have utilized it as a primary source.

union by proxy, providing the children turned out to be of opposite sex, was absolutely binding.

Unlike the West where attitudes toward women seem to have been at least in part motivated by a fear of sex, the Indians welcomed sex. The Hindu never regarded marriage as a condition inferior to virginity, nor was there any notion of sex being impure. Virginity had no special cult; lifelong celibacy was permitted for men but it was never enjoined as a permanent ideal. Celibacy for women (except widows) was actively discouraged since heaven was not open to the sacramentally unconsecrated, that is, the unwedded maiden.[17] Asceticism as practiced in India was usually a temporary discipline, a self-restraint imposed as a means for the acquisition of magical powers. Sex, moreover, was strongly emphasized in the outward aspects of Indian religions, such as the statues of the gods; in these anthropomorphic conceptions both female and male elements were portrayed in all their sensuousness.[18]

Intercourse was said to be performed for four basic reasons: for procreation, in which case it took place between a husband and wife; for pleasure, where an experienced woman or a professional courtesan served as the companion; for motives of power, as when a man desired to triumph over a husband through possessing his wife; and for magical purposes. In this last case the woman herself was equated with the sacred place: her hips and haunches with the sacrificial ground; the mons veneris to the altar; the pubic hairs to kusa grass; the moist labia to the soma press; the yellow vulva to prepared fuel; the red-tipped phallus to the ember; lust, to smoke; penetration, to the mystic chants; voluptuousness, to sparks; movement, to the burning heat; orgasm, to the living flame; and semen, to the oblation.[19] This cult sexuality appeared in both Hindu and Buddhist scriptures, but it received its fullest rationale in Tantrism. The origins of Tantrism are unknown, but it dates from very early times and is the prototype of yoga and other magical techniques.

Separate from, but also allied to, mystical sex was sex for the purposes of pleasure, and there were many Hindu love texts, the most

17. *Ibid.*, p. 375.
18. See Kanwar Lal, *The Cult of Desire: An Interpretation of Erotic Sculpture of India* (New Hyde Park, N.Y.: University Books, 1967).
19. For an excellent brief discussion of this see the articles on "Sex Mysticism" and "Tantrism," in George Benjamin Walker, *The Hindu World: An Encyclopedic Survey of Hinduism* (2 vols., New York: Praeger, 1968).

famous of which was the *Kamasutra* compiled by Vatsyayana in the fifth century A.D. According to tradition Vatsyayana remained an ascetic celibate all his life and his work was written entirely from imagination without any personal experience. There are hundreds of other books on erotics, although few of them are available to the English-speaking reader.[20]

Just as sex asceticism in the West served to justify the subjugation of women, so did sexual liberation in India. Hinduism depicted women as by far the more sexual of the two partners. Whether men or women enjoy sex the most has often been debated, but on this subject Hinduism offered definitive answers—it was women who did. The answer appeared most simply in the tale of a king named Bhangāsvana, who was known as a tiger among men, yet he was unhappy because he lacked sons. In desperation he went through a special religious ritual which served to guarantee him sons, but in the process he angered Indra, the most prominent of the Vedic gods of the heavens. Indra sought revenge, but it was not until Bhangāsvana had had 100 sons that the god was able to find a means of punishing the king. Indra's chance came when the king became lost while hunting; Indra gradually led the king to the shores of a beautiful lake where weary and tired he stopped to bathe in what proved to be magical waters. When the king emerged he found that he no longer had the body of a man but that of a woman. Though ashamed at his condition he (or now she) went back to the city and reported to her numerous wives, sons, and subjects what had occurred. Unable to be king any longer she retreated to the forest, taking up life as a companion to a holy hermit. As his mistress she soon bore as many sons as a woman as she had begotten as a man.

Indra, ever observant but still angry, felt that the ex-king had not suffered enough for his impiety in making such a sacrilegious sacrifice. As further punishment Indra hit upon the idea of having the two sets of sons of the woman-king fight against each other until they all were killed. The death of all her sons set the ex-king to weeping and wailing so loudly and piteously that even Indra was moved to have pity. He revealed himself to the woman and asked a paradoxical question: Which of the sets of sons which had been killed would she

20. For example, see the *Kama Sutra of Vatsyayana*, trans. by Richard Burton (New York: Dutton, 1962), and P. Thomas, *Kama Kalpa or the Hindu Ritual of Love* (Bombay: D. B. Taraporevala, 1959).

choose to have live again if she had the choice? The ex-king replied that she would prefer to have the sons she had born as a woman because a woman "cherishes a more tender love" than man, and it was for mother's love that she wanted her sons. Impressed by the answer, Indra not only granted the wish but also restored to life both sets of sons. Indra then asked the ex-king which sex she would be if she had a choice of remaining a woman or being changed back into a man. She chose to remain a woman because the "woman has in union with man always the greater joy, that is why . . . I choose to be a woman. I feel greater pleasure in love as a woman, that is the truth, best among the gods. I am content with existence as a woman."[21] In effect women, though subjugated to men, have the consolation of sex to keep them happy and content.

There are numerous stories in Hindu scriptures which further amplify the sensuality of women and the satisfactions of sexual pleasure for them. Ila, who was both a man and a woman during alternate months, spent his/her time as a woman in sexual pleasure, while her/his time as a man was spent in pious ways and thoughts.[22] In the *Rāmāyana*, one of the great epics of Hinduism, the insatiability of women in love appeared in the story of the woman who exhausted her husband as well as the ascetic who had taken her away from him.[23] There is an old Hindu proverb which says that woman's power in eating is twice as great as that of a man, her cunning or bashfulness four times as great, her decision or boldness six times as great, and her impetuosity or delight in love eight times as great.[24] It was commonly accepted that without sexual enjoyment a woman would pine and ache. But love was not only a tonic for a woman, it also had noble meaning since it filled her whole being, made her steadfast and faithful, and as it grew ever deeper, it strongly mingled with the altruistic.

Though emphasizing woman's sensuality and need for love, Hinduism also limited its direction by stressing that the greatest joys of love for women were found within the bonds of marriage. Love could blossom anywhere, but it was only in the garden of wedlock that the full depth of the glowing colors and innermost perfumes were re-

21. Meyer, *Sexual Life in Ancient India*, pp. 376–380.
22. *Ibid.*, p. 375.
23. There is a popular retelling of this story in Aubrey Menen, *The Ramayana* (New York: Scribner's, 1954), pp. 103–125.
24. Meyer, *Sexual Life in Ancient India*, p. 380, n. 2.

vealed.[25] Early Vedic writings seemed to hint that a certain amount of promiscuity might have once existed,[26] but if so it did not linger on into recorded history. According to Hindu tradition the blind seer Dīrghatamas ordained that woman was to have only one husband as long as she lived, and if he died, she was not to remarry. If a woman went to a man other than her husband, she lost caste, as did an unmarried woman who prostituted herself.[27]

Hindu writings portrayed women in the most favorable light, either as a sensual sexual creature or as a devoted wife and mother. This contrast of burning sensuality and devoted mother was perhaps a reflection of the dualism which seemed to be inherent in Indian thought. It has been said that nowhere in any area of the world has woman as loving wife and tender mother been more extolled or appreciated,[28] and even the misogynist Manu said, where women were not honored all other religious deeds were barren.[29] The *Rāmāyana* reported that at first all beings were alike in stature, sex, speech, and so on, but then the Maker made a distinction, taking the best from all beings, out of which he shaped woman. Good women could not be soiled or spoiled and like the pearl could be found in the most sordid of environments. On the other hand, there were passages which painted woman as the sum and substance of all that was evil. When the divine wise man Narada attempted to find the cause of evil in the world, he found that women inevitably were its basis. Women lacked the moral bonds of men, and even when they found rich and worthy husbands, they threw themselves into the arms of bad men as soon as they had a chance. Those women who remained faithful to their husbands did so only because they did not have a chance to stray or because no other man could be found who was willing to woo them. Women were envious of youth and other women, and continually in need of love. Women were death, the wind, the underworld, the ever burning entrance to hell, the knife edge, the snake, the fire; woman was each of these and she was all of

25. *Ibid.*, p. 277.

26. Altekar, *Position of Women*, pp. 29–30.

27. See Vern L. Bullough, *History of Prostitution* (New Hyde Park, N.Y.: University Books, 1964), pp. 79–90. For an account of sacred prostitution, see N. M. Penzer, ed., *The Ocean of Story*, trans. by C. H. Tawney from Somadeva's *Kathā Sarit Sagara* (10 vols., London: Charles J. Sawyer, 1924), vol. 1, app. 4, pp. 231–280.

28. Meyer, *Sexual Life in Ancient India*, p. 6.

29. *Laws of Manu*, 3, p. 56.

them. While there were good women, the glorious ones, the mothers of the world, they were more than balanced by the evil ones, who loved no man with whom they united.[30] The deception of woman was a continuing theme in Hindu literature.

There are other strains in Indian thought, particularly that represented by Buddhism which was founded in India by Buddha in the fifth century B.C. Scholars prefer to call Buddhism a system of morality or ethics rather than a religion since its essential concern is with moral precepts by which men should live. There was nothing in his life which would indicate that Buddha set out to reform Hinduism, but many of the doctrines promulgated by him were contrary to basic Hindu beliefs. As far as women were concerned Buddha emphasized their equality with men and although their activities were in general confined to domestic, social, and religious functions, their status was considered in theory as equal to men. Among the followers of Buddha the birth of girl children was not looked upon with despair and matrimony was not held before them as the end of their existence. Women were regarded as individuals in command of their own life, and not just chattels to their husbands.[31] Buddhism, however, in spite of its great contribution to India, was submerged into Hinduism within India itself, although it exercised great influence outside that country. Though in some areas in India Buddhist ideas lingered on to elevate the status of women, in general the Hindu concept of woman as somewhat of a lower animal than man remained dominant. Sikh and Parsee concepts were also different from Hindu, but it was the Hindu influence which dominated India.

Nowhere was the concept of inferiority of women more exemplified than in the custom of suttee, the Hindu rite of suicide of widows by self-immolation. The word itself is said to be derived from Sati, wife of Siva, who committed suicide because her husband had been insulted by her father. The term was extended to mean the "true" wife who remained faithful to the memory of her husband by not marrying again, and eventually it came to mean the rite by which a widow committed herself to the flames of the pyre on which the body of her husband was cremated.

There has been considerable speculation about its origins since

---

30. Meyer, *Sexual Life in Ancient India*, pp. 496–500.
31. For a discussion of this, see I. B. Horner, *Women under Primitive Buddhism* (New York: Dutton, 1930).

there were apparently no clear references to it in the Vedic literature. The one line in the *Rig Veda* which has sometimes been held to justify the custom has been shown by scholars to be a later interpolation. The interpolation, however, was important since by changing the Sanskrit word *agre* to *agneh* a sentence was changed from "Let the mother advance to the altar first," to "Let the mothers go into the womb of fire." Max Müller, the great nineteenth-century Anglo-German Orientalist and comparative philologist, called this change of text "perhaps the most flagrant instance of what can be done by an unscrupulous priesthood." The custom of suttee, however, was not established by this change of text, only encouraged, and it seems clear that by the time the modification in the scripture took place the custom must already have been in vogue in order to need scriptural justification for it.[32] The first instances of suttee were recorded in the Indian epics, and when the Greeks of Alexander the Great visited India in the fourth century B.C. they found suttee already being practiced in the Punjab. By the first or second century A.D. the rite had gained the support of some of the lawgivers who declared it a meritorious act on part of the widow. By the sixth and seventh centuries the life of a widow apart from her husband was being unequivocally condemned as sinful, and she was urged to mount the funeral pyre with him. Though the rite was probably at first restricted to the wives of princes and warriors, it also spread to other groups in society. Two kinds of suttee were distinguished: the *saha-marana*, or co-dying, in which a widow burned herself on the same fire as that on which her husband's corpse was cremated, and the *anu-marana*, in which the woman delayed her death for some reason but died on a pyre lit with embers preserved from her husband's cremation. This second type of suttee usually only took place if the widow was in a impure state at the death of her husband. Impurity could result from menstruation, and a week was to pass after the cessation of the period before she could commit suttee, or from pregnancy, and then suttee was to be delayed until two months after the birth of the child. Suttee involved a rather elaborate ceremony. The woman was given a ceremonial bath and then, dressed in her finery and ornaments, she accompanied the body of her husband to the cremation ground. Since it was believed that the woman who died in suttee would have access to the

32. Edward Thompson, *Suttee: A Historical and Philosophical Enquiry into the Hindu Rite of Widow Burning* (London: Allen and Unwin, 1928), pp. 16–18.

spheres of heaven she was entrusted with messages to carry to deceased relations. Arriving at the pyre, she gave away her ornaments which were kept by the recipients as precious mementos of her sacrifice. She then mounted the pyre and sat beside the corpse, placing her husband's head on her lap, after which the pyre was lit. Since many women would have second thoughts about their self-immolation as the flames approached, special precautions were taken to prevent them from jumping from the fire. Often the pyre was laid in a pit from which there was no escape, or the widow was tied to logs or chained to stakes. Sometimes when they still tried to escape they were hit on the head or pushed back with poles. Apparently also some women were drugged.

The custom was particularly prevalent in northern India where the ritual took on staggering proportions since polygamy and concubinage were the norm among the upper classes. It was not unknown for several hundred women, wives, concubines, daughters, and devoted female servants to burn themselves to death when their master died. During the period of Muslim domination in India there was an attempt to prevent suttee by instituting a permit system based on a declaration by the widow that she of her own free will wished to become a *sati*, but few women could resist making such a declaration under pressure of their relatives. Being descended from a woman who committed suttee or being related to one was considered a great honor. The Portuguese in their areas of control managed to eliminate suttee after 1510 by taking action against all relatives and bystanders in any suttee ritual. The British took no action in their areas at first, although they did keep records and we have some idea of how prevalent the custom was in certain parts of India. In Bengal between 1815 and 1828, for example, the British recorded some 5,100 cases of suttee, in Banaras, 1,150, and in Patna, 700, as well as hundreds of others in other parts of India. In 1829 the British finally classified suttee as a homicidal act, but the practice was slow to die out.

Scholars have advanced various reasons for suttee and all indicate the subordinate and subjugated position of women in India. Edward Thompson went so far as to argue that suttee was an inevitable consequence of the Hindu premise that "the husband stands to the wife in place of the Deity." Inevitably it became a mark of female devotion. There was also the fact that male vanity was involved. There was a half-felt belief that a man's possessions could be sent with him for use in the next world if they were burned or buried with him. His wife or wives and other women being his chief possessions, they should obviously be dispatched to the next life. There was also a kind of male jealousy at the thought of leaving a beautiful woman behind after death for others to enjoy, and the fear that one's widow without the necessary supervision might misbehave and bring disgrace to the family. There was the very real fact that relatives were reluctant to be burdened with the responsibility of having to support a widow and were happy to have her out of the way. The ancient Greeks believed that the Hindus had instituted suttee to prevent a wife from poisoning her husband since she would have to die with him as well.

Why would women follow through and commit suttee? Undoubtedly many of them believed it was essential they do so. There was also the dread of being a widow in Hindu society, probably the most unfortunate character in the whole range of Hinduism. To the orthodox family, at least in medieval India, a widow was ill luck incarnate. If she was young and childless she was even more calamitous than if she had children, since as a husbandless, barren, menstruating female, her presence brought contamination, the sound of her voice was a curse, her glance was poisonous, and her very existence was perilous. She was treated as a thing apart, as if she were already dead. Since remarriage was an impossibility, those widows whose parents would not take them back or who had no other means of support were destined for the streets, a not particularly pleasant existence. It took a long time for conditions to change in India, and as late as 1948 a survey showed that the age of widows ranged between eight and fifty-four, with the average being close to twenty, evidence of continuing child marriages. Some 16 percent of the widows had not had their marriage consummated, and another 14 percent had lived with their husband for no more than a year. The average period of married life was seven years.[33]

Chinese history covers the same period of time as the whole of Western civilization, and obviously over a span of 4,000 years there were some differences in attitudes toward women. Like the West, however, regardless of time or dynasty women have been regarded as inferior to men. Some observers have even said that women as a group were treated even more unjustly in Chinese society than West-

33. *Ibid., passim*, and see also Walker, *The Hindu World*, the articles on suttee and widows, and Mace and Mace, *Marriage: East and West*, pp. 237–244.

ern,[34] but it seems likely that most such Western observers have not really paid attention to how women were regarded in the West.

In the earliest periods of Chinese history, prior to 1100 B.C., women might have been held in more esteem than later, just as was the case in India. This is perhaps demonstrated by the fact that the family organization, and even the sexual morality, of the early Shang people was very loose, and there are even indications that a kind of matriarchy existed.[35] Again matriarchy is much too strong a term, since what evidence there is tends to show the existence of matrilineal descent and matrilocal practices rather than matriarchy. Several attitudes which later have great influence on Chinese attitudes toward women can be traced back to these early periods of Chinese history. Some of the earliest surviving texts, for example, described woman as the initiator of sex, with the male as a mere student, and throughout Chinese society this seems to be one consistent measure of attitudes toward women. The more puritanical periods in Chinese society coincided with greater hostility to women while in the more relaxed periods in which sexuality was more openly accepted women tended to be regarded with slightly less hostility. Women throughout Chinese history were revered as mothers and the Shang character for woman emphasized the large breasts of the pregnant woman. Men on the other hand were represented as a piece of cultivated land, emphasizing the male function of tiller of the land and provider for the family.[36] Women were also associated with the color red, which among other things stood for sexual potency, creative power, and happiness, while white, the color coupled with the male, was the color of death, impotency, and negative influences. The symbol for family was also closely linked with women and birth.

Later the various alchemical treatises of the third century A.D., which probably reflected earlier beliefs, also credited woman's essence, the Yin, with special rejuvenating and strengthening power.[37]

---

34. Dun Jen Li, *The Essence of Chinese Civilization* (New York: Van Nostrand, 1967), pp. 397–402.

35. Marcel Granet, *Chinese Civilization* (New York: Knopf, 1930), p. 201.

36. R. H. van Gulik, *Sexual Life in Ancient China* (Leiden: Brill, 1961), p. 5.

37. *Ibid.*, pp. 5–8. For an example of such an alchemy text see the *Nei P'ien* of Ko Hung, which dates from the early fourth century and can be found in the book of *Alchemy, Medicine, Religion in the China of A.D. 320*, trans. by J. R. Ware (Cambridge: MIT Press, 1966).

At the same time the Yin was subordinate to the Yang. The Chinese taught that the interaction of the Yin and Yang produced everything in the universe. Yin was the negative principle corresponding to shade, darkness, the moon, water, weakness or yielding, depth, and to all things feminine. Yang, the positive principle, corresponded to light, brightness, the sun, strength, fortitude, and to all things masculine. One was passive, the other active, one submissive, the other dominant, and though they were antithetical to each other, each was indispensable and necessary. In theory husband and wife, as Yang and Yin, were equal, but man's superiority over woman was clearly accepted.

This subordination was expressed under the principle of the "three dependencies": (1) dependency upon the father when a girl was young, (2) dependency upon the husband after marriage, and (3) dependency upon the son after the death of the husband. A woman could never act autonomously. On her wedding day her parents gave her their final instruction, encouraging her to be "respectful and cautious" and not to "disobey" her husband. The husband's authority replaced the father's, and the husband was regarded as ruler over his wife in much the same way as a king was to his minister or the father to a son.

Within the family woman's right to rule the household was recognized, but she ruled it for the benefit of her husband. Care of the children, cooking, washing, sewing, cleaning, and directing the maid servants were all inside tasks, and in the final analysis, were services performed for her husband. Apparently few women worked regularly in the fields, even among the peasants, although they probably joined in for harvesting. Many women were attached directly to the great households, doing various sorts of work, including silk culture, which was regarded as a woman's task. Here they were at the mercy of those above them, and this meant that the lord of the household had a perfect right to use them as he pleased. Women in such households were known as *ch'ieh*, a word which later came to mean concubine. If one of them bore their master a child this improved her status, and a male child of such a woman could even be made his father's heir, although this was not usually the case. Probably the institution of concubinage grew from such a custom, yet generally such women were regarded as little more than a means of amusement. One early prime minister was praised for his honesty and frugality with the statement that "his concubines never wore silk and his horses never ate millet."[38]

Throughout Chinese history women were accustomed to live in considerable seclusion and proper women were not usually seen at public ceremonies, although they were sometimes placed behind a screen so that they could observe without being seen. Symbolic of this subordination was the later *fu* character for woman which was a combination of the characters for female and broom and implied both to serve and to submit. Since no family could have two authorities, the woman had to submit to her husband. After his death, her son, or some other male member of the husband's family, succeeded to this position, and although a mother or grandmother was senior to her son or grandson, she could never become the family head. As an ancient proverb stated, "if a hen rules at morning the family comes to an end."[39] It was as an old woman, however, that the woman probably received the greatest respect and exercised the greatest authority.

The Chinese family included several generations occupying the same dwelling, living under the authority of the eldest generation, and holding goods and property, more or less in common. Though the authority of the male head of such families was virtually absolute, almost that of life or death, the authority of his wife was second only to his, and she exercised great influence over her daughters-in-law. If she outlived her husband, her influence increased. As one historian has written, the "authority of the old woman of position in China is a thing which defies definition."[40] Filial piety was regarded as the chief of Chinese virtues, and no son was supposed to turn against his mother. Particularly difficult was the position of daughter-in-law in such families, since she was clearly subordinate to her adopted parents and a scolding by a daughter-in-law could result in the death penalty if the parents of her husband lodged a complaint with local authorities.[41]

Like Western society, Chinese society also had a double standard

38. Herrlee Creel, *The Birth of China* (reprinted, New York: Ungar, 1954), p. 284.
39. T'ung'Tsu Ch'ü, *Law and Society in Traditional China* (Paris: Mouton, 1965), pp. 103–104.
40. Creel, *Birth of China*, p. 302.
41. T'ung'Tsu Ch'ü, *Law and Society*, pp. 118–119.

in which adultery by the husband was regarded as a mere pecadillo, if that, while adultery by a wife could be punished by death. The Chinese woman had practically no right to seek a separation or divorce from her husband, although he could divorce her for any number of reasons: disobedience to his parents, barrenness, adultery, jealousy, incurable disease, loquacity, and theft. If, however, she had no close relatives to receive her, or if she had worn mourning clothes for three years for the husband's parents, or if her husband had been poor at the time of the marriage and had since become wealthy, she could not be divorced. Divorce, however, was a drastic solution, and often a man simply took a concubine and more or less ignored his wife. In fact, in the eighth century A.D. it was held that a man without a son could be punished unless he took a concubine if his wife had failed to give him the desired heir. This was because the lack of a son might force the discontinuance of the worship of his ancestors. A wife could do little about such actions, but perhaps feel sorry for herself. There is an early poem from the Chow dynasty, first millenium B.C., expressing the feelings of a supplanted wife:

> You feast with your new wife,
> And think me not worth being with. . . .
> My person is rejected;
> What avails it to care what may come after. . . .
> You cannot cherish me,
> And you even count me as an enemy.
> You disdain my virtues,
> A pedlar's wares which do not sell. . . .
> Feasting with your new wife,
> You think of me as a provision [only] against your poverty.
> Cavalierly and angrily you treat me;
> You give me only pain.
> You do not think of the former days,
> And are only angry with me.[42]

If a wife came from a powerful family, however, she could appeal to her family for support. In general polygamy and concubinage were widespread, at least among those who could afford the practices.

Not all women submitted meekly to the taboo which forbade them to take part in public affairs. The *Odes of Yung* included a

42. See *The Chinese Classics*, ed. and trans. by James Legge (5 vols., reprinted, Hong Kong: Hong Kong University Press, 1960), vol. 4, pp. 56–58.

poem about a woman who, involved in the disaster of her state, correctly saw the course which might have saved it, but was prevented from acting because people would have dismissed her recommendations as only from a woman. "Ye great officers and gentlemen,/ Do not condemn me./ The hundred plans you think of/ Are not equal to the course I was going to take."[43] Probably, however, if she had been more discreet in her recommendations they might have been taken, since various Chinese biographies of women indicated that they often saved their menfolk from disaster by giving them timely advice.[44] Several bronze inscriptions also tell us that the wives of kings and other rulers sometimes held the reins of power while their husbands were away on military expeditions.[45] There were even a few women rulers such as the Empress Nēe Lü in the second century B.C. who ruled after the death of both her husband and son. Nevertheless the general opinion of woman as ruler or royal adviser was low. Moralists had little good to say of them but rather delighted to tell of kings and princes who met their doom through feminine intrigue. One of the worst things which could be said of a man was that he followed "the words of his woman."

> A wise man builds up the wall [of a city],
> But a wise woman overthrows it.
> Admirable may be the wise woman,
> But she is [no better than] an owl.
> A woman with a long tongue
> Is [like] a stepping-stone to disorder.
> [Disorder] does not come down from heaven;
> It is produced by the woman.
> Those from whom come no lesson, no instruction,
> Are women and eunuchs.[46]

Traditional Chinese society was deeply influenced by the teachings of Confucius and Lao-Tse, who were active about 500 B.C., and also by the teachings of the contemporary Indian thinker, Buddha. Buddhism began to permeate China shortly after his death but did not arrive in force until the first centuries of the Christian era.

43. *Ibid.*, vol. 4, p. 89.
44. Albert O'Hara, *The Position of Women in Early China* (Washington, D.C.: Catholic University Press, 1945), *passim*. This is a translation of the *Lieh Nü Chuan*, or *Biographies of Chinese Women*.
45. Creel, *Birth of China*, p. 287.
46. *Chinese Classics*, vol. 4, p. 561.

Within India itself Buddhism was gradually absorbed into Hinduism, but in China, modified by Chinese disciples, it found new force. Each of the movements founded by these men, Confucianism, Taoism, and Buddhism, helped form Chinese attitudes toward women, but probably the dominant one was that of Confucianism, and it was also the most antiwoman.

Next to nothing is known about the personal attitude of Confucius toward women, although he did state that both women and people of lowly station were difficult to deal with. "If you become close to them, they turn non-compliant, if you keep them at a distance, they turn resentful."[47] The interpreters of Confucius soon worked out a rather detailed system in which the position of women was set forth as absolutely and unconditionally inferior to man; quite simply she did not count. Woman's prime duty was to serve and obey her husband and her parents, to look after the household, and to bear male children. The biological functions of women were emphasized; psychological considerations were given only secondary importance. Chastity was a requisite for orderly family life as well as for the undisturbed continuation of the lineage. Inevitably female premarital chastity assumed almost the semblance of a religious cult. To ensure the least amount of temptation or contamination, the Confucianists advocated the complete separation of the sexes and carried this through to its most absurd consequences, even to the extent that the husband and wife were not supposed to hang their garments in the same closet. The ideal woman was one who concentrated all her efforts on her household tasks. Participation in outside affairs, especially in public matters, was abhorred as the root of all evil and the cause of the downfall of the great dynasties.[48]

A song in the *Shih Ching*, or *Book of Songs*, one of the five Confucianist classics, described the different customs observed for a newborn boy and girl, symbolizing their future status in life and the different attitudes toward the sexes.

> So he bears a son,
> And puts him to sleep upon a bed,

47. *The Sayings of Confucius*, trans. by James R. Ware (New York: New American Library, 1955), vol. 17, p. 23.

48. See van Gulik, *Sexual Life in Ancient China*, pp. 44–45; Florence Ayscough, *Chinese Women, Yesterday and Today* (Boston: Houghton Mifflin, 1937), *passim*, and L. Wieger, *Moral Tenets and Customs in China*, trans. by L. Davrout (Ho-Kien-fu: Catholic Mission Press, 1913), p. 25.

> Clothes him in robes,
> Gives him a jade sceptre to play with.
> The child's howling is very lusty;
> In red greaves shall he flare,
> Be lord and king of house and home.
> Then he bears a daughter,
> And puts her upon the ground,
> Clothes her in swaddling-clothes,
> Gives her a loom-whorl to play with.
> For her no decorations, no emblems;
> Her only care, the wine and food,
> And how to give no trouble to father and mother.[49]

The male child was dressed in bright clothes for he must one day appear in court, while the woman would remain hidden from view. The bit of jade given to the boy symbolized the badge of office which he would fill as a man, while the loom-whorl given to the girl symbolized the work of spinning which was woman's work in life.[50]

Confucianism was fundamentally a practical philosophy adapted to a patriarchal state. Its ideas were essentially ethical and they continued to be elaborated upon over the centuries. Eventually they gained the support of the Chinese rulers and Confucius was honored as the great sage; his creed became a kind of state doctrine. In the ideal state advocated by Confucius, marriage was insisted upon for all, and the chastity of women assumed the semblance of religious cult. Even the remarriage of widows was only tolerated at certain times and under the rule of certain dynasties, while during others the rigid seclusion of women was insisted upon and the remarriage of widows was considered a moral crime. A woman spent her time running the home and bringing up children, and she was supposed to have little time to devote to her own education or to perfecting herself in the arts. Too much learning was considered dangerous to her virtue, and it was not the function of wives to supply their husbands with intellectual or emotional companionship. When a man needed a woman to share his mental life with him or to teach him romantic love, he took her from among the courtesans. Proper women were barred from male society other than that of

49. *The Book of Songs*, trans. by Arthur Waley (London: Allen and Unwin, 1937), pp. 283–284.
50. O'Hara, *Position of Women in Early China*, p. 263.

their own relatives.[51] They were not supposed to share the man's intellectual interests and they were strictly forbidden to meddle with his activities outside the house. Even the young daughters in upper-class families were taught only the womanly skills such as weaving and sewing and looking after the household; they were not taught reading and writing in any regular manner. In spite of this, some women managed to leave an imprint upon history.

One who did was Lady Pan Chao (d. 116 A.D.), daughter of Pan Piao, a well-known writer and administrator, and sister of Pan Ku, a famous historian. Pan Chao was married as a girl of fourteen but when her husband died young, she, as an adherent of Confucius, never remarried. Instead she devoted herself to her literary studies, in which she had been initiated by her father, and she became famous for her polished style and wide learning. When her brother died without completing his history, the Emperor Ho ordered her to finish it; he also appointed her as instructor to the empress. Lady Pan was no feminist, but a devoted adherent of the Confucian philosophy, and accepted the inferiority of woman to man. One of her best-known works is a pamphlet, *Nü chieh*, or "Women's Precepts." In the chapter entitled "Humility," she summarized the ideal woman.

> Let a woman modestly yield to others; let her respect others; let her put others first, herself last. Should she do something good, let her not mention it; should she do something bad, let her not deny it. Let her bear disgrace; let her even endure when others speak or do evil to her. Always let her seem to tremble and to fear. [When a woman follows such maxims as these,] then she may be said to humble herself before others.
>
> Let a woman retire late to bed, but rise early to duties; let her not dread tasks by day or by night. Let her not refuse to perform domestic duties whether easy or difficult. That which must be done, let her finish completely, tidily, and systematically. [When a woman follows such rules as these,] then she may be said to be industrious.
>
> Let a woman be correct in manner and upright in character in order to serve her husband. Let her live in purity and quietness [of spirit] and attend to her own affairs. Let her love not gossip and silly laughter. Let her cleanse and purify and arrange in order the wine

51. Eloise Talcott Hibbert, *Embroidered Gauze* (New York: Dutton, 1941), pp. 21–41.

and the food for the offerings to the ancestors. [When a woman observes such principles as these,] then she may be said to continue ancestral worship.

No woman who observes these three [fundamentals of life] has ever had a bad reputation or has fallen into disgrace. If a woman fail to observe them, how can her name be honored; how can she but bring disgrace upon herself?[52]

She gave other characteristics of the proper woman.

To guard carefully her chastity; to control circumspectly her behavior; in every motion to exhibit modesty; and to model each act on the best usage, this is womanly virtue.

Man is honored for strength; a woman is beautiful on account of her gentleness.

To wash and scrub filth away; to keep clothes and ornaments fresh and clean; to wash the head and bathe the body regularly, and to keep the person free from disgraceful filth, may be called the characteristic of womanly bearing.

With whole-hearted devotion to sew and to weave; to love not gossip and silly laughter; in cleanliness and order [to prepare] the wine and food for serving guests, may be called the characteristics of womanly work.

To choose her words with care; to avoid vulgar language; to speak at appropriate times; and not to wear others [with much conversation], may be called the characteristics of womanly words.[53]

Though Lady Pan felt that girls should be educated, her whole ethical system was based on the belief that woman's place was in the home. The purpose of education was to teach girls right from wrong, but other than this defense of female intelligence, she accepted female inferiority. Women were not to assemble together in groups, nor if they traveled outside the home were they to attract attention. Lady Pan believed that a widow should not marry again because a wife could not ever leave a husband, and taking a second husband would have meant she deserted her first one.

To obtain the love of one man is the crown of a woman's life; to lose the love of one man is to miss the aim in woman's life.

52. A translation and discussion of these can be found in Nancy Lee Swann, *Pan Chao: Foremost Woman Scholar of China* (reprinted, New York: Russell and Russell, 1968), pp. 83–84.

53. *Ibid.*, pp. 85–86 (chaps. 3 and 4).

For these reason a woman cannot but seek to win her husband's heart. Nevertheless, the beseeching wife need not use flattery, coaxing words, and cheap methods to gain intimacy.

Decidedly nothing is better [to gain the heart of a husband] than whole-hearted devotion and correct manners.[54]

Lady Pan's advice to women was similar to a whole series of manuals advising women how to behave, all of which emphasized woman's submissiveness to men. A related genre was the *Lieh-nü-chuan,* or *Biographies of Eminent Women,* the prototypes of which dated from the first century B.C. Essentially these biographies consisted of edifying stories of women who sacrificed themselves for their husbands, virtuous widows who preferred death to remarriage, and women who when their husbands needed it gave them wise advice.[55]

How much do these reflect reality? It would seem obvious that the place assigned to woman in theory and that in practice might well be quite different. That reality might have been somewhat different is evident from a statement by Ko Hung, a third-century philosopher, who felt that the failure of women to observe their proper place in society was leading to the decay of the family and the ruination of the state. He urged the wise men to keep their womenfolk under more effective control. He claimed that women and girls no

longer engage in spinning and weaving, they do not like any longer to make cap-tassels, they do not make hemp, but they love to gad about on the market place. They neglect the supervision of the kitchen, but devote themselves to frivolous pleasures. They go out visiting to see their relatives, they proceed there by the light of the stars or carrying torches, night after night. . . . Along the road those ladies indulge in unseemly jokes and pranks. . . . These women also make pleasure trips to Buddhist temples, they go out to watch hunting and fishing. . . . They even travel beyond the district-boundaries. . . . They proceed there in open carriages with curtains raised.[56]

Not all philosophers, however, were misogynists, and a contemporary of Ko Hung, a scholar by the name of Fu Hsüan, lamented the low status of women.

Bitter indeed it is to be born a woman,
It is difficult to imagine anything so low!

54. *Ibid.,* p. 87 (chap. 5).
55. O'Hara, *Position of Women in Early China.*
56. Quoted in van Gulik, *Sexual Life in Ancient China,* pp. 103–104.

Boys can stand openly at the front gate,
They are treated like gods as soon as they are born.
Their manly spirit bounded only by the Four Seas,
Ten thousand miles they go, braving storm and dust.
But a girl is reared without joy or love,
And no one in her family really cares for her.
Grown up, she has to hide in the inner rooms,
Cover her head, be afraid to look others in the face.
And no one sheds a tear when she is married off,
All ties with her own kin are abruptly severed.
With bowed head she tries to compose her face,
Her white teeth biting her scarlet lips.
Now she has to bow and kneel times uncounted,
Behave humbly even with maids and concubines. . . .
She is blamed for all and everything that goes wrong.
In a few years her gentle face will have changed,
As her husband often goes after new loves.
While at first they were as close as shape and shadow,
Now they are as far apart as Chinese and Huns.
But whilst even Chinese and Huns do sometimes meet,
Husband and wife stay as far apart as Lucifer and Orion.[57]

Taoism represented another side to Chinese life. If not basically modifying attitudes toward women, it emphasized the importance of the female principle. Lao-Tse, the great prophet of Taoism, concentrated on individual life and tranquility. He and his followers reasoned that the greater part of man-made activities had served only to estrange man from nature, giving rise to an unnatural and artificial human society with its family, state, rites, ceremonials, and arbitrary differentiation between good and bad. The Taoist philosophy instead advocated a return to pristine simplicity, to a golden age where people would live long and happily, where there would be no good or bad, where everyone would live in perfect harmony with nature, where the Yin and the Yang were united. Woman was venerated by the Taoists because she was considered to be closer to the primordial forces of nature than man, and because it was in her womb that new life was created and fostered. It was the female who possessed the indispensable element for achieving the elixir of life.

The Spirit of the Valley never dies.
It is called the Mystic Female.

57. *Ibid.*, pp. 111–112.

The Door of the Mystic Female
Is the root of Heaven and Earth.

Continuously, continuously,
It seems to remain.
Draw upon it
And it served you with ease.[58]

Water, the female, and the infant were Lao-Tse's symbols to Tao, and all three were passive, receptive, and quiet.

He who is aware of the Male
But keeps to the Female
  Becomes the ravine of the world
Being the ravine of the world
  He has the original character which is not cut up
  And returns again to the [innocence of the] babe.[59]

Seekers after the One were to be aware of their masculine assertiveness, and instead keep in mind the way of women, who were passive:

The Female overcomes the Male by quietude,
And achieves the lowly position by quietude.[60]
Before the Heaven and Earth existed
There was something nebulous:
  Silent, isolated,
  Standing alone, changing not,
  Eternally revolving without fail,
  Worthy to be the Mother of All Things.
I do not know its name
  And address it as Tao. . . .[61]

Though in later Chinese history this role of the primordial mother was ignored or explained away by Confucian exegesis, it remained in esoteric Taoist writing and also had considerable influence on Chinese sexual practices. Sexual activity for the Taoist was a requirement in the search for longevity, and hence immortality. The object of such practices was to promote the happy union of Yin and Yang. Man could not live without woman any more than the sky could be separated from the earth. It was necessary, however, to

58. Lao-Tse, *The Tao te Ching,* or *The Wisdom of Laotse,* ed. and trans. by Lin Yutang (New York: Modern Library, 1948), bk. 1, chap. 6, p. 64.

59. *Ibid.,* bk. 4, chap. 28, p. 160.

60. *Ibid.,* bk. 6, chap. 61, p. 279.

61. *Ibid,* bk. 3, chap. 25, p. 145.

know the proper technique, and for this several works were written on the *Art of the Bedchamber*. The contradictory attitudes toward women as emphasized by Confucianism and Taoism were seemingly resolved by following the Confucian ideal regarding the social position of the sexes, but their sexual relations were governed by Taoist ideology.

The aim of sexual intercourse was to escape, to transcend the material world, and to replace the body by a heavenly and immortal substance which was nothing less than pure Yang. Even though Yin was the feminine force and Yang the masculine, both sexes had elements of each. Clearly the man had more Yang but the female, finding herself in the passive position, had the advantage of possessing that sweet power which in Taoist theory ended up by gaining the upper hand. Thus the Taoist sex manuals often assumed an antifeminist position. They believed that the key to the One was by storing up the male semen, and the various sex manuals instructed the men how to do this but warned them not to make this knowledge available to the female. What benefited him was really injurious to her, so he was advised to get women who were innocent of the Way and to indoctrinate them so as to ensure his sexual well-being. The man was also to absorb woman's Yin essence, and at the same time give her physical benefit by stirring her latent Yin nature. According to Chinese sex literature a man's semen was his most precious possession, the source not only of his health but also of his life; every emission of semen diminished his vital forces unless it was accompanied by the acquisition of an equivalent amount of Yin essence from the woman, which all women possessed in unlimited supply. Men only received this Yin essence from women during their orgasm; they should therefore strive to give women complete satisfaction every time they performed the sexual act. The man, however, should control his passion so that he reached orgasm only occasionally, in order to build up his Yang. If he could get his semen through mental concentration to revert upward through the center of the spinal cord into the brain, he was well on his way to becoming a sage. In effect even the Taoists, with their belief in sex as a way to Tao, would emphasize that women be kept ignorant of the Key, since if women knew the path as well as men they would have an advantage over them.[62]

62. Chinese prudishness later suppressed many of these texts but they were pre-

In the sixth century A.D. the Taoist communities began to organize themselves into monasteries on the line of the Buddhists, and thereafter the Taoist movement was almost entirely in the hands of the monks. It was only in isolated country districts that a married secular clergy was able to exist. For the monks marriage was forbidden, as were all forms of lewdness, but sexual union occupied too important a place in the philosophy to be condemned. Sexually, in fact, there were courtesans who specialized in Taoist erotic techniques in most of the major cities, but their customers were not usually men of true religion. Increasingly the merging of the Yin and Yang was to take place within the body, with the heart and the loins representing the two principles, and the true Taoist tried to merge these vital forces, freeing himself from any dependence of any kind on others, alimentary, physical, or sexual.[63] Through this the male adherents could ignore women all together.

Buddhism, the third of the great intellectual movements in China, never achieved the dominance that Confucianism did, perhaps because it taught that women were equal to men. The Buddhist creed of universal love and compassion, preaching equality of all beings, appealed particularly to the spiritual needs of the Chinese women, while the various female deities such as the compassionate Goddess Kuan-yin helped them in distress and lent some color to their rather monotonous daily life. The early Buddhist texts which were translated into Chinese, while mentioning Buddha's position on women, essentially glossed over it to avoid antagonizing what was felt to be Chinese sensibilities. Buddhism, however, allowed women to serve as nuns, and these women who by virtue of their sex had free access to the women's quarters were the favorite counselors of the ladies of the household. Buddhist nuns officiated at intimate household ceremonies, such as prayer meetings for the recovery of a sick child, advising on cures for sterility, and acted as personal advisers and physicians. They often taught young girls reading, writing, and feminine skills.

Inevitably public opinion, as represented by the male establishment, regarded nuns and convents with disfavor, and during Ming

---

served in Japan and many of them have been translated by Akira Ishihara and Howard S. Levy, *The Tao of Sex* (Tokyo: Shibundo, 1968). See also Michel Beurdeley, *et al.*, *Chinese Erotic Art* (Rutland, Vt.: Tuttle, 1969).

63. Ishihara and Levy, *The Tao of Sex, passim.*

times (1368 to 1644 A.D.) a series of novels and short stories painted their alleged iniquities in lurid colors. Even before this a writer of the Yuan dynasty (1280 to 1368 A.D.) had cautioned against various women visitors to the woman's quarters because they would only stir up trouble. He broke the visitors down into nine groups, three "aunts" and six "crones."

> The three "aunts" are the Buddhist nun, the Taoist nun, and the female fortune-teller. The six "crones" are the procuress, the female go-between, the sorceress, the female thief, the female quack, and the midwife. These are indeed like the three punishments and the six harmful cosmic influences. Few are the households which, having admitted one of them, will not be ravaged by fornication and robbery. The men who can guard against those, keeping them away as if they were snakes and scorpions, those men shall come near the method for keeping their household clean.[64]

In effect almost all women visitors to the women's quarters were frowned upon, and there was an attempt to keep women in even greater isolation.

One of the reasons for male hostility to the nuns was that the monastery offered refuge to girls who abhorred the idea of having to marry a man they had never seen, as well as to those wives or concubines who wanted to escape from a cruel husband or a tyrannical mother-in-law. Many girls, however, had no choice in the matter, and parents would often make a vow that an unborn daughter would become a nun in order to avert a calamity, or in the case of existing daughters promise them to the monastery in order to help them recover from a disastrous illness. The idea that women might abandon their sacred duty of propagating the family to live in self-contained communities free from male jurisdiction was also abhorrent to the Confucianists.

Buddhism probably had its greatest influence on Chinese society under the T'ang dynasty (618 to 907 A.D.), and during this period several women poets emerged into literary history. Not all of these poets were Buddhists, however, and perhaps the two most prominent, Yü Hsüan chi and Hsüeh T'ao, were Taoist nuns.

Following the T'ang dynasty there was a strong revival of Confucianism which undoubtedly influenced the free association of men and women. Several Confucian philosophers, such as Chou Tun-i

64. This is quoted by van Gulik, *Sexual Life in Ancient China*, p. 254.

and Shao Yung (eleventh century), borrowed concepts from Taoism and founded a syncretic system called Neo-Confucianism. They formulated a new theory on the basis of the system embodied in the *I Ching*, the ancient *Book of Changes*,[65] which was given its final form by Chu Hsi (twelfth century). He stressed the inferiority of women and the strict separation of the sexes, and it was this theme which continued until fairly recent Chinese history. This, however, did not necessarily reduce the number of educated females since the introduction of wood-block printing at about the same time made it somewhat easier to publish and acquire books. Women also painted, and perhaps the greatest woman literary genius of China appeared, namely, Li ch'ing-chao, better known by her literary name I-anu (twelfth century). Most of her poetry has been lost, and only about fifty surviving poems are definitely identified with her. These, however, serve as a mirror to the emotions of a proper upper-class woman and express her feelings at various times in her life, when her husband left home for a short period, when he was away for a longer period at an official post, and after he died. The last seems particularly moving:

> The wind has subsided, the earth is scented with fallen
>   flowers.
> The day being late, I am too tired to comb my hair.
> His things remain, but the man is gone, and life has
>   ceased to be.
> I want to talk but tears begin to flow.
>
> I have heard that spring is still fair at the Twin Stream
> And intend to go there, sailing in a light boat.
> But I am afraid that the skiff at the Twin Stream
> Cannot hold sorrows so heavy. . . .[66]

Increasingly the chastity of women became a veritable cult, and women were more and more confined. The best evidence for the imposition of greater restrictions was the introduction of footbinding, a practice which made it almost impossible for women to move about without great effort. In fact there is a Chinese verse: "Why must the foot be bound?/ To prevent barbarous running around!"[67]

65. There are various translations of the *I Ching*, including one by James Legge which is easily available (reprinted, New York: Dover, 1963).

66. Liu Wu-chi, *An Introduction to Chinese Literature* (Bloomington: Indiana University Press, 1966), p. 147.

67. Howard S. Levy, *Chinese Footbinding: The History of a Curious Erotic Custom* (New York: Walton Rawls, 1966), p. 41.

Scholarly opinion about the introduction of footbinding into China varies but most would agree that it became almost standard in the twelfth century. Chinese folklore attributed the custom to a fox who tried to conceal its paws while assuming the human guise of a Shang empress in the twelfth century and thereby set a fashion. Another semilegendary account says it was started by this same empress who was known for her small feet which she accentuated by binding. Still another version of the story claims that the empress had a club foot which she concealed by binding and persuaded her husband to make compression of feet obligatory for all young girls so that she would not stand out.[68]

A Chinese historian of the twelfth century attributed its introduction to the ruler Li Yü (961 to 975 A.D.), who controlled one section of China prior to its reunification by the Sung dynasty. He had a favored palace concubine for whom he constructed an artificial lotus plant out of gold and on which she danced with her feet tightly bound. Her admirers said she was giving rise to lotuses with every step, and "golden lotus" became an euphonym for bound feet. In spite of the mythical aspects of such stories it probably did begin as a dancing measure, was encouraged in the royal harem, and its diffusion was facilitated as a device for suppression of women. Increasingly as the Neo-Confucianists became more important, there was growing hostility to any feminine liberty and intellectual freedom, an emphasis on female chastity, and a hostility to any remarriage by women. There was also a growing belief that a woman of virtue should be a conventional lady of little talent. Though women were permitted to read proper classical works, they were discouraged from singing or writing poetry. Chu Hsi (1130 to 1200 A.D.), who introduced footbinding into southern Fukien, felt that it was better for a woman to starve than remarry after her husband's death and he thought of footbinding as a "means of spreading Chinese culture and teaching the separation of man and woman." By the twelfth century it had become accepted as the hallmark of gentility and correct fashion. Families which claimed aristocratic lineage came to feel compelled to bind the feet of their girls as a visible sign of upper-class distinction. The diminutive feet and hands and slender waist of the upper-class woman indicated that she was incapable of useful effort and had to be supported in idleness by her owner. Several

68. *Ibid.,* pp. 37–39.

treatises justified the practice as guaranteeing feminine chastity, since though it made women more attractive, it also made it difficult for them to leave their quarters. Gradually footbinding was transmitted from the north to the center and south of China, and the Chinese emphasized it in order to draw a clear cultural distinction between themselves and their large-footed Mongol conquerors. Soon upper-class Manchu and Korean women bound their feet, and it was also practiced among the Jewish colony in Honan. It remained primarily an upper-class phenomenon and women of the poorer classes were usually barefooted. Nevertheless, any family ambitious for their daughter's future bound her feet. As early as the seventeenth century various Chineses rulers tried to abolish the custom, but it was not successfully abolished until the middle of the twentieth century.[69]

Women were not particularly highly regarded as human beings in China. They were admired for their beauty, and during the period of footbinding, there was a cult of foot fetishism; they were sought after as sexual mates, and they were respected as mothers. The ideal mother in Chinese literature was the mother of Mencius, a disciple of Confucius. After the death of her husband the mother of Mencius settled with her young son in a house near the cemetery, but she soon realized that she had made a mistake because the boy at play imitated the ceremonies of burial which he saw enacted. She then moved to another house near the market, and this time to her distress she saw the boy play at buying and selling. Finally she moved to a house near a school and there she had her reward. Her little son was soon busy imitating the learned scholars he saw about him as they applied themselves to their tasks. She emphasized the necessity of female devotion by a saying attributed to her: "A woman's duty is to care for the household and she should have no desire to go abroad."

This in essence was the ideal of the Chinese women, sacrificing herself for her family and recognizing her subordination. If she adhered to the role she might as an old woman exercise considerable power over her family and demand filial respect from her sons and her daughters-in-law. As a child, however, she might be sold into prostitution or into concubinage, or given to a convent, or even, if it was believed it would propriate the gods, killed. If she was born into the upper classes she was somewhat more protected from such fates,

69. *Ibid.*, pp. 44–63.

but after the introduction of footbinding her life was tremendously circumscribed. Though China geographically includes a large area and there were differences in customs in various parts of China, women almost everywhere were regarded as inferior.[70]

Whether these Eastern women were any worse off than Western women at comparable stages in development, however, is debatable. Although footbinding seems a particularly cruel form of confinement, in many ways it was not any more debilitating than the attempts of Western women to narrow their waistlines to eighteen or twenty inches, and it had the same effect of limiting women's physical activity. Obviously, however, there must have been compensations for their confinement, and women themselves, as Lady Pan so ably demonstrated, accepted the idea that they were inferior. Even the love relationship, which sometimes removes antagonism between the sexes, became increasingly restrictive as Chinese society became formalized. As Marcel Granet, the French scholar, argued: "The absence of intimacy is the dominant feature of family organization. This was a significant feature at first in the relations between husbands and wives, and between fathers and sons. It appears to become the rule for all family relations. Dominated by ideas of respect, domestic morality seems in the end to become mixed up with a ceremonial of family life."[71] Gradually a regulated system of relations developed in which the proper actions were dictated in sex, in social situations, as well as in other situations, and spontaneity became impossible. Chinese society was organized on the inferiority of women and the superiority of men. To change this, it was necessary to almost challenge the very foundation of Chinese society.

70. Edward H. Schafer, *The Vermillion Bird: T'Ang Images of the South* (Berkeley: University of California Press, 1967), pp. 81–82.
71. Granet, *Chinese Civilization*, p. 427.

chapter eleven

Role Change and Urbanization

One of the difficulties the amateur has in studying history is the tendency to look at the past from the perspective of the present, to imagine that people lived under conditions similar to our own. Such a practice can only lead one to draw erroneous conclusions, and this is particularly true about the role and status of women. Continually throughout this book we have emphasized that women have been confined to the home, subordinated to their husbands, denied any existence apart from their menfolk. It is important to emphasize, however, that such a condition in the past would be different from a similar one today, if only because the home was such a different place. The overwhelming majority of people, probably as many as 90 percent, earned their living at agriculture and lived in a village. This meant that though women were subordinate to men they worked alongside them in the fields at crucial times and both men and women used their home or hut as an operational base. Even in the developing cities of medieval and early modern Europe the craftsmen carried on their trade in their homes, assisted by their wives and children. Most retail shops were simply an extension of the home, and only larger enterprises occasionally had a separate warehouse.

Under such conditions women were not only useful but also essential. A wife was not only a mother and a bed companion, but also an economic necessity, carrying out hundreds of tasks which assisted in bringing income to the family. Women usually had control of tasks such as spinning, weaving, making clothes, manufacturing beer, and so forth. Though the ordinary woman might well cook the meals for her family, this was not a particularly time-consuming task. Meals for the ordinary person were simple, and often meant little more than taking something from the ever stewing pot. There were no dishes to wash, no utensils to clean, since all but the richest ate with their fingers. Bread, the staple food in most of Europe, was not made at home by a devoted housewife but in a bakery, since the expense of having an oven in the home was beyond the means of most people. The higher nobility, and a few of the richer burgers, had servants, and in the great houses there were a lot of servants, but most of the great houses were isolated in the countryside, and the women of such houses had little time for social affairs. Like the ordinary peasant women they had numerous tasks to perform in running the household, seeing that the wool or other material was spun, woven, and made into clothes, keeping track of the larder, making beer, cheese, and performing other such tasks. Unless there were houseguests, the social season was limited, confined to a few weeks of the year, and usually meant moving to the royal court or to a nearby city. During this brief social season women as well as men could put on a display of the latest fabrics and fashions and get ideas to keep them occupied for the rest of the year. During the absence of her husband at war, or for other purposes, the wife was in charge of the household. Though women of the upper classes obviously had an easier time than those of the lower, the point to be emphasized is that women, regardless of the male attitude toward them, were essential, and the tasks which they performed were as important to the economic survival of the family as those of the males.

In the sixteenth and seventeenth centuries the nature and function of the nobility changed. In the early medieval period nobility had justified their existence by their military function, but with the invention of gunpowder and the development of cannon, their cavalry charges and individual prowess had become less meaningful. Ambitious kings had further attempted to weaken them because they were the greatest rivals of the kings for power. In the process the kings had turned to the developing cities for income and with this purchased soldiers and established bureaucracies which made royalty more or less independent of the nobles. The nobles, however, still existed, and it was the genius of the seventeenth-century Louis XIV to turn fighting men into courtiers, a trend which had started earlier but was now sanctioned and encouraged by the king. One of the vestigial functions of the nobility was to offer advice to the king, to attend his court, and Louis made his court such an important event that no noble ambitious for royal preferment could afford to miss it. Louis also brought women into the royal court, and by emphasizing their social functions, gave them a new kind of importance. Historians are divided on the merits of Louis XIV as a ruler or of the benefits which the French received from his rule, but as a pattern-setter and fashion-innovator he was unexcelled. Though he often seems a megalomaniac to more democratic modern readers, his imperious manner and the way in which he spent his money made his court the fashion center of Europe, and led all other European rulers to try to imitate it. Within France every person of importance tried to attend the king, and he made this a rare privilege difficult to achieve. Only noble men and women could formally be presented to him, and the way in which a person was presented or the length of time he spent with the king became a method of measuring status within France. In effect status depended upon the whim of the king. To emphasize the importance of his court Louis built a new, lavish, as well as extremely uncomfortable, palace at Versailles. It cost a fortune to build, so much that Louis tried to hide the cost from his advisers, and it has been estimated by some that six out of every ten francs collected in taxes during the later part of his reign went to support Versailles and its attendants.

From Versailles emanated the dress, manners, speech, and fashions of Europe, and though court life, because of its artificiality, must have been basically dull, no ambitious French noble or would-be noble could ignore it. Ballet, opera, drama, art, literature were all sponsored by the court, and inevitably those who achieved the patronage of the king had their reputations made. As the court grew in size, and the king's patronage became so important, factions arose between those who received royal favor and those who did not, and those who received more royal favor and those who received less. Even by the death of Louis XIV these factions were evidenced by the fact that some of the French intellectuals either preferred to work away from Versailles or were denied access to the court. When Louis eventually died in 1715, the nature of patronage changed radically. His successor, his great-grandson who took the name of Louis XV, was only a child of five, in no position to serve as patron; moreover, there was a decided intellectual reaction to the policies of Louis XIV. Louis, however, had brought men and women together

in a social setting, and even his detractors continued to follow the
same procedure, albeit on a smaller scale. The result was the rise of
the salon. Perhaps inevitably, since it was the only acceptable way in
which they could express themselves, certain powerful and ambitious
women dominated the salons.

Literally a salon was a drawing room, but it came to be the term
applied to any reception at which society gathered for balls, dances,
gambling, or even conversation. The purpose of a salon was nomi-
nally the pleasure of meeting congenial acquaintances, but it was also
a method of displaying new fashions, new talents, and new ideas. A
few women, perhaps tired of the trivia at some of the social gatherings, turned their salons into intellectual gathering places where philosophy could be discussed and important intellectuals invited. It
was through such salons that the *philosophes*, the philosophers or
intellectuals of France, spread their rather revolutionary ideas. Nevertheless the purpose of such gatherings was essentially social, and
even though philosophy was one of the favorite games, the interest
was not in deep detailed philosophical questions but rather in living,
amusing, and fascinating discussion. Even the most serious topics
almost always had a tone of artificial levity, and to be effective it
was necessary to veil major thoughts in graceful conversation.

The key to a good salon was a host or hostess who could keep the
conversation scintillating, introducing the right people, making the
kind of statement or exclamation calculated to send the guests off
on another round of discussion. Women proved particularly adept
at this, perhaps because they could appeal to the mighty egos of some
of their guests without threatening them as equals. Though the role
of hostess traditionally belonged to women, these women made it
something more than it had been in the past, and in the process influenced history. Madame de Tencin, an unfrocked nun, managed
to effect the appointment of two cardinals (her brother and her
lover) while running one of the most brilliant salons in Paris. Madame du Deffand, regarded by Voltaire as an equal, felt free enough
to criticize Rousseau. She was also a friend of the English prime
minister, Horace Walpole, who periodically escaped to France to see
her. Later the illegitimate daughter of her brother, Mademoiselle de
Lespinasse, usurped her place, and induced many of her aunt's
brightest guests to come to her salon instead. Madame Geoffrin, a
member of the bourgeoisie, and therefore never able to be presented

at court, turned her salon into a brilliant social empire and counted among her friends the tsarina of Russia and the king of Sweden.[1]

Salons in imitation of the French sprang up in most other European countries. The sponsors of such affairs in England came to be known as bluestockings, originally a rather derogatory term which implied that persons who attended them were interested more in conversation than in dress. Though the origin of the term is somewhat debatable it is believed to have resulted from the fact that Benjamin Stillingfleet, unable to afford the correct black silk stockings then worn by fashionable society, made do with some blue or black worsted stockings. Whether this was true or not, women who pretended to any intellectual abilities afterwards were called bluestockings. In London the major hostesses were Mrs. Elizabeth Montagu, and her rivals Mrs. Elizabeth Vesey and Mrs. Frances Boscawen. London, however, never rivaled Paris in the eighteenth century, in part because London was not the intellectual center of Great Britain in the same way that Paris was of France, but also because Englishmen were more addicted to clubs exclusively composed of men. In fact a larger number of women, known for their own intellectual accomplishments, attended the salons in England than they did in France.

In spite of the fact that the salon was widely imitated, its era was limited to a rather brief moment in the history of high society when it was fashionable to sponsor intellectual gatherings. Fashions, however, change, and women turned to other kinds of social activities, if only because the number of intellectual guests who met all the requirements was limited and only a few hostesses could compete in this arena.[2] Much of the decline, however, had nothing to do with the women involved but with the nature of changes taking place in the eighteenth century. As the century turned from discussion to action, women found themselves losing out, and by the time of the French Revolution the salon had disappeared all together. During the directory period in France at the end of the eighteenth century there was a rather deliberate attempt to revive the salon, but the new

1. For a discussion of some of these women see Evelyn Beatrice Hall, *The Women of the Salons* (reprinted, Freeport, N.Y.: Books for Libraries Press, 1969), and J. Christopher Herold, *Love in Five Temperaments* (New York: Atheneum, 1961).

2. See Edmond de Goncourt and Jules de Goncourt, *The Women of the Eighteenth Century*, trans. by Jacques Le Clercq and Ralph Roeder (New York: Minton, Balch, 1927).

leaders of France were unaccustomed to the refined play acting of the aristocratic society, and viewed the salons more as places for ostentatious display of newly acquired fortunes or power than centers of intellectual conversation. It was this same exaggerated display which carried over into the nineteenth century, as women, cut off from any real competition in the world at large, attempted to make their societal activities meaningful by throwing all their thwarted energies into competition for place and status.

Since women were so important in the salons, or more probably because equality followed naturally from other ideas, the *philosophes* paid considerable attention to the position of women in society. At the core of their thought was an attempt to formulate new political and social views based on the discoveries and theories of science. They believed that societies operated in accordance with natural laws as binding as the mathematical laws governing the functioning of the universe. The key words for the *philosophes* were "reason" and "natural," terms which they interpreted to mean that man, unmolested by arbitrary authority and dependent upon his own reason and observation, could find the laws governing human nature and then act accordingly to make a better world. Without intending to be revolutionary, the *philosophes* were soon at odds with many established institutions which seemed to them to have no real reason for existing and which they felt were contrary to natural law. Society had to remove such institutions because once man found truth, he should act accordingly and live in greater virtue and happiness. To find truth it was necessary to gather knowledge, to challenge old assumptions, and to eliminate obstacles. This could best be done by education, since only through the intellect could man distinguish between good and evil, become virtuous and therefore happy.

Women's "defects" of which the *philosophes* were conscious were no longer regarded as imposed by the laws of nature but instead were believed to have been acquired as a result of the conditions under which women lived. This meant that if the conditions were changed, the shortcomings of women could be eradicated. Therefore, it was essential that women develop their native mental ability as it was only by becoming enlightened, knowledgeable so to speak, that they could become virtuous and shun evil. A number of the intellectual leaders of the eighteenth century spoke out on the question. Voltaire denounced the injustice of woman's lot. Diderot felt that woman's

inferiority had largely been made by society. The Marquis de Condorcet in two pamphlets, *Letters of a Citizen of New Haven* and
On the Admission of Women to the Suffrage, pleaded that women
be granted equal social and political rights but felt that to do so they
would also have to be equally educated. Without education they
could only be dangerous rulers. In England William Wollaston's
The Religion of Nature Delineated included a section devoted to
"Truths Concerning Families and Relations," in which he stated
that marriage not only involved the propagation of the species but
also mutual happiness of the couple. David Hume wrote on such
subjects as "Of Polygamy and Divorce" and "Love and Marriage,"
and held that the subordination of woman was a sign of a barbarian
society. Frances Hutcheson in his *A Short Introduction to Moral
Philosophy* published in 1747 held that the powers vested in husbands by civil laws of many nations were monstrous. Some of the
writers did more than talk and write; they also acted. Voltaire, for
example, fell in love with the Marquise du Chatelet who "thought
as I did, and who decided to spend several years in the country, culti-
vating her mind." He wrote that he was "tasting in absolute peace
and a fully occupied leisure, the sweets of friendship and study with
one who, unique among women, can read Ovid and Euclid and who
possesses the imagination of one allied to the precision of the other."[3]

Nevertheless the intellectual woman was suspect, and it was the
reaction more than the revolt, if it can be called that, which set the
pattern. Part of the difficulty was that, in France at least, the eighteenth century was an age of debauchery and the leader was the
king of France, Louis XV. When his queen, Maria Leczinska, denied
the king access to her bedchamber, the king turned to other women,
and there were a succession of royal mistresses, the most famous of
whom was Madame de Pompadour. Madame Pompadour realized
quite early that in order to maintain her position she had to keep the
king continually distracted. To meet this need a special house in the
Deer Park (*Parc aux Cerfs*) district of Versailles was purchased to
house two or three mistresses at a time. The girls in the house lived a
rather secluded life, except for visits from their patron and lover
whom they were taught was a Polish nobleman. When a girl ceased
to attract the king, they were paid off with some jewels or a sum of

3. See for example, Nancy Mitford, *Voltaire in Love* (New York: Harper, 1957),
p. 83.

money and married off to some discreet husband. When Madame Pompadour died, her place was taken by Jeanne Comtesse du Barry, and during her reign as royal whore the Deer Park became less important, if only because Louis was growing old while Jeanne was still very young. With the king setting an example, however, the rest of French society followed, and inevitably much of the sexual excess was blamed upon women. The Goncourt brothers in their *Woman in the Eighteenth Century* held that the influence of "women was highest" during the eighteenth century, and they claimed that in France women ruled throughout the whole century. Though the Goncourts held that it was the influence of women which had raised the cultural level of France,[4] if such an argument is accepted the implication is also clear that it was women who had caused France all the misery as well. The Goncourts, however, exaggerated the position of women in eighteenth-century France, since the only way women could effectively act was through men. There was, moreover, a new kind of hostility to women which appeared in force during the eighteenth century, different than the misogynism of an earlier period, namely, the so-called libertine literature which emphasized the sensuous and unstable nature of the female.

Several of the *philosophes* wrote erotic works which tended to put down women as victims of their passions, motivated by self-seeking, pleasure, and vanity. This fact makes one wonder how deep their commitment was to female equality, since even Denis Diderot supposedly wrote such literature in his *Bijoux Indiscreets*. The most famous names in this respect, however, were Choderlos de Laclos and the Marquis de Sade in French, Casanova in Italian, and in English John Cleland, famous for his *Memoirs of a Woman of Pleasure* or *Fanny Hill*. Laclos's *Liasons Dangereuses* told how two young men seduced an innocent girl who then became a whore and how a young religious matron was systematically driven to infidelity and finally to death. The Marquis de Sade went further. He believed that since a woman's sensation of pleasure in sex can be shammed, while pain cannot, pain rather than pleasure was the highest form of sexual activity for women. Nothing, to him, was so monstrous that it could not be a source of joy. Though de Sade wrote to his wife that his sole wrong in life was to love women too much, and he gave some

4. Goncourt and Goncourt, *Women of the Eighteenth Century, passim.*

of them wickedly triumphant roles in his novels, the opposite seems to have been true. Simone de Beauvoir, for example, said that his novels effectively demonstrated the contempt and disgust which de Sade felt for servile, tearful, mystified, and passive women. She wondered whether de Sade might not have hated women so much because he saw in them his double rather than his complement and because there was nothing he could get from them. "De Sade felt himself to be feminine and he resented the fact that women were not the males he desired. He endows Durand, the greatest and most extravagant of them all, with a huge clitoris which enables her to behave sexually like a man."[5] Though Casanova has been called a skilled lover rather than a libertine, he wrote that his chief business in life was "to cultivate the pleasures of the senses." Casanova's descriptive narrative made his story something more than an account of his love affairs. It became, in fact, a valuable picture of the manner and morals of the period and perhaps in Havelock Ellis's words, a "dignified narration of undignified experiences." John Cleland's erotic account of the adventures of Fanny Hill again emphasized women as sexual objects, although he managed to do so in the most chaste English using no "vulgar" words at all.

Inevitably when the French Revolution swept away much of the ancient regime, it also swept away what were regarded as the evils of that society. Essentially it was a middle-class revolution, respectful of middle-class institutions, and in its attitudes toward women it leaned more on Rousseau than on Voltaire. Rousseau's attitude toward the female probably was most felt in the field of education, and this attitude in turn looked back to Fénelon, whose treatise on the education of girls had been published in 1686. That year also saw the establishment of the first boarding school for girls by Madame de Maintenon, the uncrowned queen of France, and the publication of Abbe Fleury's *De Choix et de la Methode des Études*, which had a chapter on studies for females. Fleury, Madame de Maintenon, and Fénelon all agreed that moral and intellectual education were inseparable. There was no need for women to study the classics because then they might become bluestocking intellectuals; even a knowledge of modern language had its dangers because it might lead to a

5. Simone de Beauvoir, *Must We Burn de Sade?*, trans. by Annette Michelson (London: Peter Nevill, 1953), p. 38.

taste for novel reading, but girls should learn to read and write their own language correctly. Arithmetic was of value to a future housewife, and girls should be trained to carry the responsibilities that managing an estate entailed. Above all girls should learn to exercise reason, because then they could be led by intelligent discussion rather than unreasoning flattery. It must always be kept in mind that women were weaker than men:

> A woman's intellect is normally more feeble and her curiosity greater than those of a man; also it is undesirable to set her to studies which may turn her head. Women should not govern the state or make war or enter the sacred ministry. Thus they can dispense with some of the more difficult branches of knowledge which deal with politics, the military art, jurisprudence, philosophy and theology. Even the majority of the mechanical arts are not suitable to them. They are made for exercise in moderation. Their bodies as well as their minds are less strong and robust than those of men.[6]

Fénelon thought that girls were best brought up in their own home, although some convents might be permissible. If a girl was educated at home it was up to her mother to oversee the process, although a governess might be called upon for help. It was for this reason that he composed his treatise. Though he felt a curious woman might be unhappy because of the restricted nature of her education, she was wrong to be so because this meant that she did not recognize the importance of the subjects on which she was instructed.

Though St. Cyr was founded by the wife of a king, it effectively demonstrated the hostilities to any education for females. In spite of rigorous control over the girls in the school, St. Cyr, perhaps because it was a boarding school located in Versailles, soon achieved a reputation as a place for training royal mistresses. Though there was no truth in such rumors, they forced revision of the curriculum and this led to the girls being put under even more stringent controls. In spite of such changes the gossip continued, until in 1692 St. Cyr became a regular Ursuline convent. Its graduates, nonetheless, were the best-educated women in France and St. Cyr became not only the best convent boarding school in France but also a teachers' training college

---

6. Francois de Salignac de la Mothe-Fenelon, *Education des Filles* (reprinted, Paris: Ernest Flammarion, 1937), chap. 1, p. 6. There is an English translation entitled *Fenelon on Education* by H. C. Barnard (Cambridge: Cambridge University Press, 1966).

sending out an annual batch of graduates who either made good wives and mothers or became teachers in other convent schools.[7]

It was with this background of female education in France that the educational writings of Jean Jacques Rousseau appeared. Rousseau thought that before progress could take place a moral revolution was necessary and such a revolution could only occur when government itself had been transformed into an expression of popular will. Part of such a revolution would establish the ideal relation between the sexes, where men would be active and strong, and women passive and weak. Rousseau held that it was necessary that one sex have the power and the will, and the other be subordinate. He believed that those who advocated equality of the sexes with reciprocal duties and obligations were indulging themselves in idle declamations. To cultivate the qualifications of the male in the female implied the neglect of those qualities which were peculiar to her sex, and therefore he felt, contrary to human nature.[8] In his *Emile,* or more fully *Emilius and Sophia or a New System of Education,* he argued that women existed only by reference to man; she was made to please him and to obey him, so nature willed it. His model of the ideal may be taken from his description of Sophie's musical ability:

> Sophie has natural talents; she feels them and she has not neglected them, but not having been in a position to put much art into their cultivation, she has contented herself with using her pretty voice to sing in tune and with taste, her feet to walk lightly, easily, and with grace, to make a reverence in all sorts of situations without embarrassment or awkwardness. Otherwise, she has had no singing master save her father, no dancing mistress save her mother; an organist of the neighborhood has given her a few lessons on the harpsichord in accompanying, which she has since cultivated by herself. At first she only thought to have her hand appear to advantage upon the lower keys; thereupon she found that the sharp dry sound of the harpsichord made the sound of the voice sweeter. Little by little she became aware of harmony; finally, in growing up, she began to feel the charms of expression and to love music for itself. But it is a taste rather than a talent; she is completely unable to decipher a tune from the notes.[9]

7. For a description of the school and its curricula see W. H. Lewis, *The Splendid Century* (reprinted, Garden City, N.Y.: Doubleday, 1957), pp. 239–259.

8. Jean Jacques Rousseau, *Emile*, trans. by Barbara Foxley (London: J. M. Dent, 1911).

9. *Ibid.*, p. 357.

From the standpoint of women's rights even the women of the salon were essentially conservative; they knew their place and dared not usurp that of the male. The truly learned woman throughout the eighteenth century was an anachronism, and the accent remained not so much on knowledge as on accomplishments. Since a woman's position in society was to be a good wife, she was to be taught those things that would make a better wife, reading, writing, household management, perhaps some modern language, French if she was English, Italian if she was French, needlework in all its branches, music, and dancing. Lady Mary Wortley Montagu (1689 to 1762), who must be classed as a rebel against the assigned female role and who is best known for introducing smallpox innoculation into Europe, wrote in 1752 that women were "educated in the grossest ignorance, and no art omitted to stifle our natural reason. If some few get above their nurses' instructions, our knowledge must rest concealed and be as useless to the world as gold in the mind. I am now speaking according to our English notions, which may wear out, some ages hence, along with others equally absurd." [10]

There were few women like Lady Montagu. Most women were content to accept their status even though they might desire a better education. Hester Mulso (Mrs. Chapone), Lady Mary's contemporary, in *Letters on the Improvement of the Mind*, warned against the danger of pedantry and presumption in a woman—of the dangers of exciting envy in one sex or jealousy in the other, of exchanging the graces of imagination for the preciseness of a scholar. Instead of having women study the classics, she wanted them to learn to enjoy the conversation of persons of sense and knowledge. Girls should be taught history, poetry, nature, geography, chronology, moral philosophy, French, and dancing, but they had to be careful in their reading and in their conversation never to offend propriety. Hannah More, one of the most famous of bluestockings, proved equally reactionary in her attitude to female education. Her goal was not equality with males in education but recognition of women as different, more moral, creatures than men. Her purpose was not to make scholarly ladies or female dialecticians but to raise the moral tone of society. Though she condemned female "accomplishments" and the emphasis upon dancing, music, and sketching, and wanted girls to be

10. Josephine Kamm, *Hope Deferred; Girls' Education in English History* (London: Methuen, 1965), pp. 102–103.

thoroughly grounded in the basic elements, she felt that emphasis should be on the "corruption of our nature" and the instillation of a disposition to counteract it.[11] Girls should also be taught to be submissive, to submit to restraint, and not to carry on a dispute even if they knew themselves to be in the right. "I do not mean that they should be robbed of the liberty of private judgment, but they should by no means be encouraged to contract a contentious and contradictory turn. It is of the greatest importance to their future happiness that they should acquire a submissive temper, and a forbearing spirit."[12] A sound grammatical knowledge of English was considered essential, as well as an appreciation of the best English authors, though Hannah feared the reading of novels. She went so far as to urge that girls not learn French since English girls were unlikely to marry Frenchmen or live abroad, and a knowledge of the language would lead even more surely to corruption than reading the English novelists. Her reputation was such that she was consulted on the education of Princess Charlotte, the daughter of George IV, and here she urged somewhat broader learning, including Latin, French, and German, but still the emphasis was on forming moral judgment.[13]

She probably would have agreed with Dr. Erasmus Darwin, the grandfather of Charles Darwin, who wrote that the "female character should possess the mild and retiring virtues rather than the bold and dazzling ones; great eminence in almost any thing is sometimes injurious to a young lady; whose temper and disposition should appear to be pliant rather than robust; to be ready to take impressions rather than to be decidedly mark'd; as great apparent strength of character, however excellent, is liable to alarm both her own and the other sex; and to create admiration rather than affection."[14]

Inevitably any woman who went further and demanded that women be granted equality would be regarded as deviant by other women and by society as well. One woman who dared to believe in equality was Catherine Macaulay Graham, who wrote an eight-

11. Hannah More, *Strictures on Female Education* (London: T. Cadell, 1779), vol. 1, p. 64.

12. Hannah More, *Essays on Various Subjects Principally Designed for Young Ladies* (Philadelphia: Young, Stewart, and McCulloch, 1786), p. 145.

13. Hannah More, *Hints towards Forming the Character of a Young Princess* (5th ed., 2 vols. in 1, London: Cadell and Davies, 1819), chap. 1.

14. Erasmus Darwin, A *Plan for the Conduct of Female Education in Boarding Schools* (reprinted, New York: Johnson Reprint Corporation, 1968), p. 10.

volume history of England covering the reign of the Stuarts. She also achieved considerable notoriety when at the age of forty-seven she took as her second husband a young man of twenty-one. She wanted coeducation for boys and girls to get rid of the notions that the education of females should be of an opposite kind to that of males. Instead she urged that boy and girl children be brought up together, following the same studies and playing the same games. "By the uninterrupted intercourse which you will thus establish, both sexes will find that friendship may be enjoyed between them without passion. The wisdom of your daughters will preserve them from coquetry. . . . Your sons will look for something more solid in women than a mere outside."[15] Mrs. Graham deplored the exclusion of women from the political arena, and held that once women had been educated they would give up indirect influence for rational privileges.

Her plea was picked up by her younger contemporary, Mary Wollstonecraft (1759 to 1797), who regarded Mrs. Graham as the woman of greatest ability ever produced in England. Her manifesto of woman's liberation, the *Vindication of the Rights of Woman*, which appeared in 1792, was a passionate plea for the education of women to be improved until they became the intellectual equals of man.

> Men complain, and with reason, of the follies and caprices of our sex, when they do not keenly satirize our headstrong passions and groveling vices. Behold, I should answer the natural effect of ignorance! The mind will ever be unstable that has only prejudices to rest on, and the current will run with destructive fury when there are no barriers to break its force. Women are told from their infancy, and taught by the examples of their mothers, that a little knowledge of human weakness, justly termed cunning, softness of temper, outward obedience, and a scrupulous attention to a puerile kind of propriety, will obtain for them the protection of man; and should they be beautiful, everything else is needless, for at least twenty years of their lives.[16]

She held that all the writers on female education from Rousseau to her own contemporaries had done little more than render women weaker and more artificial than they would otherwise have been.

15. Quoted in Kamm, *Hope Deferred*, p. 129.
16. Mary Wollstonecraft, *A Vindication of the Rights of Women* (London: J. M. Dent, 1929), p. 23. The new biography of *Mary Wollstonecraft* by Eleanor Flexner (New York: Coward, McCann, and Geoghagan, 1972) was published too late to serve as a reference for this chapter. It is invaluable.

Let woman share the rights, and she will emulate the virtues of man; she must grow more perfect when emancipated or justify the authority that chains such a weak being to her duty. If the latter, it will be expedient to open a fresh trade with Russia for whips: a present which a father should always make to his son-in-law on his wedding day, that a husband may keep his whole family in order by the same means; and without any violation of justice reign, wielding this sceptre, sole master of his house, because he is the only thing in it who has reason: the divine, indefeasible earthly sovereignty breathed into man by the Master of the universe. Allowing this position, women have not any inherent rights to claim; and, by the same rule, their duties vanish, for rights and duties are inseparable.[17]

For expressing such sentiments Mary Wollstonecraft was abused and ridiculed. Horace Walpole called her a hyena in petticoats. In spite of such attacks the work must have hit a responsive chord since it went through three editions in a few years, and probably the greatest support came from women of the middle class who lacked the protection of an aristocratic marriage settlement and could never hope for divorce from a bad husband. Hannah More, the indomitable spinster, however, spoke out against it: "I have been much pestered to read the Rights of Women, but I am invincibly resolved not to do it. Of all jargon, I hate metaphysical jargon: besides there is something fantastic and absurd in the very title. How many ways there are of being ridiculous! I am sure I have as much liberty as I can make good use of, now I am an old maid: and when I was a young one, I had, I dare say, more than was good for me."[18] As Doris Mary Stenton put it, "old maids," such as Hannah More, showed a crass indifference to the possibility of other women's suffering, particularly those who were well enough off to live in comfort and intelligent enough to find something to do. It was such women who suffered least from the attitude of the law,[19] and it might be added, who had the most to lose if married women achieved some of their privileges.

Following the writings of Mrs. Catherine Macaulay Graham and Mary Wollstonecraft were a whole series of pamphlets arguing for greater equality for women, an issue which had become more important because of the changing role of women in society. The major

17. Mary Wollstonecraft, *Vindication*, p. 215.
18. Quoted in Doris Mary Stenton, *The English Woman in History* (London: Allen and Unwin, 1957), p. 313.
19. *Ibid.*

factor in bringing about such a change was the industrial revolution. In simple terms this was the application of machine power to tasks formerly done by hand. In the process it removed industry from the home to the factory and lessened the economic importance of a wife. Industrialization, particularly with the development of steam power, led to a rapid growth in cities and marked the shift in the nature of population from rural to urban. The consequences of this at first were disastrous, not so much for attitudes toward women, but in the social functions of women. As industry moved into the factory, a wife for a workingman was no longer an economic asset but more likely a liability, while children could prove economic disasters. Even in the upper classes woman's role changed. At the beginning of the eighteenth century the mistress of the house was actively concerned in the management and productive work of a large household, but by the end of the eighteenth, and beginning of the nineteenth, she had become much less important economically, replaced by a bailiff or butler. The wife of the small freeholder or tenant farmer who lost his land became dependent upon her husband because with the loss of land went her opportunity of contributing to the resources of the family. If ultimately she became a wage-earner it was at a scale on which she could not adequately maintain herself, still less contribute to the support of the family. As middle-class women found their role changing and their numbers increasing, they tended to copy the manners and accomplishments of upper-class women, but without the property rights or responsibilities such women once had. Inevitably it came to be a sign of status for a man to have a beautiful, well-dressed, and well-decorated wife, and in some ways, leisured wives became a sign of success, a means of conspicuous consumption. The middle class, though aping the pretensions of the upper classes, nevertheless retained essentially middle-class values, emphasizing that they were more moral than the upper classes. The result was the elevation of female virtue and chastity to a new dogma, and a further limitation on women's activities. As women in such classes found themselves cut off from other activities, they got compensation by emphasizing the importance of motherhood and homemaker.

There was also a very real distinction in roles between the middle-class and the working-class women. The latter, for example, could work, but the former could not. This was because in England where industrialization began, the citizens of the time were not unconscious of its effects upon the life of the ordinary person. In fact, the moralists of the period worried about the growth of illegitimacy, the increase in orphans, and the decline in sexual and other morals. Since wages originally were very low in the factories, few laboring men could support a wife, let alone a family, and there was a rapid increase in prostitution. The problem of adequate alternatives to prostitution received particular attention. John Campbell, who wrote under the pseudonym of M. Ludovicus, thought that a foundling hospital should be established for young girls and other females.[20] Campbell's recognition of the economic factors in prostitution was further amplified by John Fielding, who, with his brother Henry Fielding, the novelist, founded the first police system in London. Fielding felt that the reason for the high crime rate in England was the existence of great numbers of homeless children which led boys to become thieves from necessity and their sisters "Whores from the Same Cause."[21] In order to cut down on prostitution, Fielding proposed a "public laundry," which would help "preserve the deserted Girls of the Poor of this Metropolis; and also to reform those Prostitutes whom Necessity has drove into the Streets, and who are willing to return to Virtue and obtain an honest livelihood by severe Industry."[22] Fielding wanted the girls in his laundry to learn as well as work, and part of his plan called for teaching girls under twelve to read, those between twelve and sixteen the housewifely tasks of knitting, cooking, and so forth, while only those over sixteen were to work in the laundry, helping to support themselves until they were married.[23]

Jonas Hanway, another reformer, felt that Fielding's idea of a laundry was not as good as his own suggestion of a factory for manufacturing carpets. He stated that the Turks had already found that

20. M. Ludovicus (John Campbell), *A Particular but Melancholy Account of the Great Hardships, Difficulties, and Miseries, that Those Unhappy and Much-to Be Pitied Creatures, the Common Women of the Town, Are Plung'd into at This Juncture. The Causes of Their Misfortunes Fully Laid Down; and the Bad Effects that too Much Rigour against Them Will Produce* (London: printed for the author, 1752), pp. 6–16. We could not resist giving the title in full.

21. John Fielding, *An Account of the Origin and Effects of a Police Set on Foot by His Grace the Duke of Newcastle in the Year 1753, upon a Plan Presented to His Grace by the Late Henry Fielding, Esq.; To Which Is Added a Plan for Preserving Those Deserted Girls in This Town, Who Become Prostitutes from Necessity* (London: A. Millar, 1758), p. 32.

22. *Ibid.*, p. 49.

23. *Ibid.*, pp. 51–53.

carpet weaving kept the women in the harems busy, and the same occupation would work for English girls who were inclined to prostitution.[24]

It was the textile factories, however, which provided the greatest source of employment for women. Though there were many critics who opposed female employment in factories, in effect women were doing there what they had done at home. Many of the English reformers believed that those factories which provided work for women and children were doing a great benefit for the country as well as providing an advantage for the poor. Daniel Defoe, best known for his *Robinson Crusoe*, explained the importance of female employment in *A Plan of the English Commerce*:

> . . . a poor labouring Man that goes abroad to his Day Work, and Husbandry, Hedging, Ditching, Threshing, Carting, etc. and brings home his Week's Wages, suppose at eight Pence to twelve Pence a Day, or in some Counties less; if he has a Wife and three or four Children to feed, and who get little or nothing for themselves, must fare hard, and live poorly; 'tis easy to suppose it must be so.
>
> But if this Man's Wife and Children can at the same Time get Employment, if at next Door or at the next Village there lives a Clothier, or a Bay Marker, or a Stuff or Drugget Weaver; the Manufacturer sends the poor Woman comb'd Wool, or carded Wool every Week to spin, and she gets eight Pence or nine Pence a day at home; the Weaver sends for her two little Children, and they work by the Loom, winding, filling Quills, etc., and the two bigger Girls spins at home with their Mother, and these earn three Pence or four Pence a Day each: So that put it together, the Family at Home gets as much as the Father gets Aboard, and generally more.
>
> This alters the Case extremely, the Family feels it, they all feed better, are cloth'd warmer, and do not so easily nor so often fall into Misery or Distress; the Father gets them Food, and the Mother gets them Clothes; and as they grow, they do not run away to be Footmen and Soldiers, Thieves and Beggars, or sell themselves to the Plantations, to avoid the Gaols and the Gallows, but have a Trade at their Hands, and every one can get their Bread.[25]

24. (Jonas Hanway), *Letters Written Occasionally on the Customs of Foreign Nations in Regards to Harlots* . . . (London: John Rivington, 1761), p. 13.

25. [Daniel Defoe], *A Plan of the English Commerce Being a Compleat Prospect of the Trade of This Nation* (2nd ed., 1730, reprinted, New York: Augustus M. Kelley, 1967), pp. 90–92.

To many people it seemed evidence of a good deed if the factories would employ women and children as well as men, and several industrialists appealed to Parliament for special favors on the grounds that they employed so many women and children. One woolen manufacturer backed up his plea for privileges by claiming that his factory enabled the workers to "take their children from the highways and from their infant idleness, and bring them to wool and wheel."[26] Defoe wrote admiringly of those areas in the country which managed to enable children of four or five to earn their own bread.

In the nineteenth century, reformers, motivated by a changing attitude toward women which held a proper woman did not work, fought to remove women and children from the factories. The factory women themselves, however, did not agree. A group of them wrote:

> Living as we do, in the densely populated manufacturing districts of Lancashire, and most of us belonging to that class of females who earn their bread either directly or indirectly by manufactories, we have looked with no little anxiety for your opinion on the Factory Bill. . . . You are for doing away with our services in manufactories altogether. So much the better, if you had pointed out any other more eligible and practical employment for the surplus female labour, that will want other channels for a subsistence. If our competition were withdrawn, and short hours substituted, we have no doubt but the effects would be as you have stated, "not to lower wages, as the male branch of the family would be enabled to earn as much as the whole had done," but for the thousands of females who are employed in manufactories, who have no legitimate claim of any male relative for employment or support, and who have, through a variety of circumstances, been early thrown on their own resources for a livelihood, what is to become of them?
>
> In this neighbourhood, hand-loom has been almost totally superseded by power-loom weaving, and no inconsiderable number of females, who must depend on their own exertions, or their parishes for support, have been forced, of necessity, into the manufactories, from their total inability to earn a livelihood at home.
>
> It is a lamentable fact, that, in these parts of the country, there is scarcely any other mode of employment for female industry, if we except servitude and dressmaking. Of the former of these, there is no chance of employment for one-twentieth of the candidates that

26. M. Dorothy George, *England in Transition* (London: Penguin Books, 1953), p. 117.

would rush into the field, to say nothing of lowering the wages of our sisters of the same craft; and of the latter, galling as some of the hardships of manufactories are (of which the indelicacy of mixing with the men is not the least), yet there are few women who have been so employed, that would change conditions with the ill-used genteel little slaves, who have to lose sleep and health, in catering to the whims and frivolities of the butterflies of fashion.[27]

Eventually instead of abolishing the right of women to work in the factories the English Parliament turned to regulating the conditions under which they worked. This suited the notion that women, even lower-class women, were made of finer material than men, but also recognized the economic realities of female employment. Middle-class attitudes of the housewife, however, also began drifting downward into society and in 1841 a group of factory operatives, anxious to raise their own wages and influenced by middle-class attitudes toward women, demanded the "gradual withdrawal of all females from the factories" on the grounds that the home, its care, and its employment was the true sphere of women, and women brought up in factories could not "make a shirt, darn a stocking, cook a dinner, or clean a house." They further held that the employment of women was an "inversion of the order of nature and of Providence—a return to a state of barbarism in which the woman does the work, while the man looks idly on."[28]

In spite of such criticism, the factories in the long run gave women an opportunity to move from the home and ultimately led to a shift in their outlook. Before the industrial revolution, marriage, even though it had been a kind of economic partnership, confined women to the home. With the factory system and urbanization eventually they were brought outside of the home into closer contact with other women, and this made the confining nature of the traditional home much more evident. It also further roused their antagonism toward the legal inequalities which existed. Traditionally a married woman had never possessed a legal right to her own earnings or to a share of the family wages, but in an earlier age where much of the life of both the men and women centered around the home this had not been a burning issue. When a husband could take the cash wages of his

27. Quoted by Ivy Pinchbeck, *Women Workers and the Industrial Revolution 1750–1850* (London: Frank Cass, 1969), pp. 199–200.
28. *Ibid.*, p. 200.

working wife or daughter, however, it became a real issue and roused women to greater consciousness of their own inequalities. Factories for the most part by the nineteenth century were discriminating against married women.

Increasingly it was the single woman, not the married woman, who worked in the factory and such a discrimination was probably accepted by a married woman on the grounds that her earnings usually did not make up for the loss to the family resulting from the nonperformance of other domestic duties. It was only in the twentieth century as more labor-saving devices for running a house appeared that this became the case. The exclusion of married women from the factory was also encouraged by the growth of humanitarianism, encouraged by the workers anxious to improve their own working conditions. Since the mores of the day, following the ideas of Adam Smith, emphasized the nature of a contract freely entered into between the employer and the employee, the government found it difficult to interfere. Since women and children, however, were not fully free individuals, their employment conditions could be regulated, and this was where the factory legislation was most effective. Indirectly of course the male also benefited. As the middle-class idea of homemaker spread downward, it became a common assumption that a man's wages should be paid on a family basis. This further encouraged the idea that a married woman's place was in the home, and homemaking and childrearing were regarded as the economic contribution of the female. This helped stabilize the family even though it discriminated against women. Single women could work but they also found more and more restrictions put upon the work they could do and their wages declined proportionately to those of men. Certain tasks were declared unsuitable for women because they were too heavy or required working in confined spaces which were not conducive to the best of moral behavior. Still in a crisis a woman of the working class, married or unmarried, could work outside the home. No such outlet was permitted to the middle-class woman, who found outlets for her energies more and more restricted. The effects of this were summed up by Margaretta Greg in 1853. She wrote that a lady must be a mere lady, and nothing else:

> She must not work for profit, or engage in any occupation that money can command, lest she invade the rights of the working classes, who live by their labour. Men in want of employment have

pressed their way into nearly all the shopping and retail businesses that in my early years were managed in whole, or in part, by women. The conventional barrier that pronounced it ungenteel to be behind a counter, or serving the public in any mercantile capacity, is greatly extended. The same in household economy. Servants must be up to their offices, which is very well; but ladies, dismissed from the dairy, the confectionery, the store room, the still room, the poultry yard, the kitchen garden, and the orchard have hardly yet found themselves a sphere equally useful and important in the pursuits of trade and art to which to apply their too abundant leisure.[29]

It was from educated middle-class women, as they became more and more unhappy with their confined role in society, that the demands for female emancipation began to appear.

The new model of the genteel woman which appeared among the emerging middle classes was one where the woman did not manage an estate or closely supervise the work of her household; instead gentility came to be associated with inactivity. Women, who were already items of conspicuous consumption, became more useless by social convention which they themselves adopted. To make matters worse such women were not only useless, many were also uneducated and terribly bored. To compensate for this there was a growing tendency to set women apart from the rest of mankind; women were a species of men who had reached a higher moral level. They were a special creation called upon to perform a special function, motherhood—and children received more attention.

Though epidemics were still widespread and large numbers of children died before achieving maturity, the eighteenth century as a whole saw a shift in emphasis from treating them as little adults to treating them as children requiring special care. In the process the role of the mother increased in importance. Cardinal Bernis wrote during the period that "nothing is more dangerous for the morals and perhaps also for the health than to leave children too long in the care of servants."[30] The importance of the family was also increased by the growth of privacy. Until almost the seventeenth century it was rarely possible for anyone to be left alone. People lived close together, and the density of social life made isolation virtually impossible. People who shut themselves up in a room for some time were regarded

29. *Ibid.*, pp. 315–316.
30. Philip Aries, *Centuries of Childhood: A Social History of Family Life*, trans. by Robert Baldick (New York: Knopf, 1962), p. 117.

as exceptionally eccentric. In the eighteenth century, due in part to increased prosperity, the style of living changed and houses themselves were altered to establish new ways of privacy. Rooms, for example, were made independent of each other, opening on a corridor or a hallway instead of passing from one to another. Rooms also developed specialization, and the concept of comfort was born. Beds were confined to the bedroom, which was also furnished with cupboards or alcoves, often fitted out with the new toilette and hygenic equipment. In France and Italy the word *chambre* began to be used to denote the room in which one slept, as distinct from *salle*, the room where one received visitors and ate. In England, though the word "room" was kept for all functions, a prefix was added to give precision, the dining room, the bedroom, and so forth. This specialization of rooms among the middle class and nobility confined servants to out of the way quarters and required that bells be arranged in order to summon them. It became quite improper to call on a friend or acquaintance at any time of the day without warning. The proper lady had a day at home or sent formal invitations.

The greater emphasis on family life also led to an emphasis on children, and since it was recognized that the husband might have to be away from home, the burden of holding the family together fell upon the mother. It was recognized that the child was not ready for life, that he had to be subject to a special treatment, a sort of quarantine before he was allowed to join the adults. Since the child was to be isolated from society, it seemed obvious that woman also, the natural guardian of the children, should be isolated. Motherhood was a special calling, demanding equal time with other occupations, and the tendency to put a woman on a pedestal which had started in the Middle Ages reached a new height.

This new elevation of woman was evident in the instructions of the Presbyterian minister, Dr. Gregory, to his motherless daughters, entitled *A Father's Legacy to His Daughters.*

> Though the duties of religion, strictly speaking, are equally binding on both sex, yet certain differences in their natural character and education, render some vices in your sex particularly odious. . . . Your superior delicacy, your modesty, and the usual severity of your education, preserve you, in a great measure, from any temptation to those vices to which we are most subjected. The natural softness and sensibility of your dispositions particularly fit you for the practice of

those duties where the heart is chiefly concerned. And this, along with the natural warmth of your imagination, rends you particularly susceptible to the feelings of devotion. . . . One of the chief beauties in a female character, is that modest reserve, that retiring delicacy, which avoids the public eye and is disconcerted even at the gaze of admiration. . . .[31]

The capstone of gentility was the attainment of a higher moral susceptibility and delicacy in feeling. The genteel woman was to be a model of self-control, to attenuate sexual attraction as the mode of relation between the sexes, and to favor discreet withdrawal and even retreat in the face of vulgarity. Even Hannah More, the bluestocking teacher, dramatist, writer, and essayist, felt that woman's knowledge was not to be reproduced in some literary composition but to come out in conduct. The ideal gentle woman would be the woman who

had been accustomed to have an early habit of restraint exercised over all her appetites and temper; she who has been used to pent bounds of her desires as a general principle, will have learned to withstand a passion for dress and personal ornaments; and the woman who has conquered this propensity has surmounted one of the most domineering temptations which assail the sex. Modesty, simplicity, humility, economy, prudence, liberality, charity, are almost inseparable, and not very remotely connected with an habitual victory over personal vanity.[32]

Chastity was the mark of the new gentility, and though chastity or the lack of it might be difficult to prove, the assumptions of chastity were not. Thus there were a lot of things that a proper lady could not or would not do. If a girl's dress was too revealing, her ornaments too provocative, her speech and gestures too bold, then some people would assume that she lost her chastity. Appearance counted for more than reality. It was absolutely essential that a proper girl look and behave with a respectable "modesty." Since women in the wealthier classes were also relieved of all kinds of physical exertion, it was expected that their appearance exhibit a meticulous personal daintiness, their gestures an absence of violent muscularity, and their clothes and hairdress an unfunctional fragility. This meant that even

31. Quoted in John Langdon-Davies, *A Short History of Women* (New York: Blue Ribbon Books, 1927), pp. 329–330.
32. Quoted in Fred K. Vigman, *Beauty's Triumph* (Boston: Christopher Publishing House, 1966), p. 48.

her "creative" activities, the form in which women were permitted to direct some of their energies, had to be very limited. As far as music was concerned, and music was a favorite because it could be shown off best, certain activities were very unladylike. If a girl played a flute she had to purse her lips, a very unladylike gesture; this was also true if she played a horn, and the brass instruments had the added difficulty of requiring visceral support for tone quality, which meant they were even more unladylike. The cello required a girl to spread her legs; if she played the violin she had to twist her upper torso and strain her neck in an unnatural way. The clothes of the time added to the difficulties of playing and remaining ladylike. In fact about the only instrument a proper girl could play was a keyboard one; the harpsichord, clavichord, or pianoforte allowed the girl to sit properly before the keyboard, arrange her clothes neatly, put a polite smile on her face, keep her feet demurely together, strike the key lightly with no unseemly vehemence, and act gentle and genteel, an outward symbol of her family's ability to pay for her education and her decorativeness. Her abilities, which should be adequate but not professional, were signs of her family's status of life, of its striving for culture, of its pride in the fact that she did not have to work nor did she have to chase after men.[33]

Inevitably the life of the proper woman came to be filled with a kind of genteel idleness in which she tried to fill her time with a number of trivial occupations superficially related to the fine arts, known as "accomplishments": fancy needlework and embroidery, framing pictures in shellwork, embellishing cabinets with a tracery of seaweed, filigree, and varnish work, working with chenille, crepe, ribbon, or netting, making artificial flowers of wax or fabric, cutting out paper ornaments, drawing or painting slightly, and playing the piano adequately. When anything untoward appeared the lady was either to withdraw, or if this was impossible, to faint. There were even ways to faint elegantly:

> The eyes grow dim, and almost closed; the jaw fallen; the head hung down; as if too heavy to be supported by the neck. A general inertia prevails. The voice trembling, the utterance through the nose; every sentence accompanied with a groan; the hand shaking, and the knees tottering under the body. Fainting eventually produces a sudden re-

33. For a discussion of this see Arthur Loesser, *Men, Women and Pianos: A Social History* (New York: Simon and Schuster, 1954), pp. 65ff.

laxation of all that holds the human frame together, every sinew and ligament unstrung. The colour flies from the vermilion cheek; the sparkling eye grows dim. Down the body drops, as helpless, and as senseless, as a mass of clay, to which, by its colour and appearance it seems hastening to resolve itself.[34]

Though the prudery associated with the new gentility has often been labeled Victorianism, it predated the advent of Queen Victoria and remained a dominant theme for much of the nineteenth century. The new mystique of motherhood granted women special status but at the same time guaranteed them inferiority. Common women went to work in the factories, neglecting their families, and aristocratic women remained outside the bounds of middle-class morality, but the good woman, the true middle-class woman, as befitted her new-found moral purity and spiritual genius, had to devote herself to the task of homemaking, something which in the past had not been regarded as particularly important. Because she was pure she was also weak and had to be safeguarded at all costs from the corrupting effects of the man-made world beyond the domestic circle. William R. Taylor and Christopher Lasch have suggested the

> cult of women and the Home contained contradictions that tended to undermine the very things that they were supposed to safeguard. Implicit in the myth was a repudiation not only of heterosexuality but of domesticity itself. It was her purity, contrasted with the coarseness of men, that made woman the head of the Home (though not of the family) and the guardian of public morality. But the same purity made intercourse between men and women at least almost literally impossible and drove women to retreat almost exclusively into the society of their own sex, to abandon the very Home which it was their appointed mission to preserve.[35]

The burden put upon women by such an attitude was one that many of them did not want and could not bear, but the only outlet for their discontent was in church work and in literary pursuits. Religion in a sense became a justification for what they wanted to do and could not do, and even women suffrage became a movement to raise the standards of morality by allowing the purer and finer species,

34. Quoted in *The Genteel Female: An Anthology*, ed. by Clifton Joseph Furness (New York: Knopf, 1931), p. 9, from *An Essay: In which Are Given Rules for Expressing Properly the Principal Passions and Humours* (1782).

35. William R. Taylor and Christopher Lasch, "Two Kindred Spirit: Sorority and Family in New England, 1839–1846," *New England Quarterly*, 36 (March, 1963), 35.

the woman, to vote. Victorianism taught women to think of themselves as a special class, and having become conscious of their unique sexual identity, they could no longer accept uncritically the role definitions drawn up for them. Denied liberty they sought power, and not infrequently the easiest way to gain power was over their children. Motherhood came to be elevated into a kind of mystique which Freud made into a kind of pseudo-scientific basis of existence. Though the Victorian concept of women as wan, ethereal, spiritualized creatures bore little relation to the real world where women operated machines, worked the fields, handwashed clothing, toiled over great kitchen stoves, it was endorsed by science and religion. Fashion materially assisted by keeping women in bustles and hoops, corsets and trailing skirts, and other items of clothing in which they remained encased throughout much of the period. The ideal waistline came to be the span of a man's two hands, and since few women could achieve this naturally they did so by tight lacing. Feminine delicacy which was so much admired was at least in part due to constricting corsets rather than visible evidence of the superior sensibilities, the "finer clay" of which women were made. Women who were not delicate by nature became so by design. Women themselves came to believe in their own special genius, and those who did not conform were usually ostracized. The world came to be made up of good girls and bad girls. The bad girls represented sexuality, the good girls purity of mind and spirit, unclouded by the shadow of any gross or vulgar thought. The largest collection of bad girls were the prostitutes, and they were thought to have had poor moral inheritance. The literature of the time, particularly the novels, represented sexuality as dangerous and evil, thereby reinforcing respectable young women and anxious wives in their moral code of chastity and virtue. With overpowering mothers who were brought up as young girls to fear sex, the nineteenth-century home often became a nest of psychological difficulties which have not yet disappeared today.

Since women, in spite of their sensibilities, were reading in increasing numbers, it became essential that their reading material be controlled. By the end of the eighteenth century it was assumed that most fiction was much too delicate for women who had to be shielded from the grosser facts of life. Even Aphra Behn, the late seventeenth-century writer, and usually regarded as the first professional woman of letters, became suspect for the new generation of women readers.

Though Mrs. Behn had been considerably less ribald than some of her masculine contemporaries, the standards of Charles II's age, even in a mild form, were much too risque for young ladies of a more squeamish age. Samuel Richardson's *Pamela*, strongly recommended as a moral tale for young girls in the last part of the eighteenth century, by the nineteenth was considered much too daring for virtuous young ladies. This in spite of the fact that Pamela was successful in fending off all assaults on her virtue until she was safely married.

Indicative of the change in literature was the success of Thomas Bowdler, a well-to-do physician who never seriously practiced medicine but did take a great interest in "good" works of nearly every kind. Bowdler was university educated and widely traveled, a man of the world who nonetheless enjoyed reading aloud the great writers to his family. He became concerned at the overt sexuality in Shakespeare and his concern led him in 1818 to produce a ten-volume expurgated version which he felt included only what was fit to be read "by a gentleman in the company of ladies." *Othello*, however, was too much for even Bowdler's purifying activities, and he advised that this play be transferred from the parlor to the locked cabinet. Bowdler's efforts had been anticipated by others, including James Plumptre, who in 1805 published an expurgated song book. One British writer went so far as to urge the perfect hostess to see "to it that the works of male and female authors be properly separated on her bookshelves. Their proximity unless they happen to be married should not be tolerated."[36]

At the same time that the concept of feminine sensibility was being refined, the concept of marriage was also changing, and this ultimately led to a different attitude toward the woman as wife—from being a helpmate and mother only to one of lover and companion as well. Usually this change is attributed to the movement known as romanticism, which can be traced to some of the writings of Jean Jacques Rousseau and Johann Wolfgang von Goethe. This movement reached its greatest influence in nineteenth-century Germany, from whence it spread outward. In romanticism the claims of the intellect gave way to those of passion and emotion, the critical spirit was replaced by the imaginative one, although romanticism could be

36. Quoted in Milton Rugoff, *Prudery and Passion* (New York: Putnam's, 1971), p. 61.

better defined as a "mood" rather than a movement because it is difficult to confine it to a rigid definition. The romantics reacted against the views of the *philosophes* who they felt had overstressed the role of reason in discovering truth and had not paid enough attention to emotion. Romanticism was pro-sex in that the romantic was encouraged to go against social convention, to emphasize physical passion, to recognize the fact of sexual inconstancy, to cultivate emotion and sensation for their own sake. Put in this way the actions of the romantics were not particularly different than those of the *philosophes*, although the thought processes by which they arrived at conclusions were different. As far as marriage was concerned, the romantics held that the only true basis for marriage was a mutuality of feeling and attraction, and carried logically to a conclusion this meant the romantic union was one freely made between equals. The "inequality" of women in the marriage relationship, in fact, was one of the principal points of agreement among the romantics.

The threads of the romantic movement trace back to the chivalric epics, but added to its medieval heritage was the belief that love itself involved an intense psychological relationship as well as a physical one. The adherents revived Plato's theory that every individual was but one-half of a complete entity so that somewhere there was to be found the twin-soul, the missing half, the only person in the world who provided the full complement for one's own personality. For the romantics sex had a positive value but only if it took place within an intense psychological relationship. In fact sexual union was illegitimate unless the lovers were joined by emotional and intellectual ties as well as physical ones. Sex was only possible with the beloved, and its purpose was to link together two individuals motivated by the highest emotions. The female partner should be in Percy Bysshe Shelley's terms "as perfect and beautiful as possible, both in body and in mind, so that all sympathies may be harmoniously blended, and the moment of abandonment be prepared by the entire consent of all the conscious portions of our being." [37]

Marriage relationships which were loveless and oppressive ought to be dissolved, and the German Johann Fichte went so far as to state

37. Percy Bysshe Shelley, "A Discourse on the Manners of the Ancient Greeks Relative to the Subject of Love," in *Shelley's Prose*, ed. by David Lee Clark (Albuquerque: University of New Mexico Press, 1954), p. 222.

that marriage without love should be regarded as an automatic divorce.[38] Generally the romantics would hold that once a true love was found the lovers became so perfectly united in body and soul that true love was identical with fidelity.[39] Not all would agree that love was eternal and immutable, and Shelley, for example, held that in the normal course of life one could fall in love more than once. "A husband and wife ought to continue so long united as they love each other: any law which should bind them to cohabitation for one moment after the decay of their affection would be a most intolerable tyranny. . . . The connection of the sexes is so long sacred as it contributes to the comfort of the parties, and is naturally dissolved when its evils are greater than its benefits."[40]

In essence the romantics were a kind of feminist. They believed that woman had been denied her humanity in a world ruled by men and that she needed to be liberated from masculine tyranny; at the same time, however, they were ambivalent about how far woman should go. This was because while they recognized the disabilities under which women lived, they still emphasized the nature of opposites in the male and female psychology. Marriage was the union of opposites and the female complemented the male, and thus if he was aggressive, she was passive, if he was rational, she was emotional. As Victorianism settled in, the free-love aspects of romanticism were also modified, and marriage was the be all and end all of romantic love. The romantics were conscious of their inherent masculine bias and some of them attempted to soften traditional sexual identities by preferring "delicate and dreamy men, free and daring girls." The German Friedrich Schlegel wondered what "is uglier than overemphasized womanliness, what is more repulsive than the exaggerated manliness which prevails in our mores, our opinions, yes even in our art? . . . Only self-reliant womanliness, only gentle manliness, is good and beautiful."[41] In his novel *Lucinda* his male protagonist says to

38. Johann Fichte, *Grundlage des Naturrechts nach Principien der Wissenschaftslehre von Johann Gottlieb Fichte's Sammtliche Werke*, ed. by J. H. Fichte (Berlin: Veit, 1845), vol. 3, p. 336.

39. For a discussion of this see the unpublished paper by Paul A. Robinson, "Romantic Sexual Theory," presented at the American Historical Association, Boston, 1970, *passim*, but esp. pp. 16–17.

40. Shelley, "Notes on Queen Mab," *Works*, p. 806.

41. Friedrich von Schlegel, "Über die Diotima," in *Friedrich von Schlegel: Seine prosaischen Jugendschriften*, ed by J. Minor (Wein: Verlagsbuchhandlung Carl Konegen, 1906), vol. 1, p. 59.

his mistress: "We exchange roles and with childish delight try to see who can best imitate the other; whether you succeed best with the tender vehemence of a man, or I with the yielding devotion of a woman. . . . This sweet game has for me quite other charms than its own. . . . I see in it a wonderful and profoundly significant allegory of the development of man and woman into complete humanity."[42] Unfortunately, however, since sexual roles were not blurred but only exchanged, it must be assumed that they eventually reverted to their original owners, that men continued to be vehement and women yielding.

> This is indeed what happens over and over with the Romantics: after struggling toward an affirmation of female equality and a new concept of sexual roles, they invariably fall back upon the old categories, emphasizing the essential differences between male and female postures, whether in bed, in interpersonal relations, or in society at large. These differences are variously described by Romantic authors, but they all boil down to the same thing: the old distinction between male assertiveness and female passivity. Women are made for love, men for friendship; women are subjective, men objective; women have peculiar gifts for poetry and religion, men for science and philosophy; women are patient and receptive, men are volatile and spontaneous.[43]

Though the romantics ultimately only rarely carried their feminist ideas to the logical conclusion of equality, they did place the ideal of romantic love within marriage, and in the process emphasized both the need for psychical and physical capability of the marriage partners.

The fact that the romantics eventually accepted the idea that women were essentially different from men in the long run proved to be the most successful weapon that women had in demanding greater equality. If women were made of finer fabric, more concerned with morals, with man's inhumanity to man, then this allowed them to enter the political arena on these grounds. The battle for woman's suffrage was not fought on the grounds of basic equality but on bringing a higher moral plane to politics. Women were active in the moral causes, in the fight to free the slaves, in the battle to

---

42. Schlegel, *Lucinda*, trans. by Bernard Thomas in *The German Classics*, vol. 4 (Albany, N.Y.: J. B. Lyon, n.d.), p. 131.
43. Robinson, "Romantic Sexual Theory," p. 22.

outlaw liquor, in the struggle to eliminate prostitution, and in the campaign to extend education. These were moral causes, or were concerned with children, causes which women could join in and, even within the limits of the masculine prerogatives of the time, assume a leadership. Middle-class women were expressing themselves in the arts, in literature, and in poetry, but they were not really confronting men on their own terms. Women rulers had come to be an accepted part of life, and there were a large number in the seventeenth and eighteenth century from Maria Theresa to Catherine the Great of Russia, but they usually were only allowed to rule when the male line had defaulted.

If women could not come in the front door, they would enter stealthily by the back door of equality, fighting on the unequal terms assigned to them by the males. Though physically this put them at a disadvantage, it probably allowed them to move forward without appearing too deviant. Though many women must have admired the freedom of a Mary Wollstonecraft who had an illegitimate child and did not believe in marriage and believed that women were equal, they did so secretly, rarely in the open. The romantic notions of feminine sensibility emphasized women's weakness but also established the battleground for greater freedom.

chapter twelve

The American Experience

The American colonists carried European attitudes toward women with them as part of their intellectual baggage. There were, nonetheless, certain conditions and developments unique to America that materially affected the status of woman. One of the ways in which colonial America differed from Europe was in the existence of a great sexual imbalance. The scarcity of women was proverbial and colonial documents offer a constant refrain that single girls would find America a paradise of bachelors eager to wed. One early Swiss settler wrote home with the advice that penniless girls ought to emigrate to America because "here men do not care for money. . . ."[1]

In fact, the first permanent English settlement in Virginia, Jamestown, was an all-male enterprise. Since the Virginia Company made no provisions for sexual matters the gentlemanly adventurers were left to their own devices, and though Indian women were used as sexual companions only rarely did the Virginia settlers marry them. The only official marriage between an Indian and European in the early days of Virginia was that of John Rolfe and Pocahontas. Though this marriage was an important factor in preserving peace between the Indians and Europeans, Rolfe's own attitude toward his wife and offspring is indicated by the fact that he failed to provide in his will for his child by Pocahontas.[2]

As a rule interracial marriages were frowned upon. Even before the colonists had set out for Virginia they were warned in a sermon that just as Abraham's posterity was to keep to themselves so the

1. Mildred Campbell, "Social Origins of Some Early Americans," in James M. Smith, ed., *Seventeenth Century America* (Chapel Hill: University of North Carolina, 1959), p. 74.
2. Arthur W. Calhoun, *A Social History of the American Family* (3 vols. reprinted in 1, New York: Barnes and Noble, 1945), p. 324.

English settlers were not to "marry nor give in marriage to the heathen. . . . The breaking of this rule, may breake the neck of all good success of this voyage."[3] This did not mean, however, that they could not sleep with the "heathen," and colonial records were full of such alliances. It was not just social pressure and prejudice that accounted for the lack of Indian wives, but also the fact that Indian women were simply not qualified by their background to assume the household tasks which the European-oriented men of the time assumed that a wife would do. Unless a man wanted to live on the frontier among the Indians or isolated from the rest of the settlers, an Indian wife put him at a disadvantage because she could not spin and weave the type of material to which he was accustomed, churn or make sausages, brew beer, make cheese, or any number of other tasks. In fact, the profitability of housekeeping operations usually depended on a woman's administrative and business ability.

The scarcity of European women caused some difficulty since many of the women who did come found so many offers that they attempted to keep several men happy, an activity much frowned upon by the authorities. The Virginia Great Charter of 1619 set up machinery so that the church could search out such "skandalous offences as suspicions of whoredomes, dishonest keeping with women, and such like."[4] In New England the most scandalous settlement was that of Mare Mount of Thomas Morton, where contacts between Indian women and colonial males upset the Pilgrim colony at Plymouth. It was ultimately destroyed by the combined forces of New England.[5] Even when sex ratios began to be equalized in theory, they were not in practice, since men kept moving to the frontier and most of the frontier settlements at least for a time went through periods of unequal sex ratios. Later, in fact, some of the eastern more settled communities developed a surplus of eligible females which also had an effect upon concepts toward women in the United States.

It is interesting to note that even while females were scarce, they were still regarded as inferior by the establishment and the institutions of the day. The churches, except for the Quaker, remained

3. Quoted in *ibid.*, p. 323.
4. George F. Willison, *Behold Virginia: The Fifth Crown* (New York: Harcourt, Brace, 1951), p. 200.
5. William Bradford, *Of Plimoth Plantation* (Boston: Wright and Potter, 1898), pp. 285–286.

male-dominated institutions, and laws were made by males. Holding or willing of property by women was restricted, and what a woman might say, do, or learn was delineated by social custom that was at least as binding as the statutes. Though female education was not disregarded among the colonies since the women had of necessity to be prepared for the search for grace, it was restricted. When education was available girls as well as boys were taught to read, write, and do basic arithmetic, but the education of girls ended at a much lower level than that of boys. The decision to limit female education was reinforced by the widespread belief that female capacities were limited.

When the wife of Governor Hopkins of Connecticut, for example, became mentally ill, her insanity was blamed upon the fact that she had spent so much time in reading and writing. "If she had attended her household affairs, and such things as belong to women, and not gone out of her way and calling to meddle in such things as are proper for men, whose minds are stronger, etc., she had kept her wits, and might have improved them usefully and honorably in the place God had set her."[6] Those women who attempted to exceed their assigned role usually found themselves in hot water. A good illustration of this is Anne Hutchinson (1591 to 1643), who was banned from Massachusetts because she had exceeded "woman's place" by holding informal weekly meetings of women to discuss the sermons of the previous Sunday and to interpret them for her listeners. Such activity was held to be "a thing not tolerable nor comely in the sight of God nor fitting" for a woman to do. When Mrs. Hutchinson retorted that the Bible gave permission for women to teach the young (Titus 2:3–5), she was warned that such teachings were to be restricted to teaching young women "about their business to love their husbands," not religious views that differed from the majority.[7]

The Puritans in New England found biblical justification for their subjugation of women in the fifth commandment and its reference to honoring a father and mother. Though both sexes were clearly mentioned in the commandment it was held that "father and mother" were to be interpreted as meaning not only parents but all

6. John Winthrop, *The History of New England 1630–1649* (2 vols., Boston: Thomas B. Wait, 1826), vol. 2, p. 216.

7. David Hall, ed., *The Antinomian Controversy, 1636–1638* (Middleton, Conn.: Wesleyan University Press, 1968), pp. 312, 315–316.

superiors and since the husband was the superior of the wife by the
law of conjugal subjection, as well as by nature, she had no choice
but to respect his wishes.[8] When one New England woman wrote a
book her brother publicly rebuked her by stating that your "printing
of a Book beyond the custom of your sex, doth rankly smell."[9] Anne
Bradstreet (1612 to 1672), America's first woman poet, conscious of
the male hostility to the educated female, prefaced her book:

> I am obnoxious to each carping tongue
> Who says my hand a needle better fits.
> A poets pen all scorn I should thus wrong,
> For such despite they caste on Female wits:
> If what I do prove well, it won't advance,
> They'l say it's stoln, or else it was by chance.[10]

Even when women went to school they often read special text-
books prepared for them in order to limit the strain on their faculties.
Such titles as *Newton's Ladies Philosophy, The Lady's Geography,
The Female Academy, The Ladies Complete Letter Writer,* and the
Female Miscellany were often advertised.[11] Women were not always
happy with such restrictions and Anne Bradstreet was one of those
who protested against the generalizations about female inferiority.
She pointed to Queen Elizabeth as an example of a woman who had
made considerable contributions to civilization and concluded:

> Now say, have women worth or have they none?
> Or have they some, but with our Queen is't gone?
> Nay Masculines, you have thus taxt us long,
> But she, though dead, will vindicate our wrong.
> Let such as say our Sex is void of Reason,
> Know tis a Slander now, but once was Treason.[12]

Women of course were invaluable as economic adjuncts to their
husbands and they did other jobs which either required no formal
education or little technical knowledge. Others served in more skilled

8. For a discussion of this see Thomas Cobbet, *A Fruitful and Useful Discourse
Touching the Honour Due from Children to Parents* (London, 1656), p. 18.
9. Thomas Parker, *The Copy of a Letter Written to His Sister* (London, 1650),
p. 13.
10. Anne Bradstreet, *The Works of Anne Bradstreet,* ed. by John Harvard Ellis
(New York: Peter Smith, 1932), p. 101.
11. Julia Cherry Spruill, *Women's Life and Work in the Southern Colonies*
(Chapel Hill: University of North Carolina Press, 1938), p. 202.
12. Bradstreet, *Works,* p. 361.

capacities as private tutors, as school mistresses, or as midwives and herb doctors. Many served as nurses but usually as a sideline rather than a real occupation. Women were also shopkeepers, although their shops were usually run from their own homes. Maria Provost, wife of James Alexander, kept one of the largest shops in New York City. One evening in 1721 she gave birth to a daughter after having spent the day behind the counter and the next day with the help of her sixteen-year-old apprentice she opened the shop and sold thirty pounds worth of merchandise from her bed. Her husband bragged that he was very lucky to have such a good wife who "alone would make a man easy and happy had he nothing else to depend on."[13] Women, of course, served as seamstresses, milliners, laundresses, dyers, and stay-makers, but they also had other occupations; Jane Inch of Maryland was a silversmith, while Mary Willet took over her husband's pewter business after his death. In South Carolina Anna Maria Hoyland advertised that she would do any kind of "braziery and tinwork" as her mother had done. Maria Warwell mended china and Cassandra Ducker of Maryland owned and ran a fulling mill.[14] It was only when cities grew larger and occupations more specialized and professionalized that women were cut out of most jobs. This was because as cities became larger the business districts centralized and it became much more difficult for women to run a store from their home or to compete with the specialized stores. As specialization increased in importance, more training was required and women were denied the opportunity to be apprentices or in the cases of the professions to attend the necessary colleges or universities. Continental ideas about what constituted the fashionable women also exercised more influence as Americans reached higher levels of prosperity. Increasingly those women who pretended to any culture or status imitated their English cousins in their ideas about women's role.

Still the vastness of America often allowed different norms to be followed. On Nantucket Island, for example, the whaling fleets kept the men away from home on voyages from two to five years in length, with the result that much of the island's business was handled by the women. Status for such a woman came from her ability to best

13. Alice Morse Earle, *Colonial Days in Old New York* (Port Washington, N.Y.: Friedman, 1962), p. 163.
14. Spruill, *Women's Life*, p. 288.

make or protect her husband's money during his absence. Under such conditions it was very difficult for a woman to be a "clinging vine," if only because as one islander remarked, there were "no sturdy oaks" for her to cling to. Though mainlanders characterized Nantucket women as "homely and ungenteel," and their Quakerism kept their dress plain, they performed many of the tasks reserved for men in other parts of America. One preserved anecdote, perhaps apocryphal, tells the tale of a good wife who while at a store decided to buy a whole barrel of flour rather than make several trips to the store, and then to save delivery time, picked up the barrel and carried it home.[15] It was perhaps no accident that women from Nantucket contributed out of proportion to the leaders of the women's rights movement in the nineteenth century. Lucretia Mott, one of the early feminists, and Maria Mitchell, professor of astronomy at Vassar and militant champion of a new place for women, were both natives of the island.

Attitudes toward women were influenced by slavery, particularly in the south. Though there was always a double standard in America, the availability of vast numbers of slavewomen in the south lent further encouragement to the practice and eventually led to a concept of female gentility which was not matched in the north or in the west. Every planter tended to regard himself as the supreme source of law in his own bailiwick, the creator of his own slave code. Inevitably Negro women suffered from being his unwilling sexual partners, while his wife suffered from her inability to do anything about the situation. Peter Fontaine claimed that in 1757 "the country swarms with mulattoe bastards."[16] Thomas Anburey, who traveled throughout much of America during the eighteenth century, also reported seeing a number of mulattoes on southern plantations and added that many of the young women "are really beautiful, being extremely well made, and with pretty delicate features; all of which I was informed were the colonel's own. . . . It is a pleasant method to procure slaves at a cheap rate."[17] White women on the other hand were protected from the male Negro slaves, and the result

15. William Oliver Steven, *Nantucket, the Far Away Island* (New York: Dodd, Mead, 1966), p. 103.

16. Robert E. Brown and B. Katherine Brown, *Virginia, 1705–1786* (East Lansing: Michigan State University Press, 1964), p. 68.

17. Thomas Anburey, *Travels through the Interior Parts of America* (2 vols., Boston: Houghton Mifflin, 1923), vol. 2, pp. 342–343.

was an eventual exaltation of the white female almost as a guilty compensation for the philandering activities of the men. W. J. Cash wrote that she became

the South's Palladium, this Southern woman, the shield-bearing Athena gleaming whitely in the clouds, the standards for its rallying the mystic symbol of its nationality in face of the foe. She was the lily-pure maid of Astolat and the hunting goddess of Boetian hill. And she was the pitiful Mother of God. Merely to mention her was to send strong men into tears—or shouts. There was hardly a sermon that did not begin and end with tributes in her honor, hardly a brave speech that did not open and close with the clashing of shields and the flourishing of swords for her glory. . . .[18]

Such gyneolatry did not lead to political power or equality for women but it had its compensations. The difficulty was that while many women were satisfied with being subjugated and exhalted, not all were. Men were recognized as different creatures, able to assume different tasks, but women were all set apart by biology and qualified only to be wives and mothers.

In the western states, the sexual imbalance continued to favor women until well into the twentieth century. How much such an imbalance affected ideas about women is perhaps debatable but that it had some effect is indicated by the fact that it was the western states which restored the right of women to vote. Legally in many of the early colonies women often had the right to vote, although there were only a few recorded instances of their use of the ballot. As the colonies grew in size the colonial legislatures gradually withdrew such rights. New Jersey during the revolutionary fervor of 1776 restored it but there is little reported about it until an Elizabethtown election in 1796 where a group of conservative "widows and maids" organized by the Federalist candidate nearly defeated his opponent. The *Newark Centinel* proudly reported that the residents of New Jersey not only preached the rights of women but also boldly pushed such ideas into practice. Apparently the New Jersey provisions were rather loosely enforced, since after an election in 1806 in which women, Negroes, servants, and boys were herded into polling booths, the New Jersey legislature moved to restrict the suffrage to "free, white, male citizens," cutting out aliens, females, and Negroes all

18. W. J. Cash, *The Mind of the South* (New York: Random House, 1960), p. 89.

together.[19] Female suffrage, however, had not yet become the issue it later became, and during its existence in New Jersey there was no real female political leader of any importance, or for that matter any real feminist.

It was the western territories that first restored female suffrage, although the reasons probably had little to do with female equality as such. The men in Wyoming in 1869, who first gave women the vote, were in part motivated by a desire to preserve the "white, rural, middle-class American virtue." This they felt they could do by doubling the vote of the "respectable" people who settled as family units against the "undesirables," such as gamblers, the hustlers, and the mentally unbalanced who were so often attracted to the frontier.[20] Women were in short supply in Wyoming and it was also hoped that more women would be attracted to the territory. Women, wrote one local humorist, "can give this territory a boom that will make her the bonanza of all creation." Even though equality for women probably was not the motivating factor in giving women the vote, woman suffrage did serve as a case study for those women who argued that women could vote as intelligently as men.

The second territory to give women the vote, Utah, faced a somewhat different situation than Wyoming, since women were as numerous as men, but again the motivation was to gain backing for the establishment, this time the Mormon church. Obviously in both Wyoming and Utah the men thought they could control their women. At least two reasons seemed to have motivated the Mormons in Utah to give women the vote. The overwhelming majority of women in the territory were Mormon while large numbers of men were non-Mormons attracted by the mining industry. By giving women the vote the Mormons could assure themselves of dominance. The Mormons at this time also practiced polygamy and the Mormon church was intent on proving that if women were given the vote they would vote to retain polygamy, thus assuring an increasingly hostile America that women were not forced into polygamy. In fact, when the Utah women did not vote out polygamy the United States Congress in 1887 took away their right to vote. It was restored,

19. E. R. Turner, "Women's Suffrage in New Jersey: 1790–1807," *Smith College Studies in History*, 1 (July, 1916).
20. Alan P. Grimes, *The Puritan Ethic and Woman Suffrage* (New York: Oxford University Press, 1967).

however, in 1896 when Utah was admitted to the Union with a constitution making polygamy illegal. Wyoming in 1890 was admitted as a state with woman suffrage. Not all western states, however, gave women the vote, and California rejected it by referendum in 1896.[21]

The unequal sex distribution had given women even without the vote considerable freedom of action, and it was not until the nineteenth century, particularly in the eastern sections of the country, that there were attempts to curtail this. The mounting pressure was social rather than political and was tied in with a changing concept of womanhood being introduced from Europe. In the mid-eighteenth century Dr. Alexander Hamilton, a Scottish observer, reported that it was not unusual for young couples to go on long walks together and that he even went on such a hike himself with a woman companion and friends, enjoying "all the pleasures of gallantry without transgressing the rules of modesty or good manners."[22]

The American custom of dating can be traced back into the early colonial period. One observer reported that before the dangers of the wild had been eliminated it was not unusual to see in Albany, New York, adolescent boys and girls going off on picnics together with the girls carrying their sewing baskets and young men their rifles.[23] European travelers, in fact, often remarked on the amazing innocence of Americans on such ventures, although some of the American guardians of morals were not so sure. Jonathan Edwards, for example, condemned all kinds of frolics where mixed groups were out at night.[24] Often the Europeans were shocked at what was permissible. The French traveler, François de Chastellus, observed a young man and woman holding hands and kissing in the presence of the family. He assumed that the couple were betrothed and when he discovered that this was not the case he marveled that it was not a crime "for a girl to kiss a young man."[25] Kissing, pinching, and fondling in the eighteenth century usually were regarded as mere flirta-

21. See Andrew Sinclair, *The Better Half: The Emancipation of the American Women* (New York: Harper and Row, 1965), pp. 208–219.

22. Alexander Hamilton, *Gentleman's Progress: The Itinerarium of Dr. Alexander Hamilton, 1744* (Chapel Hill: University of North Carolina Press, 1948), p. 155.

23. Anne Grant, *Memoirs of an American Lady* (New York: Dodd, Mead, 1903), pp. 114–116.

24. Mary Sumner Benson, *Women in Eighteenth-Century America* (New York: Columbia University Press, 1935), p. 276.

25. François de Chastellux, *Travels in North America in the Years, 1780, 1781, 1782* (2 vols., London: Robinson, 1787), vol. 1, p. 120.

tions, not to be taken too seriously. There were, however, limits and, to our minds, contradictions. Hannah Logan, a young Quaker, had to receive her father's permission before she could press the suit of her lover, but it was perfectly all right for the two to sit alone past midnight, embracing each "other in pure Love and perfect Confidence."[26]

One of the things that distinguished early America from Europe was the great distances between settlements, and this coupled with a lack of hotels and restaurants, early bedtimes, and shortage of beds meant that strangers were dependent upon individual hospitality. The result was the development of bundling, putting another person into the same bed. Lt. Thomas Anburey, stopping in a storm at a Massachusetts cabin, was offered a portion of the bed of the daughter of the house. Unaccustomed to American hospitality the lieutenant offered to sit up all night rather than share the bed of the teenaged daughter. The father rejected this response out of hand and laughingly explained that he was not the first man Jemima had bundled with. His daughter Jemima, however, volunteered the information that he was the first Britisher.[27] Bundling was also part of the courtship process.

Marriage in the colonies usually involved a formal betrothal or precontract before the final marriage vows. This put the couple in an ambiguous position, not yet married but more than single. In several of the New England colonies, for example, sexual intercourse of an espoused woman with another man was punishable not as fornication but as adultery, but if it took place with her betrothed the couple was punished only half as severely as an uncontracted couple for the same offense.[28] Many of the betrothed couples courted each other in bed, with a board between them for safety, although from the church confessions it seems that the board did not always work. In spite of the attempts to stamp out the custom it continued through the eighteenth century, at least until greater sophisication and urbanization and more adequate housing became the norms of the American opinionmakers.[29] Memories of the custom, if not the custom itself,

26. John Smith, *Hannah Logan's Courtship: The Diary of Her Lover*, ed. by Albert C. Myers (Philadelphia: Ferris T. Leach, 1904), pp. 160, 222, 224.

27. Anburey, *Travels*, vol. 2, pp. 25–26.

28. Geoffrey May, *Social Control of Sex Expression* (New York: Morrow, 1931), pp. 248–249.

29. There are several accounts of bundling in America. Probably the most famous

continued to exist in the numerous traveling salesman jokes about farmers' daughters.

American women were also relatively free and open in their discussions about sex.[30] Again it was not until the nineteenth century, and then primarily in the east, that euphemisms replaced the Anglo-Saxonisms and the cult of gentility made it difficult for a lady to function biologically. Dr. Alexander Hamilton, already mentioned, was not a little embarrassed when in the presence of women, a New Yorker recommended a "good mowing" as a cure for female hysterics. Hamilton felt that such language was a piece of inexcusable rudeness, "especially when it is practised before wifes and daughters whose ears should never receive anything from husbands and fathers but what is quite modest and clean."[31]

In short women in colonial America and later on the frontier, though regarded as intellectually inferior to men, were not regarded with overt hostility if they kept their place. Within the confines of their inferiority they had considerable freedom. Married women were under the control of their husbands, but single women of age could usually run their own affairs. Legally of course women were at a disadvantage in comparison to men and had few rights under the law. There was also some continuation of the clerical misogyny which had so dominated earlier references to women. Pastor John Cotton, Jr., in particular was fond of lecturing women on their sin of "pride, increase of sensuality," overdressing, and their abilities to tempt men to sin, but he spoke from experience. It was later found that his prayer vigils with sinful women often ended in intercourse.[32] Most colonists would have agreed that: "Women are Creatures without which there is no comfortable Living for man: it is true of them what is wont to be said of Governments, That bad ones are better than none: They are a sort of Blaspheremers then who dispise and

---

is that by Henry Reed Stiles originally published in 1871 but available in several editions, including one under the title *Bundling: Its Origin, Progress and Decline in America* (reprinted, New York: Book Collectors Association, 1934). See also C. F. Adams, "Some Phases of Sexual Morality and Church Discipline in Colonial New England," Massachusetts Historical Society, *Proceedings*, 2nd. ser., 6 (June, 1891), pp. 503–510.

30. George Francis Dow, *Everyday Life in the Massachusetts Bay Colony* (New York: Benjamin Blom, 1967), p. 118.

31. Hamilton, *Gentleman's Progress*, p. 177.

32. Willison, *Behold Virginia*, pp. 368, 372.

decry them, and call them a necessary Evil, for they are a necessary Good." [33] Perhaps the only overt attack on women was the witchcraft trials which did result in the death of a number of women. Among the colonists, at least the male colonists, it was a truism that women were neither as strong nor as intelligent as men. It became natural then to equate women of ability with witches and several such women were executed. In New England, for example, a female herb doctor who objected to the conventional medical treatment of bleeding and the administration of violent emetics was hanged as a witch, while another suffered for simply "having more wits than her neighbors." [34]

Even though the colonists had left Europe, America was not un-affected by the currents of European thought, and these tended to have their greatest influence first on the eastern seaboard where the more settled colonies were and then gradually spread westward. Mary Wollstonecraft's *Vindication of the Rights of Women*, men-tioned earlier, appeared in two independent editions in 1792, one printed at Philadelphia and the other at Boston. Still a third edition appeared in 1794. Though there was undoubtedly hostility to her ideas, there was also acceptance. One reviewer reported that there were only a few "thinly scattered weeds" in the book but "many durable trees, which unite the beauties of Flora with the firmness of the elm." William Godwin's *Enquiry Concerning Political Justice and Its Influence on Morals and Marriage* was published in the United States three years after it appeared in England. Godwin, the husband of Mary Wollstonecraft, held that monogamous marriages were inconsistent with men's psychological makeup, and that remov-ing the unnecessary bindings of law and property would allow man to apply a kind of reasonable virtue and moderation to his sex life. [35]

Americans, such as Benjamin Franklin and Benjamin Rush, also picked up and modified European ideas for their American audience. One of Franklin's earliest efforts was his *Reflections on Courtship and Marriage*, originally published in 1746. Franklin chided his fel-

33. Edmund S. Morgan, "The Puritans and Sex," *New England Quarterly*, 15 (1942), 591–607.

34. John Fiske, *New France and New England* (Boston: Houghton and Mifflin, 1904), p. 125.

35. Sidney Ditzion, *Marriage, Morals and Sex in America* (New York: Bookman Associates, 1953), pp. 22–48.

low males for inflating women's conceit and vanity by flattering female beauty and petty accomplishments which only prevented women from achieving anything solid in the realm of reason. Franklin, in spite of the fact that he held it was contrary to reason and nature for one sex to tyrannize the other, was not for female equality. He firmly believed that nature as well as the circumstances of life seemed to design for "man that superiority, and to invest him with a directing power in the more difficult and important affairs of life." Nevertheless, it was essential for women to be educated since only then could man give them proper direction. Women who had been taught to reason would listen to their husbands "with delicacy, coolness, and good temper, supported by a solidarity and strength of judgment." Franklin also held that though love might come by chance it was retained by art. He realized that the "hard to be governed passions" of youth had driven him into intrigues with "low women that fell" his way, and he advised others that marriage was the best solution to such problems. He offered similar thoughts in his *Advice to a Young Man on the Choice of a Mistress*, but then added that if the young man rejected his advice he might give thought to choosing a mistress. Franklin advised an older woman rather than a young one for a mistress since the older was more likely to be knowledgeable, would be unable to have children, and also would make fewer demands upon her patron. Franklin added that it was easier to make an old woman happy than a young one, and besides all mares looked the same in the dark.[36]

How much such writings modified attitudes toward women is perhaps debatable. Franklin clearly was no feminist. Others, however, went somewhat further, including Charles Brockden Brown, who is usually regarded as the first professional author in the United States. His *Alcuin: A Dialogue* (1798) portrays a utopia where sexual equality was the norm. Brown believed it was unfortunate that in the actual world women were regarded more or less as animals existing only for the convenience of the more dignified sex. In his attempt to do something about it he wrote a series of "gothic" ro-

36. Franklin's advice on mistresses can be found in various editions, but it is also in *Satires and Bagatelles*, ed. by Paul McPharlin (Detroit: Fine Book Circle, 1937). His *Reflections on Courtship and Marriage* was published anonymously and it was not until the third edition of 1758 that he is listed as the author. The complete works of Franklin are in the process of being published.

mances emphasizing his ideas on sexual equality, including *Wieland* (1798), *Arthur Mervyn* (1799), *Ormand* (1799), *Edgar Huntly* (1799), *Clara Howard* (1801), and *Jan Talbot* (1801). He also edited several magazines which carried his ideas on sexual equality, love, marriage, and society across the emerging United States.

Even liberals, such as Benjamin Rush, the physician who was also a founding father, seemed conservative about women. In a treatise on female education he urged women to concentrate on learning useful things, such as reading, writing, arithmetic, bookkeeping, and elementary sciences. Science instruction was not studied so women could become scientists but to help "prevent superstitions." Rush also urged girls to study vocal music in order to participate in worship and to soothe the cares of domestic life, and to study dancing because it promoted good health. He saw no need for higher learning. It was, nonetheless, important that women be educated since it was so difficult to govern the ignorant, and like Franklin he felt men would have an easier time in dealing with women if things could be explained to them.[37]

If these were the radicals in their attitudes toward the female, it seems obvious that American women had a long way to go to achieve any kind of equality at the beginning of the nineteenth century. Charles Brockden Brown was one of the few male Americans who believed in equality. Even Thomas Jefferson held that girls were unfit in brains and character for serious study. Probably the most significant intellectual movement in the first half of the nineteenth century was transcendentalism, a sort of American version of the romantic movement. Many of the transcendentalists espoused greater equality for women. At the center of the movement were such authors as Henry Thoreau and Ralph Waldo Emerson on the male side, and Louisa May Alcott and Margaret Fuller on the female. From the very fact that women such as Alcott and Fuller were recognized intellectuals indicates that there was a changing attitude toward the capacities of the American woman. Margaret Fuller, in fact, is usually regarded as the author of the first major woman's right tract to be written in America. Her "The Great Lawsuit—Man Versus Men; Woman Versus Women" portrayed the campaign for

37. Benjamin Rush, "Thoughts upon Female Education," in *Essays, Literary, Moral, and Philosophical* (Philadelphia: Thomas and Samuel Bradford, 1798), pp. 75–92.

feminine equality as a divinely ordained fight to exalt the human race.[38]

Not all the transcendentalists, however, were feminists. Orestes Brownson, who at least in one phase of his life could be classified as a transcendentalist, wrote that female independence was unthinkable. The submissive woman, he held, was a companion, comforter, ministering angel, but a woman as equal was something else. When a woman is allowed an "independent existence, free to follow her own fancies and vague longings, her own ambition and natural love of power, without masculine direction or control, she is out of her element, and a social anomaly, sometimes a hideous monster, which men seldom are, excepting through a woman's influence."[39]

Part of the difficulty with any attempt to change basic attitudes toward women was that it required a change in woman's attitudes toward herself. Increasingly in the eighteenth and nineteenth centuries individual women were allowed to break through some of the bastions of male prerogatives, but women as a group were not. The institutions and formalized structures of power outside of the family remained under the control of men. Few women seemed willing to mount a frontal assault on male prerogatives, and even if a small minority of hardy pioneers tried to do so it was necessary for their success to carry the bulk of womanhood with them. Most women before the nineteenth century, however, were unwilling to demand radical changes in their status either because they saw little chance for change or were more or less contented with things as they were. For women to go out in the business world or have a profession when the bulk of her earnings could be claimed by her husband was not particularly attractive. This legal inequity, however, was only part of the reason. Within the home the woman was essential, and though the man might go out in the world, woman ran the home and her job was as important as her husband's.

Industrialization only began to reach America in the nineteenth century, and with the growth of factories, the home began to lose out as the key economic unit. This cut down the economic impor-

38. Margaret Fuller, "The Great Lawsuit. Man Versus Men. Woman Versus Women," *The Dial*, 4 (July, 1843), 1–47, and further amplification of the ideas appeared in her *Woman in the Nineteenth Century* (Boston, 1855). An extract of "The Great Lawsuit" can be found in Aileen Kraditor, *Up from the Pedestal* (Chicago: Quadrangle Books, 1968), pp. 66–70.

39. *Ibid.*, p. 193.

tance of women and probably encouraged their dissatisfaction with the traditional role assigned to them. At the same time the nineteenth century in America, as in Europe, perhaps as sort of unconscious compensation for lack of economic importance, emphasized the finer nature of women, the special qualities that it took to be wife and mother. This concept took strong root in the American soil not only because in much of America women were still in short supply, but also because it could be used by both those who wanted greater equality for women and those who opposed it. Both sides agreed that woman was created to be a wife and a mother, and equated motherhood with patience, endurance, passive courage, finer sensibilities, and greater sympathy. Though the antisuffragists argued that women for these reasons should be confined to the home, those fighting for woman's rights argued with equal logic that it was just such qualities that were needed in the electoral process. While a few of the more militant women made a frontal assault upon the male citadel of privilege, most women played the proper woman's role but in the process managed to crusade for such moral causes as the abolition of slavery, temperance, better schools, and reform of public morals.[40] Though in the long run this oblique approach to equality had limitations, something which many women are just beginning to realize, it had the advantage of bringing about change and at the same time convincing most women that change was what they wanted. Perhaps if those early pioneers of woman's rights had been able to choose their own ground on which to struggle they might have chosen a different version of women, but they were in part forced to adopt such a view because this was the one that many males also had.

The concept of women's special nature appeared very early in American history. Seventeenth-century Thomas Cobbet wrote: "Age may wear and waste a Mother's beauty, strength, parts, senses, limbs, estate, etc., but her relation of a Mother is as the Sun, where he goeth forth in his might, for the ever of this life, that is always in its meridian, and knoweth no evening; the person may be gray-headed, but her Motherly relation, is ever in its flourish. It may be Autumn, yea,

40. For an account of this see Eleanor Flexner, *Century of Struggle: The Woman's Rights Movement in the United States* (Cambridge: Harvard University Press, 1959); William L. O'Neill, *Everyone Was Brave: The Rise and Fall of Feminism in America* (Chicago: Quadrangle Books, 1969); and Andrew Sinclair, *The Better Half: The Emancipation of American Women* (New York: Harper and Row, 1965).

Winter, with the woman, but with the Mother, as a Mother, it is always Spring."[41] Later legislators refused to discuss the topic of female suffrage with "cold, dry logic," because they felt they were dishonoring the memory of their "dear old grand mother, or the gentle words and caressing hand of that dear blessed mother gone to the unknown world." A New York constitutional convention, for example, turned down a woman's suffrage amendment because women were enshrined "forever in the hearts of the father, the husband, and the son," and the only way for women to achieve their goals would be to teach true religious principles to their children and their husband.[42] California voters originally turned down woman's suffrage because they were afraid it would mean prohibition since women were so concerned with their homes.

Some of the women militants ridiculed the motherhood rhetoric. Olive Schreiner, for example, wondered whether a husband, after portraying his wife as a sacred childbearer, requested that she not work any more because it was enough that she "should have the holy and mysterious power of bringing the race to life."[43] Most women accepted such rhetoric as compensation for other privileges which they did not have. To be effective any movement for feminine equality had to come to terms with such attitudes, both female and male.

Most people were horrified that any woman would reject motherhood, although there was compassion for the spinster since it was generally believed that she had lacked the opportunity to be married and become a mother. Any distribution of contraceptive information or devices in the nineteenth century was punishable by law, and a majority of medical men believed that the practice of birth control harmed health. Books with information on contraceptives were equated with obscenity and Anthony Comstock, who was given powers of censorship by the United States Post Office in the last part of the nineteenth century, even prosecuted physicians who wrote on the subject. Some writers even compared the obligation of women to bear children with the duty of military service for men. Though both tasks caused suffering, such a pattern had been set by biology,

41. Thomas Cobbet, *A Fruitful and Useful Discourse*, p. 25.
42. This is a paraphrase of some of the antisuffrage writings of the time. A good example can be found in Aileen Kraditor, *Up from the Pedestal*, pp. 192–198.
43. Olive Schriener, *Woman and Labor* (New York: Frederick A. Stokes, 1911), pp. 208–213.

and one prominent writer claimed that any person who interfered with either of these duties should be regarded as a traitor.[44]

The effect of such rhetoric is evident from the fact that Mother's Day, the day Americans express their respect for the women who bore them, was established at about the same time that women received the suffrage. The first Mother's Day was observed at the urging of Anna Jarvis in a Philadelphia church in 1908 on the anniversary of her own mother's death. It spread rapidly because the rhetoric of motherhood had become so engrained in the American conscience. Perhaps Americans felt guilty because they had failed to properly revere their mothers and such a sin needed a penance. For such people Mother's Day proved a godsend since it only cost money and interrupted a day (Sunday) which was otherwise not useful. By 1914 Mother's Day was so popular that President Wilson proclaimed it a national observance, a time when all government flags were to be displayed as a "public expression of our love and reverence for the mothers of our country."

Beneath the surface of the rhetoric over the finer sensibilities which developed in the nineteenth century, woman often found herself in conflict. Part of the difficulty was that the myth, at least for most of the country, conflicted with reality. While Americans were officially adopting the belief that women were made of finer fabric, not suited for the more mundane tasks of life, the vast majority of Americans were still living on farms where women worked, and in fact, pulled a fair share of the load so the family farm would not collapse. The result was a continuing contradiction between myth and reality which often led foreign visitors to make fun of the Americans. When myth and reality clash the result is often a kind of hesitancy about what is proper, and when the myth is adopted as proper there is still no certitude of what is right conduct because it is so far from reality. Reality, except in the more backward parts of the country, was considered poor manners, and this meant that women were caught in a kind of trap in which they were damned if they did and damned if they did not.

Some of these conflicts are evident in the observations of the nineteenth-century traveler, Frederick Marryat, whose *Diary in America* is often cited as proof of the prudishness of American wom-

44. G. Stanley Hall, *Adolescence* (2 vols., New York: Appleton, 1904), vol. 2, p. 609.

anhood. In one incident Marryat wrote that when he asked a lady if she had hurt her leg after she had stumbled and fell, she expressed shock at his language. Finally with considerable reluctance she explained that in the presence of ladies a gentleman refers to a leg as a limb. In spite of such delicacy, however, women went walking around "without chaperons" much to the surprise of Marryat. It was also Marryat who claimed that American women were so prudish that they denied pianos had legs but instead referred to such supports as limbs. He reported a visit to a ladies' seminary where the piano had each of its four "limbs clothed in modest little trousers, with frills at the bottom of them."[45] This incident seems to have been a kind of sophisticated hoax played upon Marryat, but even if the incident were true it does not so much represent a total picture of American attitudes as an instance of "perverted" prudery in a low-ranking status-conscious girls' school whose staff was trying to imitate what it thought proper ladies would do. On the other hand, Max O'Rell, another observer, was greatly impressed with the emancipation of American girls who had their own friends, their own pocket money, and went unescorted to concerts and theaters.[46]

American women knew the attitudes and actions for the proper woman in the nineteenth century, but large numbers lacked the leisure to cultivate the necessary manners, and many of them who did lacked the conviction that they were doing the correct thing. The results were often contradictory. This is most evident in the survey of American manners compiled by Mrs. Frances Trollope who had gone to Cincinnati from England in 1829 to open up a "moorish bazaar." The store failed and Mrs. Trollope recouped her investment by writing a gossipy account of the gaucheries of American womanhood. She tells, for example, how a well-mannered young German offended one of the principal local families by using the word "corset" in the presence of ladies.[47] She regarded this as an example of inverted prudery, yet Mrs. Trollope herself was shocked by the openness of two young women who described to her how they had tried to embarrass a male acquaintance as he left the rooms of a local prostitute. The girls had engaged the young man in conversa-

45. Frederick Marryat, *A Diary in America* (New York: Knopf, 1962), pp. 273–274, 419.

46. Max O'Rell, *Jonathan and His Continent* (New York: Cassell, 1889), p. 68.

47. Frances Trollope, *Domestic Manners of the Americans*, ed. by Donald Smalley (New York: Vintage Books, 1949), p. 136.

tion and made it clear to him that they knew where he had been. The "emancipated" Mrs. Trollope was only able to write the story by using linguistic circumlocutions, the brothel becoming "a mansion of worse than doubtful reputation," and the story one "hardly fit to tell." This she said only indicated how Americans feigned delicacy.[48]

Her son, the novelist Anthony Trollope, wrote his own account of American morals some thirty years later and found American women still troublesome, particularly in the west. He reported that though women in the east had acquired "womanly grace," by which he probably meant that they acted like proper English women, women in the west were a different matter. "I cannot fancy myself much in love with a western lady, or rather with a lady in the West. They are as sharp as nails, but then they are also as hard. They know, doubtless, all that they ought to know, but then they know so much more than they ought to know. They are tyrants to their parents, and never practise the virtue of obedience till they have half–grown-up daughters of their own."[49] Anthony Trollope resented both the independence of the American working classes and the American woman, and although he realized that the working people were better off than their British counterparts, he was not so understanding of American women. Instead he held that "Eve would have had no charms had she not recognized Adam as her lord."

As the nineteenth century progressed the freedom of action of American women became more eroded as the veneer of what was proper stretched westward. The wealthier classes adopted the custom of chaperonage as a device to prevent unsuitable marriages, and the middle-class girls and women, in spite of their better education, found themselves bound with more and more restrictions as to what was proper. Respectable women were cautioned not to ride in omnibuses alone or enter restaurants or theaters without a male escort. Even though many women must have resented such restrictions, only a few of them were willing to break with the new respectability which equated outward forms with virtue and chastity. Those women who did break were often ostracized by the "proper" lady, although not necessarily by men. In fact some of the most iconoclastic women,

48. *Ibid.*, pp. 137–138.
49. Anthony Trollope, *North America* (London: Chapman and Hall, 1862), p. 400.

provided they did not overtly threaten the male when they broke conventions, had the strongest male backers. This was true of the two Claflin sisters, Victoria Woodhull and Tennessee Claflin, who achieved considerable notoriety in the nineteenth century for their refusal to abide with the feminine stereotypes. The sisters did do things with a kind of style that their more timid sisters would probably have found painful. For example, when they were refused service at Delmonico's in New York because they lacked a male escort, the sisters simply went outside and invited a cabbie to join them for dinner and then enjoyed their meal.[50]

Most women were careful, however, not to antagonize other women, and this meant they always had to retain their decorum even when they threatened masculine privilege. Masculine privilege could be easily threatened and even when speaking on such moral uplifting causes as abolitionism women had to be careful what they said. The Grimke sisters, Sarah and Angelina, who spoke on the evils of slavery in the 1830s, were severely censored by the Massachusetts Congregationalists for mentioning the fact that slave women were often sexually abused by their masters and overseers. The clergy felt it was wrong for women to speak on subjects which "ought not to be named." Some nineteenth-century clergymen even held that it was beyond woman's capacity to speak from the platform, and when the Grimke sisters and others demonstrated that this was not the case, the reactionary clergy retorted as did the Reverend Jonathan F. Stearns that the "question is not in regard to ability, but to decency, to order, to Christian propriety."[51] The Grimke sisters were not silenced by the censure of the Massachusetts Congregationalists, and Sarah Grimke, in fact, took the offensive with her "Letter on the Equality of the Sexes and the Conditions of Women." She held that whatsoever was "morally right for a man to do" was also morally right for a woman. Sarah Grimke admitted that by such a statement she was asking women to sacrifice the adulation, the flattery, the attentions of trifling men, but she held that this was the only way women could elevate her own character.[52]

50. Emanie Sachs, *The Terrible Siren* (New York: Harper, 1928), p. 63.
51. Kraditor, *Up from the Pedestal*, pp. 49–52. Part of the quotation is from the "Pastoral Letter of the General Association of the Massachusetts (Orthodox) to the Churches under Their Care."
52. William L. O'Neill, *The Woman Movement* (London: Allen and Unwin, 1969), pp. 103–107.

Men seemingly became excited over the silliest things, even women banding together to collect funds for a worthy cause. In Boston, for example, the Bunker Hill Battle monument still was unfinished in the 1840s because of lack of funds. To raise money to finish it a group of women under the leadership of Sarah Joseph Hale held a handicraft fair. The funds raised permitted construction to continue, but the managers of the project accepted the money only on condition that no credit be given to the women who had so ignored their natural incapacity by attempting (successfully) to raise money.[53] The list of don'ts for women during the period would fill a book.

During the Civil War when northern women organized the Women's Central Association for Relief it was headed by a man since it was assumed that women would be incapable of chairing such a body. Nevertheless, the women's organization eventually led to the formation of the United States Sanitary Commission, which was an important factor in the northern victory. In the aftermath of the Civil War, however, a number of women's clubs were organized, and these had the merit of allowing women to exercise leadership positions in their own right. Other organizations such as the Woman's Christian Temperance Union also gave women a chance to demonstrate their abilities, and finally in 1896 the first professional association in which women were dominant, the American Nurses Association, was organized. Hostility, however, still remained. When a Board of Lady Managers was established to oversee the women's activities of the 1893 Chicago World's Fair, journalists expected they would accomplish nothing of importance since many still held women to be innately incapable of governing or administering anything. When the innovation proved not to be a disaster but a success, some of the chauvinistic male journalists invented stories and exaggerated incidents of "quarreling and Hysterics" among the women members of the board to demonstrate the incapabilities of woman. One woman militant attempted to show the double standards used by journalists by comparing the newspaper accounts of female discussion on the board with coverage of a debate on the floor of the British House of Commons where the members fought on the floor until the "whole space between the front benches was

53. Charles W. Ferguson, *The Male Attitude* (Boston: Little, Brown, 1966), pp. 222–223.

filled with a struggling, cursing, mass of members, striking, clawing and up-setting each other." She concluded that the males might well follow the precepts they "always so generously dealt out to women" instead of continually setting such a bad example.[54]

Not all women, however, were looked upon with the mixture of reverence and disdain that was the lot of middle-class women. Excluded from the category of creatures with finer sensibilities were women below the poverty line, and in particular Negro women. Following the abolition of slavery and the northern and western migration of many blacks it turned out to be easier for a woman to get a job than a man. Black women were in demand as domestics and servants, and while there was also a limited market for males in this same area, there was considerable fear and suspicion about employing males in houses where the woman was home alone, regardless of color. Unfortunately most other occupations were closed to black males and few had the money, the resources, or the education to go into business for themselves. This meant that in spite of the rhetoric about female weaknesses and sensibilities, the Negro woman often became the economic mainstay of her family and the male held a much less important role as a father figure. Richard Wright, one of the great writers of the first part of the twentieth century, pictured the situation graphically and poignantly in one of his stories which recounts the continued failure of a Negro male to get a job. In desperation he finally dressed up in his pregnant wife's clothes and was hired almost immediately as a domestic. He then found that he was also expected to satisfy the sexual appetite of his male employer, and when he/she refused he was fired.[55] As a Negro middle class developed, black men adopted some of the white male attitudes toward the proper role of the female, but a higher proportion of Negro women at all socioeconomic levels work than do white women. On the lower economic levels much of the sex discrimination in jobs still exists to the detriment of the male, which means that even today the position of the black women is still different from that of the white.

In the Richard Wright story a man dressed as a woman in order to gain employment, but usually in American history it has been the

54. *The Woman's Column*, Aug. 12, 1893, vol. 6 (Boston: American Woman Suffrage Assoc.).

55. Richard Wright, "Man of All Work," *Eight Men* (New York: Avon Books, 1961).

other way around. One way in which women could escape the confinement of their role was to don the clothes of the male, although after exposure most of them settled down to become good wives and mothers. Such impersonation was rather lightly regarded by males, since one of the arguments used to justify the inferiority of women was to point to their desire to be men, ignoring in the process that it might not have been so much a desire to change sex as to enjoy some of the freedoms which most women felt men had. Perhaps the most famous of American women to impersonate a male was Deborah Sampson, who fought in the Continental Army under the name of Robert Shirtliffe. Deborah had donned male clothes in order to travel and see the world. To get money for adventure, Deborah, who had completed a term as an indentured servant, joined the Continental Army. She wore a bandage about her breasts during her enlistment to disguise herself and reportedly augmented her waist, although just how is unknown. Though Cornwallis had already surrendered at Yorktown when she enlisted, she did see action with scattered units of British troops and Tory bandits and was wounded. When she was finally discovered in 1783 she was given an honorable discharge, and shortly after married Benjamin Gannett. She received a pension for her wartime services and thus can be listed as one of the first, if not *the* first, woman to serve in the United States Army. As her story reached the public she became an object of considerable curiosity and gossip, but she also eventually came to be regarded as a kind of heroine. She was the mother of three children.[56]

Following her example, several such women served in the Civil War as men. Private Frank Fuller, alias Frances Hook, of the 90th Illinois, carried a rifle and served until wounded and captured at the Battle of Chattanooga. A private of the 25th Michigan Cavalry turned out to be Elizabeth Compton. Matilda Joslyn Gage, a nineteenth-century feminist, collected incidents of at least ten other

56. An early account of her escapades appeared under the title of *The Female Review: Or Memoirs of an American Young Lady* (Dedham: Nathaniel and Benjamin Heaton, 1797). Though no author was listed, it was written by a Herman Mann. This account was republished with introduction and notes by John Adams Vinton (Boston: J. K. Wiggin and William Parsons Lunt, 1866). Vinton's work was republished as Extra Number 47 of the *Magazine of History with Notes and Queries*, 1916. The most recent and scholarly investigation was by W. F. Norwood, "Deborah Sampson, Alias Robert Shirtliff, Fighting Female of the Continental Line," *Bulletin of the History of Medicine*, 31 (1957), 147–161.

women with similar experiences.[57] One woman wrote a book about her experiences, namely Loretta Janeta Velazquez, who served in the Confederate Army. She had first disguised herself to be with her husband but she continued to serve long after his death. According to her story she had a New Orleans tailor make her a half-dozen wire net shields which she wore next to her skin in order to disguise her true form since a "woman's waist, as a general thing, is tapering, and her hips are very large in comparison with those of man, so that if I had undertaken to wear pantaloons without some such contrivance, they would have drawn in at the waist and revealed my true form. . . . So many men have weak and feminine voices that, provided the clothing is properly constructed and put on right, and the disguise in other respects is well arranged, a woman with even a very high-pitched voice need have very little to fear on that score." Over her wire net shield she wore a tight-fitting undershirt of silk or lisle thread, held in place by straps across the chest and shoulders. Around her waist she had a band with eyelet holes arranged so that the pantaloons would stand out. When her true sex was eventually discovered, in part she felt because her apparatus was out of order, she was sentenced to ten days in jail and fined ten dollars.[58]

On the union side the most famous case was Sarah Emma Edmonds, alias Franklin Thomson. As a girl in New Brunswick, Canada, Emma, the name by which she was known, read a novel by M. M. Ballou entitled *Fanny Campbell: Or, the Female Pirate Captain* published in Boston in 1844. The novel told about a girl whose lover was captured by pirates and she, cutting her curls and stepping into "freedom and glorious independence of masculinity," managed to rescue him. How much the story influenced her is uncertain, but young Emma in order to escape marriage fled at fifteen from her family home and then to support herself donned male garb and worked as a Bible salesman. After the outbreak of the Civil War, she managed to enlist, and served for two years until illness forced her to retire, still undetected. Soon after she published her memoirs under the title of *Nurse and Spy* (Hartford, 1864) and became famous. She later married and became a mother but her adventures were recog-

57. Cited in Stewart H. Holbrook, *Dreamers of the American Dream* (Garden City, N.Y.: Doubleday, 1957), p. 187.
58. Loretta Janeta Valezquez, *The Woman in Battle*, ed. by C. J. Worthington (Hartford, Conn.: T. Belknap, 1876).

nized in 1897 when she was officially accepted into the George B. McClellan Post, Grand Army of the Republic, and thus became the only woman member of the GAR, the nineteenth-century equivalent of the American Legion.[59]

There were several other women who also disguised themselves in order to see the world.[60] Some were not discovered until their death. This was the case of Charles Durkee Pankhurst, who must be listed as the first woman to vote in California, since on "his" death in 1879 Charles was found to be a woman. "He" had driven a stagecoach in the various mining towns of California.[61] Several women were known as Mountain Charley, a woman who lived as a man in the western territories in the 1850s, and at least two wrote books claiming to be the legendary person.[62] It was perhaps also poetic justice that women took to playing men's parts on the stage, and instead of men impersonating women as they had in sixteenth-century England, many women impersonated men. Almost all of the leading actresses in the nineteenth century at some time played a male part and some became quite famous in such roles, as did Adah Isaacs Menken, who played the character of Ivan Mazeppa in a poem of the same name by Lord Byron.

Other women began wearing some items of male clothes as a rebellion against the confinement of female clothing. The most famous of these was Amelia Bloomer who urged the "Daughters of the American Republic" to "abjure the feminine fashion adopted at profligate courts in Europe." Mrs. Bloomer and her allies were basically fighting with foresight and common sense what was one of the most inhibiting factors women had to face, their confining clothes. It is estimated that women in the nineteenth century wore over fif-

59. Her story is recounted by Sylvia Dannett, *She Rode with the Generals: The True and Incredible Story of Sarah Emma Seelye, alias Franklin Thompson* (New York: Nelson, 1960).

60. See for some examples, Rosanne Smith, "Women Who Wanted to Be Men," *Coronet* (September, 1957), pp. 62–64; C. J. S. Thompson, *Mysteries of Sex: Women Who Posed as Men and Men Who Impersonated Women* (London: Hutchinson, n.d.), pp. 139–152.

61. Mary Chaney Hoffman, "Whips of the Old West," *American Mercury*, 84 (April, 1957), pp. 107–110.

62. For a discussion of the various Mountain Charleys and the biographical account of two of them see Mrs. E. J. Guerin, *Mountain Charley or the Adventures of Mrs. E. J. Guerin, Who Was Thirteen Years in Male Attire*, intro. by Fred W. Marzulla and William Kostka (Norman: University of Oklahoma Press, 1968).

teen pounds of skirts and petticoats plus their lung-squeezing stays, all of which would limit their activity. Her solution by our standards was rather modest. She proposed that women cut their skirt lengths to half way between the knees and ankle, and under their various petticoats they were to wear trousers "cut moderately full and gathered in above the footwear." Actually Mrs. Bloomer did not invent the costume which eventually bore her name but adopted it from a feminist dress-reformer, Libby Smith Miller. She did, however, publicly advocate it, and the costume became associated with her name. Perhaps not so surprisingly the greatest opposition to the costume came from the clergy, who felt it was immoral for women to wear pants because they had to spread their legs to put them on. Mrs. Bloomer and her friends wore the costume primarily to publicize the cause of women's rights, but quietly dropped it after several years because they felt it was not particularly becoming to them.[63]

There were, however, women who continued to wear trousers, in spite of the hostility which such a costume aroused, and the most notorious of these was Dr. Mary Walker. Dr. Walker served for a brief period in the United States Army during the Civil War and claimed the right to wear trousers by special Congressional action, although no record of such action is now available. She was an advocate of woman's rights and held that it was only by reforming the female costume that women could advance. She at first wore a short dress over long trousers but after the Civil War she began wearing the full masculine apparel. She died in 1919 still advocating trousers for women, not long before women started to wear "slacks" as a matter of course.[64]

An interesting example of changes in this century toward women's clothing can be found in the recommendations of the Sierra Club, the conservationist and outdoor club which in 1901 allowed women

63. For a popular account of this see Charles Nelson Gattey, *The Bloomer Girls* (New York: Coward-McCann, 1968).

64. I know of no full length biography of Mary Walker but she has often been the subject of study. See Lida Poynter, "Dr. Mary Walker—Pioneer Woman Physician," *Medical Woman's Journal*, LIII:10 (October, 1946); James A. Brussel, "Pants, Postage, and Physic," *Psychiatric Quarterly Supplement*, 35 (1961), 332–345; Linden F. Edwards, "Dr. Mary Edwards Walker (1832–1919): Charlatan or Martyr," *The Ohio State Medical Journal*, 54 (1958), 1296–98. Contemporary descriptions of her activities can be found in the *New York Medical Journal*, 4 (1867), 314–316, and 5 (1867), 167–170. See also "Dr. Mary Walker's Eccentric Dress Drew Attention from Her Real Achievements," *The Literary Digest* (March 15, 1919).

on their outings. At that time women were advised to wear a durable shirtwaist for "tramping" and a light one around the camps. The skirts were to be "short, not more than half way from knee to ankle," and under them it was recommended that women wear, "shorter dark-colored bloomers." For the women who planned to ride horse-back, the woman's guide recommended divided skirts since "it would be unsafe to ride otherwise than astride on portions of the trip." By 1914 there was a radical departure and women were advised to always wear "bloomers or knickerbockers" under skirts, since pants were "es-sential for the more difficult mountain climbs where skirts are dan-gerous to wear." By 1920 the guidebook indicated that women often prefer to wear "knickerbockers or trousers on the entire trip to the ex-clusion of skirts," and finally in 1925 women were regarded as able to make up their own minds about the kind of hiking clothes they were to wear and no further recommendations were made.[65]

If woman's dress was a half-way comical interlude in the struggle to change male attitudes, it was nevertheless important. It was only one obstacle to changing attitudes toward women. Religion, as has been apparent throughout this book, was also an obstacle, but so was medicine and science. Just as women were beginning to make ad-vances in the last part of the nineteenth century they ran into scien-tific proofs of their inferiority. Medical historians have often debated among themselves when the physician actually began to cure more people than he killed, and most would agree that in spite of the medi-cal pretensions of some of the physicians of the past, it was not until the first quarter of the twentieth century that medical knowledge and techniques had reached the level of being able to cure rather than simply relieve symptoms. It was perhaps no accident then that medi-cine, a profession dominated by men, was perfectly willing to accept the idea that women were inferior. In fact the intensity of medical hostility seemed to increase as women became more active in their struggle for equality. For example, a Dr. Edward H. Clarke in 1873 argued that women could not possibly plan to devote the number of hours to schooling required to become educated and still hope to emerge whole and healthy women. He said their attempts to com-pete with men would only reduce them to unhealthy invalids and un-fit childbearers. Symptomatic of their inferiority was their menstrual

65. Francis P. Farquhar, *History of the Sierra Nevada* (Berkeley: University of Cali-fornia Press, 1969), p. 228.

period, and he advised that during it girls should be kept from hard work, whether physical or mental. If they were not thus protected they would suffer from ill health, and perhaps even death.[66]

An Oregon physician insisted that most girls were hurt by education, that hard study killed sexual desire in women, took away physical beauty, and led to sterility. He believed in the inheritance of acquired characteristics and held that academic application not only arrested the natural development of the female pelvis but also increased the size of the brain of the offspring. This in turn caused women with college educations to have more difficult childbirths. Moreover most of the women of the past had not had the education of some of the modern girls but managed to possess the womanly qualities which would permanently enshrine them in humanity's memory, while the "name of the last graduate of the woman's college shall have faded from the recollection of men forever."[67]

Another medical practitioner held that in the educated woman the "nervous system has been developed at the expense of other bodily organs and structure. The delicate organism and sensitive and highly developed nervous system of our girls was never intended by the creator to undergo the stress and strain of the modern system of higher education, and the baneful results are becoming more and more apparent as the years go by." Proof of this, he said, came from the fact that in 1902 a New York commission on lunacy found that 42 percent of the women admitted to asylums were well educated but only 16 percent of the men. Obviously this could only mean that men were more fit for education than women. Moreover educated women lost the characteristics of the female, bcame discontented, selfish, and critical. Everyone would be happier, he claimed, if women married young and did not bother with any intellectual pretensions.[68]

In general physicians held that during the menstrual cycle women were inclined to a natural piety and sense of dependence. Inevitably this made women more religious than men and more inclined to intuition than rationality. Such inherent biological characteristics

66. Edward H. Clarke, *Sex in Education; or, a Fair Chance for Girls* (Boston: James R. Osgood, 1874).

67. F. W. Van Dyke, "High Education a Cause of Physical Decay in Women," *Medical Record*, 67 (1905), 296–298.

68. Ralph W. Parsons, "The American Girls Versus Higher Education, Considered from a Medical Point of View," *New York Medical Journal*, 85 (1907), 115–119.

forced women into subordinate roles, and any challenge to such roles could only lead to an increase in mental illness. Coeducation in adolescence, for example, was bad because in academic competition with males the female lost her bloom and delicacy as well as other innate feminine characteristics. Girls could only retain their modesty and good health if they were educated alone, given long rest periods during their menses, and encouraged in intuitive, not mental, accomplishments. It was a common belief that bookishness was a "bad sign in a girl."[69]

If too much intellectual stimulation was bad for women, so was too much interest in sex. The majority of women of the nineteenth century, including the feminists, probably subscribed to the ideology that sex was a "low passion confined almost entirely to men, and that pure and sexless wives endured male importunities merely as their wifely duty." Even as late as the beginning of the twentieth century a marriage manual could claim that the happiest marriages were those that seldom had sexual relations.[70] This kind of female prudishness had been emphasized through most of the nineteenth century and undoubtedly increased the frustrations under which most women had to live. The Reverend John Ware in a pamphlet originally written in 1850 emphasized that the physical aspects of sex were something that was filthy and not usually discussed between persons of good reputation.[71]

One of the reasons that legalized prostitution was advocated in the mid-nineteenth century was to protect women from such base male desires as sex. Dr. William Sanger, the nineteenth-century American authority on the subject, wrote that "the full force of sexual desire is seldom known to a virtuous woman," and that this lack of sexual desire was all for the best. He felt that only evil could result if there was a "mutual appetite equally felt by both."[72] If the wife did not temper the demands of her husband for sex the result would be overindulgence which could only contaminate the wife and lead to her corrup-

69. G. Stanley Hall, *Adolescence, Its Psychology and Its Relations to Physiology, Anthropology, Sociology, Sex, Crime, Religion and Education* (2 vols., New York: Appleton, 1904), vol. 2, p. 562.

70. William H. Walling, *Sexology* (Philadelphia: Puritan Publishing, 1909).

71. John Ware, *Hints to Young Men on the True Relation of the Sexes* (Boston: A. Williams, 1879).

72. William Sanger, *A History of Prostitution* (New York: Harper, 1858), pp. 488–489.

tion. Once a woman enjoyed sex she entered into the bottomless pit of sexuality; it was inevitable that she would become promiscuous, and from this she probably would turn to prostitution, and suffer from a horrible death. It was to protect women from such dangerous knowledge that much of the nineteenth-century concern with pornography grew.

The rather notorious Victoria Woodhull was one of the few nineteenth-century feminists who demanded reforms in marriage and openly admitted her sexuality, but she was ostracized by most "proper" women. Some other feminists, like Elizabeth Cady Stanton, also felt that the sexual taboos would have to be broached if women were to gain any kind of equality. Most women, however, seemed to accept the idea that sex was evil. A few, like Mrs. Elizabeth Osgood Goodrich Willard, believed that sexual orgasm was more debilitating to the system than a "whole day's work." She wrote in 1867: "It is this constant abuse of the sexual organs, producing constant failures and the most loathsome diseases; it is this ridiculous farce of a strong man putting forth all the nervous energy of his system, till he is perfectly prostrated by the effort, without one worthy motive, purpose or end; it is this which has so disgraced the act of impregnation. . . . We must stop this waste through the sexual organs, if we would have health and strength of body. . . ."[73]

Why such hostility to sex? It might be that at least some of the feminine hostility or alleged hostility to sex was based upon experience. Sexual intercourse led to pregnancy and though women desired children in the nineteenth century there was a limit to the number of pregnancies that most wanted to endure. Venereal disease was also widespread in the nineteenth century and there was no particularly effective cure. The number of women who actually suffered from venereal disease is difficult to estimate but the existence of widespread blindness caused by a gonorrheal infection at birth is one indication that many wives and mothers must have contracted it. During the nineteenth century there was also growth in the use of medications for "female complaints," such as the one sold by Lydia E. Pinkham. The illnesses such medications relieved, however, were not so much in the reproductive organs as in the urinary tract. Though many women suffer from urinary tract infections, an infec-

73. Mrs. Elizabeth Osgood Goodrich Willard, *Sexology as the Philosophy of Life* (Chicago: J. R. Walsh, 1867), pp. 306–308.

tion which can make intercourse painful, the number of such infections probably increased in the nineteenth century. This was because of the increased use of various methods of birth control, particularly among middle-class women.

The decline in the number of children among college-educated and middle-class women in the last part of the nineteenth century can be documented and resulted either from women barring the marital bed to their husbands or else attempting to use some form of birth control. Modern research has demonstrated that without the use of any contraceptives the ordinary woman engaging in intercourse with any degree of regularity would probably become pregnant every other year. In spite of censorship we know that the whole subject of birth control reached public attention at that time and some of the methods would have increased the likelihood of urinary infection. Robert D. Owen, a nineteenth-century advocate of birth control, urged his readers to practice coitus interruptus, which might have increased the likelihood of infection by allowing mucous into the uretha. Charles Knowlton's classic work, *Fruits of Philosophy*, recommended douching with various solutions of alum, astringents, sulphates of zinc, and so forth, some of which would also have damaged the external genitalia as well as the vagina since he was not always precise in his recommended dosages. With the vulcanization of rubber in 1843 to 1844, condoms also began to be widely used, but these required some lubricants which with the lack of effective hygiene in the nineteenth century were probably contaminated and increased the likelihood of infection. Other writers advocated that women insert various items into their vagina, such as sponges or toward the end of the century, the rubber cervical cap,[74] all of which, unless proper hygienic precautions were taken, probably increased the rate of infection. In short, even when women might have taken some tentative steps toward the enjoyment of sex, they were likely to suffer from infection which tended to emphasize the sinfulness of birth control. It was not until the introduction of sulfa drugs following World War II that such infections could be easily cured.

To gain publicity for their cause feminists often had to adopt radical positions, but to win converts they also had to act like proper

74. For a discussion of these see Norman E. Himes, *Medical History of Contraception* (reprinted, New York: Schocken Books, 1970).

ladies. With nineteenth-century attitudes this was no easy task, particularly for middle-class women who assumed leadership of the movement. Working-class women were allowed to work in the factories in the United States as they were in England, although it was usually only considered desirable to work if a girl was single. Middle-class women, however, even lacked this outlet, and to change the situation they had to assault the bastions of male prerogative yet remain proper women. Sometimes it seems as if the women were schizophrenic. One of the major documents in the history of female emancipation was the *Declaration of Sentiments* adopted at the first Woman's Right Convention held in Seneca Falls, New York, in 1848. Paraphrasing the *Declaration of Independence*, it stated: "We hold these truths to be self-evident; that all men and women are created equal. . . . The history of mankind is a history of repeated injuries and usurpations on the part of man towards woman, having in direct object the establishment of absolute tyranny over her."[75] The document listed specific grievances and called for the removal of various liabilities. The Seneca Falls convention also voted to secure woman's sacred rights to the elective franchise. Such radical stands and statements antagonized many women, even the strong feminist Lucretia Mott, and though it was a manifesto of the movement it did not lead to any immediate change in attitudes. Most women of the time ignored it, and yet these very women had to be aroused before attitudes could be changed. This meant that the feminists to avoid antagonizing their sisters had to be ladies and fight on ladylike terms. In the process some sounded like terrible prudes. In 1850 Martha Coffin Wright, an early feminist, attended a rural dance and was righteously indignant because of the women "sitting in gentlemen's laps and thinking nothing of being kissed."[76] Francis E. Willard, a feminist and leader of the Woman's Christian Temperance Union, reported that when she was at an Evanston Boarding School in 1858: "a young woman who was not chaste came to the college there through some misrepresentation, but she was speedily dismissed; not knowing her degraded status I was speaking to her when a schoolmate whispered a few words of explanation that crimsoned my face

75. The document is reproduced in Kraditor, *Up from the Pedestal*, pp. 183–188.
76. Robert Riegel, *American Feminists* (Lawrence: University of Kansas Press, 1963), p. 25.

suddenly; and grasping my dress lest its hem should touch the garments of one so morally polluted, I fled from the room."[77]

Not all the feminists were quite so prudish, although there was some dicussion among them about how much submission a wife owed to her husband. Lucy Stone wrote to Elizabeth Cady Stanton about a woman who had "fled from her husband to the Shakers, because he gave her no peace." "I very much wish," she later wrote, "that a wife's right to her own body should be pushed at our next convention." One way in which some of the more radical feminists thought they could solve the problem was by allowing divorce, and this caused a split in the feminist movement. Page Smith in his history of American women has said that the base of the split between what came to be the New York and the New England wings of the woman's suffrage movement was in part due to personality and temperament of the women involved but also because some had better relations with the opposite sex than others. Elizabeth Cady Stanton had a difficult marriage and Susan Anthony, perhaps the most anti-male, was a spinster. Antoinette Brown, Lucy Stone, and Julia Ward Howe were happily married.[78] Though this is undoubtedly true, from the point of view of today, Stanton and Anthony probably were more far-seeing than the others, and as Smith states they hit at the heart of the issue, the basic relationship between man and woman.

Probably, however, this was much too big a problem to deal with at the beginning of the movement and one which would have posed too much a threat to the woman's image of herself. There were just too many obstacles to overcome before even the tentative beginnings of equality could be approached. One of the major barriers was that of education. Though there had been various female seminaries, the first coeducational institution of higher education was Oberlin College, founded in 1833. A few other colleges also were established as coeducational schools while the first woman's college, then known as Mount Holyoke Female Seminary, was established shortly after Oberlin. Almost immediately the schools were faced with such major problems as what degree to confer because some felt that it would be improper to award a woman a degree as bachelor or master of arts.

77. Francis Willard, *Glimpses of Fifty Years*, quoted in Leo Markun, *Mrs. Grundy* (New York: Appleton, 1930), p. 406.
78. Page Smith, *Daughters of the Promised Land* (Boston: Little, Brown, 1970), pp. 163–165.

Some institutions tried to get around the dilemma by issuing such degrees as "Laureate of Science," "Maid of Philosophy," and "Mistress of Polite Literature," but eventually most women were given the same degree as men. Though the number of coeducational schools continued to increase, it was more socially acceptable to go to a girls' school, and in the period after the Civil War these rapidly increased with the foundation of Vassar in 1865, Smith and Wellesley in 1875, and Radcliffe and Barnard, the female annexes to Harvard and Columbia, shortly after. Though the women's colleges, particularly the counterparts to the male Ivy League, contributed immeasurably to helping recognize the intellectual abilities of women, they also set women apart as a separate class, and encouraged the treatment of them as somehow being of finer fabric than man. Throughout the nineteenth and well into the twentieth century most of the women's colleges continued to emphasize that women were different from men, and to deny that any of their graduates might really want a career. Except for giving some teacher training, almost none of them ever established a professional school.

This meant that when women graduated from the women's colleges they had a difficult time finding jobs because they were unprepared to compete with males looking for positions. In a sense perhaps the women's colleges took the inevitable position and to be much more revolutionary would have negated what positive effect they had. Americans thought that women were meant to be mothers and if a woman's college had claimed that they were training women to be other than mothers they would not have had the public support they did. In fact almost until World War II the only way a woman could have a career was to sacrifice marriage and a family, to be a professional spinster, and this status was generally regarded as being second to that of wife and mother.[79]

Women who did enter the professions often went to extremes to try to assert their feminity. This is perhaps best exemplified by the case of Elizabeth Blackwell, who has been given the title of America's first woman doctor. Miss Blackwell was admitted to Geneva Medical College in 1847 after being rejected by twenty-seven others. Geneva accepted her because the faculty of the school, unwilling to

79. For a survey of attitudes toward the single woman see Dorothy Yost Deegan, *The Stereotype of the Single Woman in American Novels* (New York: Columbia University Press, 1951).

antagonize her sponsor, an influential physician whose support they needed, turned the decision over to the students with the provision that one negative vote would prohibit her entry. The students, some because they saw an attempt to embarrass their teachers, others because they saw it as an exciting prank, and a few because they believed in woman's rights, voted to admit her. One student had started to vote "no" but the other students pounced on him and either in real or mock fear he changed his vote. When she graduated less than eighteen months later Dr. Blackwell refused to walk in the commencement procession because it was unladylike. It was the custom for all women to be seated in the church before the graduating students marched in, and then the various male guests followed. To show that in spite of her medical degree she was every inch a lady, she entered the church, firmly corseted, with the other ladies.[80]

Even those few women who did earn professional degrees found themselves handicapped by existing prejudices, and rather than fight men head on women tried to find ways to earn a living in which they would not be competing with men. Middle-class women tried to latch on and claim for themselves newly developing professions or occupations which were as yet not dominated by men. At the end of the nineteenth century four such professions appeared and were quickly dominated by women: nursing, social work, elementary teaching, and library work. In a sense all of them had been traditionally women's jobs which were becoming professionalized, but the fact that they were taken over by women almost immediately led to them being lower paid than jobs held by men requiring similar education or ability. Most of the women who went into these fields only worked until they were married, and this meant that there was a rapid turnover of personnel which helped to keep wages down. It also meant that the women who emerged as leaders in these professions were generally those who did not marry, and so leadership went not necessarily to those most qualified but those who chose not to marry, which was quite a different thing. Moreover since the women who did achieve positions of authority within their occupation, be-

80. Elizabeth Blackwell wrote her own story, *Pioneer Work in Opening the Medical Profession to Women* (London: Longmans, Green, 1895). Ishbel Ross, *Child of Destiny* (London: Gollancz, 1950) is a popular biography of Miss Blackwell but there is also an excellent biography of the whole Blackwell family, a rather remarkable collection of individuals, by Elinor Rice Hays, *Those Extraordinary Blackwells* (New York: Harcourt, Brace, and World, 1950), p. 18.

cause they had either consciously or unconsciously sacrificed marriage, had a great resentment to the married woman who tried to combine marriage and a career. This has meant that some of the greatest objections to married career women have not come from men but from women in positions of leadership. Women's professions have also been handicapped by the fact that women who did emerge in leadership positions had to be careful to act in proper feminine ways, and perhaps for this reason their leadership has almost never been as aggressive as in male-dominated organizations.

It was in these so-called women's fields that women were able to emerge as individuals in their own right and several achieved national and international fame. Jane Addams, the winner of the Nobel Peace Prize in 1931, was a pioneer social worker who founded Hull House in Chicago in 1889. She was a major figure in most of the battles for the rights of the poor, the Negro, the laborer, women, and children, and also helped found the Women's International League for Peace and Freedom as well as the National Conference of Social Work. Only slightly less well known is Lillian Wald, the nurse and social worker, who founded the Henry Street Settlement in New York. Margaret Sanger, one of the key figures in the birth-control movement, was a nurse. Jeannette Rankin, the first woman to serve in Congress, was a social worker, as was Frances Perkins, the Secretary of Labor under Franklin D. Roosevelt and first woman to serve in the cabinet.

Even in these fields it was difficult to combine a marriage and a career and three of the five were spinsters, Addams, Wald, and Rankin, and though Margaret Sanger and Frances Perkins were married, Mrs. Sanger was divorced and Mrs. Perkins married late and had only one child. Until after World War II this pattern seemed to hold true of most so-called women's professions. The literary field which women in theory could carry on at home also was dominated by spinsters. Louisa May Alcott, Willa Cather, Ellen Glasgow, and Gertrude Stein represent a continuing line of unmarried women. Pearl Buck, the only American woman writer to win the Nobel Prize for Literature (in 1938), was married but she had also been divorced. Edna St. Vincent Millay, one of the major poets, did marry but fairly late in life, while Dorothy Parker was married and divorced. Mary Baker Eddy was married and widowed or divorced several times. The list could go on. The implication seems to be that the woman who wanted to succeed in her own right had to sacrifice almost everything else to get ahead, regardless of her chosen field. The more acceptable way of earning recognition was through sharing in the achievement of a husband, and few women went beyond this. Eleanor Roosevelt was one of the major exceptions. She was the wife of a President, but also took independent action.

In the lower socioeconomic groups married women worked, if only because they had to, but the better jobs were available usually only to the single girl awaiting marriage. This was generally true of the two occupations in the business world which women were most effectively able to claim as their own: typist and telephone operator. In 1870 there were only seven women in the United States who were classified as secretaries, but by 1950 there were over one million. The first woman telephone operator was hired in 1878, in part because it was found women could be hired at lower wages than men. Women were also able to take over selling jobs, particularly of women's goods, but it was not until the twentieth century that it was considered respectable for a woman to be a saleslady in a department store. When Gilchrist Department store in Boston hired its first woman salesclerk in 1877 people came to stare at her for several weeks. It was Gilchrist's which in 1972 announced that it would issue charge cards to women customers in their own names without getting their husband's permission, indicating only that it takes a long time to modify long-standing prejudices. Women could also work in the emerging factories in the nineteenth century but here they ran into organized opposition from males who felt they were cutting them out of jobs. Organized labor, feminists, and various reformers worked to establish legislation designed to establish certain minimum working conditions for women and children which were important in bettering the working conditions for men as well, but also handicapped women in the job market. Probably the majority of women who worked did so as domestics or in jobs allied to women's tasks in the home, such as laundress, cook, practical nurse, hairdresser, and so forth. Most married women, however, regardless of class, did not work outside of the home.

One of the major factors in opening up new roles for middle-class women was the demands put upon society by both World Wars I and II. As men were drafted and as defense and then war industries demanded ever more workers, women entered the work force in greater and greater numbers. During World War I when the Navy ran short of clerks and lacked appropriations for more civilian help, the Secretary of Navy Josephus Daniels publicly questioned whether there was any law that said a yeoman must be a man. When he found out there was not, the Navy proceeded to enroll some 11,000 uniformed "yeomanettes," although the only women to reach France were nurses, ambulance drivers, and Salvation Army "lassies." Women also entered industry in greater numbers and found themselves making grenades, collecting streetcar fares, running elevators, and washing locomotives, as well as scores of other tasks previously regarded as being "unsuitable" for women. Even those women who did not work for pay found new kinds of demands put upon their time and new volunteer tasks such as managing many of the volunteer charitable activities which in the past had been run by men. After the war the vast majority of women lost their jobs or voluntarily returned to their housewifely tasks, but many of them expressed an unwillingness to be relegated to a restricted list of occupations.

In the interwar period women continued to break down past barriers. Women such as Isadora Duncan in dance, Gertrude Ederle in swimming, Amelia Earhart in aviation, and Aimee Semple McPherson in religion broke new grounds for women, and although much of the public attention lavished on them was undoubtedly due to the fact that they refused to conform to old images, girls could have a different model to follow. The depression of the 1930s was no less influential in forcing women to readjust to new values since vast numbers were no longer willing to assume that with the proper marriage they would be comfortably established for the rest of their life. Though there was great hostility to those working wives who also had working husbands, and many a married woman with a job or career found herself under attack for preventing a man from working, women continued to enter the labor force.

All such hostility ended with the outbreak of World War II, and what had been a trickle of women before mushroomed into an avalanche. All told some six million new female war workers appeared, that is, women who had never worked before. Some 200,000 women enlisted in the auxiliary military units of WAAC, WAVE, SPAR, and women MARINES, and the changing status of women was recognized by finally authorizing nurses to be regular commissioned officers, eligible for all the wartime benefits of men instead of serving outside the official military structure as they had in World War I. The end of the war saw a mass return to home and to motherhood as women who had delayed their families because of economic difficulties of the depression and the absence of their husbands during the war settled down to become housewives, at least temporarily. Conditions, however, could not be the same.

Part of the change was due to the fact that Americans were increasingly urbanized and the home was no longer the all-consuming job it had been, especially when children entered school. The technological developments of the twentieth century made housekeeping a part-time job. Vacuums, washing machines, automatic dryers, dishwashers, refrigerators, electric irons, regulated ovens, and introduction of running water, electricity, natural gas, and modern plumbing fixtures inside the house cut down the number of hours the average woman had to do housework. Outside the home self-service markets cut down the time she had to spend shopping, and canned, dried, frozen, and freeze-dried foods meant she had to shop less frequently. Many women found that what for their grandmothers and even their mothers had been an all-consuming job could be done in a few hours. This was especially true of women who no longer had small children at home. This in turn meant that women had more freedom to enter the job market. Though discrimination continued to exist the barriers were more psychological than legal. Girls who had been taught as children not to compete with men had to undo generations of training. This problem is discussed in the next chapter. Women also had political power, or at least the possibilities of power through their vote, and this meant that they could not be ignored as they had in the past.

chapter thirteen

Some Questions about the Past and the Future
by Bonnie Bullough

With the sweep of history behind us, it is fitting to raise some questions and reach some tentative conclusions about the attitudes which society (that is, men) holds toward women, their role, their status. Though women in the past have had varying conditions, they have never held a position of equality with men nor have they been viewed either by themselves or by their menfolk as entitled to such a position. The footbinding of the upper-class Chinese women and the suttee of the loyal Hindu wife might stand out as particularly brutal and dehumanizing customs, but more subtle kinds of discrimination have been quietly accepted by women. Generations of children have been socialized to accept inequality without protest. Why has this male-female inequality persisted in such a variety of societies?

In large part the answer seems to be biological. In the early development of society physical strength was a significant variable in helping to establish the subordinate position of women. The greater size and strength of the male made him better able than the female to fight off animal and human enemies, and even though the female in individual cases might have been equal to the male in strength, as a group they were not. In return for male protection woman offered obedience. If man's asserted superiority to woman was only due to simple brute strength, it would seem logical that as civilization progressed and physical strength became less important the position of woman should have improved. Nonetheless, the nature of the reproductive processes with the attendant responsibilities in caring for offspring still kept women at a disadvantage in the world of work, and it was the world of work rather than that of home and family which has carried the higher status in most societies. In effect women's greatest disadvantage until fairly recently was their unlimited fertility.

It is also possible that most women in the past simply lacked the strength to compete effectively with men even if they desired to do so. While the comparative lack of muscular strength in women is fairly obvious, it is not so obvious that large numbers of women were further weakened by inadequate diet. Women in many societies ate less than men, and often the comparative deficit in their diet was in the more expensive protein foods. This lack coupled with their continual childbearing and their biological proclivity to anemia, further weakened them, making them even less likely to compete or to rebel.

The physical differences between the sexes became the basis for building a system of reciprocal roles, and in the process the wife role, including the nurturing functions, was defined as inferior and subordinate while the economic functions of the male were defined as superior and superordinate. Boys and girls were socialized to fill these roles and children of both sexes were taught that males were superior while females were inferior. Once the discriminatory pattern was set up the socialization process carried it forward.

Essential to the differential socialization process was a belief in psychological and intellectual differences between men and women. This belief system allowed males to deny females the right to higher education or political participation. John Stuart Mill, in the classic essay on *The Subjection of Women*, wrote that woman was a "man in petticoats," a radical enough statement for the time, but then he contradicted himself by arguing that women were an essential counterpart to the abstractness, narrowness, and rigidity likely to beset the male.[1] In short he insisted on basic differences in the masculine and feminine natures and felt that the political equality of women would have a great moral effect upon men. This contradictory view of women, of even the enlightened Mill whose work was among the most influential on the subject of woman's emancipation,[2] has continued to plague the efforts of women to achieve greater liberation.

As a result it seems that for every step forward in the liberation of women in the past century or so, there has been a half-step backward

1. See John Stuart Mill, *The Subjection of Women*. There are several recent reprints. One of the paperback editions has an introduction by Wendell Robert Carr (Cambridge: MIT Press, 1970).

2. This was the claim of Havelock Ellis, *The Task of Social Hygiene* (Boston: Houghton Mifflin, 1914), p. 11.

or sideward, and sometimes more, as women demonstrated their uncertainty about the role they wanted to play. The contradictions appear in segregated education for women, as exemplified by the women's colleges, and women's reluctance to compete directly with men in the professions, as exemplified by their scarcity in medicine and their dominance in nursing, or their scarcity in educational administration, and their dominance in many aspects of teaching. When women did enter into medicine, they usually selected specialties which were regarded as particularly suitable for females, and stayed out of others which for no rhyme or reason were regarded as more suitable for males. Sigmund Freud and his followers have given a significant theoretical rationale to the belief in psychological differences between the sexes and have furnished an intellectual justification for the subordination of women. Freud argued that women were incomplete men,[3] and as such could not compete in the world of men. One of the most influential popularizations of Freud in America, that of Ferdinand Lundberg and Marynia Farnham, *Modern Woman: The Lost Sex*, appeared right after the end of World War II, just as women who had made great advances in breaking down some of the sex barriers during the war were having second thoughts about their role in society and were also anxious to start their long-delayed families.[4] Lundberg and Farnham diagnosed feminism as an illness, a delusion, which had destroyed the integrated home and cast women adrift. Though they felt there was merit in some of the feminist arguments, they saw most of the feminists as victims of emotional sickness. They held equality to be a fetish and went on to argue in Freudian terms that feminists wanted to be males and suffered from penis envy. Lundberg and Farnham instead wanted to glorify the family, female submission, and motherhood.

Similar arguments were common in the education field. Lynn

3. See Kate Millet, *Sexual Politics* (Garden City, N.Y.: Doubleday, 1970); for the Freudian view itself see Sigmund Freud, *Civilization and Its Discontents*, trans. by James Strachey (New York: Norton, 1961), his essay on feminity in the *New Introductory Lectures on Psycho-Analysis* (reprinted, New York: Norton, 1964), and various essays in his *Collected Papers*, ed. by Joan Reviere (New York: Basic Books, 1959) and in the standard edition of the *Complete Psychological Works* (London: Hogarth Press, 1953).

4. Ferdinand Lundberg and Marynia Farnham, *Modern Woman: The Lost Sex* (New York: Grosset and Dunlap, 1947).

White, Jr., a former president of Mills College and a distinguished historian, emphasized that women were not to compete with men but to be different. "On my desk lies a letter from a young mother, a few years out of college: 'I have come to realize that I was educated to be a successful man and now must learn by myself how to be a successful woman.' The basic irrelevance of much of what passes as women's education in America could not be more compactly phrased."[5] His book, *Educating Our Daughters*, dedicated to this theme, seemed to dominate much of American thought in the 1950s. It took several years for the voice of dissent to catch up with the new critics. Mirra Komarovsky, however, pointed out that what would defeat the various appeals to women to find dignity in domesticity was the fact that society was saturated with values which emphasized that being a housewife was not a particularly important job. She argued that it might have once been possible to maintain a system of values for women only and to insulate them against the dominant masculine goals of society, but the conditions and ideologies which once encouraged a sharp demarcation between the feminine and the masculine goals of life have greatly changed. Since the majority of women are now employed at least part of the time they are exposed to the incentives of the economic world. With suffrage and the more recent political reforms women can participate in a greater variety of cultural and political activities. In the process they are bound to absorb values pervading those sectors of life and realize that being just a housewife is a low-status job, regardless of how one attempts to enhance it. Komarovsky held that the modern antifeminists have attempted to shame women into renouncing achievement goals by claiming that such goals lure only the neurotic women and that the male emphasis on achievement was but a compensation for his inability to bear children. She concluded that such an ideology could succeed only if one accepted as dogma many unproved theories about feminine personality and suppressed all that has been learned about the overlapping of mental traits of men and women.[6] Still the mythology remains. Herbert Marcuse, the Marxist Freudian philosopher, in his *Counterrevolution and Revolt*, holds that women are less brutalized than men because economic discrimination keeps

5. Lynn White, Jr., *Educating Our Daughters* (New York: Harper, 1950), p. 18.
6. Mirra Komarovsky, *Women in the Modern World: Their Education and Their Dilemma* (Boston: Little, Brown, 1953), pp. 292–293.

them out of the competitive world and confines them to the home, where they exemplify bourgeois virtue.[7]

Thus Marcuse, perhaps unwillingly, joins what Mary Daly calls the "pedestal pedlars," those who argue that woman's nature has set her apart and who see the significance of women not in the light of her psychological or biological, her historical or social position, but her symbolic aspect.[8] The "eternal woman" is said to have a vocation to surrender and hide; selfless, she achieves not individual realization but merely generic fulfillment in motherhood, physical or spiritual. She is said to be timeless and conservative by nature and is shrouded in "mystery" because she is not recognized as a genuine human person.[9] The latest manifestations of this are the adherents of "fascinating womanhood," where women are taught to be feminine and to always obey the male.[10] The already classic criticism of this concept has been Betty Friedan's *Feminine Mystique*,[11] and there have been a whole host of books since it appeared. Woman's lib, as much as anything, has attempted to challenge these assumptions.

That there must be rewards to being subjugated and subordinate should by now appear obvious to readers of this book, and the rewards of the inferior position have been a major factor in maintaining inequality. Probably the simplest behavioral explanation of this finding can be approached by thinking of behavior as a product of the expectations of rewards and punishments. Women who submitted to the stereotypes of the past were rewarded for their inferior position. Sometimes the reward was a direct one. Lack of power protected one from the risk of decisionmaking and the anxiety over punishments for wrong decisions. It is much simpler to be relieved of these decisions. Upper-class women were also often rewarded directly for their obedience and passivity by gifts and a life of luxury. With the industrial revolution these rewards for wives have been extended down the social-class ladder to include middle-class women,

7. Herbert Marcuse, *Counterrevolution and Revolt* (Boston: Beacon Press, 1972).

8. Mary Daly, *The Church and the Second Sex* (New York: Harper and Row, 1968), pp. 105ff.

9. Perhaps the classic example of such a theme is Gertrud von le Fort's *The Eternal Woman*, which was first published in Germany in 1934. It was translated into English by Placid Jordan (Milwaukee: Bruce, 1962).

10. Helen Andelin, *Fascinating Womanhood* (Santa Barbara: Pacific Press, n.d.). According to news releases the book has sold 300,000 copies and millions of women have taken the course.

11. Betty Friedan, *The Feminine Mystique* (New York: Norton, 1963).

as more men made more women items of conspicuous consumption, flattered them, comforted them, and displayed them.

Sometimes the reward for a lack of formal power was indirect and came in the form of great informal power. In China the power of the old mother was almost absolute, and in various polygamous societies, the mother whose son reached a position of power could lord it all over the other women. Although these women lacked the physical power to confront men directly, they could take satisfaction in their ability to manipulate them. Manipulation has traditionally been the role of the subjugated, and for those who followed the rules it could be a position of considerable influence. Mary R. Beard wrote an interesting study documenting just such informal power in her *Woman as Force in History*.[12] Being the power behind the throne is apparently satisfying to many. It might well be that in the past when physical strength and military ability were frequently the deciding factors in any power confrontation, manipulation was the only possibility which was open to the ambitious woman. This does not need to be the case today.

One of the assets of being in the subordinate role is that status can be ascribed and so achievement is not necessary. The most obvious example of this today is the beautiful girl with the right measurements who catches the attention of a rich sponsor and simply by being female in a male-dominant society can advance far beyond her own social origins. Men on the other hand are more likely to have to earn their status through hard work. The fact that women share the status of their husbands also means that they have been able to change social classes much more easily than a man.

Few women in the past have openly rebelled, but this is not saying much about role satisfaction, since few slaves have ever rebelled on a mass scale either. Even Marx came to believe that the lumpen proletariat tended to lack the spark of revolution. Punishments in the past have been much too severe for those women who rebelled, and the rewards too great for those who conformed, for any large number of women to rebel. The best they could do was attack the edge of the glacier of prejudice or to claim for themselves the role of woman who was different from all other women. In the long run probably those who attacked prejudice were more important in changing attitudes

12. Mary R. Beard, *Woman as Force in History* (New York: Macmillan, 1946).

than those who claimed special privileges, but in any case the process of change was slow.

Part of the difficulty with trying to change woman's role in society is that no role is exclusive. Roles are defined by a series of expectations and they tend to be reciprocal. The role wife relates to the role husband, and if she changes her role he is forced to change his. It is understandable why fights against such change occur. The woman who leaves home for work may cause great adjustment pangs for her husband whose role must change almost as much as hers. He tends to lose his personal servant, and while he can replace some of the services formerly done by his devoted housewife with hired help or an electronic device, manipulating a dishwasher effectively does not give the sense of power that bossing a wife does, and hired help, particularly if the labor market is scarce, can refuse to meet his more outrageous demands. Although much of what we identify as sexually assigned roles has nothing to do with biological sex but with tradition and culture, it will be a long struggle to change them, and to do this most women will have to want to change.

Even changing the roles played by one husband and wife has implications for society. This is because as a few women do emerge who can combine an occupation with marriage, many of the women who do not change feel threatened. The result is often a kind of backlash movement as these women struggle to preserve the old order. Thus the career woman often faces greatest hostility from her sisters rather than from her masculine friends. The real difficulty with housework is that there is no effective measuring rod for the competent as against the incompetent, except in the most drastic of cases, and the woman who has a husband, family, and job seems to threaten other women by implying that they are either incompetent or lazy. The comparison then becomes obvious for all to see. This is why a conscious women's liberation movement is so essential to bringing about change.

There is one area, however, where the devoted housewife far outshines her working sister, and that is as a volunteer worker and charitable specialist. For the past hundred years or so large numbers of middle-class women have utilized their free time to do good works of one kind or another and most of the charitable institutions in society could not run without their legions of devoted nearly full-time female volunteers. Churches in particular will be in difficulty as the trend toward working wives continues to grow. The present-day crisis in Catholicism caused by the reassessment of the role of nuns is one such situation. Though superficially it seems that the nuns are interested in modifying or eliminating their traditional habits, in reality what they are attempting to do is to reject some of the feminine stereotypes about what a nun's role should be. They see no reason why a nun cannot be as dynamic a college president as a male clergyman, or why they cannot be scientists instead of just elementary teachers. In the process of their rebellion, the Catholic parochial school system has been forced into a crisis since it relied upon nuns and other devoted women to work at low wages. Nuns, however, are only symbolic of the changes since they do not have the obligations of family to attend to, but if PTA's, museums, churches, and all the other volunteer fund-raising groups have to rely upon working women for their free help, they will, if the present trend continues, be faced with an even greater crisis than the Catholic school system is with the desertion of the nuns. Obviously these institutions and individuals in need of such free volunteers will be hostile to a changing role for women.

Changes are occurring which will propel women toward greater equality, even if many of them do not want to change. In fact the role of women and the attitudes toward them have changed more in the past hundred years than in the previous thousand. Several factors seem to have been at work, some of them anticipated by past advocates of greater freedom for women and others almost entirely unanticipated. Probably the single most important factor in bringing about radical change is not economic or political but simply the development of reliable methods of contraception. Though methods of birth control are as old as man the only really effective method of control before the nineteenth century was abstinence, which was adopted by some societies in the form of late marriages, or by select people such as clergy or members of religious orders on a life-long basis. When a woman has to accept motherhood as an inevitable consequence of sexual intercourse her freedom vis-à-vis the male must be constricted. Often in the past the only way a woman could be free of pregnancy was to deny the marital bed to her husband, not always a particularly friendly solution to the problem.

As the birth control movement grew in the late nineteenth and early twentieth centuries a variety of methods of contraception were tried. The vulcanization of rubber made condoms cheaper and safer than the older types which were made from such materials as fish bladders. Condoms are a fairly reliable method of contraception but have the disadvantage of being controlled by the male, and in our opinion to be really effective in raising the power and status of woman the method needs to be under her control as much as possible. Rubber diaphragms were also developed and could be used by women, although they had the disadvantage of requiring a fairly high level of sophistication to manage. Douches and chemicals were also tried with varying amounts of success. Early attempts were also made to develop an intra-uterine device, but until recently all of the devices proved to be too irritating to the uterine mucosa to be tolerated by most women. Two effective methods of birth control, oral contraceptives and plastic intra-uterine devices, are little more than a decade old, and in this brief period of time these more effective methods are creating rapid social change.

The rapid change in attitudes toward contraception, however, has not necessarily resulted from an organized campaign by women to free themselves of unwanted prenancies. Though women have been the beneficiaries the motivation has been as much the belated public realization that the world is already overpopulated for the available food supply and that high fertility levels are no longer necessary for the survival of the species. In effect an antinatalist philosophy is replacing the pronatalist position which has necessarily characterized most past societies because it was needed for survival. Other evidence of this changing position on fertility is the growing number of vasectomies, of tubal ligations, and the rapidly changing public view of abortion. While Japan and some of the eastern European countries such as Hungary have allowed abortions for several decades the change in this country is less than a decade old. It was not until 1973 that abortion became a matter of constitutional right, although in many areas it is still a very expensive proposition. This changing philosophy has freed the woman who does not want to bear children—or who only wants one or two children—from the stigma of neglecting her female role. In effect she is now in a position of making a choice.

Equally as important as the development of birth control technology has been the democratization of the availability of these methods, a process which is only now beginning. Twenty years ago birth control information and services, in spite of planned parent-hood clinics, were primarily available to the middle-class women. It was possible, for example, for a public health nurse to be fired in the city of Chicago in 1952 if she were caught directing patients who requested such information to the family planning clinic.[13] Most women who obtained contraceptives went to private physicians. Services for the poor mother were simply not available, although she was the one who was most likely to have a large family and have need for this type of service. Now the United States government itself is in the business of helping to disseminate birth-control information, and contraceptives are slowly becoming available to women of all ages and social classes. Such a step cannot help but have revolution-ary consequences.

The revolution is still in process, if only because there are large numbers of women who have not yet been reached. Low-income women are still less likely than affluent ones to use preventive health services, including contraceptives. The practical barriers to preven-tive care such as transportation, the expense of babysitting, and a general lack of sophistication about health facilities tend to be re-inforced by the feelings of alienation and powerlessness which are associated with poverty. These barriers make it difficult for the low-income mother to achieve the level of control over the reproductive process which the middle-income woman enjoys.

Another group which still has problems are the young unmarried college or high school students. Because the norms of the society have not all caught up with the advancements in technology and the growing antinatalist philosophy, the girls who take oral contracep-tives or use some other means of preplanned birth control still feel guilty and are often labeled as not respectable by their peers. The rapid changes in philosophy create confusion so that young women must respond to two sets of contrary expectations. While some of the norms about premarital sex have changed, many young women still accept only unplanned premarital sexual activity and end up with unplanned prenancies.

Though overlooked in popular histories, perhaps second only to woman's ability to control the number of her offspring has been her

13. Personal testimony of Bonnie Bullough, who was at this time a public health nurse in Chicago.

ability to overcome the physiological and psychological effects of menstruation. The belief that menstruating women were unclean, cursed, or jinxed is as old as recorded history. Even those women in the past who were emancipated enough to ignore popular superstitions about menstruation were handicapped in their activities by the physical fact. They made various kinds of diapers and pads for themselves, but one of the reasons they wore so many petticoats was to cut down possible odors and hide the bulges; inevitably they also cut out many physical activities during such times. For this reason the development of the modern disposable, hygenic, and comparatively inexpensive sanitary napkin or pad was an important breakthrough in the emancipation of women. It first appeared on the market in 1920 as a direct result of the development of cellucotton products for surgical dressings during World War I. As the demand for such bandages declined with the end of the war, the manufacturers attempted to find other uses, and the Kimberly Clark Company hit upon the concept of selling them as sanitary pads under the name of Kotex. To be effectively merchandised the company had to bring the subject out in the open, and this also cut down some of the fears and misinformation. In this the manufacturers were assisted by the fact that science was also finally able to explain the whole process of ovulation. The success of Kotex was followed by a whole host of imitators and new products such as tampons and cups. One of the first effects of the introduction of the pad was the shedding of petticoats by women, and it was no accident that the new age of the emancipated flapper coincided with the introduction of Kotex and its competitors.

Not to be overlooked in removing some of the handicaps of being a woman was the development of alternative means of nursing infants. The chemical composition of breast milk had been analyzed by 1880. This, coupled with means of keeping cow's milk safe for infants through pasteurization, condensation, and refrigeration, and the invention of the rubber nipple following the vulcanization of rubber, made it possible for a baby to thrive without being dependent upon the supply of its mother's milk or that of a wet nurse. As a result women of even comparatively newborn infants enjoy greater freedom than most women in the past, and men are able to assume a greater role in infant care, if they can be persuaded to do so.

Control of these biological processes has helped women enter the labor market, and though most women still do not compete on anything like equal terms with men, increasing numbers are beginning to do so. The change in the job situation has been due in part to the industrial revolution which has freed women from some of the tasks formerly carried out at home and also offered them jobs in the newly developed industries. Simply having access to jobs outside of the home, however, does not in itself lead to equality, as most women have long since found out. Women in America are still more likely to be hired in low-paying jobs than men, and even when they are hired at the same kind of jobs as men, they are likely either to be paid less or promoted more slowly. It is only recently that women have started to protest these inequities.

Many of the Marxist theoreticians of the past held that discrimination against women was inherent in bourgeois culture, and though woman as an item of conspicuous consumption is mainly associated with a middle-class pattern, the problem is not that simple. This is indicated by the experience of the Soviet Union where more than 75 percent of women over twenty work full time.[14] On the surface it seems when simple statistics are cited that the Soviet women have all the advantages over their American sisters. For example, 79 percent of the physicians in 1959 were women, but the statistics do not always tell the full story, since within Soviet medicine there is a ranking of physicians, and the overwhelming majority of high-level, research-oriented, university physician professors are men. In fact, the massive entry of women into the Soviet labor force, in part a consequence of the casualties of World War II, has too often meant that women while free to work also have to fulfill all the other roles traditionally assigned to women. A 1960 letter published in the Moscow daily *Sovetskaia Rossiia* complained that "We work like our husbands often in the same shop. . . . But in the home the duties are unequally divided. . . . And when you ask a husband to help, the answer is always the same: 'Do you want me to do a woman's work? Why, the neighbors would laugh at me.' "[15] Lenin was conscious of this ingrown male prejudice and many years ago wrote that it would be only fair and desirable if Soviet husbands lent a hand to their wives, but Soviet men in general have been slow to take up either the

14. H. Kent Geiger, *The Family in Soviet Russia* (Cambridge: Harvard University Press, 1968), p. 17.
15. *Ibid.*, p. 184.

dishpan or the diaper. Recent studies of patterns of Soviet household activity demonstrated that the husband is finally beginning to share in some of the jobs labeled as woman's work, such as housekeeping and childcare, but it is reluctant participation, and the available statistics indicate that the husbands of working wives sleep longer and enjoy more free time than their wives.

In Soviet fiction where women are enthusiastic in the performance of their professional and occupational duties, and are portrayed as eloquent in expression of loyalty to the party, always ready to put duty above love, women are still shown as more or less subservient to the male. As yet a "heroine has not been allowed merely to exchange feminine virtues for masculine ones. In Western terms one may say that a Soviet heroine, having assumed a gentleman's code of behavior, has not been excused from being a lady. Kind, modest, unselfish, chaste, she thus has a double set of distinguished qualities, civic and feminine. Correspondingly, she also has a double set of duties, civic and domestic." While the male hero after providing for his family is free to engage wholly in the pursuit of larger goals, social, ideological, and professional, the heroine, while similarly engaged and no less busy, is also expected to "look attractive, to take an interest in the hero's career, and if married, to run a household and to bear and raise the children."[16] Though Article 122 in the U.S.S.R. Constitution of 1936 stipulated that women were to enjoy the same rights as men in all aspects of economic, official, cultural, public, and political life, and though laws helped to change attitudes while economic changes have helped to alter the status of women, the historical pattern of regarding women as somehow inferior to men still persists in Russia as in the United States.[17] Change will not come easy nor will it come without considerable agitation by women themselves.

It is not only the ability to enter the labor market that counts but the kind of job that is available to women which is also important. Education is a key to equality. In modern society the better paying jobs are the professional ones, and this has meant that as long as

16. Xenia Gasiorowska, *Women in Soviet Fiction: 1917–1964* (Madison: University of Wisconsin Press, 1968), p. 11.

17. For a discussion of the legal barriers still handicapping the liberation of women see Leon Kanowitz, *Women and the Law: The Unfinished Revolution* (Albuquerque: University of New Mexico Press, 1969).

women were cut off from higher education or educated in the women's academies, they could not move up the occupational ladder or gain the power which the manipulation of words and ideas brings about.[18] Once women became workers in the world outside the home, they were in a better position to demand equal education, although the occupations which they at first entered are still not as well established in the college curriculum as the male ones. To further advance women have to attack the bastions of male privilege, in education as elsewhere.

Economic changes and improved education have also helped stimulate political changes. Suffrage gave women a tool which they could use to achieve more power and though they have been slow to effectively utilize the ballot box to advance their own sex (witness the comparatively few women legislators and public officials), the potential of power is there and most legislators realize the possibilities of an aroused female vote. Some women have risen to positions of real power in the world or on the national scene, such as Indira Gandhi in India, Golda Meier in Israel, or Margaret Chase Smith in America. Such women in politics are still few in number, and part of the reason for this, at least in the United States, is that women have not attempted to play the political game. The most powerful women's political group is the League of Women Voters, and while their stand on issues is well researched and thought out, their nonpartisanship is a handicap in the real world of politics. Success in politics is due not so much to issues as it is to partisanship and the effective use of power. When the league confronts these realities it breaks down because it was not set up to deal in this arena and has to depend upon the good will of the politicians with whom it lobbies. The league, however, has served as a training ground for women who do want to enter politics and more of them are beginning to do so. The task is not an easy one because to be effective women have to not only be elected but also break down the informal barriers which exist for women officeholders. This is because the informal male stag committee meeting is often the key to decisionmaking and the woman politician is still excluded from these. There is the further difficulty in

18. We have developed this theme somewhat in an historical context in Bonnie and Vern Bullough, "Intellectual Achievers: A Study of Eighteenth-Century Scotland," *American Journal of Sociology*, 76 (1971), 1048–63. See also Vern Bullough, *The Development of Medicine as a Profession* (Basle: Karger, 1966).

that politics is more than a full-time job and requires the neglect of family and home that few women are as yet willing to do.

One indicator of the changing role of the sexes in society is the present crisis in marriage. In the American past marriage required much more adjustment on the part of the woman than the man and it was usually assumed she would adopt her husband's religion, his politics, and his way of life. As indicated she was legally under the control of her husband. If the role and status of women in society is to change then it becomes obvious that marriage as it was in the past must also change. In 1927 Judge Ben B. Lindsey, a controversial and noted reformer, called for a new kind of marriage, the companionate marriage with legalized birth control and the right to divorce by mutual consent for childless couples, usually without payment of alimony. This in effect has finally begun to materialize with the no-fault divorce laws adopted in states such as California, where marriages can be ended even when children are involved without the necessity of affixing fault.[19] Earlier states such as Nevada capitalized on their easy divorces, and such developments helped to give freedom to those women who felt they were a prisoner of their spouses.

Liberalized divorce leaves many problems. Children are often involved, and the trauma inherent in such separations have never been fully assessed. In most divorces women are given the custody of the children, even though they are not always the most qualified to take care of them, or in some cases not particularly interested in them. Child custody is a leftover vestige of the belief in women's biological role as nursing mother, and women's liberation will not really have arrived until some basis other than supposed maternal instinct is used to determine the custody of children. Divorce also has financial consequences which most women have never fully been conscious of until they find themselves involved. Theoretically a father is supposed to pay child support, but only rarely, contrary to popular impression, does the woman receive alimony. In over 90 percent of the divorce cases in the United States the wives do not ask for alimony, and in the case of the 10 percent who do, a significant proportion will not receive it. The United States Census Bureau kept statistics on alimony until 1922, when the item was dropped, and the all time high for alimony was reached in that year when alimony was given in 14.7

19. Judge Ben B. Lindsey and Wainwright Evans, *The Companionate Marriage* (New York: Boni and Liveright, 1927).

percent of the cases. Since then it has declined. This means that women, no matter how unsatisfactory the marriage may have been, often find themselves in middle age without a job and with no real skill to earn a living. The effect of this is seen in the welfare statistics, which even in the prosperous decade of the 1960s found six times as many families headed by a female on welfare than were headed by a male. Most of the women in such situations (over 90 percent) had once been married. This figure becomes even more significant when it is realized that the number of families with children headed by a woman is gradually increasing. In 1971 the figure stood at 12 percent of all American families, while for the decade or so before that the number had remained constant at 10 percent. Most fathers who are required to give child support do not. A Wisconsin study found that 79 percent of the fathers simply did not obey the court orders while only 13 percent were in full compliance and 8 percent made only token payments. Most states eventually give up taking legal action against the delinquent males. Only 36 percent of those defying the court order in Wisconsin had legal action taken against them.[20] Inevitably divorce also leaves the ex-mates, both male and female, with serious problems of readjustment. Many of the meetings of Parents Without Partners or any of the numerous other groups in the world of the formerly married contain a great many embittered people.[21]

Many commentators of today are upset about the high divorce rate, and anyone who has observed families in which there are her children, his children, and their children realize that there are some ludicrous contradictions in present-day marriage and divorce customs. Divorce is only a symptom of changing conditions and probably reflects the strains of the changing social mores in much the same way as do the increasing numbers of younger couples who practice a kind of companionate marriage without benefit of ceremony before deciding to stay together. Many decide not to marry. More-

20. Marian P. Winston and Trude Forsher, "The Myth of the Easy Life on Alimony," *Los Angeles Times*, July 16, 1972. Other information from various editions of the *Stastical Abstract of the United States* (Washington, D.C.: Government Printing Office), which is published annually.

21. For a discussion of divorce on a popular level see Morton M. Hunt, *The World of the Formerly Married* (New York: McGraw-Hill, 1966), and for a history of divorce in the United States see Nelson Manfred Blake, *The Road to Reno* (New York: Macmillan, 1962).

over, in spite of the difficulties inherent in a divorce, increasing numbers of women are initiating divorces, willing to go through the emotional and financial difficulties rather than stay in their present state. Since in the past the woman has probably been the key factor in a successful marriage, this in itself is indicative of changing roles and attitudes of women, changes to which the law and social custom have not yet adjusted. Often it seems that it is only as a divorcée that women who have never run a household or exercised their independence find out, sometime to their own surprise, that they are capable of conducting their own affairs, a rather sad commentary on the way many women have entered into marriage.

Another sign of the growing emancipation of women is the elimination of some of the restrictive clothing of the past. Thorsten Veblen, the famed American economist and sociologist, once described the corset as substantially "a mutilation, undergone for the purpose of lowering the subject's vitality and rendering her permanently and obviously unfit for work." [22] In the not too distant past proper young girls were put into training corsets while still in primary school, and this meant that even during their childhood they were inhibited from engaging in any real physical activity. Though many of the dress reformers of the nineteenth century had inveighed against the evils of the corset and other aspects of the female costume such as the bustle or the hoop, it was only after World War I that women as a group began to adopt the new freer styles, aided undoubtedly by the development of the sanitary pad. Eventually the old-fashioned corset became not only obsolete but an anathema. Lawrence Langner in his study of clothing argued that in the past much of the differentiation in clothing between the sexes has been the result of the desire of the male to assert his superiority over the female and to hold her to his service. Man, regardless of period or culture, has usually devised clothes for himself, whether trousers, knickerbockers, pleated kilts, or tunics that permitted freedom of movement, while at the same time he has encouraged his womenfolk to wear clothes that impeded their movements. In the East where women often wore pantaloons or trousers they sometimes were hampered by other restrictions. In China this impediment was the crippling footbinding. Elsewhere women's ankles were shackled, they wore sandles provided

22. Quoted by Lawrence Langner, *The Importance of Wearing Clothes* (London: Constable, 1959), p. 213.

with stilts, or they went out of the home only with their faces and bodies heavily veiled. In the West women were further restricted by tight bindings, such as corsets, or by high-heeled shoes, which made walking a kind of acrobatic feat. The "main purpose of all these costumes and customs was to make it difficult for her to run away. Thus, by imposing confining garments on women, or by otherwise hobbling her, man was enabled almost universally to keep her in a state of inferiority and subjugation to him as a personal possession."[23]

Though not all of the changes in female costume have served to encourage greater freedom of movement, the mini-skirt for example was impossible for sitting or bending, in general there has been a tendency for women to shed their restrictive clothing, at least for work and playtime activity, and for young girls to be almost entirely free. Though the "proper" female costume for dress of hose, girdle, and high heels still restricts physical activity more than any costume worn by the male, there are acceptable alternatives for women who do not want such confinement. Even here there are changing standards, since the girdle is more likely to be found among older than younger women, and among the young, it is sometimes difficult to tell the male from the female.

One of the assumptions which proved not to be entirely valid in this book was that attitudes toward sex would be an indication of how women would be regarded. It was hypothesized as part of a broader study on sex that a sex-negative culture would be more inclined to emphasize the subjugation of women while a sex-positive culture would be more inclined to liberate women. Though a sex-negative culture is inclined to downgrade women, it seems clear that a sex-positive one, as evidenced by the Greeks, the Arabs, or the Indians, is not necessarily likely to upgrade her position. At the beginning of this study we surveyed several theories as to why women had keen kept in subordination through much if not all of history, and at the completion it seems that most such theories are invalid. Though we have no earthshaking theory to account for female subjugation, it would seem that the biology of women in the past tended to confine them to the home, to make them submissive to man, and this biological submissiveness was transferred very early in man's history into a subordinate role. This subordinate role has been maintained through a system of rewards and punishments, and through

23. *Ibid.*, pp. 51–55.

childhood socialization processes which supported a view of women as the subordinate sex.

Though woman in the past remained dominant in the home, the man was chief outside, and it was only with the advent of the industrial revolution when women were forced to leave the home that a real drive for equality could be mounted. Religion, government, and education early moved outside of the home, and eventually so did manufacturing and agricultural production. Women were left with the children, and it was only by holding onto them that they could exercise any kind of control. Finally women themselves began to leave the home, and though they still talked in terms of home and children, they were able to make their way into the community and to demand equality. They did this, however, in a somewhat ambivalent fashion. In their demand for the vote, for example, they tended to believe that they would raise the moral tone of politics. In effect women were able to move forward only if they visualized themselves as fulfilling what they thought of as a female role.

There were of course the extremists, represented by those today who class all males as chauvinist pigs. Such extremists are in fact essential. The very extremes of their demands make it possible for more moderate women to demand concessions and keep the bulk of womanhood behind them. If such demands can be expressed in the traditional terms of home and family (or perhaps even equality?), instead of just a demand to quash the male, and if the past is any guide, women are more likely to rally around the cause. Even then, however, there has to be veiled power behind the demand and women with their potential at the ballot box and in the economic arena now have such power. Progress, however, will probably still be slow, or at least appear to be to those demanding change, although in the long run of history changes are taking place at a rapid pace. To really gain ultimate equality it will be necessary to remodel many of our institutions, to change the socialization process so that a girl who wants to be an administrator or a physician or a basketball star is regarded as normal and encouraged in her ambitions as much as if she wants to be a wife and mother. Girls will also have to be taught to be somewhat more competitive instead of disguising their competitive instinct, but these kind of changes cannot be effected by one woman or by a small group. They require the backing of society.

It is important that history be reinterpreted to give at least some attention to women in the past who, even though behind the scenes, exercised power. Even at the first-grade level the Dick-and-Jane books will have to be rewritten to allow the future Jane to fulfill some of the tasks now limited to her brother. Freudian theory will have to be reassessed and much of it discarded. Religious traditions which have been interpreted by men to keep women in subordinate roles will have to be abandoned. With all of this many of the special privileges now given to women because of their inferior position will be abolished. Obviously women will continue to bear children, and it is quite possible that many of them will take ten years or so out of their careers to do so, or will be comparatively inactive for a similar period in their occupational role, but there is no reason this should make them less than equal to men. To aid them in meeting the demands of what still remains a male society, we should encourage the development of child-care centers, and perhaps even go so far as to give paternity leaves for fathers, since fathers should have the opportunity to be as responsible for the family as the mother.

In short, times are changing, and though women have not yet achieved real equality, and will probably not do so in our lifetime, it at least seems that they might well sometime in the future if they care to keep pursuing the goal. This is the decision that women themselves will have to make. Like the Black revolution, the role of the sympathetic outsider is no longer in a leadership position but as a supporter. Men can encourage but women will have to take the lead. The Black militants, although they speak with a strident voice, also give impetus to a movement that was beginning to slow down. So do the militants of women's liberation. It is interesting how all reform movements have peaks and valleys. This current peak seems to have brought some substantive changes, aided by some of the basic modifications in society which make the liberation of women more likely. The biological burdens of the past have been more or less overcome, the economic burdens are in the process of being overcome, political power is real, but the psychological, sociological, and historical barriers are still there. These might well be the most difficult to overcome.

Guide to Further Reading

Throughout this study I have tried to footnote the sources ultilized as well as note some of the available secondary and reference materials. It is not my intention to repeat this information again but instead to give a kind of summary guide to materials for those interested in further exploring the field, both historians and the general reader. Obviously anyone attempting to do research or explore further in the history of women has to have some knowledge of history in the conventional sense of the word. For Western civilization in general my own survey, *Man in Western Civilization* (New York: Holt, 1970) might serve as a guide. It has the advantage of being short, although like most such histories it neglects the role of the female and ignores Eastern cultures. To remedy this last defect the work by William H. McNeill, *World History* (New York: Oxford University Press, 1971) is helpful. No general survey that I know of deals adequately with the role of women and it was in part to correct this deficiency that I undertook the present study. For the reader able to tackle a longer and more detailed survey the works of Will and Ariel Durant might be consulted. Their *The Story of Civilization* (New York: Simon and Schuster, 1935 ongoing) has so far reached eight volumes and is based upon wide reading in the secondary sources. Some of their concepts and interpretations would not meet the approval of many scholars but I know of nothing better in English. At a more sophisticated and scholarly level there are the many volumed Cambridge series, all published by Cambridge University Press and comprising an enormous and generally reliable encyclopedia of history: *Cambridge Ancient History, Cambridge Medieval History, New Cambridge Modern History* (in progress), *Cambridge Economic History of Europe* (in progress), *Cambridge History of India* (in progress). A standard reference series on American history is *The American Nation: A History from Original Sources*, originally published by Harper and Company in twenty-eight volumes. The series is now undergoing revision and is being updated under the general editorship of Henry S. Commager and Richard B. Morris. Also helpful is *A History of American Life* (12 vols., New York: Macmillan, 1929–44).

Until recently there was a lack of bibliographic tools for those interested in studying the history of women, but the interest aroused by the woman's lib movement has begun to remedy this situation. How many of the publications will survive only time will tell. Currently attempting to act as an information center in the burgeoning field is the Clearinghouse on Women's Studies, College at Old Westbury, State University of New York, Old Westbury, New York. The Westbury group issues periodic "fact sheets" on female studies. There is a *Women's Studies Abstract*, ed. by Sara Stauffer Whaley, Post Office Box 1, Rush, New York, 14543, which abstracts periodical articles about women. The Barnard Women's Center at Barnard College is in the process of compiling an annotated bibliography which they then plan to issue annually. The Modern Language Association's Commission on the Status of Women has published syllabi dealing with content for women's studies courses as well as bibliographies. Some of their material has been printed in *Female Studies*, published by KNOW, Inc., Post Office Box 10197, Pittsburgh, Pa., 15232. The Coordinating Committee on Women in the Historical Profession issues a periodic bulletin, *Current Research on the History of Women*, available from the American Historical Association. Lucinda Cisler, 102 West 80th Street, New York City, N.Y., 10024, has compiled a twelve-page mimeographed bibliography entitled "Women: A Bibliography," which she sells for 25¢. Andrea Hinding and Rosemary Richardson compiled a brief listing of the "Archival and Manuscript Resources for the Study of Women's History," copies of which are available from the University of Minnesota Libraries. Joan Hoff Wilson of California State University, Sacramento, did a more detailed survey on "West Coast Archival Manuscript Resources for the Study of Women's History." Most of the bibliographies are in mimeographed form and this undoubtedly will change as new journals appear in the field. Several journals have been announced, including *Women's Studies: An Interdisciplinary Journal*, edited by Wendy Martin, Department of English, Queens College, City University of New York, and *Feminist Studies*, edited by Ann Calderwood, 606 West 116th Street, New York City, N.Y., 10027. Closely allied, although somewhat broader in scope, is *The Family in Historical Perspective*, a newsletter established by the Newberry Library in Chicago as part of a project to establish a center devoted to research on the topic. Most professional associations, including sociologists and psychologists as well as those cited above, have established sections dealing with women and publish newsletters on the topic. In addition several of the so-called women's magazines deal periodically with various aspects of what might be called the women movement. *Cosmopolitan* under the editorship of Helen Gurley Brown achieved considerable publicity with its first nude male centerfold. In 1972 *Redbook*, which like most women's magazines in the past is still edited by men for women, ran the first cover ever portraying a pregnant female on an American woman's magazine, which interestingly enough aroused as much controversy in the magazine industry as the nude male centerfold of *Cosmopolitan*. *Ms.* is a new magazine founded by Gloria Steinem designed to carry the ideas of the woman's liberation movement to a wider audience. Other journals or magazines or newsletters which have appeared in recent years include *Aphra, Female Liberation Newsletter, A Journal of Female Liberation,* and *Women.* Undoubtedly there will be many more but it is too early to indicate which ones will survive.

Several readers about women in history have been published, including Elsie Adams and Mary Louise Briscoe, *Up against the Wall Mother* (Beverly Hills: Glencoe Press, 1971) and Aileen S. Kraditor, *Up from the Pedestal* (Chicago: Quadrangle Books, 1968). New ones are beginning to appear with great rapidity. What so far has been lacking is the dedicated monographic scholarship which is so necessary to advance our knowledge. Some monographs have appeared, and more will follow, but I have not cited most of the existing ones in this bibliography.

The present study is by no means the first attempt to survey women throughout history. One of the pioneering works on the subject was that of Hermann Heinrich Ploss, Max Bartels, and Paul Bartels, *Woman: A Historical Gynaecological and Anthropological Compendium,* edited and translated by Eric John Dingwal (3 vols., London: Heinemann, 1935). The first German edition appeared in 1885 but the English edition was based upon a revised German edition, typeset but never published because the plates were destroyed by Hitler. Another early work on the subject was Emily James Putnam, *The Lady: Studies of Certain Significant Phases of Her History,* which was originally published in 1910 (New York: Sturgis and Walton, republished, Chicago: University of Chicago Press, 1970). Mrs. Putnam was the first dean of Barnard College and under her guidance it became part of Columbia University. She retired when she married in 1899, but later rejoined the faculty. Also important are the pioneering works of Charlotte Gilman, *Women and Economics,* originally published in 1898, with a new edition edited by Carl N. Degler (New York: Harper and Row, 1966), and *The Home: Its Work and Influence,* originally published in 1903, with a new edition edited by William O'Neill (Urbana: University of Illinois Press, 1972). Mrs. Gilman, born as Charlotte Perkins, published some of her work under the name of Stetson. She later divorced Stetson and married Gilman. She was a disciple of Lester Ward, the early sociologist who held that women were the true type of the human species and the male characteristics of aggression, combativeness, and so on, were secondary sex manifestations. Her work dealing with this theme, *The Man Made World: Or Our Androcentric Culture*, was originally published in 1911 (reprinted, New York: Science Book Press, 1970). There were other surveys of women in history, such as Willis J. Abbot, *Notable Women in History* (Philadelphia: Winston, 1913), or Sarah Parker White, *A Moral History of Woman* (Garden City: Doubleday, Doran, 1937) but most such works are little more than pot boilers and include little basic research. The title of Sarah White's book is indicative of a view toward women which has been difficult to overcome. A good anthology of such views can be found in Clifton Joseph Furness, *The Genteel Female: An Anthology* (New York: Knopf, 1931). Probably the classic work expounding this view was a nineteenth-century book by Artemas Bowers Muzzey entitled *The Young Maiden* (4th ed., Boston: William Crosby, 1843). Muzzey claimed that although women have lesser intellects than men they have greater moral qualities and it is their duty to feel and suffer.

Quite different in concept is Mary R. Beard, *Woman as a Force in History* (New York: Macmillan, 1946), written by a professional historian and contrasting conventional myths with the reality of women in history. Mrs. Beard gives an effective portrayal of the informal power of women. Also invaluable is Doris Mary Stenton, *The English Woman in History* (London: Allen and Unwin, 1957), which does for England what this study attempts on a larger scale. Similar to this work is a French one by Maurice Bardèche, *Histoire des Femmes* (2 vols., Paris: Stock, 1968). For a scholarly analysis of women at mid-century see Mirra Komarovsky, *Women in the Modern World* (Boston: Little, Brown, 1953). Whether it reflects the power of women's lib is unclear but Professor Komarovsky has moved to the forefront of American sociologists, and as of this writing is president-elect of the American Sociological Association. For American women see Page Smith, *Daughters of the Promised Land* (Boston: Little, Brown, 1970). One of the most interesting studies of American women is the illustrated study by Oliver Jensen entitled *The Revolt of the American Women* (New York: Harcourt, 1952). Some twenty years ago this seemed an apt title and it still seems so today. A good recent survey of British women in the nineteenth century appears in *Suffer and Be Still: Women in the Victorian Age*, edited by Martha Vicinus (Bloomington: Indiana University Press, 1972). Included is an excellent bibliography.

H. R. Hays, *The Dangerous Sex: The Myth of Feminine Evil* (New York: Putnam's Sons, 1964), surveys the history of women from the viewpoint of an anthropologically and psychologically oriented writer.

Both his methodology and content differ from my study and it might be interesting for the reader to compare and contrast this work with his. Eleanor Flexner's new biography *Mary Wollstonecraft* (New York: Coward, McCann, and Geoghegan, 1972) is invaluable. Misogyny has been a strong strand in Western literature and Katharine M. Rogers, *The Troublesome Helpmate: A History of Misogyny in Literature* (Seattle: University of Washington Press, 1966), is an invaluable study of this aspect of literature. A more detailed and more confined study on the same subject is Frances Lee Utley, *The Crooked Rib: An Analytical Index to the Argument about Women in English and Scots Literature to the End of the Year 1568* (Columbus: Ohio State University Press, 1944). Another history is Barbara Welter, ed., *The Woman Question in American History* (Hinsdale, Ill.: The Dryden Press, 1973). R. E. L. Masters and Eduard Lea collected some of the most misogynistic writings in their *The Anti-Sex: The Belief in the Natural Inferiority of Women* (New York: Julian Press, 1964). One of the most hateful of all books is Edouard de Beaumont's, *L'Epee et les femmes*, published in 1882 but translated into English under the title of the *Sword and Womankind* (New York: Panurge Press, n.d.). An effective antidote to Beaumont is Simone de Beauvoir, *The Second Sex* (New York: Knopf, 1957), translated by H. M. Parshley. Madame de Beauvoir is one of the key voices in woman's struggle for equality. Recently some attention has been paid to the writings of women themselves and my colleague Ann Stanford has compiled an *Anthology of Women Poets in English* from Eadwacer in the Anglo-Saxon to the present (London: Herder and Herder, 1972). Alison Adburgham, *Women in Print* (London: Allen and Unwin, 1972), gives a full account of the woman writer of the past. An old collection of the way men have looked upon women can be found in Frederick W. Morton, *Woman in Epigram* (Chicago: A. C. McClurg, 1895).

A more specialized study of the male scientific attitude toward women appears in Ilza Veith, *Hysteria: The History of a Disease* (Chicago: University of Chicago Press, 1965). Medical attitudes have been extremely influential in justifying the subordination of women and some of these can be found in histories of gynecology and obstetrics. See Harvey Graham, *Eternal Eve* (Garden City, N.Y.: Doubleday, 1951), or E. Jameson, *Gynecology and Obstetrics* (reprinted, New York: Hafner, 1962). An outstanding history of contraception is Norman E. Himes, *Medical History of Contraception* (Baltimore: Williams and Wilkins, 1936). Equally outstanding but approaching the subject from a different viewpoint is John T. Noonan, Jr., *Contraception: A History of Its Treatment by Catholic Theologians and Canonists* (Cambridge: Harvard Belknap Press, 1966). Noonan also edited an historical survey of abortion, *The*

Morality of Abortion (Cambridge: Harvard University Press, 1970), which were the papers given at a conference on the subject at the Harvard Divinity School under the sponsorship of the Joseph P. Kennedy, Jr., Foundation. See also C. Thomas Dienes, *Law, Politics, and Birth Control* (Urbana: University of Illinois Press, 1972). Laws and attitudes about abortion are changing rapidly, but Lawrence Lader's survey for the mid-sixties still has value, *Abortion* (Indianapolis: Bobbs-Merrill, 1966). Lee Rainwater and Karol Weinstein did a study on working and lower-class attitudes toward contraception and sex entitled *And the Poor Get Children* (Chicago: Quadrangle Books, 1960).

For other aspects of woman's role in history see my *History of Prostitution* (New Hyde Park, N.Y.: University Books, 1964). This was my first attempt to look at male attitudes toward women. The thesis of the book was that prostitution was a male-tolerated occupation for women and was correlated with the way in which men have regarded women in the past. Though I would now rewrite some parts of the book and expand others, it contains much information not available elsewhere. My wife and I also attempted to survey another of the women's "occupations," and for this see Vern and Bonnie Bullough, *Emergence of Modern Nursing* (New York: Macmillan, 1964 and 1969). In the first edition Bonnie is listed as first author and I am second, and the procedure was reversed for the second edition in an attempt to demonstrate that we both were equal participants in the writing. So far few of the other so-called women's occupations have been studied historically, nor has there been much effort in tracing the role of women in other fields. Kate Campbell Hurd Mead wrote *A History of Women in Medicine* (Haddam, Conn.: Haddam Press, 1938), a pioneering study which others might emulate. Margaret Cussler, *The Woman Executive* (New York: Harcourt, Brace, and World, 1958); Jacqueln A. Mattfeld and Carol G. Van Aken edited an MIT symposium on *Women and the Scientific Professions* (Cambridge: MIT Press, 1965). A survey of working mothers published over ten years ago is still valuable, F. Ivan Nye and Lois Wladis Hoffman, eds., *The Employed Mother in America* (New York: Rand McNally, 1963). Their findings disproved the oft-quoted theory that working mothers are ogres. Cynthia F. Epstein, *Woman's Place: Options and Limits in a Professional Career* (Berkeley: University of California, 1970), indicates some of the current problems faced by professional women. The *School Review* published by the University of Chicago devoted its February, 1972, issue (vol. 80, no. 2) to an invaluable discussion of "Women and Education." Also worthwhile is the special edition of the *American Journal of Sociology*, 78 (January, 1973), edited by Joan Huber and devoted to "Changing Woman in a Changing Society."

The three-volume *Notable American Women 1607–1950*, edited by Edward T. James, Janet Wilson James, and Paul S. Boyer (Cambridge: The Belknap Press of Harvard University, 1972), better than anything shows some of the difficulties that American women have had to face. Most women were either spinsters, or widows, and the usual adjective to describe them was "plain in appearance" or some similar term, and had to overcome almost insurmountable difficulties to become listed as a Notable American Woman.

The Marxist, Socialist, and Communist views which are not always the same thing are summarized in *The Woman Question: Selections from the Writings of Karl Marx, Frederick Engels, V. I. Lenin, Joseph Stalin* (New York: International Publishers, 1951). Included are sections on "The Enslavement of Women," "The Exploitation of Women," "The Bourgeois Family," "Women in the Struggle for Socialism," and so on. The reader should also consult the classic works in the field, such as Frederick Engels, *The Origin of the Family, Private Property and the State* (New York: International Publishers, 1942), and August Bebel, *Woman under Socialism*, translated from the 33rd German edition by Daniel de Leon (New York: Labor News, 1904). An interesting recent summary of Marxist-Leninist views is a pamphlet by Clara Colón, *Enter Fighting: Today's Woman* (New York: New Outlook Publishers, 1970). *The "Little Red Book" of Mao Tse-Tung*, which had various publishers in this country, also had a chapter on women.

For the controversy over matriarchy the reader might start with Robert Briffault, *The Mothers* (3 vols., New York: Macmillan, 1927), which contains a massive collection of materials. The contrary view was set forth in an equally comprehensive work by Edward Westermarck, *The History of Human Marriage* (3 vols., New York: Allerton Books, 1922). A radio debate between Robert Briffault and Bronislaw Malinowski on the topic which took place in 1930 was later published as *Marriage: Past and Present* (Boston: Porter Sargent, 1956). The classic work on mother right can be found in selections of the writings of J. J. Bachofen, *Myth, Religion and Mother Right*, translated by Ralph Manheim (Princeton: Princeton University Press, Bollingen Series, vol. 84, 1967). See also Ernest Crawley, *The Mystic Rose*, revised and enlarged by Theodore Besterman (2nd ed., London: Methuen, 1927). Theodore Besterman on his own wrote *Men against Women* (London: Methuen, 1934). There is an interesting collection of writings on women edited by T. R. Smith published under the title of *The Woman Question* (New York: Boni and Liveright, 1918). Included are selections from such people as Westermarck, John Stuart Mill, Rebecca West, and Havelock Ellis. The controversy over matriarchy is not yet ended and it has been revived in a slightly different form by Elaine Morgan, *The Descent of Woman* (New York: Stein and Day, 1972), which pictures women as the key factor in the evolution of man and civilization. Her book to me seems to belong to the category of pseudo-science rather than science but the reader can judge for herself or himself.

Freud dealt with the subject of women in his *A General Introduction to Psychoanalysis,* translated by Joan Riviere (reprinted, Garden City, N.Y.: Garden City Publishing, 1943), and in his *Civilization and Its Discontents* (London: Hogarth Press, 1930), among other places. Additional citations can be found in the introductory chapter to this volume. The views of C. G. Jung have been analyzed by Ann Belford Ulanov, *The Feminine in Jungian Psychology and in Christian Theology* (Evanston: Northwestern University Press, 1971). See also Helen Deutsche, *The Psychology of Women* (New York: Grune and Stratton, 1945), and Karen Horney, *Female Psychology* (New York: Norton, 1967) for the feminine viewpoint. Deutsch, however, argued that to be an adult, a woman must be narcissistic, masochistic, and passive. Horney is cut more in the mold of women's liberation and gives an effective rejoinder to the penis-envy theory of Freud. Theodore Reik's, *The Creation of Woman* (New York: Braziller, 1960) is a kind of archaeological psychoanalysis. A combination of the Freudian and Marxian views are found in Herbert Marcuse, *Counterrevolution and Revolt* (Boston: Beacon Press, 1972), and in other books by him. Marcuse argues that women are less brutalized under capitalism than men because economic discrimination has kept them out of the dog-eat-dog competitive world. Another viewpoint is expressed by Viola Klein, *The Feminine Character* (reprint, Urbana: University of Illinois Press, 1972). She includes a discussion of the concepts of Karen Horney and Clara Thompson.

The sexual studies of recent decades have been responsible for helping to change attitudes about women. A good sampler of the view of the 1920s can be found in V. F. Calverton and S. D. Schmalhausen, *Sex in Civilization* (New York: MacCauley Company, 1929). For the studies themselves see K. B. Davis, *Factors in the Sex Life of Twenty-Two Hundred Women* (New York: Harper, 1929); G. V. Hamilton, *A Research in Marriage* (New York: Boni, 1929), and most especially Alfred C. Kinsey *et al., Sexual Behavior in the Human Male* (Philadelphia: W. B. Saunders, 1948) and *Sexual Behavior in the Human Female* (Philadelphia: W. B. Saunders, 1953). The physiological processes of sex have begun to receive scientific attention and here the team of Masters and Johnson holds prime importance, in particular their pioneering first volume, William H. Masters and Virginia E. Johnson, *Human Sexual Response* (Boston: Little, Brown, 1966). Several histories of sexual attitudes have been written which are helpful in studying attitudes toward women. Among those which should be listed is Richard Lewinsohn, *A History of Sexual Customs* (New York: Harper, 1958). This originally appeared in German and was translated by Albert Mayce. Another German work, Jos van Ussel on sex repression, has not yet been translated into English but has appeared in a French edition which I consulted under the title of *Histoire de la répression sexuelle* (Paris: Robert Laffont, 1972). Several other works have appeared in German and some of these are cited in the footnotes. A work which contains a lot of invaluable information but with whose interpretation I disagree is G. Rattray Taylor, *Sex in History* (London: Thames and Hudson, 1954). A pioneering work on the subject was Geoffrey May, *Social Control of Sex Expression* (New York: Morrow, 1931). Jeannette H. Foster who was associated with the Kinsey team for a time did a study of *Sex Variant Women in Literature* (London: Muller, 1958). Derrick Sherwin Bailey has done pioneering work in studying Christian attitudes toward sex and his *Sexual Relations in Christian Thought* (New York: Harper, 1959) is invaluable. Other works which should be listed include Wayland Young, *Eros Denied: Sex in Western Society* (New York: Grove Press, 1964), Sidney Ditzion, *Marriage, Morals and Sex in America* (New York: Bookman Associates, 1953), and Edwin M. Schur, *The Family and the Sexual Revolution* (London: Allen and Unwin, 1966), as well as the numerous works cited in the footnotes.

The subject of love has been much studied, and attitudes toward love influence attitudes toward women. Included in any listing should be Denis de Rougemont, *Love in the Western World* (rev. ed., New York: Pantheon Books, 1956), Erich Fromm, *The Art of Loving* (New York: Harper, 1956), and Fernando Henriques, *Love in Action: The Sociology of Sex* (New York: Dutton, 1960). A satisfactory bibliography of the subject can be found in Morton M. Hunt, *The Natural History of Love* (New York: Knopf, 1959). A popular history of courting, E. S. Turner, *A History of Courting* (New York: Dutton, 1955), throws some humor on the subject. More scholarly, although somewhat outdated, is George Elliott Howard, *A History of Matrimonial Institutions*, which first appeared in 1904 and has since been reprinted (3 vols., reprinted, New York: Humanities Press, 1964). An old classic in the field is Bernhard A. Bauer, *Woman and Love*, translated from the German by Eden and Cedar Paul (New York: Boni and Liveright, 1927). For the medieval period, in addition to works cited in the footnotes, see Norman R. Shapiro and James Wadsworth, *The Comedy of Eros: Medieval French Guides to the Art of Love* (Urbana: University of Illinois Press, 1971).

The relation of clothes to the emancipation of women is discussed by Lawrence Langner, *The Importance of Wearing Clothes* (London: Constable, 1959). C. Willett and Phillis Cunnington surveyed *The History of Underclothes* (London: Michael Joseph, 1951) and include a discussion of the hostility of the clergy to women wearing underpants. The corset has received attention from Norah Waugh in *Corsets and Crinolines* (London: B. T. Batsford, 1954). A kind of encyclopedia of clothing can be found in Ludmilla Kybalová, Olga Herbenová, Milena Lamarová, *The Pictorial Encyclopedia of Fashion*, translated by Claudia Rosoux (London: Hamlyn, 1968). R. Riegel, "Women's Clothes and Women's Rights," *American Quarterly* (Fall, 1963), is a kind of documentation of the theme put forth by Thorstein Veblen in "The Economic Theory of Women's Dress," *Popular Science Monthly*, 46 (November, 1894).

Religion has been a major factor in the way society has looked at woman, and a good summary of this from a Catholic viewpoint is Mary Daly, *The Church and the Second Sex* (New York: Harper and Row, 1968). Derrick Sherwin Bailey also surveyed the field from an Anglican viewpoint in *The Man-Woman Relation in Christian Thought* (London: Longmans, Green, 1959). In Western thought attitudes toward women have also been influenced by ideas toward celibacy and for this see H. C. Lea, *History of Sacerdotal Celibacy in the Christian Church* (London: Watts, 1932). Closely connected with the topic are attitudes toward witchcraft. An excellent survey is Rossell Hope Robbins, *The Encyclopedia of Witchcraft and Demonology* (New York: Crown Publishers, 1959). One of the more recent studies which appeared too late to utilize in this study is Jeffrey Russell, *Witchcraft in the Middle Ages* (Ithaca, N.Y.: Cornell University Press, 1972).

Leo Kanowitz, *Women and the Law: The Unfinished Revolution* (Albuquerque: University of New Mexico Press, 1969), surveys the legal difficulties that women face in trying to achieve equality. Peggy Lanison, *Few Are Chosen: American Women in Political Life Today* (Boston: Houghton Mifflin, 1968), and Alva Myrdal and Viola Klein, *Women's Two Roles: Home and Work* (London: Routledge and Kegan Paul, 1968), report difficulties in other fields. There are numerous works dealing with women which have appeared in the last decade or so analyzing the female psyche and trying to place woman in an important role in society. The most influential American work in this area was Betty Friedan, *The Feminine Mystique* (New York: Norton, 1963), although a male writer preceded her, Morton M. Hunt, *Her Infinite Variety: The American Woman as Lover, Mate and Rival* (New York: Harper and Row, 1962). Some of the other works include Kate Millett, *Sexual Politics* (New York: Doubleday, 1970), Germaine Greer, *The Female Eunuch* (New York: McGraw-Hill, 1971), Elisabeth Mann Borgese, *Ascent of Woman* (New York: Braziller, 1963). Millett's work was an analysis of the masculine bias of some major American literary figures as well as Freud himself. Greer argued that men have deformed women by making them eunuchs and in the process of recounting her thesis gives an insight into the female role not available in most of the other books I have read. Borgese equates the ascent of women with the rise of the collective and the replacement of the individual. She argued that the feminine psyche is deeply rooted in the collective and as societies become more collectivist women will become more important. Borghese's work is handicapped by some rather far-fetched biological speculations. One of the most valuable studies is Elizabeth Janeway, *Man's World, Woman's Place* (New York: Morrow, 1971). Betty and Theodore Roszak, *Masculine / Feminine* (New York: Harper and Row, 1969), collect some of the writings for and about women and have some pertinent things to say about role-playing. Caroline Bird, *Born Female: The High Cost of Keeping Women Down* (New York: McKay, 1968), is good on the economic facts of life for women. Joseph Carson, *Silent Voices: The Southern Negro Woman Today* (New York: Delacorte Press, 1969), deals movingly with the overwhelming poverty, drudgery, and struggle that is the lot of lower-class Negro woman in the south. For a historical view of the Negro woman see Gerda Lerner, *Black Women in White America: A Documentary History* (New York: Pantheon Books, 1972). Anne F. Scott's *The Southern Lady* (Chicago: University of Chicago Press, 1970) and *The American Women: Who Was She* (Englewood Cliffs, N.J.: Prentice Hall, 1971) are good studies. Women have been deeply influenced by male attitudes and for some of these see Charles W. Ferguson, *The Male Attitude* (Boston: Little Brown, 1966). Ferguson argues that the male psyche has used the gun, the machine, and slavery to dominante American history. Eva Figes, *Patriarchal Attitudes* (London: Faber and Faber, 1970), examined historical attitudes toward woman, somewhat as does the present study, and is particularly good on Rousseau and Freud. Robin Morgan, *Sisterhood Is Powerful: An Anthology of Writings from the Women's Liberation Movement* (New York: Vintage Books, 1970), represents a good overview of some of the more militant members of women's liberation. Representing the opposite view is Karl Stern's *The Flight from Woman* (New York: Farrar, Straus, and Giroux, 1965). He is a strong believer in sexual polarities, "masculine rationalism" versus "feminine intuitiveness." Arguing against such innate differences in masculine-feminine behavior is Robert J. Stoller, *Sex and Gender: On the Development of Masculinity and Feminity* (New York: Science House, 1968). Also of interest is Eve Merriam, *After Nora Slammed the Door: American Women in the 1960's* (Cleveland: World, 1964). Most such works emphasize or are written from the point of view of the middle-class woman. Somewhat different is Lee Rainwater, Richard P. Coleman, and Gerald Handel, *Workingman's Wife: Her Personality, World and Life Style* (New York: Oceana, 1959).

Midge Decter, in *The New Chastity and Other Arguments against Women's Liberation* (New York: Coward, McCann, and Geoghegan, 1972), argues that women's liberation expresses not a demand for equal rights or a yearning for freedom but an inability to manage the rights and freedoms women already have.

For a survey of women in America in 1970 see the special issue of *Trans-Action* magazine (November-December, 1970). For a more official view see *American Women 1968* compiled for the Citizen's Advisory Council of the Status of Women, United States Department of Labor, and published by the United States Government Printing Office. One of the most interesting studies of the effect of the strict sex-role pattern advocated by some groups in society is Ruth E. Harley, "Children's Perceptions of Sex Preference in Four Culture Groups," *Journal of Marriage and Family,* 31 (1969), pp. 380–387. She held that in male-oriented cultures where sex roles were clearly separated and women relegated almost wholly to the home and motherhood most young boys believed girls were the preferred sex. This belief obviously had implications for them in later life. Arguing just the opposite view is a psychiatrist, Robert P. Odenwald, *The Disappearing Sexes* (New York: Random House, 1965). He blamed many of the ailments of contemporary society on a lack of clear sex-role distinction. For a somewhat less biased view see Jessie Bernard, *The Sex Game* (Englewood Cliffs, N.J.: Prentice Hall, 1968). She concluded that each generation has to work out its own sexual destiny.

Women have begun to write about the nature of female sexuality instead of leaving the topic for males to discuss. Perhaps the best of recent books on the subject is Mary Jane Sherfey, *The Nature and Evolution of Female Sexuality* (New York: Random House, 1972), although Barbara Seaman, *Free and Female: The Sex Life of the Contemporary Woman* (New York: Coward-McCann, 1972) runs it a close second. J. Chasseguet-Smirgel, *Female Sexuality: New Psychoanalytic Views* (Ann Arbor: University of Michigan Press, 1970), might be consulted. Del Martin and Phyllis Lyon wrote *Lesbian / Woman,* a book by and about lesbians published by Glide Publications, 330 Ellis Street, San Francisco, California, 94102.

The listing could go on and on without being exhaustive. No journal articles have been cited in the bibliography nor have works dealing with specific periods or areas, and for some of these the reader should consult the footnotes. The literature on the subject is expanding in almost a geometric ratio and will continue to do so for some time as new journals enter the field and scholars focus their attention on the area. It is my hope that this book will be useful both to the general reader and to scholars in the field, now and in the future.

Index

Abdon, 44
Abortion, 343
Abraham, 44
Adad-nirari III, 26
Adams, Henry, 14
Addams, Jane, 331
Adultery, 8, 22, 23–24, 37, 44, 45, 61, 90, 98, 112, 115, 124, 143, 153, 163, 164, 174, 181, 183, 243
Aeneas, 83
Africanus, Scipio, 91
Agrippina, 92
Ahab, 46
Akhenaton, 35
Alberti, Leon Battista, 190, 193
Albizzi, Cardinal, 224
Alcestis, 73
Alcott, Louisa May, 308, 331
Alexius I, 127
Ali, 143
Amazons, 9
Amenhotep III, 35
America, 50
American Nurses Association, 316
Amnon, 44
Amon, 33
Anaxadrides, 74
Anburey, Thomas, 300, 304
Anglicanism, 203
Anthony, Susan, 328
Anu, 20
Aphrodite, 57, 70
Apocalypse, 103, 112
Aquinas, Saint Thomas, 174–176, 205–206, 223
Archbishop of Mainz, 198
Archilochus, 69–70
Aregunda, 156
Aristophanes, 73
Aristotle, 12, 58, 61, 62, 63–64, 66, 67, 68, 174, 211

Arynas, 230
Asceticism, 122
Ascham, Roger, 221
Aspasia, 66, 75
Asshur, 20
Assyrian kingdom, 26–27
Athena, 57
Athenagoras, 114
Athens, 50, 51, 55, 60, 65, 67
Augustus, Emperor, 25, 80, 90, 92
Aurelius, Marcus, 91
Ayesha, 142
Aylmer, John, 202

Baal, 46
Babylon, 19, 25
Bachofen, J. J., 6
Balsdon, J. P. V. D., 79
Barak, 46
Barberino, Francesco, 211
Barnard College, 329
Bathild at Chelles, 158
Bath-sheba, 46
Beard, Mary R., 340
Bebel, August, 9
Becon, Thomas, 203
Beguines, 161–163
Behn, Aphra, 289
Beorthtric, 155
Besterman, Theodore, 10
Bhangāsvana, 237
Bible, 41, 45, 46, 104
Bilhah, 44
Birth control, 140, 326, 342–344
Blackwell, Elizabeth, 329
Bloomer, Amelia, 320–321
Bluestockings, 274
Boccaccio, Giovanni, 192–193
Boece, 168
Boleyn, Anne, 219

Borgia, Lucrezia, 3
Boscawen, Frances, 267
Bowdler, Thomas, 290
Bradstreet, Anne, 298
Brahmans, 110
Briffault, Robert, 9, 30
Brown, Antoinette, 328
Brown, Charles Brockden, 307, 308
Brownson, Orestes, 309
Brunner, Emil, 105
Buck, Pearl, 331
Buddhism, 240, 257, 258
Burckhardt, Jacob, 210
Butler, Samuel, 55
Byzantium, 127, 132

Caesar, 90
Caesarius, Bishop of Arles, 158
Cajeta, Cardinal, 205
Caliph Muqtadir, 149
Calvin, John, 195, 199–200
Campbell, John [M. Ludovicus], 279
Campbell, Joseph, 11
Canterbury Tales, 173
Capellanus, Andreas, 183
Casanova, 270
Cash, W. J., 300
Cassia, 127
Castiglione, Baldesar, 215
Cather, Willa, 331
Catherine the Great, 3, 294
Catholicism, 201, 205, 206–207, 208–
    209, 219, 342
Cato, 87, 92
Cecil, William, 202
Celibacy, 102, 115, 117, 118, 119, 122,
    172, 174, 196, 236
Cerny, Jaroslav, 32
Chaperonage, 314
Charlemagne, 156–157, 165
Charlotte, Princess, 275
Chastity, 249, 259, 260, 286
Chaucer, Geoffrey, 173, 187–188
Cheops, 34
Childbearing, 29, 67, 76, 102
China, 230, 243, 351
Chou Tun-i, 258
Christianity, 19, 41, 42, 49, 97, 99, 103,
    105, 111, 114, 119, 121, 137, 164,
    166, 190, 215
Chrysostom, St. John, 98, 115–116
Chu Hsi, 259, 260
Cicero, 81, 212
Cinderella, 126
Cistercians, 160, 170

Civil War, American, 35, 316, 319, 321,
    329
Claflin, Tennessee, 315
Clarke, Edward H., 322–323
Claudius, 92
Cleland, John, 270, 271
Clement of Alexandria, 114
Cleopatra, 3, 36
Clergy, 180
Clitorectomy, 143
Clotaire II, King, 156, 157
Cluny, 160
Cobbet, Thomas, 310
Coke, Edward, Sir, 222
Coke, Frances, 222
Collatinus, 85
Comenius, John, 204
Commodus, 91
Comnena, Anna, 127–129
Compton, Elizabeth, 318
Comstock, Anthony, 311
Comtesse du Barry, Jeanne, 270
Concubinage, 36, 44, 91, 141, 151, 156,
    164, 242, 247, 261
Concupiscence, 118
Confucianism, 250, 256, 257, 258
Confucius, 248, 250, 261
Constantine, 91, 126
Constantine IX Monomachus, 125
Constantine X, Emperor, 127
Contenau, Georges, 21
Continence, 18, 97, 105, 111, 113
Convents, 157–160
Cooke, Alexander, 228
Corsets, 226
Cotton, John, Jr., 305
Coulton, G. G., 173
Council of Trent, 207
Council of Vienne, 162
Courtesans, 67, 75
Crassus, 90
Crawley, Ernest, 10
Cyprian, 211

Daitya, 230
Daly, Mary, 339
Damascius, 127
Dānavas, 230
Darwin, Charles, 6
Darwin, Erasmus, 275
David, 44, 46
de Beauvoir, Simone, 271
Deborah, 46
de Bury, Richard, 187
de Chastellus, François, 303

Declaration of Independence, 327
de Condorcet, Marquis, 269
de Die, Beatrice, Countess, 191
Deer Park (*Parc aux Cerfs*), 269–270
Defoe, Daniel, 280
de France, Marie, 191
de Gournay, Marie, 218
de Laclos, Choderlos, 270
de l'Escale, Pierre, 218
de Lespinasse, Mademoiselle, 266
Delilah, 46
de Lorris, Guillaume, 184
de Maintenon, Madame, 271
de Medici, Catherine, 211
de Medici, Giuliano, 215
de Meung, Jean, 184
de Montaigne, Michel, 218
de Navarre, Marguerite, 218
de Novaire, Philippe, 189
de Pisan, Christine, 191, 194
de Pompadour, Madame, 269
de Romans, Humbert, 177
de Sade, Marquis, 270
Desexualization, 77
de Tencin, Madame, 266
de Troyes, Chretien, 183
Domesday Book, 155–156
Dominican order, 162, 176–177, 207
Double standard, 124
Dowry, 141, 155
Diderot, Denis, 270
Dinah, 44
Dionysius, 106
Dirghatamas, 239
Divorce, 87, 89, 124, 140, 141, 247, 349–351
Ducker, Cassandra, 299
du Deffand, Madame, 266
Duke of Saxony, 158
Duncan, Isadora, 333

Ea, 20
Eadberg, 155
Earhart, Amelia, 333
Ecclesiastes, 46
Ederle, Gertrude, 333
Edmonds, Sarah Emma, 319
Edwards, Jonathan, 303
Egypt, 13, 19, 30, 32, 34, 36, 40, 49, 109, 110
Eleanor of Aquitaine, 4, 182, 211
Elizabeth I, Queen, 3, 219, 220–221
Ellis, Havelock, 271
Emerson, Ralph Waldo, 308
Empedocles, 107

Encratites, 113
Engels, Frederick, 8, 14
England, 223, 224, 227, 285
Enheduanna, 27
Enki, 20
Enkidu, 28
Enlil, 20
Enslin, Morton S., 105
Entu, 24–25
Ephesians, 104
Epimetheus, 57
Erasumus, Desiderus, 212–213, 216
Erech, 27
Erinna, 70, 71
Esarhaddon, 26
Eshnunna, 21
Etheldreda at Ely, 158
Eudocia Macrembolitissa, Empress, 127
Euripides, 51, 68, 71, 73
Europe, 50, 210, 263
Eurydice, 106
Eve, 4
Ewen III, King, 168

Farid al-Din 'Attar, 149
Farnham, Marynia, 337
Farthingales, 226–227
Feminine mystique, 182
Feminists, 73, 326–377
Fichte, Johann, 291
Field, Nathaniel, 228
Fielding, John, 279
Fielding, Henry, 279
Fontaine, Peter, 300
Footbinding, 260
France, 210, 223, 285
Francis de Sales, 207
Franciscans, 162, 207
Frankfort, 179
Franklin, Benjamin, 306
Frazer, Sir James, 30
Freewomen, 24
Fregoso, Agostino, 215
French Revolution, 267–268, 271
Freud, Sigmund, 8, 14, 16, 53, 289, 337
Friedan, Betty, 339
Fu Hsüan, 253
Fuller, Margaret, 308

Gage, Matilda Joslyn, 318
Galileo, 224
Gandersheim, 158, 159
Gandhi, Indira, 348
Gaurī-Sankar, 230

Gautier, Leon, 167
Geneva Medical College, 329–330
Geoffrin, Madame, 266
George IV, 275
Germany, 223, 224
Gibbon, Edward, 80
Gideon, 44
Gilgamish, 27–28
Glasgow, Ellen, 331
Gnosticism, 111, 113–114
God, 41, 49, 104, 110, 121, 139, 192, 195
Godwin, William, 306
Goethe, Johann Wolfgang von, 290
Gomme, Arnold, 51
Goodman, Christopher, 202
Gough, Robert (Goffe), 228
Graham, Catherine Macaulay, 275–276, 277
Grand Army of the Republic, 320
Granet, Marcel, 262
Greek, 19, 32, 50, 65, 68, 76, 105, 210
Greek literature, 54
Greg, Margaretta, 283
Gregory of Tours, 156
Grimke, Angelina, 315
Grimke, Sarah, 315
Guilds, 179
Guise, Queen Mary, 201
Gynaeceum, 126
Gynaecocracy, 6

Hades, 106
Hagar, 44
Hale, Sarah Joseph, 316
Hamilton, Alexander, 303, 305
Hammurabi, 21–22
Hammurabic code, 22, 24, 25
Hannibal, 86
Hanway, Jonas, 279–280
Hapsburgs, 219–220
Harems, 36, 144, 145, 151, 180, 280
Harun al-Raschid, 144
Harvey, William, 12
Hassan, 143
Hathor, 33
Hathumod, 158
Hatshepsut, 3, 34, 35, 40
Hays, H. R., 16
Hekhebet, 34
Henry II, 183, 211
Henry VIII, 211, 220
Hephaestus, 57
Herodotus, 25
Herolt, Johann, 176–177
Hesiod, 54, 56, 57, 58
Hetep-hires II, 34

Hilda at Whitby, 158
Hinduism, 231, 234, 237–238, 240, 243
Hippocrates, 63
Hippocratic corpus, 12
Holland, 223
Homer, 54, 56
Homosexuality, 53, 54, 55
Hook, Frances, 318
Hooker, Thomas, 200
Horney, Karen, 53
Horus, 33
Hotep, Ptah, 38
Howe, Julia Ward, 328
Hoyland, Anna Maria, 299
Hroswitha, 159
Hsuëh T'ao, 258
Hull House, 331
Hume, David, 269
Hungary, 343
Husein, 143
Hutcheson, Frances, 269
Hutchinson, Anne, 297

I-anu, 259
Ibzan, 44
Iliad, 56
Inagunda, 156
Inanna, 20, 27
Incest, 45, 61
Inch, Jane, 299
India, 230
Industrial revolution, 346, 353
Industrialization, 278, 309–311
Innocent I, Bishop of Rome, 122
Innocent VIII, 223
Interracial marriages, 295
Iraq, 19
Ireland, 223
Irene, Empress, 124–125, 126
Irma'al-Quais, 136
Iroquois Indians, 7
Isabella, Queen of Navarre, 178
Isabella of Castille, 211
Ishtar, 20, 27
Isis, 33
Islam, 133, 135, 136, 146
Islamic literature, 135, 137, 181
Israel, ancient, 41, 55
Italy, 86, 210, 223, 227, 285

Jacob, 44
Jair, 44
James I, King, 222–223, 227
Japan, 343
Jarvis, Anna, 312

Jason, 72
Jeanne de Chantal, 207
Jefferson, Thomas, 308
Jesuits, 207
Jesus, 97, 98, 99, 100, 104, 112, 119, 192
Jezebel, 46
Joan of Arc, 224
John of Salisbury, 186
Joseph, 45
Judaism, 19, 33, 40, 41, 42, 44, 49, 100, 105, 110, 137, 144, 164
Jung, Carl Gustav, 15
Jus maternum, 7
Jus paternum, 7
Jus primae noctis, 167
Juvenal, 93, 96

Kādravey, 230
Kadrū, 230
Kalakh (Nimrud), 26
Kierkegaard, Soren, 196
Kepler, Johannes, 224
Khadijah, 142
Khons, 33
Kitto, H. D. F., 50
Knowlton, Charles, 326
Knox, John, 201
Ko Hung, 253
Komarovsky, Mirra, 338
Koran, 134, 140, 144
Kramer, Heinrich, 223
Kulmashitu, 25

Lakshmī-Nārāyan, 230
Langner, Lawrence, 351
Lao-Tse, 248, 254
Lasch, Christopher, 288
Latin, 209
League of Women Voters, 348
Leah, 46
Lenin, 346
Lesbianism, 70
Licentiousness, 61
Li ch'ing-chao, 259
Lindsey, Ben B., 349
Lipit Ishtar, 21
Liudolf, Duke, 158
Livia, 92
Livy, 79–80, 88
Li Yü, 260
Logan, Hannah, 304
London, 267
Louis VII, 183
Louis IX, 178
Louis XII, 219

Louis XIV, 264–265
Louis XV, 265, 269
Loyola, Saint Ignatius, 206
Lucretius, 94
Lundberg, Ferdinand, 337
Luther, Martin, 195, 198–199

Magic, 18
Maine, Sir Henry, 6, 11
Malinowski, Bronislaw, 10
Malory, Sir Thomas, 184
Manicheanism, 116–117
Manu, 231, 239
Map, Walter, 187
Marcion, 112
Marcuse, Herbert, 338
Marduk, 20
Maria Theresa, Queen, 294
Marriage. *See* Adultery; Celibacy; Continence; Double standard; Harems; Incest, Interracial marriages; Matriarchy; Misogyny; Monogamy; Patriarchy; Polyandry; Polygamy; Prostitution; Suttee
Marryat, Frederick, 312–313
Martel, Charles, 164
Martyr, Justin, 113
Marx, Karl, 14, 16, 33, 340
Marxists, 8, 9
Maspero, Gaston, 31, 37
Matilda, Empress, 211
Matriarchy, 10, 40, 56, 244
Matrilineal societies, 11
Matrilocal societies, 11
Matrist Society, 13–14
Mayflower, 57
McPherson, Aimee Semple, 333
Mead, Frank S., 46
Medea, 71–72
Meier, Golda, 348
Memphis triad, 33
Mencius, 261
Menken, Adah Isaacs, 320
Menopause, 25
Menstruation, 45, 62, 141, 172, 241, 345
Merici, Angela, 207
Mertz, Barbara, 32
Meshkhent, 34
Mesopotamia, 20, 26, 29, 30, 33, 36, 41, 49
Methodius, 104
Middle Ages, 43, 151, 153, 157, 164, 169, 179, 180, 182, 187, 192–193, 209, 227–228, 285
Mill, John Stuart, 5, 336
Millay, Edna St. Vincent, 331

Miller, Libby Smith, 321
Millet, Kate, 15
Milton, John, 225
Minnesingers, 183
Misogyny, 54, 55, 69, 71, 73, 81, 84–85, 86, 93, 95, 98, 103, 104, 105, 118, 121, 132, 134, 177, 186, 191, 192, 202, 208, 270
Mitchell, Maria, 300
Monastery, 258
Monasticism, 122
Monogamy, 19, 22, 78, 306
Monophysites, 126
Montagu, Elizabeth, 267
Montagu, Mary Wortley, 274
Morality, 97
More, Hannah, 274, 277, 286
More, Thomas, Sir, 212
Morgan, Lewis N., 7
Mormons, 302
Morton, Thomas, 296
Motherhood, 38
Mother's Day, 312
Mott, Lucretia, 306, 327
Mount Holyoke Female Seminary, 328
Mu-allaqat, 136
Muhammad, 134, 146, 149
Mulcaster, Richard, 214
Müller, Max, 241
Mulso, Hester, 274
Muslim, 166, 208
Mut, 33
Mythology, 58, 80–81, 86

Nabu, 26
Naditu, 25
Naomi, 47
Near East, 19, 49
Nefertiti, 35
Nefertum, 33
Neo-Platonists, 107, 109
Neo-Pythagoreans, 107, 109
Nephthys, 33
New England, 296, 298
New Testament, 97, 99, 105
Newton, Sir Isaac, 224
Nicolaites, 112
Ninus, King, 25
Nitocris, 25, 26
Notre Dame de Paris, 170
Numenius of Apamea, 110
Nuremberg, 179

Oberlin College, 328
Odyssey, 56

Omar Khayyam, 149–150
O'Rell, Max, 313
Origen, 100
Orpheus, 106
Orphics, 106–107
Osiris, 33
Ostler, Willie, 228
Ovid, 94–95, 181, 183
Owen, Robert D., 326

Painter, Sidney, 180
Palestine, 41, 49
Pallavicino, Count Gaspar, 215
Pan, Lady, 262
Pan Chao, Lady, 251
Pan Ku, 251
Pan Piao, 251
Pandora, 57
Paris, 267
Parker, Dorothy, 331
Pater familias, 83
Patriarchy, 11, 51, 61, 68, 230, 250
Patrist society, 13–14
Patronage, 180–181
Paul, Apostle, 41
Pederasty, 55
Peloponnesian War, 60, 65
Penelope, 56
Pepi II, 35
Pericles, 66, 75
Perkins, Frances, 331
Persia, 32, 144
Petrie, W. H. Flinders, 30
Philip of Spain, King, 219
Philo, 109
Philosophes, 266, 268, 291
Pilgrims, 57
Pius, Antoninus, 91
Planned parenthood clinics, 344
Plato, 58–59, 60, 75, 108, 110, 190, **211**, 212, 291
Playboy, 11
Pliny the Younger, 89
Plotinus, 111
Plumptre, James, 290
Plutarch, 69, 212
Pocahontas, 295
Polyandry, 19
Polygamy, 44, 151, 156, 242, 247, 302, 340
Pompey, 89
Ponet, John, 202
Pope Gregory XV, 208
Pope Pius V, 207
Pope Urban VIII, 208

Porphyry, 111
Portuguese, 242
Potiphar, 45
Premonstratensians, 160
Priestesses, 24–25
Procopius, 125, 132
Prometheus, 57
Prostitution, 22, 23, 24, 67, 75, 90, 261, 324
Protestantism, 195, 201–204, 206–207, 208–209, 224
Proverbs, 46, 47
Provost, Maria, 299
Psellus, Michael, 126
Ptah, 33
Ptolemies, 32
Pulcheria, 127
Punic War, 86, 87
Purdah, 142, 151
Puritanism, 225
Pythagoras, 107, 110
Pythagoreans, 107

Qadishtu, 25
Quakerism, 296–297, 300
Quinta, Claudia, 86

Rabelais, François, 225
Rachel, 44, 46
Radcliffe College, 329
Radegunde at Poitiers, 158
Rāha-Krishna, 230
Ramses II, 36
Rankin, Jeannette, 331
Rape of Lucretia, 84
Rehoboam, 44
Remus, 83
Renaissance, 191, 210
Renée of Ferrara, 219
Renenet, 34
Rhodopis, 34
Richardson, Samuel, 290
Robin Hood, 186
Robinson, Richard, 228
Rolfe, John, 295
Roman, 19, 42, 50, 77, 78, 83, 96, 105, 122, 153, 196, 210
Romanticism, 292–294
Romulus, 83
Roosevelt, Eleanor, 332
Roper, William, 213
Rousseau, Jean Jacques, 271, 273, 290
Rush, Benjamin, 306
Russia, 267, 347
Ruth, 47

Sabines, 84
Saint Ambrose, 116
Saint Athanasius, 97
Saint Augustine, 118, 211
Saint Basil of Caesarea, 121, 124
Saint Bernard of Clairvaux, 160, 170
Saint Francis de Sales, 206
Saint Jerome, 74, 116, 211
Saint Luke, 102
Saint Paul, 102, 104
Saint Peter, 112
Saint Theresa of Avila, 205
Saint Vincent de Paul, 207
Sāktas, 230
Sammuramat, 26
Sampson, Deborah, 318
Samson, 46
Sanger, Margaret, 331
Sanger, William, 324–325
Sapphism, 70
Sappho, 70–71
Sarah, 44
Sargon, 21, 27
Saturninus, 112
Scandinavia, 223
Schlegel, Friedrich, 292
Schreiner, Olive, 311
Scotland, 223
Scott, Sir Walter, 167
Semiramis, 25
Seneca, 81
Sennacherib, 26
Sex objects, 145, 165
Sextus Tarquinius, 85
Sexual intercourse, 18, 95, 103, 111, 117, 140, 164, 171, 181, 182, 183, 236, 256, 325, 342
Shamash, 20
Shamshi-Ada V, 26
Shao Yung, 259
Shaw, George Bernard, 167
Shechem, 44
Sheherazade, 148
Shelley, Percy Bysshe, 291
Shi-ite, 143
Shuhda bint al-Ibari, 149
Sicilus, Diodorus, 25
Sierra Club, 321–322
Simon, 112
Sin, 20
Sisera, 46
Sitta Zubayda, 149
Skhmet, 33
Slater, Philip, 51
Slaves, 24, 67, 89
Smith, Adam, 283

Smith, Margaret Chase, 348
Smith, Page, 328
Smith College, 329
Socrates, 59, 60
Sodomy, 61
Solomon, 44
Song of Solomon, 49
Soranus of Ephesus, 95
Soto, Dominic, 206
Soviet Union, 346
Spain, 223
Sparta, 60, 68
Spengler, Oswald, 12, 14–15
Sprenger, Jakob, 223
St. Cyr (school), 272–273
Stanton, Elizabeth Cady, 325, 328
Stearns, Jonathan F., 315
Stein, Gertrude, 331
Stenton, Doris Mary, 277
Stephens, William, 15
Stillingfleet, Benjamin, 267
Stone, Lucy, 328
Stone Age, 8
Sufism, 149, 150
Sulla, 89
Sumerian society, 19
Sunni, 143
Suttee, 241–242
Sweden, 267

Tacitus, 153
Tamar, 44
Tantrism, 236
Taoism, 254, 256
Tatian, 113
Taueret, 34
Taylor, G. Rattray, 13, 195
Taylor, Jeremy, 203
Taylor, William R., 288
Terence, 159
Terhatum (bride money), 22
Tertullian, 97, 114
Theban triad, 33
Theodora, 3, 125, 132
Theophrastus, 74
Thompson, Edward, 242
Thoreau, Henry, 308
Thousand and One Nights, 147
Thutmose III, 34–35
Tiber River, 86
Tigris-Euphrates Valley, 19
Tiy, 35
Transcendentalism, 308
Trollope, Anthony, 314
Trollope, Frances, 313–314

Tubal ligations, 343
Tudor, Mary, Queen, 201–202
Tudors, 219–220
Tynan, Kenneth, 228
Tyndale, William, 203

Ulysses, 56
United States, 296, 347
Unwin, J. E., 15, 77
Urbanization, 54, 161, 282, 334
Ur-Nammu, 21

Vaerting, Mathilde and Mathias, 12, 30
Vasectomies, 343
Vassar College, 329
Vatsyayana, 237
Veblen, Thorsten, 351
Velazquez, Loretta Janeta, 319
Venereal disease, 18, 325
Venus, 20, 83
Versailles, 265
Vesey, Elizabeth, 267
Vespasian, 91
Victorianism, 288, 289, 292
Villiers, Sir John, 222
Vinateya, 230
Virgin Mary, 4, 116, 169–171, 172–173,
    174, 182
Virginia Company, 295
Virginity, 25, 45, 66, 95, 103, 104, 109,
    113, 118, 159, 171, 174, 236
Vives, Luis, 211
Voltaire, François, 167–168, 266, 269,
    271
Volunteer workers, 341
von Bora, Katherine, 196
von Nettesheim, Henry Cornelius
    Agrippa, 217

Wald, Lillian, 331
Walker, Mary, 321
Walpole, Horace, 266, 277
Ward, Mary, 207–208
Ware, John, 324
Warwell, Maria, 299
Wellesley College, 329
Wessex, 155
Westermarck, Edward, 9
White, Lynn, Jr., 337–338
Wife of Bath, 173, 187–188, 189
Wilde, Oscar, 4

Willard, Elizabeth Osgood Goodrich, 325
Willard, Francis E., 327–328
Willet, Mary, 299
William IX, 181
William of Aquitaine, Duke, 182–183
William the Conqueror, 155–156, 164
Wilson, John A., 31
Winick, Charles, 77
Witchcraft, 223, 306
Wollaston, William, 269
Wollstonecraft, Mary, 276–278, 294, 306
Woman's Christian Temperance Union, 316, 327
Woodhull, Victoria, 315, 325
World War I, 333
World War II, 329, 333
Wright, Martha Coffin, 327

Wright, Richard, 317
Wyatt, Thomas, 220

Xanthippe, 59
Xenophon, 65, 66

Yājñāvalkya, 233
Yang, 244–245, 254, 256
Yin, 244–245, 254, 256
Yü Hsüan, 258

Zell, Katherine, 203–204
Zenophon, 211
Zeus, 56
Zoe, 125
Zoroastrians, 117